BEAUMARCHAIS

BEAUMARCHAIS

LE MARIAGE
DE
FIGARO

Caron Beaumarchais

BEAUMARCHAIS

A Biography

MAURICE LEVER

TRANSLATED FROM THE FRENCH
BY SUSAN EMANUEL

Farrar, Straus and Giroux
New York

Farrar, Straus and Giroux
18 West 18th Street, New York 10011

Originally published in three volumes as
Pierre-Augustin Caron de Beaumarchais,
copyright © 1999, 2003, and 2004
by Maurice Lever and Librairie Arthème Fayard, France
This condensed one-volume edition first published
in the United States in 2009 by Farrar, Straus and Giroux,
copyright © 2009 by Farrar, Straus and Giroux, LLC
Translation copyright © 2009 by Susan Emanuel
All rights reserved
Distributed in Canada by Douglas & McIntyre Ltd.
Printed in the United States of America
First American edition, 2009

Grateful acknowledgment is made for permission to reprint the following material:
Excerpts from *The Figaro Plays*, translated by John Wells, reprinted by
permission of United Agents Limited on behalf of Michael Rosen,
copyright © 1997 by John Wells, as printed in the original volume.
Frontispiece copyright © The Print Collector / Alamy.

Library of Congress Cataloging-in-Publication Data
Lever, Maurice.
    Beaumarchais : a biography / Maurice Lever.— 1st American ed.
        p.   cm.
    Includes bibliographical references and index.
    ISBN-13: 978-0-374-11328-5 (alk. paper)
    ISBN-10: 0-374-11328-9 (alk. paper)
    1. Dramatists, French—18th century—Biography.   2. Beaumarchais,
Pierre Augustin Caron de, 1732–1799.   I. Title.

PQ1956 .L455 2008
842'.5—dc22
[B]
                                                                    2008055449

Designed by Jonathan D. Lippincott

www.fsgbooks.com

1   3   5   7   9   10   8   6   4   2

To Évelyne

If time were measured by the events that fill it, I have lived two hundred years. —Beaumarchais

Of all the famous men of the eighteenth century, he is probably the one about whom the greatest number of fabulous statements have been circulated. Watchmaker, musician, songwriter, dramatist, comic writer, man of fashion, courtier, man of business, financier, manufacturer, publisher, shipowner, contractor, secret agent, negotiator, pamphleteer, orator on certain occasions, a peaceful man by taste and yet always at law, engaging like Figaro in every occupation, Beaumarchais was involved in most of the events, great or small, which preceded the Revolution. —Louis Léonard de Loménie

CONTENTS

ACKNOWLEDGMENTS

This book pays homage to Mme. Jacques de Beaumarchais and to her son, Jean-Pierre de Beaumarchais, who have long worked in the service of their ancestor's memory. I cannot forget the interest they took in my research, nor the charming welcome they gave me, nor the generosity with which they opened their archives to me. I pray that they will find here the expression of my deepest gratitude.

Madame Anne Vassal freely shared letters from her distant relative, Nicolas Ruault, who was Beaumarchais's editor, friend, and confidant, and I am grateful to her. My friends Donald Spinelli, a professor at Wayne State University whose work is well known; Thierry Bodin, a handwriting expert and adviser; Chantal Thomas, an eminent specialist in the Enlightenment; and finally Pierre Assouline have all contributed to the progress of this enterprise with their information, advice, and encouragement. I thank them from the bottom of my heart. I also cannot forget François Bessire, professor at the Université de Tours and a distinguished eighteenth-century scholar. —Maurice Lever

Maurice Lever, a leading historian of eighteenth-century France, published his magisterial biography of Pierre-Augustin Caron de Beaumarchais (1732–1799) in three volumes with Fayard between 1999
and 2004. Known in the English-speaking world primarily as the
author of the plays *The Barber of Seville* and *The Marriage of Figaro*,
Beaumarchais was one of the most fascinating figures of his century:
a self-made man under a regime that would have confined him to a
workshop, an inventor and an entrepreneur, a musician and a dramatist, a diplomat and a spy, a confidant of both kings and revolutionaries, a libertine and a family man—and a social reformer who was one
of America's prime advocates at the court of Louis XVI. Whether or
not his plays contributed to the downfall of the aristocracy, his work
on behalf of the American War of Independence certainly contributed
to its victory. His life was as rich in adventure as any novel.

Maurice Lever's biography was published in three volumes: *The
Irresistible Ascension* covers his birth in 1732 up to 1774; *The Citizen
of America*, the decade of his fight on behalf of the United States and
personal freedom in France; and the final *Into Torment*, 1785 to
1799, the period of the French Revolution and his escape from the
guillotine and return to France. Liberal quotations from his writings
are identified in hundreds of endnotes and an authoritative bibliography (the latter reproduced here), to which I refer readers. Shortly
after Lever's death, his widow, Évelyne, started to condense these
tomes into a single volume, though I have modified the selection
considerably.

One

A YOUNG MAN IN A HURRY

'Tis the chance of birth decided
Who's a shepherd, who's a king.
Cruel fate their lives divided
Wit alone a change may bring.
—*Figaro, in* **The Marriage of Figaro**

"Paris is the only city in the world where such a man could be born!"
the Prince de Conti once exclaimed; in those days "the world" was
confined to Europe. But it was indeed in Paris that Pierre-Augustin
Caron first saw light, not in the elegant Faubourg Saint-Germain,
like those who "took the trouble to be born and nothing else," but
rather in the heart of working-class Paris, halfway along the rue
Saint-Denis, where his father kept a watchmaker's shop, almost at the
corner of the rue de la Ferronnerie, a few steps from Les Halles market. This street was then called the grande rue Saint-Denis, not so
much because of its length as for its liveliness and the swarms of
shops, of which it was the artery. With its maze of dark crisscrossing
alleys, cluttered with various artisans' workshops, the whole quartier
formed one of the liveliest neighborhoods in the capital.

It was on this site that master watchmaker André-Charles Caron
set up shop around 1725, after having moved from within the parish
of Saint-André-des-Arts. Born in 1698 in Meaux, a town strongly
tinged with the Calvinist heresy, André-Charles was the son of Daniel

Caron, another watchmaker, and Marie Fortin, both Protestants. Since the revocation of the Edict of Nantes in 1685, marriages between Huguenots were illegitimate, as were the children born of such unions, so the Carons were probably married clandestinely. But when André-Charles came to Paris in 1721, he abjured "Calvin's heresy." His return to the traditional faith was apparently sincere, and he practiced its duties fervently.

To open a workshop in Paris, a watchmaker had to obtain mastery after eight years of apprenticeship. Their number being limited to seventy-two, one had to wait for a vacancy. A year after converting to Catholicism André-Charles made a request to the king and was granted the title of master watchmaker; five months later he married Marie-Louise Pichon, a young middle-class girl from the neighborhood. An excellent housekeeper with a tender and indulgent heart, she gave him ten children, of whom Pierre-Augustin was the last, born on January 24, 1732—and the only surviving son amid five daughters. His first years were blissful. Caressed, coddled, pampered, fawned over, and spoiled, while preening his male plumage and relishing the coquetry of his young ladies, this only boy was at an early age apprenticed to voluptuous pleasures, seeking his sisters' caresses, sniffing their perfume, spying on their secrets.

The Caron home was a nest, full of chirping from dawn to dusk; the incessant household rowdiness mingled with the babbling chatter of the chickadees, the mischievous squawks of the boy, and the shouting at the maidservant. Slaps flew here and there when someone tried to restore a bit of order or quell the racket. In all corners of the household, from attic to office, from common hall to shop backroom, there resonated trills and singing exercises, lines quoted from Molière and banter from Voltaire, as family members declaimed or versified or composed ariettas, or as they played the viol or flute or harpsichord or even the pedal harp, an instrument recently imported from Germany. In short, it was not the home of a simple artisan but a back-of-the-shop academy: with its intimate concerts and amateur dramatics, the entertainment was permanent, and Pierre-Augustin played his part honorably. Having begun by strumming the strings of a guitar, he turned to the viol, then to the flute, and finally to the harp, with which he had a true fascination.

The Caron parents did not scold, so great freedom reigned in the household. Paternal gravitas was felt only at the daily mass. Since André-Charles Caron had been obliged to abjure the Protestant religion in order to exercise his profession, he did not compromise on religious observance. Although born Catholic, young Beaumarchais would never renounce his origins and would campaign as much as he could in favor of Protestants. In 1777 he would write to Minister of State the Comte de Maurepas: "I will never have a day of happiness if your administration does not achieve three illustrious projects: the abasement of the English in the union of America and France, the reestablishment of finances on the Sully plan . . . and civil rights returned to Protestants by a law that . . . will legally combine them with all the King's subjects." Traces of Protestantism recurred later in life, in his appetite for freedom, his independence of thought, and perhaps most of all, his relation to money and his pragmatic and very modern conception of commerce and industry.

The Caron tribe was raised culturally well above its social condition, for André-Charles was not an artisan like others; watchmaking as a mechanical art required aptitudes going beyond manual skill: knowledge of astronomy, taste, and accuracy. As an engineer as well as an artist, he possessed a curious mind and a love of literature. Watchmaking required artistic sensibilities and presupposed familiarity with the privileged classes. If he never made a fortune in his calling, father Caron acquired an uncommon general education that he transmitted to his children—the only wealth he would bequeath them. Like the Genevan father of Jean-Jacques Rousseau (also a Protestant watchmaker), he loved belles lettres; he became familiar with Enlightenment culture and with the cultural melting pot that was the eighteenth-century theater.

Beaumarchais's childhood was set in the rue Saint-Denis, so lively and gay with its shops and merchants. Under shop signs paraded a colorful crowd, where people of all social conditions mingled and pressed against each other in an incessant coming-and-going. The street was his classroom, where he would learn about people and life; the Paris pavements made him into the rebellious adolescent he would in many ways remain. Headstrong and big-hearted, with cheeky humor and effrontery, he calls to mind Hugo's street urchin

Gavroche, of the messy hair and sloppy dress; he wandered the quartier at the head of his band of good-for-nothings. Street life meant freedom, adventure, temptation. When Pierre-Augustin reached the age of ten, however, his studies had to be considered. Probably because Father Caron had lost three sons and wanted to have Pierre-Augustin follow in his own footsteps, he sent him neither to the Jesuits nor to the Oratorians—considered the best educators in France, who would have given his surviving son a classical education—but to a country school, about which we know little, except that he would have received a smattering of Latin. After his first communion ("at twelve, an old monk gave me sermons and a snack under a huge painting of the *Last Judgment* in the sacristy"), he was withdrawn from school and put into apprenticeship. As he would later have Figaro say, knowledge of the world was better than book learning.

At thirteen, then, his father took him as apprentice, drawing up a contract to guide his behavior. Lovers of *Figaro* will recall that thirteen was the age of the page Chérubin! Beaumarchais would not have had to look far to create his character but merely forage in his memory and depict his own youth. This precocious stripling full of fire, who flirts with Suzanne, Fanchette, and even the old Marceline (because "she is a woman"), is close to the spitting image of our Pierrot, fancifully swerving among his sisters and "young mistresses," who cajole and caress him, turning his head with their teasing. Rustling skirts, stolen ribbons, tender winks, furtive kisses, and fervent oaths: those games of love, as innocent as they might be, would warm his mind and enflame his senses. The idea of womanhood intoxicated him as it did the young page to Count Almaviva in *The Marriage of Figaro*.

Yet Pierre-Augustin was soon behaving neither as a good son nor as a model apprentice. Neglecting the workbench for the harp, he pilfered from the cash box and resold repaired watches for his own profit. Between his insolent remarks, his overly free manners, his bad company, his debts, and the "fortunate nightcap and privileged ribbon" that this budding libertine passionately sought, one can understand why Caron the father got fed up. Pushed to the limit, the master watchmaker decided one fine day to throw his son out of the house. It was a harsh punishment, but Pierre-Augustin did nothing to avoid it, his attitude arising as much from provocation as from thoughtlessness. Now he was abruptly thrown onto the street, without a penny or any shelter. Friends and relatives quickly came to his aid. He sent his father supplicating letters proclaiming his repentance and filial devotion. His mother and sisters interceded in his favor, and M. Caron let himself be swayed, but only on one condition: the prodigal must sign a contract in which he formally promised to change his conduct.*

Returned to the straight and narrow, the young Caron no longer slipped out of the workshop. Imagine him at his bench, between the four glass panes of his loge, his magnifying glass screwed into the corner of his eye, as he wielded a jeweler's file and tweezers: a royal regulation obliged watchmakers to work in a sort of glass cage within sight of passersby. Under the reign of Louis XV, watchmaking had reached its highest degree of refinement, and watches were all the rage. To ornament the casings, chasers and painters rivaled one another in inventiveness. However, one did not expect to learn the exact time from these precious works of art. They ran more or less fast, often advancing a half hour per day, if not more. Barely nineteen years old, Pierre-Augustin decided to solve this problem and perfected an escapement that revolutionized the art of watchmaking and rendered timepieces slim and reliable. In the course of his research, which occupied him for almost an entire year, he committed the imprudence of confiding in M. Le Paute, His Majesty's watchmaker, whose reputation exceeded the frontiers of the kingdom. After congratulating the young man on his discovery, Le Paute tried to claim Pierre-Augustin's invention as his own in a notice published in the *Mercure de France* in September 1753.

In disbelief, Pierre-Augustin hurried to spread the news. To his great surprise, the friends to whom he confided his misfortune were astonished at his naïveté. Le Paute was known for this kind of dirty

---

*The penitent wrote, "Honored Father—I sign all your conditions in the full intention of executing them, with the assistance of the Lord; but how sadly all this recalls to me the time when these conditions and laws were far from being necessary to make me do my duty. It is just that I should suffer a humiliation, which I have greatly deserved; and if this and my good conduct can induce you to give me back your kindness and affection, I shall be only too happy."

trick. The young Caron reasoned: "The evil deed is done, what good lamenting my imprudence? Better to seek a way of defending myself." First, he would need judges, a forum, and urgent action, or else he would be suspected of having concocted his evidence. He deposited with the office of the Academy of Sciences a memorandum describing his escapement and a sealed box containing all the pieces on which he had worked, thus retracing the successive stages of his research. This precaution taken, he asked for a hearing with the Comte de Saint-Florentin, minister of the king's household (who was showering M. Le Paute with his bounty), in order to present the wrong that the eminent king's watchmaker had done him; he begged the count to hear both sides in open debate. Saint-Florentin indeed charged experts to hear both parties, separately and then in cross-examination, so that the truth would come to light. Meanwhile Pierre-Augustin had printed and distributed in Paris a letter "on the subject of a discovery that sire Le Paute wanted to seize from him." The story stuck to the facts, which conferred on it an incomparable power of conviction. The conclusion appeared evident without vain declamation or coaxing: Le Paute was a thief. Two days later Pierre-Augustin sent the *Mercure de France* a response to the previous notice. For the first time he appealed to the public as witness. This procedure, which he would exploit masterfully later in life, won over public opinion and put pressure on his judges (in this case, the Academy of Sciences). Enchanted with the publicity, Beaumarchais neglected nothing in order to gain the sympathy of a public that he knew for its "fairness" and "the protection it gives to the arts." A fine lesson in insinuating himself into the public's good graces!*

But Le Paute could not let the matter rest. Furious to have been challenged by this young lout and embarrassed in having to defend himself, he replied maladroitly; his reply had the sole result of making him appear as a vain "mandarin" who despised his disciples but did not hesitate to steal their credit. While the quarrel raged in the gazettes, the Academy of Sciences designated two commissioners to render a judgment. Their conclusion found in favor of the young

---

*"With my escapement and my mode of construction, excellent watches can be made as flat and as small as may be thought fit."

Caron by a unanimous vote that was confirmed by the Academy in February 1754. The *Encyclopédie* of Diderot and d'Alembert soon recorded (with apparent satisfaction) the victory of young Caron over M. Le Paute. This rather flattering mention testified that its editors shared the views of Pierre-Augustin on the subject of intellectual property. His own struggle to contest favoritism with ability was akin to their concern to base an individual's esteem and benefits upon his merit alone, and so his triumph was one for their ideas, too.

Intoxicated by his victory in the Academy, he aspired to draw as much profit from it as possible. It got him spoken of in high places, even at Versailles. Not very often within the stultified society of the ancien régime did one see a greenhorn, aged twenty-one, stand up to a powerful and royally lauded man and reduce him in a shameful rout. If there was one thing of which Pierre-Augustin was fully aware, it was that reputations do not last long. Nothing is more capricious than public favor, and nothing is more ephemeral than what is fashionable. If he wanted to profit from his notoriety, he had better do so right away. The discovery that public opinion, although invisible and silent, is a power to be reckoned with is no doubt the major lesson of Beaumarchais's years of apprenticeship.

The most startling result of the press campaign that Pierre-Augustin orchestrated around this affair was his entry into Versailles as a purveyor to the king, to his mistress Mme. de Pompadour, and to Mesdames, the daughters of Louis XV. From this momentous reception in the summer of 1754 dates his good fortune. He executed a fob watch for the sovereign, miniaturized one in a ring setting for Mme. de Pompadour, and made a small pendulum clock for Mme. Victoire—this was his consecration. From one day to the next, all the court nobles gave him their orders. He could now adopt the prestigious and enviable title of "horologist to the king." Although only twenty-two years old, he did not let himself be easily intoxicated with success. He spent these months at court scrutinizing people as he scrutinized his mechanical devices, with the same penetrating gaze; he took apart the social cogs to understand how they functioned, and soon he learned how to manipulate the lowly springs called egotism, vanity, and self-interest.

From the moment Beaumarchais appeared at Versailles, women

were struck by his height, his narrow and neat waist, his regular features, his healthy and animated complexion, his self-assured gaze, and the dominating air that seemed to lift him above his surroundings—as well as the involuntary ardor that the female aspect ignited in him. The portrait painter Jean-Marc Nattier painted him thus during this time, dressed in his gilt embroidered waistcoat and fine red coat. Nobody could deny that he was a charming young man. If his face retained the round softness of childhood, his gaze was imposing in its aplomb; its sardonic and arrogant gleam bewitched or disconcerted, or did both simultaneously, but did not leave people indifferent—especially the ladies, over whom he exercised an irresistible influence. By all accounts, Pierre-Augustin belonged to the race of seducers: he played at being one and enjoyed the part.*

One fine day in the spring of 1755 a very beautiful woman around thirty years old entered his father's workshop; she blushed while presenting a watch to be repaired. This was only a pretext: ever since the woman had noticed Pierre-Augustin at Versailles, she had dreamed of making his acquaintance and had found this means of approaching him. It was the start of an affair that would change young Caron's life. Madeleine-Catherine Aubertin was the wife of Pierre-Augustin Franquet, comptroller of the king's victuals. This modest office was one of a thousand court posts that had been created at the sovereign's will, which had no substance but were expensively bought when the king needed money. These offices were then transmitted to heirs or sold to other buyers, with the prince's agreement. Mme. Franquet was fifteen years younger than her husband but ten years older than Pierre-Augustin. The difference in age scarcely troubled the young man. Shortly after this meeting Madeleine-Catherine persuaded her husband to cede his office to her young lover. By the autumn of the same year, the deal was concluded, and Pierre-Augustin gave up the profession of watchmaker. Only two months after the young man took up his post in January

---

*According to Gudin, "As soon as he appeared at Versailles, the women were struck with his lofty stature, his slender and elegant figure, the regularity of his features, his bright, animated complexion, his confident bearing, that air of command which seemed to raise him above all who surrounded him, and finally, with that involuntary ardor which he exhibited at their appearance."

1756, M. Franquet discreetly passed away. It was a very opportune death, for the charming widow was in a hurry to legitimize her liaison. The Caron parents tried everything to discourage their son from entering this marriage, but Pierre-Augustin stood his ground, pleaded passion, and ended up securing their consent in front of the notary. On November 27 the wedding was celebrated at the Church of Saint-Nicolas-des-Champs.

It was then that Pierre-Augustin traded the name Caron, decidedly too plebeian, for that of Beaumarchais, truly much more elegant. This new patronymic came to him from his wife and had nothing aristocratic about it. It was quite simply the name of the former owner of a house that old M. Franquet had bought in the village of Vert-le-Grand, in Alsace. But what is a name without a coat of arms? Soon after his marriage the newly named Beaumarchais had a seal engraved with his arms, "the muzzle of a gold lion surrounded by a band of vair." But he did not achieve the status of gentleman, for his modest office did not confer nobility. While Beaumarchais waited to take the next step up the class ladder, he enjoyed other advantages: he had two lackeys and ordered his clothes from the best tailors. He now affected an arrogance toward the common folk that bespoke at ten leagues his being a parvenu.*

Inconstant by nature and frivolous by caprice, Beaumarchais would never be a faithful lover or husband. A lover of women but a refined *amateur*, he loved them "passionately" (as he said)—as a man of taste savors delicacies. From childhood, when he seemed the handsomest boy in the neighborhood, he knew the secret of pleasing women without ever having learned it. He knew how to charm them, court them, entertain and admire them in love notes; his instinct and love of pleasure enabled him to seduce. But this Lovelace† was no corrupter; he amused himself with seduction, but his play was never cruel. Beaumarchais respected women as much as he relished making

---

*Loménie: "What a difficult situation was that of a young *parvenu*, who was sufficiently favored by nature and fortune to inspire a great deal of jealousy, and too recently emerged from the shop to be received on a footing of equality. It is not astonishing that Beaumarchais's character was formed early in the midst of so many obstacles."
†Translated as *Clarisse Harlowe* in 1752, Samuel Richardson's epistolary novel had a major impact on the philosophes.

love to them. "Any woman has more spirit than a man of letters": whether he meant it sincerely or simply as gallantry, he would repeat this compliment throughout his life. He was undoubtedly a libertine, but not at the cost of degrading women. Neither a grand seigneur nor a bad man, he would never be a Don Juan!

But as taken as he was with the fair sex and not knowing how to resist it, and reputed to be himself irresistible, he lacked the virtues of an ideal husband. Endowed with a particularly strong clan spirit (his whole family would end up living at his expense), he would always disdain the joys of the conjugal home. Barely was his union with Mme. Franquet sealed than he proved less tender and less attentive. Very quickly the new bride had cause to complain of his inconstancy. Tormented by jealousy, she grew bitter, became authoritarian and irritable. Alas, poor Madeleine did not have long to suffer. Struck with a "putrid fever," she expired on September 29, 1757, less than a year after her marriage. Pierre-Augustin had summoned the best doctors to visit her regularly during her illness.

The death of his wife plunged Beaumarchais into grave financial difficulties, since the provisions of his marriage contract did not permit him to inherit from her. Incapable of maintaining his lifestyle, he accumulated debts and argued with bailiffs, occupying his moments of freedom with improving his education, of which he was only too aware of the gaps. He devoured the great classics of literature, perfected his Latin, studied history and geography, and deepened his knowledge of mathematics. He also scribbled pell-mell his own thoughts onto scraps of writing, throwing himself into this new apprenticeship with the same ardor he had formerly applied to establishing himself as a watchmaker. His first attempts leave the reader with scarcely any doubt about his true aptitudes; these are the first stammerings of a writer who has not yet found himself.

Two

THE ROAD TO FORTUNE

I invented a few good machines, but I did not belong to the mechanics; people spoke ill of me. I made verses and songs, but who would have recognized me as a poet? I was the son of a watchmaker.   —*Beaumarchais*

Amazing! I have something you want, and social barriers just disappear!   —*Figaro, in* The Barber of Seville

As if I didn't know that being a lover, or a poet, or a musician entitles anyone to any kind of lunacy . . .
                    —*Count Almaviva, in* The Marriage of Figaro

Finally Providence consented to send Beaumarchais a favorable sign. The harp was the instrument he loved most in the world and the one he played the best, to the great joy of his sisters and the despair of his father. He had never abandoned study of it and ceaselessly perfected its musical mechanism. Rumor spread at Versailles that M. de Beaumarchais composed music and that he was in a perfect position to teach anyone who asked how to play—especially if a pupil boasted a fine name and paid well for lessons. Chance came his way—and how!—in the form of the daughters of the king, collectively called Mesdames. The most famous of the quartet of princesses, Mme. Adelaide, was then twenty-five years old; Mme. Victoire was twenty-four,

Mme. Sophie was twenty-three, and Mme. Louise twenty. Strangely, historians have tended to consider the four sisters as one and the same person. Under the name Mesdames, they appear to have formed a single body and mind, like a sort of four-headed hydra. In fact, these unfortunate young women suffered their condition as single women deprived of love. The sole passion that ever reigned in the deserted hearts of Mesdames was their passion for their father, so exclusive and absolute that it left no space for any other. For his part, Louis XV responded with a tenderness that he expressed in an offhand and gruff fashion.

When Beaumarchais assumed his task as harp master for Mesdames, it was not as a stranger, for his talents had endowed him with a kind of court notoriety. With his enterprising disposition, he was not content to simply place their august fingers on the strings or reveal to them the secrets of the pedals. Quickly he exceeded his initial assignment to become the princesses' official music steward. Each week he organized a chamber music concert given before the king, the queen, the dauphin, the dauphine, and some regular visitors. He himself took part, playing either flute or harp. Such concerts and lessons represented royal favor, which allowed those who had been recently ennobled to lift themselves to higher offices. The monarchical state was lowering the aristocracy by reducing the power of seigneurs and by creating a new nobility, conferring titles on servitors who arose from among commoners. Beaumarchais quickly grasped that this new sort of man, adept at economic realities as he was, would soon be part of the dominant class. He applied all the resources of his energy to a single purpose: to obtain wealth, without which there was neither rank, nor prestige, nor power. This would be his revenge on the idiots. Hence his efforts in these days to cultivate useful friendships, which would carry the name Beaumarchais as high and as far as possible, as the name Voltaire had been carried thirty years earlier. Persuaded that money would soon be worth the "quarters" of nobility, he frequented the milieux of financiers and men of mercantile affairs.

Around 1757 or 1758 he made the acquaintance of Charles Borromée Le Normant, the hapless husband of Mme. de Pompadour who owned the magnificent château of Étoilles. Both men shared a love of money and a taste for business affairs, a similar joie de vivre and generosity. The fabulously wealthy seigneur of Étoilles enjoyed brilliant social connections. It was on the stage of the theater created for his château that Pierre-Augustin made his debut as a dramatic author, with *parades** that he composed expressly for the master of the house. What could be more titillating for the impromptu actors than to enact on the stage outrageous things that propriety forbade in daily life! The salons were crazy about these bawdy sketches. Beaumarchais composed six of them in one act for the Étoilles stage.

At the château he met a financier of great stature, Joseph Pâris, known as Pâris-Duverney, the third and best known of the four Pâris brothers, sons of an innkeeper, who was then more than seventy-five years old. Possessed of a veritable passion for finance and an uncommon capacity for work, this former protector of Voltaire had benefited from lofty patronage, stretching from Mme. de Prie, mistress of the regent, to Mme. de Pompadour, who called her friend "my silly billy." Duverney had conceived a project to found a royal military college, where five hundred sons of French officers, aged eight to eleven, would receive free board and lodging and tuition for four years until they earned the rank of sublieutenant. Mme. de Pompadour, remembering Mme. de Maintenon, the mistress of Louis XIV who had founded a school for girls, wanted to make her own version of "Saint-Cyr." Construction of the École Militaire began in 1751 and the first boarders were taken in, although the building was not finished. By 1755 funds were lacking, despite prodigious expenditure by the king's favorite, the energy of the financier, and the shrewdness of Giacomo Casanova, who proposed creating a lottery. Only the king could save the situation, but Louis XV was scarcely interested in this academy for officers: too many people were opposed because they perceived it as the project of the royal mistress.

Dazzled by Beaumarchais's intelligence, seduced by his spirit, and flabbergasted by his aplomb, Duverney saw the advantage he could draw from the protégé of Mesdames. Who could have predicted that one of the richest and most powerful men of the kingdom would ask Pierre-Augustin, the son of a shopkeeper, for a favor! The young man

---

Parades were short farces, rather smutty in nature.

promised to help Duverney obtain the royal intervention he had sought for nine years. Pierre-Augustin pleaded the case to the princesses, vaunting the usefulness and philanthropic purpose of this grandiose project. Understanding that serving a man who might make his fortune would advance his own interests, he persuaded the princesses to visit the establishment. They were only too happy to escape their golden cage for a day, and some days later, on August 17, 1760, the king himself, charmed by the tale of his daughters, consented to come in person to inaugurate buildings that were already the talk of Europe. Beaumarchais was well along the path to fortune.

From the start of their relationship, Pâris-Duverney held his young friend in affection. Everything about Beaumarchais was seductive: his audacity, his love of risk, his spirit of enterprise, his political intelligence, his keen sense of public relations, his unshakable self-confidence, and above all, an appetite for wealth that he did not even try to hide. Far from sharing the prejudices of the great, Beaumarchais saw nothing ignominious about wanting to get rich. He considered business, despised by the nobility, as a perfectly respectable activity and as one of the essential foundations of a peaceful world. Duverney and Beaumarchais belonged to the same species of humankind, and henceforth the financier would treat Pierre-Augustin on an equal footing and as a trusted collaborator in whom he could confide his most secret thoughts without fear of being betrayed. He promised to help him build his fortune: "My dear boy, I will now regard you as my son." To start with, he gave him 6,000 livres in annuity income and involved him increasingly in his financial speculations. The budding entrepreneur listened to his mentor's advice with keen deference, soaking up his conversation, following him around, asking a thousand questions, involving himself in everything, and demonstrating the most tender devotion to his master. Later he would remember that Duverney "initiated me into financial affairs, where everybody knows he was a consummate master. I commenced making my fortune under his direction; on his advice I started several speculations. In some he helped me with his money or his name and in all of them with his counsel." In the garden of the residence that he would build in the Faubourg Saint-Antoine at the end of his life, Beaumarchais would erect a bust in Duverney's memory, on which was engraved this simple line: "If I am worth anything, it is thanks to him."

Knowing that if he were to push himself farther ahead in society—and in finance—he must accede to the nobility, Beaumarchais resolved to buy a patent as secretary to the king, an office called a *savonette à vilain* (soap for the lowborn), which consisted of signing letters to the large and small chancelleries and putting them before a wax heater to be sealed. This post would confer the first degree of nobility, transmittable to heirs if performed for twenty years. But no man whose father owned a shop could obtain nobility, and so Pierre-Augustin induced his father, not without difficulty, to retire.* He had no illusions about the moral value of social promotion: in his eyes, it was a simple formality to be undergone in order to advance his career. But he would take advantage of his newly minted nobility and view it with the same pride as if it were a thousand years old, perhaps more, since he knew he owed it to his merit alone. We recall Figaro's famous audacity in disparaging birth to make talent triumphant: "Being an aristocrat, having money, a position in society, holding public office—all that makes a man so arrogant! What have you ever done for all this wealth? You took the trouble to be born and nothing else! Apart from that you're rather an ordinary man. And me, God damn it, a nobody, one of the crowd, and I've had to use more skill and ingenuity simply to stay alive than they've expended in a hundred years in governing the whole of Spain!"

His parchment now in his pocket, Beaumarchais went in quest of a new and more lucrative office. Having failed to secure the office of Grand Master of Rivers and Forests because of his father, he was now able to acquire Lieutenant-General of the Hunt in the Bailiwick and Captaincy of the Preserves of the Louvre, which meant he judged any individual who trespassed on the royal monopoly on hunting in the Louvre's parks. Hearings were held twice a month at the Louvre Palace, most often under the presidency of the lieutenant—

---

*"Changing the inscription above your shop-front [. . .] will make a great difference in my prospects, owing to the foolish manner in which matters are viewed in this country. Not being able to alter the prejudice, I am obliged to submit to it, as there is no other channel open to the advancement which I desire for our happiness, and for that of all the family."

to wit, Beaumarchais—decked out in a long robe and wearing a vast wig crowned with a velvet mortarboard, his countenance severe.

Now endowed with an office that allowed him to live comfortably for many years, Beaumarchais bought a large and fine house at 26, rue de Condé, into which he moved his father and his two unmarried sisters, Julie and Tonton, resuscitating the jolly atmosphere of former days at the rue Saint-Denis. Laughter resumed, along with music, songs, and skits, as before. "Our home," wrote Julie, "is a bear-pit of suitors who live on love and hope." The preoccupation with love started with the young widower himself, who was still under thirty and did not remain unconsoled. Even had he felt the strongest aversion to libertinage, his ascension in society made its practice an obligation: one could not pass oneself off as a man of quality unless one was a libertine. His social elevation imposed loose living on him, which happily happened to correspond to his taste and led him to opera girls, with whom he had several liaisons that we know of from police reports. But these were trifles to which he attached no greater importance than they merited. He regarded debauchery as the luxury of a great lord, not as a principle of life, and still less as an end in itself. Unlike certain nobles who exhausted their whole raison d'être in women's boudoirs, he abandoned only a tiny part of himself there. To the feudal nostalgia that entrained a Marquis de Sade in every sort of perversion, he opposed the lucid and hardy vision of a modern adventurer. If he colluded with this decrepit world, it was so as to better dominate it later. M. de Beaumarchais, ex-Caron, might adopt the famous reply of Voltaire to an elder: "Sir, I am starting to make my name and you are finishing yours."

Was it the perfume of youth that filled the house from top to bottom? Was it the songs and laughter, or the passing fancies blossoming behind every door? The pleasant company or the dear maidservant? The champagne that flowed? Or the solicitude of his children, in particular the cherished son? Whatever the reason, Father Caron appeared rejuvenated and reinvigorated, experiencing a new spring by discovering love with a still fresh widow, whom he married in January 1766, at the age of sixty-five.

The romantic banter that reigned at rue de Condé touched everybody, particularly Beaumarchais's sisters and Pierre-Augustin himself, who did not wish to remain alone on the banks of the river while the rest of the household was embarking for the land of Venus. Tired of the beauties up for auction, Pierre-Augustin had dreamed of something more ever since he met Pauline Le Breton. It was not that he aspired to passionate love, the absolute and eternal: he belonged too much to his times to give himself up to such romantic excesses. There was nothing foolishly sentimental in him: no mawkishness, no outbursts; he admired Samuel Richardson but belonged to the race of the tragedian Crébillon and of Laclos, the author of *Les Liaisons Dangereuses*. According to him, love was no different from self-love. "Whoever says *amour propre*," he wrote,

> also says love, for the latter is merely an extension of the former toward an object that one thinks worthy of oneself. One loves oneself in one's mistress, in the judicious choices that justify our good taste. One loves oneself in the tenderness that is showered on someone and which makes that heart interesting for us, in the caresses that are given her and which are produced in us, all the more flattering when the return is sincere. Finally, one loves oneself in the lively and delicate pleasure of inspiring love, of giving it to one's beloved; every happiness or unhappiness in life has only one veritable way of being envisaged, and that is in relation to ourselves. Without this love of ourselves, no passion has entry into our soul.

Pierre-Augustin's avowed libertine egotism did not prevent the young girl of seventeen from awakening in him the desire for a stable domestic establishment. Six years after the death of his wife, he yearned for a home that might flatter his present situation and sustain him in his future ambitions, while ensuring the survival of a name that he was the first to bear and of which he could already boast. Pauline Le Breton corresponded point by point to what he was looking for: she was very pretty and an excellent musician; she had "a tender, childlike, and delicate air" and "the voice of an enchantress." Raised in the Antilles colony of Santo Domingo by an uncle who was a wealthy planter, she made frequent visits to the rue de Condé, where Pierre-Augustin courted her assiduously. She would later be an inspiration for his theatrical women in love: Pauline of *Deux Amis* and Rosine of *The Barber of Seville* (originally called Pauline) would both borrow more than one feature from the gracious Creole girl.

Marriage seemed to Pauline to be the natural result of this idyll. People soon regarded the pair as affianced, awaiting their forthcoming union. Mesdames of France, to whom she was presented, found her "charming." But one question still bothered the future husband and held him back from getting engaged: the young woman's fortune was said to be quite diminished. To have a clearer understanding of her estate, he started an inquiry, sending his own agent, Pichon de Villeneuve, to Santo Domingo on a mission to evaluate the exact holdings of Mlle. Le Breton and to see how much could be drawn from the plantation. Meanwhile he played the difficult role of a passionate suitor who is not in a hurry to conclude the affair. His letters to Pauline show him oscillating between amorous élan and concern for his interests; tenderness and calculation shared his heart, although unequally. If only the holdings in Santo Domingo could prove profitable! What delicious days he would spend there in the arms of his adored wife, served by slaves! He dreamed of becoming a planter—when he was not in the alcoves of his beautiful mistresses, companions of one night, whose follies amused him and offered the advantages of "ready-made love." Pushed toward the altar both by his promise and by his mother, he declared his impatience to be united with the one he loved—and at the same time applied the brakes. It was an untenable dilemma—hymen without a guarantee, or rupture without hope—which he was pressed to resolve. Beaumarchais counted on his guiding star to get him out of his embarrassment. No doubt it was shining on him, for a theatrical coup intervened, like the ones he would know throughout his life. In a few hours he had to prepare his baggage and rush to Spain: the honor of his family was at stake, and there was not a second to lose! The marriage would have to wait.

Three

"EN CAPA Y SOMBRERO"

A wig, a waistcoat, or clogs should not scare people away when the heart is excellent and the mind acceptable.
    —Beaumarchais, in a letter to his father

When there's a call for my services I am a man of initiative who goes to work with a will.   *—Figaro, in* The Barber of Seville

In a case where I can't see any prospect of making a profit, I think at least I can have a bit of fun. Enjoy life, that's my motto.
    —Figaro, in The Barber of Seville

In 1748 two of Pierre-Augustin's older sisters, Marie-Josèphe (wife of former master mason Louis Guilbert, who had been promoted to architect to the King of Spain) and Marie-Louise (nicknamed Lisette), had left the Caron family shop to settle in Spain. A correspondent of their father's had suggested they take over a dress shop on calle de la Montera, one of the most elegant avenues in Madrid. They accepted the invitation. Soon a suitor presented himself for the younger sister, in the person of José Clavijo y Fajardo, an industrious and modest pen pusher toiling in the Ministry of War. Physically, Clavijo resembled Sancho Panza: short legged and pudgy, with a rubicund face. But he was lacking in neither education nor ambition. Lisette had promised him her hand, but nothing was to be concluded until the future bridegroom had an assured position. Six years passed, during which Clavijo advanced himself as best he could, publishing a book on the Spanish army, and launching a philosophical journal, pompously titled *El Pensador*, which won him the position of keeper of the Crown's archives. However, no longer finding Lisette so fresh or to his taste and telling himself that his ascension merited a more brilliant match, he withdrew his commitment—without even dreaming that, during this long wait, she had sacrificed several advantageous suitors for his sake. After a reconciliation, he broke it off altogether, thus putting the reputation of Mlle. Caron in danger.

In February 1764 a tearful letter from Mme. Guilbert apprised Beaumarchais of Lisette's misfortune. Moved by his sister's fate, the protégé of Mesdames rushed to Versailles to ask for leave. "Go and be careful," answered the indulgent princesses, "for what you are doing is good, and you will not lack support in Spain if your conduct is reasonable."

An innocent victim, a treacherous blackguard, and a hero who dispenses justice flying to the aid of his unfortunate sister! It was a tale to make sensitive souls swoon. And what a fine drama it would have been for the French theater!

But family honor was only the simple pretext for this expedition— it was business that truly called Beaumarchais to Spain. For several months Pâris-Duverney and his associate Le Ray de Chaumont had been negotiating with the Spanish government for several exceptionally important contracts, both financially and politically. They wanted to obtain concessions for Louisiana for a period of twenty years, for the general supply of all black slaves to the colonies of the New World, for the provisioning of Spanish troops there, and finally for the right to colonize the Sierra Morena. Owing to a lack of direct contacts, discussions were dragging. Having an agent on the spot became necessary to ensure that the French got the *asiento*, meaning the monopoly of these various business affairs. It goes without saying that a mission of this kind required serious preparation. Pierre-Augustin spent a month profitably making various arrangements in high places, taking the necessary instructions, gathering substantial documentation on the American colonies, and devouring treatises on political economy. More prosaically, he plunged into his father's account books, for in addition to handling Lisette's marriage, he was charged with recovering some old debts owed to the Caron estate. Finally, a few days before his departure, he asked the Duc de Choiseul, the secretary of state for war and the navy,* for a letter of introduction to the French ambassador in Madrid, the Marquis d'Ossun.

The final formalities accomplished and his baggage packed, Pierre-Augustin took to the road at the end of April 1764. Arriving in Madrid on May 18, he had a suit pulled from his trunks, hastily changed his clothes, found a carriage, and went to see Sir Clavijo, to whom he delivered a glacial and resolute indictment. Stunned, incapable of uttering a word, the Spaniard gathered himself, tried to stammer an explanation, and ended up writing (under his interlocutor's dictation) a declaration of repentance that would save Lisette's honor. Without further delay, Beaumarchais rushed to Aranjuez to give an account of his initiative to the ambassador to France, who ardently advised him to marry his sister to Clavijo, invoking mysterious "considerations that he could not explain to him." When Pierre-Augustin returned to his sisters, he found Clavijo there, come to renew his marriage request. Blushing, Lisette agreed to unite herself with this traitor, and the ceremony was set for June 7. Beaumarchais was satisfied, since the formation of this alliance would facilitate his negotiations with the Spanish government. After all, Clavijo enjoyed powerful protection, directing an influential periodical and contributing to spreading French ideas in Spain. The proposal had only to be in writing.

On the wedding morning the apostolic notary summoned by Beaumarchais revealed that the day before he had received an objection to the marriage of Mlle. Caron: a *dueña*, a landlady, asserted that she had had a marriage promise from Clavijo in 1755. Furious, Beaumarchais rushed to Clavijo's house, shook him rudely, and accused him of fabricating his previous declaration. He promised to reveal his infamy to the Spanish minister of foreign affairs and swore

---

*Beaumarchais's first diplomatic patron would soon become the minister of foreign affairs and pursue a vehemently anti-British policy when the rival countries engaged in a series of technological, trade, and military wars.

that he would oblige him to marry his *dueña*. The Spaniard protested his good faith, acknowledged that he had formerly had a certain weakness for this woman, but a few *pistoles* would suffice, he said, for her to withdraw her complaint. Disconcerted, Beaumarchais wondered if this scoundrel had not once again tricked him and his sister. Whatever anguish came over him, he decided to suspend judgment until evening. At the wedding hour, he went back to Clavijo, accompanied by two friends. Nobody was home: the lodging was empty.

Suddenly a messenger arrived from the French ambassador warning Pierre-Augustin that Clavijo had filed a complaint against him, accusing him of having threatened him with death if he did not marry his sister. The diplomat advised Beaumarchais to take a powder, for an order for his arrest had been issued. In a fury, Beaumarchais took just enough time to write a memo in his own defense and to gather a few pieces of evidence, then ran to the Marquis d'Ossun. In the ambassador's antechamber, he had the good fortune to meet a former minister who still enjoyed the confidence of King Charles III. Beaumarchais told him his story in compelling detail and was attentively listened to. A few days later the traitor Clavijo was removed from his post as keeper of the archives and chased out of the Spanish court.

We cannot be certain of the perfect accuracy of this account of the Clavijo affair, as it is reported only in Beaumarchais's account, written and published ten years later. However, the principal witnesses were then still alive and could easily have contradicted him in case of manifest falsification. Evidently Pierre-Augustin thought of bringing the story of this adventure to the stage, and no doubt he would have done so had the enterprise not seemed too risky. It was in effect a painful family tale in which he did not play the finest role, far from it: governing the loves of his sisters for the benefit of his personal convenience. Ultimately, he was anxious to throw Clavijo into the arms of Lisette because the Spaniard could be useful to him in his own negotiations. The enterprise a failure, he prevented his unhappy sister from marrying another suitor in order to obtain Clavijo as a personal collaborator. And so Lisette would remain unmarried. Decency may have prevented Beaumarchais from exploiting this theme in the theater, but others did not deprive themselves of the story; Goethe drew from it a drama in five acts (*Clavigo*) in 1774, and others would follow suit in the nineteenth century.

The Clavijo affair was settled in less than three weeks; Beaumarchais gave himself six months to bring his negotiations with the Spanish government to fruition. But this plan did not take into account the eminent inertia of the Iberian people. "I am here in the country of *poco a poco*," he grasped after a while, "and the *vivacidad francesca*, mother of perpetual impatience, has to hide under the veil of patience that must be superbly exercised here." In the course of this enforced leisure, he explored the capital at whim, letting himself be nonchalantly led by serendipity along alleys and squares, soaking up his surroundings. Instinctively his gaze turned toward the common folk, to whom he paid particular attention. At night he paced the lower-class neighborhoods of the town *en capa y sombrero*, sat down at the tables of smoky taverns, and let himself be intoxicated by the song of guitars and the wild eroticism of the fandango. Bewitched by the charm of this music, he studied it with delight, appropriating it and composing French lyrics for seguedillan airs. Only by the intercession of music did he learn to love this nation. The passion that eventually carried him away came not from intellectual or cultural adherence but from a sensual attachment. Spain exercised on Beaumarchais a durable and decisive influence, to which the great part of his oeuvre bears witness. Neither Figaro, nor Almaviva, nor Bazile, nor Bartholo, nor Rosine—not any of these comic types, now universal, would have seen the light of day if Pierre-Augustin had not conceived the first sketch in the country of Cervantes.

It was also as a philosopher that Beaumarchais visited the Kingdom of Spain: his observations on Spanish manners and beliefs, on the power of the Church and the rigors of the Inquisition, on the mode of government and the practice of justice, are not just those of a man of the Enlightenment, freed from all superstition; they issue from an independent mind. Always suspicious of dogma developed far from concrete situations, political economics appealed to him because it applied to practical experience and to topics that were central to the Enlightenment, like demographics, consumption, agriculture, trade, free exchange, production of wealth. He wrote in his memoirs of Spain: "Philosophy, when freed from dust and jargon, has been successfully applied since the start of the century to enlightening Europe on useful subjects. Humanity owes to it the turning of every person's and every government's regard to the people, to agriculture and commerce, the only true foundations of the prosperity of states and the happiness of subjects."

"It is in the good company for which I was born that I find my means," he declared proudly to his father. Barely arrived in Madrid, he set out in quest of "good company" and managed without difficulty to be received in high society, visiting the ambassadors of France, England, and Russia, taking his place as a favorite of their wives. Evidence suggests that the relationship between the Russian ambassadress and Pierre-Augustin went farther than was appropriate. But this was not his only gallant adventure in Spain. He needed many, and good fortune did not fail him—no doubt one reason for his constant good humor, despite the troubles caused him by the ongoing negotiations. Beaumarchais overflowed with optimism and joie de vivre. "My inexhaustible good humor never leaves me for an instant," he confided to his father. ". . . In truth, I laugh into the pillow when I think how the things of this world mesh, how the paths of fortune are great in number and all quite bizarre, and especially how a soul superior to events may always enjoy itself amid this whirlwind of business, pleasure, and various interests, sorrows, and hopes that collide with each other and then break up against that soul."

Pierre-Augustin soon made the acquaintance of a certain Comtesse de Fuen-Clara, a highly placed lady who lived in a magnificent townhouse by the park at the gates of the capital, whose salon was the rendezvous of Madrid aristocracy. By introducing him to the best houses in Madrid, she merited the nickname of "good angel" that he soon gave her. At the first reception to which he was invited, only a month after his arrival, she presented him to a woman of exceptional beauty. Aged about twenty-five, the Marquise de La Croix was the daughter of a Provençal gentleman, M. de Jarente, Marquis de Sénas, and niece of the Bishop of Orléans, a notorious libertine. Married to a French lieutenant-general who had moved into the service of the King of Spain, Mme. de La Croix had formerly been the mistress of Cardinal Acquaviva, the vice legate of Avignon.

She had a figure full of grace and character, a piercing eye, an aquiline nose, a haughty head, superb bearing, and a majestic walk. Sensual, free in her manners, and following only her own inclinations—a headstrong, lively, and willful woman—she led a grand life, frequenting diplomatic circles. Everybody praised her sovereign aspect, her intelligence, and her sense of intrigue. Beaumarchais painted her as "the most spirited and most beautiful of the Frenchwomen who has ever surpassed all possible Spanish women." But nobody knew anything of her activities. To all appearances, she was one of those adventuresses, half-courtesans, half-secret agents, whose services Louis XV employed in all the courts of Europe. No doubt her apparently fortuitous encounter with Pierre-Augustin had been organized by the Comtesse de Fuen-Clara at the request of the young Frenchman. Whether by calculation or a *coup de foudre*, Pierre-Augustin became without delay the lover of this mystery woman: an infallible means, he thought, of attracting a woman whom one intends to use for political ends—and that was indeed his intention. Moreover, he found in her a temperament as gay as his own: she bit into life enthusiastically and fled boredom like the plague.

Most biographers address only the picturesque or literary aspects of Beaumarchais's trip to Spain, but I cannot fully evoke this period of his life without alluding to his political role with the Spanish government. Despite his lack of success, his mission in Spain appears to have been exemplary because it laid the foundations of what ten years later, during his fight for the American insurgents, would become his principles of moral conduct and business dealing. Retaining a taste for work well done from his apprenticeship in the paternal workshop, Beaumarchais inherited the methodical spirit and sense of organization from his Huguenot origins. Add to these qualities a pronounced taste for the politics of the private study cabinet, an innate feeling for negotiation, an enveloping charm that disarmed any distrust, and a muffled cynicism that masked self-interest beneath the most flattering exterior—it was the ideal model for a diplomatic agent. Not to mention his genius for "imbroglio"—he deployed it in his political maneuvers with as much virtuosity as he would later exercise in the theater. Beaumarchais was perfectly aware of all that. Moreover, he felt he was master of himself, in full possession of his powers at full strength, ready to put into action all procedures without exception—from the most legitimate to the least admissible—to fulfill his mission worthily and to draw the greatest possible personal profit. In a true sense his political vocation preceded his literary vocation. Politics would be his real passion, much more than the composition of dramatic works (six in total), of which only two would merit being passed to posterity as masterpieces. "It was only furtively that I dared give myself up to the taste for literature," he admitted to the Duc de Noailles. Beaumarchais was not a writer who dallied in politics, but rather a politician who amused himself by writing. Despite the many activities that he exercised throughout his life, it was this image that he always claimed in preference to any other.

As a perfectly organized man, he devoted his days to work and his nights to pleasure. His various memoranda and reports reveal his economic and geopolitical expertise and understanding of the complexity of Franco-Spanish relations. "I do not want small stuff. Everything or nothing": this remark expresses the spirit in which he engaged in negotiations.

Thus, without losing sight of the commercial mission entrusted to him, Beaumarchais managed to meld it into the larger realm of imperial politics, whose objectives were clear: guarantee the Spanish Empire against British ascendancy, restore the finances of Spain, and finally unite the French and Spanish powers by means of a "political knot" against their common adversary, England. He acted on his own authority, but went further, without worrying about the position of Foreign Minister Choiseul vis-à-vis Spain. He thereby compromised his chances of success by alienating that cultivated diplomat—whom some have taken as a model for Almaviva. Had he envisaged the asiento on the trade in Negroes as merely a business, instead of broadening it into wide-ranging political activity, he would undoubtedly have obtained it. But he committed the double fault of politicizing the whole commercial plan and of undertaking his own initiatives, without Choiseul's support, although they engaged the higher interests of the nation. More than impatience or clumsiness, it was presumptuousness that lost the monopolies for him.

Yet the discussions had been carried out under the best auspices. Entirely won over to his ideas, the Spanish minister of foreign affairs,

Grimaldi, treated him as a friend. King Charles III did not appear indifferent to the French proposals. Yet these fine projects were sharply criticized by certain ministers and ran up against the hostility of the Prince of Asturias (the future Charles IV), who had been raised to hate France.

Unfortunately, Beaumarchais would apply his genius for intrigue, his virtuosity in ruses (which he would later transmit to Figaro), in one of the most foolish plots that can be imagined. His plan was to make himself the absolute master of the King of Spain, to infiltrate himself skillfully inside his thoughts, to orient his judgments, direct his actions, and inspire his decisions, while leaving him to think that he kept his free will. To this end Beaumarchais employed his own mistress, the Marquise de La Croix. He had no trouble flattering her amour propre and "the novel in her head" by painting a shimmering picture of the glorious results of her idyll with the king: for her first of all, then for her husband (who would derive a thousand advantages), and finally for the French nation, in whose eyes she would appear as a heroine. The marquise pretended to defend her virtue; Beaumarchais spent treasures of eloquence to convince her to accept his plan, and she ended up stifling her scruples.

Everything unfolded magnificently at first. Charles III took the bait, faster than one might have expected, but ten times in a row he fixed a rendezvous with the beauty and then canceled. Torn between his attraction to this young woman and the sacrosanct memory of his wife; tormented by the specter of sin, a slave to his confessor; pierced by fears of others and of himself, Charles never became the marquise's lover. So ended an adventure upon which Beaumarchais had founded so many hopes. Nor had he reached the end of his disappointments: castles in Spain are made for crumbling. If the boudoir intrigue came to naught, the business deals were scarcely advancing; the talks were making no progress, and the discussions were bogged down, much to the despair of this incurable man-in-a-hurry. The provisioning deal ended in failure; the Louisiana concession was vetoed by the Spanish Indies Council; and the asiento was given to Pâris-Duverney's principal competitor.

Beaumarchais felt the failure of these negotiations as a personal defeat, for this program, founded on a correspondence of interests between the French company and Spain, had been his idea. "To work and to suffer has long been my lot," he wrote to his father, when he learned that his emissary to Santo Domingo had just died there, having given him an even grimmer assessment of the inheritance of Pauline Le Breton.

Spring was approaching, and there was no question of remaining longer in Madrid. A thousand tasks were waiting for Beaumarchais in Paris, starting with his functions as lieutenant-general of the hunt in the preserves of the Louvre. On March 22, 1765, he left Madrid and the following April 9 alighted at rue de Condé, "covered in mud and filth" but very happy to be embraced by his father and dear sisters.

Barely recovered from his trip, Pierre-Augustin broke off his engagement with Pauline, on the pretext that she had been unfaithful to him, since a certain cavalryman was ardently aspiring to become her husband. Pauline and her suitor protested their innocence, but Beaumarchais remained inflexible, since the chances that the pretty Creole could recover her colonial property were uncertain at best. But after all, what pleasure is there in breaking things off if not rediscovering one's freedom? "Any woman is worth an homage, very few are worth a regret," he would say later. Although his dreams of fortune had evaporated, he continued to live in grand style. Modeling himself after fashionable gentlemen, he even gave himself as valet a handsome mulatto, Ambroise Lucas, a former slave who had escaped; that story led Pierre-Augustin to become aware of the realities of slavery, the trade in which he had envisaged investing only a few weeks earlier. But not many other people achieved this awareness.

Four

"MONSIEUR, THE FALLEN AUTHOR"

Not liking the game of loto, I made plays. But people said, what is he doing? He is not a writer, for he makes immense and countless business deals. —Beaumarchais, 1789

Wherever I went I rose above it: Praised by some, condemned by others, taking risks when I was on a winning streak, cutting my losses when I wasn't. —*Figaro, in* **The Barber of Seville**

Despite his failure in Spain, Beaumarchais at least brought home, not only themes to inspire his theater and music (perhaps the essential thing) but also some delicious memories of his stay on the other side of the Pyrenees. The women whom he had met lingered in his mind—always gallant, he sent them fripperies from Paris. He also brought home a grand ambition, a political one that led him quite naturally to the office of Foreign Minister Choiseul at Versailles.* Tolerably satisfied with his own activity despite its disappointing results, he strove to get the post of French consul in Madrid. Indeed, he did not doubt that he would obtain it, in recognition of services rendered.

But Choiseul, angry with him, flatly refused his request and thenceforth excluded him from all dealings with Spain, reproaching

---

*In 1765, France had just been defeated in the Seven Years' War and Choiseul was planning to restore her prestige at the expense of Britain, partly by forming an alliance with Spain.

him for having privileged Spanish interests over those of France. Beyond this misunderstanding, fundamental and insurmountable differences stood between Choiseul and Beaumarchais. Choiseul was a partisan of a political union of the two kingdoms, but he conceived of it differently from Beaumarchais; in his mind France ought to furnish manufactured products to Spain but refrain from intervening in the development of its industry or the management of its colonies. We may understand Choiseul's irritation when he learned that the impertinent former watchmaker, with no official mission, had dared to meddle in Spain's domestic affairs, stretching even into the bedroom of its sovereign.

Despite this setback, the year 1766 did not begin badly for Beaumarchais. He was now engaged in a new project: creating a company for forestry exploitation in the Touraine, using funds advanced to him by Duverney. His task was enormous: to inspect his two hundred "sales workers," to ensure the transport of felled trees, to plan new trails between forests and rivers, to repair overgrown paths, to buy horses, to go to markets for hay and oats, to equip the carts, to transport naval lumber before the winter, to construct sluices and locks on the Indre River so as to have water the whole year around at the embarkation ports, and to supervise the loading of his fifty barges that would follow the Loire toward the Atlantic. Not to mention managing seven or eight farms for the provisioning of thirty people. Not counting, either, the general inventorying of receipts and expenses that had to be regularly done. But too much work had never made him grumble; on the contrary, it stimulated him, and he plunged into these tasks with a sort of drunken fervor. As time went on, he adopted a real affection for the Touraine countryside, whose calmness he loved.

Still, "love of letters is not incompatible with a business spirit," thought Beaumarchais, now dreaming of writing plays. To get one's work performed on the Paris stage, however, one needed more audacity than that of a soldier exposing himself to enemy fire on the field of battle, for even if the attacks suffered by a playwright were not mortal, one never healed from some of them. Surviving the gibes of the critics and the catcalls and whistles of the parterre presupposed having an uncommon faith in one's own genius, or a fanatical megalomania, or even a good dose of obliviousness. But the theater was not totally foreign to Pierre-Augustin, and he had proved his skill in his days with Charles Le Normant. But *parades* stuffed with bawdiness, thrown together for coteries bribed in advance—were these really comparable to Parisian theater?

The audience he now intended to seduce had nothing in common with the charming young women blushing in the shady park of Étoilles; this audience would consist of people who paid for seats and wanted to be entertained; they had bought with their tickets the right to whistle, and their applause conferred the only guarantee of glory that counted for an author: popular approval. If Pierre-Augustin launched himself relatively late into this redoubtable adventure (he was now thirty-five years old), he nevertheless stopped himself from embracing theatrical activity exclusively. "I have no merit as an author," he declared from the start, "and the time and talent are also lacking for me to become one." "I am a dramatic writer out of amusement," he would repeat. He was seeking in letters "an honest relaxation" from his serious occupations. If he chose the theater, it was because he saw there a leisure pursuit that conformed to his tastes and his aptitudes: "Of several genres of literature from which I had to choose to try my hand, the least important might be this one, and this was how it obtained my preference." Amid his multiple activities as a big businessman, financier, diplomatic agent, and international negotiator, the theater would always occupy only a marginal place. With his innate flair for publicity, he saw writing as much more than a simple hobby; it was a formidable means of making himself talked about, of attracting public attention and building himself a reputation, for the purpose of promoting his financial projects and his political ideas. His colleagues, less well off than he and whose fate depended entirely on the caprices of the stalls, naturally saw him as a millionaire dilettante who could only succeed, before whom everything must bend, and whose social power would supplement his talent, if necessary. Was he not secretary to the king, a financier, and the spiritual son of Pâris-Duverney, one of the three or four wealthiest nobles of the century? Did he not have entrée to the royal family? And did he not pass for a man of fashion and good fortune? Rapid ascents did not occur without nasty rumors arising, and already many about Beaumarchais circulated in ministerial antechambers, business offices, and the corridors of high finance. Was he not always showing off? His self-infatuation decidedly knew no bounds, not even that of decency, as he pretended to throw himself into the melee of writers! And he was exploiting the same vein as they: serious drama, midway between tragedy and comedy.

It was in 1759, while he was still in the service of Mesdames, that Beaumarchais had put into rehearsal his first drama, *Eugénie*. The great number of drafts, sketches, and manuscript versions that have come down to us prove that he continually modified his play over the course of its long gestation. In turn enthusiastic and discouraged, he was ceaselessly split between élan and self-doubt, between assurance and repentance. His example was Denis Diderot, whom he regarded as his teacher. What seduced him in "serious comedy" (which Diderot called "bourgeois tragedy") was that it finally adapted theater to the people of its time, constructing characters who were closer to average humanity than the kings, demigods, tyrants, generals, and princesses that peopled classical tragedy. He wanted to dramatize sensitive souls who spoke the language of the heart:

> The portrait of the unhappiness of an honest man touches the heart, opens it gently, wins it, and soon obliges it to examine itself. When I see virtue persecuted but still fine, still glorious, and preferable to all even when close to misery, the effect of the drama is not at all equivocal, and in this alone am I interested; and when, if I am not happy myself, if base envy tries to blacken me, if it attacks my person, my honor or my fortune, then how pleased I am by this kind of spectacle! And what a fine moral sense I may draw from it! . . . The man who fears to weep, who refuses to become tender, has a vice in his heart, or strong reasons not to reckon with himself. It is not to him that I speak—he is a stranger to all that I have just said. I am speaking to the sensitive man, who often goes inside himself after seeing a touching drama. I am addressing someone who prefers the useful and tender emotions into which the theater spectacle has thrown him over the diverting pleasantries of the little play that, once the curtain is down, leaves nothing in the heart.

Finally—and this point appears essential to the economic and social history of that era—"serious drama" was a spectacle intended for the bourgeois public, offering a moving and moral portrait of its own milieu. In the eighteenth century a bourgeois was no longer a person whose faults Molière could freely mock and ridicule; he belonged to a class moving upward socially, a class of which Beaumarchais himself was the pure product. The bourgeoisie was no longer laughed at. As for the drama, it was the genre most suitable to Enlightenment ideology—and most representative of the triumphant Third Estate.

On January 29, 1767, the curtain of the Comédie-Française finally rose on *Eugénie, or Unhappy Virtue*, a prose drama in five acts by M. de Beaumarchais. It recounted the story (set in London for censorship reasons) of the sweet and elegant Eugénie, the secret wife of the Count of Clarendon, a corrupt libertine. Her father, a baron, is unaware of their union and wants to marry Eugénie to his old friend Captain Cowerly. Pregnant by the count, Eugénie learns that her marriage was actually a trick and that her seducer Clarendon is preparing to wed, this time legally, a rich heiress.

With what a venomous pen did an anonymous chronicler announce the forthcoming performance of his play on December 28, 1766!

They are announcing to the French a weepy comedy entitled *Eugénie* or *Unhappy Virtue*. This play, quite Romanesque, is emphatically recommended. It is by a well-known man who has no reputation; someone named *Caron de Beaumarchais*, hardly known in literature. His first years were employed in acquiring mechanical talents. Son of watchmaker Caron, he followed in his father's situation with success. But born with a certain portion of spirit and a natural disposition for the lively arts, his taste for music enabled him to cover the distance that separated him from a certain society. He has managed to get close to the court; he was rather fortunate to have pleased it through his talents and to profit from favors that put him in a position to make a considerable fortune. The successive deaths of the husband of a wife he loved and whom he then married, as well as of this same wife, after she had made him a legacy of all her property, has laid over his reputation an unsavory varnish; he has been refused various offices to which he wanted to be promoted.

The Comédie-Française mounted a fine production; the casting was brilliant. The opening night, nevertheless, was a grandiose failure. The howls from the audience Beaumarchais bore philosophically; he paid attention to critiques made in good faith and disdained the jealousy of others. By no means beaten down by this failure, he returned to his manuscript and corrected, altered, rewrote, cut, streamlined, and revised it. Forty-eight hours after the opening, on January 31, to be precise, he submitted his play once more for public approval, and this time it was received warmly. Despite its unfortunate debut, *Eugénie* had an honorable career on the principal national stage (where it would be revived many times until 1863), and provincial theaters welcomed it favorably. In London, David Garrick produced it at Drury Lane under the title *The School for Rakes*.

In this blessed era when theater and libertinage were the two great French passions, where society women tore each other apart arguing over authors who had fallen or triumphed, the author could not long remain unnoticed. He was spoken about everywhere, in the salons, cafés, and corridors, but also in studios and shops. From this point of view Beaumarchais had scored a publicity victory. Nobody in Paris could ignore his existence, least of all Geneviève-Madeleine Wattebled, the wealthy widow of the master of the wardrobe at the revels office, Antoine Lévêque.

Some friends had organized a meeting between her and Beaumarchais in a remote alley off the Champs-Élysées. Geneviève was fine featured, with transparent skin and sensual lips. Both timid and passionate, she feared tying her fate to a libertine. No doubt she had suffered from the infidelities of her late husband, for when Pierre-Augustin proposed that they unite their destinies, she reacted like a wounded woman. "Monsieur de Beaumarchais," she answered, "I am a widow. I know how little most men are restrained by the oath they swear at the altar. I feel how difficult it is to not love you. I know how much you cherish women. You are a man of honor; promise me, and I will believe you, that you will never forsake me, that you will never leave me crying in a solitary bed, prey to suspicions of jealousy." Beaumarchais so promised—and kept his word.

The marriage was celebrated at Saint-Eustache on April 11, 1768. Apart from her annuities, the second Mme. de Beaumarchais brought as dowry a house in Pantin, just outside Paris. She loved her new husband passionately and gave him a baby boy eight months after their wedding. The child received the name Augustin. Beaumarchais exulted in the thought that this son would perpetuate the name he was trying to make illustrious. Detained by business in the Touraine, he wrote to his wife: "My son, my son! How is he? I laugh when I think that I am working for him!"

One year later, in April 1769, Beaumarchais put the final touches on a new drama in five acts entitled *Les deux amis, ou le Négociant de Lyon* (*The Two Friends, or the Lyons Merchant*). In November the Comédie-Française read it and soon put it into rehearsal, scheduling it to open on January 13, 1770. Alas, despite a magnificent cast, the play was again very badly received at its opening. This time the plot privileged a description of social conditions over the depiction of characters. Beaumarchais gave free play to his own ideas and also to those of Diderot and Voltaire. Like the creator, the hero of *The Two Friends* was a recently minted noble who continues to do business although he wears a sword at his side. Again like his creator, he arouses jealousy among the nobility, both ancient and recent, who find his rapid ascension and his financial success unpardonable. Beaumarchais was addressing the bourgeoisie and more generally the Third Estate; he dedicated the play to them. "I wish," he wrote an anonymous correspondent, "for it to please merchants, this play that was made for them, and in general to honor the people of the Third Estate." The play attributed to this mercantile bourgeoisie the virtues and delicacy of feeling that until then had been reserved for the aristocracy alone. As the two friends, one a tax receiver and the other a merchant, both demonstrate extraordinary generosity, we realize that honor is not the sole property of gentlemen of the sword but exists just as much among people of commerce. A failure to keep one's word has consequences as grave for one as for the other.

In writing this apologia for financiers and more generally for the bourgeoisie, the author of *The Two Friends* was expressing his own deep convictions, certainly, but he was also flattering a public that issued from this same class. But all his fawning and fine sentiments were wasted! The regrettable response began even before the curtain fell. A joker in the stalls responded to the obscurity of the plot with a cry, "It's about a bankruptcy, and here's my twenty sous." Someone scrawled on the theater bill after the title *The Two Friends*, "By a writer who has none at all." Soon a quatrain was circulating around Paris:

> I've seen Beaumarchais's piece: it's so absurd,
> I'll tell you about it in a word.
> While capital is worked in every way,
> There's naught like interest throughout the play.

The critic Baron Grimm added that "M. de Beaumarchais must have many faults because he has no friends. His father, Caron, was a watchmaker of reputation who left him an honest fortune. It would have been better to make good watches than to [play the bully and] buy an office at court and compose bad plays for Paris."

The philosophical clan could not forgive Beaumarchais for his money, his office at court, and his brilliant contacts. Instead of parading with strivers, they felt, he should possess a little less wealth and associate more assiduously with themselves, the literati. But the literati bored him so much, he did not even try to hide it. He fled their company and avoided their salons; he never appeared at the Wednesdays of Mme. Geoffrin, nor at the home of Mme. du Deffand (who found him "bad company"), nor at the salon of Julie de Lespinasse, the muse of the *encyclopédistes*, nor in the cafés where gentlemen spoke of fashionable books. Theorizing on politics and philosophy scarcely amused him. A person could reason usefully, he thought, only with a view to action or to making a deal; the rest was vain banter. Whatever his deep convictions, he never had the fiber for partisanship; his soul was that of a dilettante who refused to take sides. As for the social recognition that the distinguished patronesses of the Enlightenment distributed to their protégés, he cared little for it: one did not beg for what one already possessed.

In truth, Beaumarchais belonged scarcely to the Republic of Letters and not at all to the Republic of Philosophers; he shared neither their taste nor their society nor their way of living—and he flattered himself for that. He perceived philosophy as a way of thinking but certainly not as a calling, let alone as a political sect. If his attitude toward its publicists was not exactly contempt, it resembled it sufficiently to warrant solid enmity. Considered from an "ideological" angle, the judgment made on his first two plays might suggest that Beaumarchais was a participant in the struggle of the "philosophical sect" against the antiphilosophers. Belonging to neither camp (even if his secret sympathies lay with the former), he found himself rejected by both. If *The Two Friends* failed, despite its melodramatic theme involving an illegitimate child (a subject to which he would return in the Figaro cycle), it was no doubt because the financial strands of the plot were so complicated that inattentive spectators could not follow them. The social stakes on which the plot relied condemned the play to a premature closing. (Beaumarchais would later beg the Comédie-Française to revive it, without success.) After eleven performances in January and February 1770, it disappeared from Paris, although it was performed in Lyons, Marseilles, and Rouen later that year.*

The year 1770 would mark a decisive turning point in Beaumarchais's life. He successively saw the deaths of several people: his daughter, at an early age; his friend and protector Pâris-Duverney; and then his second wife; two years later his son Augustin and one of his sisters would follow to their own graves. While he would mourn them all, he became embroiled in a series of court cases; the attacks grew every day more virulent; he met with disgrace, dishonor, prison, and ruin. A cruel fatalism seemed to chase him, each blow leaving its mark. Despite this bitter experience, these "seven or eight years that empoisoned his virile age" would teach him about himself, and he would draw from them tenacity, courage, confidence, and an extraordinary lesson in hope. "For a long time," he would admit, "I have known that to live is to fight; and I would feel desolate, perhaps, if I did not feel on the other hand that to fight is to live." A new man

---

*When the Comédie-Française finally did revive it in 1783, it had only two performances and then was largely forgotten (except by Balzac, who used it as inspiration for *Le Faiseur*).

would emerge from these trials, a man more combative, more sure of himself, more determined than ever to conquer the summits.

Less than two months after the failure of *The Two Friends*, Mme. de Beaumarchais offered her husband the most precious of consolations, giving birth to a daughter on March 7, 1770. But little Aimable-Eugénie lived only a few days. Scarcely had the infant been buried than Geneviève herself, already weak from her pregnancy, felt a sudden aggravation of the chest ailment (probably tuberculosis) that had bothered her for years. She was obliged to take to her bed, where her condition worsened daily, although the most eminent doctors were called to her bedside. During the next eight months of agony, Pierre-Augustin showered her with devotion.

> In her eyes he read the fears devouring her; he tried to dissipate them with his care, his caresses, a host of small attentions that are so highly prized by understanding hearts; she received them with all the more gratitude because she could no longer hide from herself that she had lost her charm and all the attractiveness that had made her desirable, that people loved in her now only the memory of what she had been and the feelings of a pure soul, already about to escape a destroyed body that barely conserved a breath of life.

He continued to sleep in the same bed as his wife, without worrying about contagion. His family did everything they could to prevent him, going to the doctors Tronchin and Lorry, who took turns trying to persuade him to take a separate room. "Why do you want me to go away when we are doing everything to remove from her mind the idea of her death?" he answered them. "Will I betray by my conduct the hope I am trying to give her by my speech? If I spend no more nights with her, whatever I say to her, I will give her a mortal blow. Her imagination will persuade her that I am abandoning her for another or that her final hour is come." "Well then," replied Dr. Tronchin, "I must get you out of this cruel situation."

And so the doctor told his patient that he proposed to visit her at various hours of the day to follow the evolution of her illness. The next day he arrived so early in the morning that Beaumarchais was still abed. Surprised and angry, the doctor reproached Pierre-Augustin for showing so little regard for his wife, who had dared not cough or moan lest she awaken him. The poor woman tried to calm the doctor and defend her husband: his excess of attention, she protested, came from wanting to care for her himself so she would lack nothing. But Tronchin told him to leave the marital bed immediately and not to come back until his wife was well. Pierre-Augustin obeyed, but so that the unfortunate woman would not think he was abandoning her, he had a small camp bed set up in the same room, preferring to breathe the "diseased miasma" rather than cause his wife the least distress. Still, all this care could only soften the last moments of an existence that was deteriorating daily. On November 20, 1770, at the end of her strength, Mme. de Beaumarchais sighed her last breath in the arms of her husband, leaving him a widower for the second time.

Of course, he still had Augustin, his little boy, thanks to whom he could believe his lineage was assured. But in October 1772, a fever took the child at the age of three years and ten months.

Five

THE LA BLACHE AFFAIR

For four years, in truth, I have seen myself ill at ease, mistreated, attacked, denigrated, badly judged, denounced, blamed, assassinated; I lost my fortune and my health . . . Is it not time for the misery to end? —*Beaumarchais, 1775*

There are people everywhere, scheming men, who will stop at nothing . . . —*Bartholo, in* **The Barber of Seville**

After Geneviève's death, strange rumors circulated about the fact of Beaumarchais becoming a widower again, almost as promptly and provocatively as they had the first time. (It was even said that when Geneviève came to have her marriage contract with Beaumarchais signed by the Duc d'Aumont, the latter cried, "Recall, Madame, the fate of the first wife. I fear that I may be signing your bill of burial.") Unknown to the hawkers of infamous rumors, however, Geneviève had possessed more than half her fortune in annuities that he could not touch, and so Beaumarchais's financial interest lay in keeping her in good health. Moreover, she had left a son as her heir. But the calumny sowed its venom regardless. "I have seen the most honest people close to being overwhelmed by it," the creator of Figaro would cry—he knew something about such emotions!*

---

*When Voltaire heard the rumor of Beaumarchais killing his wives, he quipped: "This Beaumarchais cannot be a poisoner. He is too droll for that."

Instead of money, Geneviève left him a few jewels and diamonds valued at about 40,000 to 50,000 livres. Rather than leave these precious relics asleep in their box, Pierre-Augustin resolved to sell them for coin of the realm. Cruelly lacking in liquidity as he was, he needed the money; his wife's property being tied up in the annuities, he could see no other solution. And on the following December 25, in a little less than a month, he would have to pay the annual premium for the Touraine forestry license.

The young Marquis de La Rochefoucauld-Liancourt, who was then the main topic of the scandal sheets, said he wanted to acquire the jewels to offer them to his mistress. But to the great despair of Pierre-Augustin, the marquis changed his mind and sent back the jewel box. In a few hours all of Paris knew that Beaumarchais had tried to sell his second wife's jewels only ten days after her death. People were scandalized, or burst out laughing, and the miserable man was devastated. Once more (and this would not be the last time) these aristocrats whose privileges he claimed to share were rejecting him with disdain, reminding him that a man without birth or powerful family connections would never be anything in their eyes. The parchment title that they had sold him was worth nothing, since it did not even protect him from their jibes. Less than nothing, since these people trampled on the very principles of nobility that ought to have guaranteed its value. The frustration that Pierre-Augustin would suffer his whole life in his relations with the nobility arose less from class rivalry than from jealous spite.

Misfortunes never arrive singly; it was at this moment that Pâris-Duverney was dying. For over ten years he had been passing large sums of money to Beaumarchais. The initial income of 6,000 livres; the capital advances for the Chinon forest; various loans relating to the acquisition of his office and house at the rue de Condé; the 200,000 livres advanced during the trip to Spain—in all no less than 800,000 livres had passed from the hands of Pâris-Duverney to his protégé. Yet for all these transactions over the past ten years, there was no piece of accounting, no official attestation, no signed paper—nothing! Moreover, in order to hide their affairs from indiscreet regard, the two associates had corresponded with each other in coded language; they disguised the financial operations as gallant declarations, in what they called the "Oriental style."

In 1770 Pâris-Duverney reached the age of eighty-six. His mind remained lucid, but his constitution gave signs of alarming weakness, and Beaumarchais watched with anxiety for the moment when he could raise the issue of succession. He urgently needed to obtain from the old man a settlement of accounts, officially signed by his hand, lacking which he would be exposed to the claims of unscrupulous third parties. On February 15, 1770, a last will and testament was drawn up that designated Joseph-Alexandre Falcoz, Comte de La Blache, as the sole legatee of his great-uncle, "to mark his satisfaction in the nobility of his sentiments, his conduct and his personal attachment to which he had given all the signs on all occasions." Aged thirty-one, with "a cute little face like a blowing cherub" (as Beaumarchais nicely described him), but of unbearable fatuousness, the Comte de La Blache despised the weak as zealously as he courted those of whom he had need. Haughty, irascible, and subject to sudden fits of fury, he was jealous of Pierre-Augustin's intimacy with his great-uncle and detested his rival with his usual immoderation. "For ten years I have hated this man, as a lover adores his mistress," he would repeat to anyone who would listen.

The count's hatred was soon compounded by a desire for vengeance. For the time being, he wanted to isolate his old uncle, cutting him off from the outside world. Installing himself in quarters only a short walk away, he veritably terrorized the unhappy old man, depriving him of any freedom of movement, watching over his every act and gesture—in short, treating him like a prisoner. Pâris-Duverney, eager to avoid a confrontation, bought peace at the cost of a thousand small cowardly acts and was reduced to undertaking childish ruses to escape the vigilance of his guardian. He received Beaumarchais only with the greatest secrecy, leaving his house in a carriage, then returning a moment later by the garden gate, slipping along the walls into his office, and shutting himself in with a double lock. It was his only means of freely talking with his young associate. La Blache was soon alerted and redoubled his vigilance. Moreover, he used every means to destroy his great-uncle's affection for Beaumarchais. There was no calumny, no baseness to which he did not stoop for this purpose; he even went so far as to send anonymous letters to both protector and protégé, trying to set them against each other.

Disgusted by the situation, Pierre-Augustin complained angrily one day to his spiritual father, who answered: "My friend, you are the finest passion of my soul. But I seem to be only your shameful passion."

Nevertheless, after many discussions, on April 1, 1770, Beaumarchais finally held in his hands a signed settlement of accounts. But since they had not been able to consult a notary, Pierre-Augustin had to be content with a private agreement, one not legally certified. This document, which had been preceded by several drafts, would become the subject of a court case lasting seven years. It has been kept in the family archives: it is a great double sheet of paper. The list of accounts, entirely in Beaumarchais's hand, fills the recto and verso of the first sheet; Duverney has dated and signed the second page in the lower left, and on the right is the signature of Beaumarchais. The deed was prepared in two copies, one for each party. Essentially it stated that Beaumarchais had indeed repaid to Duverney 160,000 livres in notes to the bearer, out of the 200,000 that the latter had lent him before his departure for Spain; 40,000 had been spent "for personal and secret affairs." Moreover, Duverney declared that Pierre-Augustin was quit of any debt to him, and he even acknowledged owing *him* the sum of 15,000, payable at will. He ceded him ownership of a third of the Chinon forest that he had initially financed for him, and in order "to aid him with the new funds that the affair requires," he promised to lend him 75,000 livres over eight years, without interest. Three months later, on July 17, Duverney died. Thus began one of the most famous political and judicial affairs of the eighteenth century.

Before embarking on the story, we need to introduce the man who would become Beaumarchais's friend, ally, and first biographer. Six years younger than Beaumarchais, Gudin de La Brenellerie was also the son of a Protestant watchmaker, a neighbor of Voltaire's, who had briefly studied theology in Geneva before coming to Paris to try his hand at letters. This poetaster's first tragedy was called *Clytemnestra*, but he is chiefly remembered for writing an elegy to Voltaire and for being "the humble satellite of a singularly mobile and luminous planet": Beaumarchais. Meeting in a salon in late 1770, the two men formed a friendship that nothing would shake for thirty years; Gudin became a Boswell to his Johnson. In the adversities to come, Beaumarchais knew he could count unreservedly on the absolute devotion of this modest and trustworthy friend. And he would indeed soon need an ally.

When Duverney died, none of the clauses of the settlement of account had been executed, neither the reimbursement of the 15,000 nor the loan of the 75,000. Out of respect for convention, Beaumarchais let a month pass before presenting his letter of credit to the Comte de La Blache. The count first tried to stall, alleging that he was too little informed about his uncle's affairs, that an inventory was not yet done, and that he could not find a copy of this document. Things dragged on for several weeks, as the two men exchanged bittersweet missives. La Blache had been promoted to brigadier general and was associated with Chancellor Maupeou's faction fighting the hereditary magistrature of the *parlements*, which Louis XV had just dissolved, and so matters took a political turn.*

Having given the original of his letter of credit to his notary, Beaumarchais asked La Blache to come and inspect it. But the noble heir cried imposture, denounced the document as false, and exclaimed, beside himself: "Ten years will pass before he ever gets this money, during which I will vilify him in every way!" On the matter of the 15,000 livres due to his adversary, he denounced the document as false, but he did recognize it in the sense of demanding the restitution of the 139,000 livres owed to his uncle—from which the settlement had precisely discharged Beaumarchais. Summoned shortly afterward as witnesses, Duverney's stewards, notably his cashier, testified to the authenticity of the signature, but the heir persisted in maintaining it was counterfeit, supported by his lawyer, Maître Caillard, who boldly declared: "It is thus that justice will have vengeance, and honest citizens will see with satisfaction our opponent caught in the traps that he himself had set."

A trial proceeded in a climate rendered pestilential by groundless allegations, perfidious insinuations, and heinous statements—all

---

*The parlements were regional law courts and presented the only challenge to royal absolutism. When the legal establishment balked at a tax increase in 1771, Chancellor Maupeou abolished them—this is seen by historians as a step toward Revolution. The parlements would be reinstated under Louis XVI.

orchestrated with diabolical villainy by La Blache's lawyer Caillard. Revolted by so much ingenuity in the service of evil, Beaumarchais attacked that kind of lawyer: "Oh what a miserable job for a man who, to gain the money of another, tries unworthily to dishonor a third, to shamelessly alter facts, distort texts, falsely cite authorities, and make a game of lying and bad faith!" The case was making a stir; public opinion became passionately interested, especially because the adversaries were a freshly ennobled commoner and a gentleman of the court. The Prince de Conti summarized it as follows: "Beaumarchais will be paid or hanged." To which the actress Sophie Arnould added: "If he is hanged, you will see that the rope breaks."

While La Blache's lawyers in their memoranda presented this case as a combat between a great seigneur and a nobody, Beaumarchais reduced it to an ordinary issue: "Our enemy flatters himself with arming against us the whole military corps of the nobility. What does the nobility have to do with a trial of the vilest interest? I will honor as much as you wish the man of qualities, the officer general, provided that I am left the sole legatee!" He adjured both his partisans and adversaries not to be preoccupied with "grades and ranks," for they should not subsist in a courtroom. He did not contest the "benefit" of illustrious birth, he affirmed, recognizing that, without nobles or "intermediate ranks" between king and people, France would comprise only a despot and slaves. But the issue was to decide whether La Blache was an "unjust legatee" or if he himself was a false creditor.

The trial lasted almost four months in lower court. By a first ruling in February 1772, the court rejected plaintiff Comte de La Blache's suit to annul the settlement of accounts of April 1, 1770, and recognized the writing and signature of Pâris-Duverney at the bottom of this document. A second ruling on March 14 condemned La Blache to execute all its provisions, to settle expenses, and to pay Beaumarchais damages and interests for the prejudice he had suffered. In those days a grand seigneur could believe himself to be above judges; since the Comte de La Blache thought he was essentially superior, and was certainly hopping mad and stuffed with arrogance, he went to the home of one of the magistrates who had condemned him and made a scene. "It is quite strange, Monsieur, that you have supported (perhaps formed) the opinion that was contrary to my interests at the Cour des Requêtes de l'Hôtel. My post chaise is at your door, and I am going to complain loudly at Versailles. We will see what results!" Taken aback, the magistrate, who understood that he did not have to account to anyone, least of all to this mounted whippersnapper in spurs, pushed him gently toward the door, inviting him to make his complaint at Versailles right away. Beaumarchais concluded that "this is how ridicule and vanity are inseparable companions; thus folly and pride are always holding hands." Naturally, La Blache had to have revenge and hastened to file an appeal against the two rulings to the Paris parlement, persuaded that this higher jurisdiction would be more favorable to him than the Cour des Requêtes de l'Hôtel.

And so the curtain fell on the first act of this judicial drama; Beaumarchais had won in court a success that had been meanly denied him onstage. That he emerged a victor in this first round could not be denied. But at what price? And in what state? Defeated, bruised, and humiliated, he was incapable of enjoying his victory, for it tasted so much like defeat. Perhaps never was he so aware of the abyss that separated him from the society to which he claimed to belong as in those days. In the course of the trial, ignoble insinuations were spread about him. People perfidiously recalled the abrupt deaths of his two wives and the benefits that he had drawn from them in succession. The news of the courtroom proceedings seemed to echo these rumors, quickly relayed to the foreign gazettes. Moreover, Beaumarchais's relations with Pâris-Duverney were perhaps not as pure as they appeared, people whispered. The morals of the old financier, a hardened bachelor, had caused chatter; some imputed to him the "Socratic sin." Had Beaumarchais not deployed charm and seductiveness in the old man's company? Had he not been his new Alcibiades? And did their strange letters not reflect the customary language practices used within the small community of *infâmes*? The same insinuation could very well have been made against La Blache— he had been raised from childhood by his old uncle, who treated him as a son before making him his sole heir. But people hesitated to blacken the reputation of a gentleman, while they risked nothing in dragging Pierre-Augustin Caron's name through the mud, even with his title of "de Beaumarchais." A man without a clientele is a man alone, and Beaumarchais's pretension to nobility, proclaimed with the arrogance of the parvenu, only isolated him more.

The Comte de La Blache was spreading the rumor that Mesdames of France had chased their former music master away for dishonorable acts. So in a letter of February 9, 1772, Beaumarchais asked the Comtesse de Périgord, first lady-in-waiting to Princess Victoire, to deliver public testimony as to his probity.

> Madame Countess, in a court case about money that is being pleaded in Paris, and over which my adversary has furnished only dishonest defenses, he has dared to inform our judges that Mesdames, who once had honored me with their greatest protection, have since then recognized that I rendered myself unworthy by a thousand dishonorable traits and have forever banished me from their presence. Such an outrageous falsehood, though bearing on a subject foreign to my case, might cause me the greatest harm in the eyes of my judges. I fear that some hidden enemy might have sought to damage me with Mesdames. I spent four years meriting their goodwill by the most assiduous and most disinterested care for the various objects of their amusements. These amusements having ceased to please the princesses, I did not make myself importunate with them, soliciting the favors for which I know they are always tormented. Today I ask for some recompense for an ardent zeal that will never end: not that Mme. Victoire grant any protection in my trial, but that she deign to attest by your pen that, as long as I was employed in her service, she recognized me as a man of honor and incapable of doing anything that might attract a disgrace as withering as that with which someone wants to stain me. I have assured my judges that all the defamations of my adversary will not prevent me from obtaining this testimony of Mesdames' justice. I am at their feet and at yours, penetrated in advance with the most respectful gratitude, Madame la Comtesse, etc.

The Countess of Périgord replied right away: "Monsieur, I informed Mme. Victoire of your letter and have her assurance *that*

she never said anything to anybody that might harm your reputation,
knowing nothing of you that might put her in a position to do so. She
authorized me to transmit this to you. The Princess even added that
she was aware of your lawsuit but that her references to you could
never do you any harm whatsoever, and particularly in a lawsuit, and
that you may be tranquil on this point, etc."

Beaumarchais's letter to the Lady of Honor had asked only for a
testimony of good conduct, and he had been wary of directly solicit-
ing the support of Mesdames in his lawsuit. But he committed an
error, or an imprudence, by having the Comtesse de Périgord's response printed in a pamphlet against La Blache. There he declared
that his adversary was trying "to remove from [me] the honorable
protection that Mesdames had always granted [me] . . . by running
to whisper in all the judges' ears that the princesses were saying that
sire de Beaumarchais had rendered himself unworthy of their goodness and they took no kind of interest in [me] any longer." Beaumarchais went on, writing that he had been able to reclaim the justice of
Madame Victoire before the judgment in the case. "This generous
princess indeed wants to authorize [me] to publish that all the discourse about [me] in the present affair is absolutely false, and that
she has never recognized anything that was capable of damaging
[my] reputation during the whole time that [I] had the honor of
being in her service."

If Beaumarchais faithfully summarized the countess's letter, his
commentary audaciously skewed its meaning, by making Mesdames
say much more than they had actually said. Their character reference
became under his pen a deposition in his favor in the court case that
opposed him to the Comte de La Blache. Nothing could more have
displeased these princesses than to see themselves implicated against
their will in a legal matter. They felt they had been trapped, and they
were not wrong: their protégé's "gaffe" might pass at best as an
impropriety, at worst as an imposture. In any case, his adversary fully
exploited it: he hastened to Versailles to inform Mesdames that the
impudent man dared cite their testimony in a public pamphlet,
implying that they considered themselves on his side and wished for
the success of his cause! These were not his exact statements, as we
know; Beaumarchais had simply spoken of *interest, protection, justice.*

But his intention had undoubtedly indeed been to hint at their support. The princesses judged it prudent to prevent any abuse of their name and sent La Blache these lapidary lines: "We declare we take no interest in M. Caron de Beaumarchais and his affair, and did not permit him to insert in a printed and public pamphlet any assurances of our protection."

Warned of La Blache's expedition to Versailles and foreseeing the disastrous effect of his revelation, Beaumarchais sent a copy of the printed pamphlet to the countess, accompanied by an evidently embarrassed note, dated February 14:

> I have the honor of sending you one of my pamphlets in which I make the respectful use that Madame Victoire allowed of the justice that she deigns to render me and of the letter that you honored me with. It remains for me to pray that you crown your good deed by assuring the princess that I am very touched by the honorable testimony that she has not refused to a zealous but now useless servant. There are moments when the simplest justice becomes an astounding favor, particularly when it arrives to help a wronged man. As soon as the judgment in this case has allowed me to breathe, my first duty will be to assure you of the respectful gratitude with which I am, Madame la Comtesse, etc.

Upon returning from Versailles, La Blache hurried to have printed thirty copies of the princesses' declaration, which he addressed that very evening to all the judges. At the same time he circulated the rumor that Beaumarchais had himself confected Mesdames' false letter. Beaumarchais rushed to the court recorder, M. Dufour, who accused him of producing false letters of protection. Beaumarchais then showed him the original letter. The stupefied man examined the writing and finally exclaimed: "Explain then, Monsieur, the meaning of the note from Mesdames that M. de La Blache is showing around." Beaumarchais told the whole story. Returning home, he found a summons from the chief of police, Sartine. He went there and encountered the same reproaches; he gave the same justification. "I am still charged," replied the police chief, "to ask the prosecutor to suppress the note, and I cannot do otherwise."

What was to be done? Beaumarchais buried his bitterness in the secrecy of his soul and fought, again and always, to bring out the truth. "All Paris was fooled," he would write. "All Paris believed that I had offered false letters from Mesdames, to the point that my keenest defenders, shrugging their shoulders, confined themselves to saying that this incident had no relation to the issue in our trial. And I, devastated, publicly dishonored by the most perfidious enemy, but restrained by my respect for Mesdames and by the circumspection imposed by the suit that was underway, I swallowed my resentment; I kept my silence." The court ruled in his favor; La Blache appealed.

Six

THE MAD DAY

You believe an untrue story, you come in a rage, you turn every-
thing upside down like some great roaring cataract: you are
looking for a man, you have to have [him] or you are going to
break down doors, smash holes in walls.

—*Figaro, in* **The Marriage of Figaro**

A perfectly serene Beaumarchais awaited the summons for the appeal.
Why should he worry, since his case was neither unjust nor doubtful?
After all, he had won in the lower court, and he had every reason to
think that the Paris parlement would uphold that judgment. It sufficed to be patient. While waiting, he devoted himself to his usual
activities at the tribunal of the Louvre; he relaxed from his legal cog-
itations by writing again for the theater, despite the failure of his first
two plays. Abandoning the serious genre this time, for which he was
decidedly not made, he composed a comic opera on a subject that
had been done a thousand times but that unfailingly unleashed hilar-
ity in the audience, which he summarized in three phrases: "An old
man in love wants to marry his ward. An adroit young lover prevents
it, and that very day in disguise [he] makes her [his] wife in the
house of the guardian. That is the plot." The play would be called
The Barber of Seville. He embellished it with a few satirical songs on
Italian or Spanish airs brought back from Madrid, then gave it for
reading to the Comédie-Italienne, which was then still called the
Théâtre des Chansons, specializing in this kind of entertainment.

One evening he dined at the home of Mlle. Ménard, an actress at the Comédie-Italienne and an intelligent woman, at whose home men of letters and grand lords like the Duc de Chaulnes sometimes gathered; he occupied a coveted place next to the young woman, for he protected her charms in exchange for her favors. That evening Beaumarchais told his friends that his play had been rejected. Instead of sympathizing, they congratulated him: what more could he hope for? He need only suppress some of the songs, transform his comic opera into a comedy, and present it to the Comédie-Française, where it would be welcome. In any case, *The Barber of Seville* was a hundred times better suited to the theater of Molière than to that of Harlequin. The successful playwright Michel-Jean Sedaine, who knew the mysteries of the latter, revealed the secret reason the Comédie-Italienne had rejected the play: Clairval, the principal actor there, had been a barber before going on the stage. Since it was up to him to accept or reject a play, he had shut the door on the Sevillian Figaro, out of fear that it would remind the public of his modest origins.

Transformed into a comedy, and stripped of most of its tunes and satirical songs, *The Barber of Seville, or the Useless Precaution*, was accordingly submitted to the reading committee of the Comédie-Française, which enthusiastically accepted it on January 3, 1773. The roles were cast, and work began the following month. On February 12 the play won the approval of the censor Marin, and the next day the chief of police countersigned. Two weeks later everything was stopped: no more play, no more rehearsals. The reason was unbelievable but true: the author was in prison! How did Beaumarchais find himself locked up?

Pierre-Augustin had seduced Mlle. Ménard, the mistress of his acquaintance the liberal and eccentric Duc de Chaulnes, then aged thirty. According to the king's mistress, Mme. du Barry, who cannot be denied a certain experience on the subject, the actress had

> got herself noticed for her kindness and her intellect among the girls of Paris. Courtiers, nobles of the robe, and bourgeois financiers all found her accessible: she received everybody. Gentlemen with châteaux and those with medals of honor, as well as tax collectors aspired to the honor of ruining themselves over her. She

had already satisfied a dozen of both kinds when the Duc de Chaulnes joined their ranks; he defeated his rivals, he was happy. And would have remained so for a while without the greatest imprudence that a suitor can commit.

The Duc de Chaulnes was a physical colossus with an outsize temperament: brusque, hot-tempered, and endowed with herculean strength. Observed Beaumarchais's friend Gudin:

> His character was a rare assembly of contradictory qualities: intellect and no judgment at all, pride and a lack of discernment which removed his sense of dignity and of his relations with his superiors, his equals and his inferiors; a vast and disordered memory; a great desire to educate himself and an even greater taste for dissipation; a prodigious physical strength; a violence of character that disturbed his reason, already rather confused; frequent bouts of anger in which he resembled a savage drunk, not to mention a ferocious beast. Always given to momentary impulses without regard for consequences, he was mixed up in more than one nasty affair. Obliged to leave the kingdom, he employed his exile in making a scientific voyage. He had visited the Pyramids, frequented the Bedouins in the desert, and brought back a monkey that he struck daily.

It is not known when or in what circumstances Chaulnes made the acquaintance of Mlle. Ménard. Becoming his official mistress, she bore him a daughter and, at his request, definitively gave up the stage. Although her protector lived in extreme debauchery, he proved ferociously jealous over her, demanding exemplary conduct from her and raising his hand against her over the least infraction. Her life turned into a nightmare; meanwhile her lover found himself in the worst financial difficulties and saw his inheritance shrinking day by day until he was forced to cease keeping his "protégée." The poor woman finally thought she was free of him and able to seek a more tranquil existence. But the executioner could not long neglect his victim. Several times a week he showed up at her place for the sole purpose of tormenting her, his favorite pastime. He showered her with insults and threats, had her interrogated and spied on, and harassed her with questions about her visits. The young woman secretly dreamed of the man who would deliver her and before whom she would not tremble. She would soon meet him in the person of Beaumarchais.

Gudin again noted his friend's attractiveness to women:

> One of the greatest faults I knew in Beaumarchais was his appearing so likable to women that he was always preferred; which made him as many enemies as they had suitors trying to please them. To present to such a man the sight of a young woman persecuted by her lover and who dreamed only of tender sensuality in the arms of another, was indeed to introduce the wolf into the sheepfold. This was the inconceivable error committed by the Duc de Chaulnes the day he invited the seducer to dinner with his mistress. No doubt he wanted to show his confidence—or else thank him for the loans he had been given.

A few days after their first meeting, a garden near the Père Lachaise was rented, where the two lovers saw each other in secret. Theirs was a liaison of hearts and bodies, where monetary interest had no place, where pleasure was not paid for; the young actress willingly renounced her role as kept courtesan for that of a woman in love. They were secluded from the rest of the world, sheltered from sight, in an isolated spot propitious for endearments and embraces. While they were having a perfect love affair, nobody seemed to notice the enormous cuckold's horns that were growing on the noble brow of the duke. However, a guardian spirit was watching over his honor: Mme. Duverger, his former mistress, could not stand to be abandoned and had sworn to take vengeance on her rival. By spying on Mlle. Ménard, she discovered her secret garden, her clandestine rendezvous, and her feelings for Beaumarchais. She even managed, by bribing a chambermaid, to seize a few letters bearing irrefutable proof of Ménard's crime and sent them to the Duc de Chaulnes.

Learning of his mistress's treachery, the duke went into a fury that cost him his reason. If Ménard had betrayed him with a duke or peer, he might perhaps have tolerated it, if not pardoned her. But the son of a watchmaker, a businessman, a *littérateur*—that was too much! On the morning of February 11, 1773—after intercepting Gudin, boxing his ears, and pulling off his wig—the duke rushed to his rival's house in the rue de Condé. The servants told him he was at the Varenne du Louvre, so he got back in his carriage and raced to the tribunal where Beaumarchais, who had been warned by Gudin that Chaulnes was on the rampage, was rendering justice with grand pomp. Bursting into the hearing chamber and shouting "with all the energy of Les Halles market, he swore to kill him on the spot, tear his heart out and drink the blood he thirsted for."

Beaumarchais left an account of this affair worthy of his best comedies:

> "Ah, is that all, Monsieur le Duc? Please allow business before pleasure."
>
> When the hearing was over, I came down, asking M. de Chaulnes what he wanted and what his complaints could be against a man he had not seen in six months.
>
> "No explanations. Let us go fight in a field, or I shall make a scandal right here."
>
> I told him, "At least will you permit me to go home and get a sword? In my carriage I have only a poor one, with which I hope you will not expect me to defend myself against you?"
>
> He replied, "We will go to M. le Comte de La Tour-du-Pin, who will lend you one and whom I want to serve as our witness."
>
> He jumped into my carriage first: I got in after him, and his followed us. He did me the honor of assuring me that I would not escape him, ornamenting his speech with all the superb imprecations that are so familiar to him. The sang-froid of my replies distressed him and increased his rage. He threatened me with his fist in my carriage. I observed that, if he wanted to fight, a public insult could only distance him from his goal, and I was not going to get my sword to engage in a street brawl in the meantime. We arrived at the count's, who came out and mounted on the running board of my carriage.
>
> I said, "Monsieur le Duc is kidnapping me without my knowing why: he wants to cut my throat. But in this strange adven-

ture, he makes me hope at least that you, Monsieur, will witness the conduct of the two adversaries."

M. de La Tour-du-Pin told me that a pressing affair forced him to go at that very hour to the Luxembourg Palace, and that it would keep him there until four hours after midday. (I did not doubt that M. de La Tour-du-Pin's goal was to allow enough time to pass for a hothead to calm down.) He left. M. de Chaulnes wanted to take me to his home until four o'clock.

"Oh, not that, Monsieur le Duc. Just as I would not wish to meet you alone on the field because of the risk of being accused by you of having killed you if you forced me to wound you, so I will not go to a house of which you are the master and where you will not fail to trick me. I am ordering my coachman to take me home."

"If you get down, I will stab you in front of your door." Strong oaths in the carriage.

"Wait, Monsieur le Duc. When one wants to fight, one does not chitchat. Come to my house, and I will serve you dinner, and if I do not manage to return you to good sense between now and four o'clock, and if you persist in forcing me to choose between fighting and getting my face scratched, then the fate of arms will decide."

My carriage arrived at my door. I got down, he followed me and feigned accepting my dinner. I coldly gave orders. The postman gave me a letter; he pounced and tore it from me in front of my father and all the servants. I wanted to turn the affair into joking, and he started to swear. My father was afraid, I reassured him, and I ordered dinner to be brought us in my study. We went upstairs. My valet followed me, and I asked for my sword.

"It is with the furbisher."

"Go get it, and if it is not ready, bring me another."

"I forbid you to go out," said M. de Chaulnes, "or I will knock your brains out."

I gave my valet a sign, and he left. I wanted to write, and he grabbed my pen. I told him that my house was a sanctuary that I would not violate unless he forced me to by such excesses. I wanted to have peace talks over his folly in wanting to kill me; he dashed at my poor mourning sword that had been placed on my desk and told me with all the rage of a maniac and gnashing of teeth that I would not carry it much farther. He drew my own sword, his being at his side; he was going to stab me.

"Oh, coward," I cried, and I seized him around the waist to put myself outside the weapon's reach; I wanted to push him to my fireplace in order to ring the bell-pull. With his free hand, he scratched me in the eyes and face, which flowed with blood. Without releasing him, I managed to ring, and my people came running.

"Disarm this madman," I cried to them while holding on to him.

My cook, as strong and brutal as the duke, wanted to take a log to knock him out.

I cried louder: "Disarm him, but do not hurt him; he will say that he was killed in my house." They took my sword away from him. Instantly he jumped at my head and tore out my hair at the front. The pain I felt made me release his body, and with all the strength in my arm I planted a great punch on his face.

"Wretch! You are striking a duke and peer of the realm!"

I admit that this exclamation, extravagant in the circumstances, would have made me laugh at any other time. But as he was stronger than me and took me by the throat, I was concerned only with my defense. My suit and shirt were torn, my face bloody. My father, an old man of seventy-five, wanted to throw himself across us; he knows about the furors of duke-and-peer. My servants started to separate us. I had lost my own composure, and blows were given back as soon as taken. We found ourselves at the edge of the stairs, where the bull fell, rolling over my servants and taking me with him. This horrible mess returned him to sanity somewhat. He heard knocking at the street door, ran there, and saw enter this same young man [Gudin de La Brenellerie] who had warned me that very morning in my carriage. He took him by the arm, pulled him into the house, and swore that nobody would enter or leave unless by his order until he had torn me to pieces. Due to the noise he was making, people were gathering in front of the door; a woman of my house called out a window that her master was being killed. My young friend, frightened to see me disfigured and bloody, wanted to take me upstairs. The duke would not permit it. His rage revived, he drew his sword that had remained at his side, for it is noteworthy that none of my people had dared to take it from him, believing, according to what they told me, that it would show a lack of respect that would have had bad consequences for them. He made as if to stab me, eight people jumped on him and disarmed him. He wounded my valet in the head, my coachman had a cut nose, my cook a slashed hand.

"Shameful coward!" I cried. "This is the second time he comes at me, who am unarmed, with a sword."

He ran into the kitchen to look for a knife; they followed him and locked up anything that might inflict a fatal wound. I went back to my study. I armed myself with fire tongs. I was going to go back down when I realized something that proved that this man had become absolutely mad: as soon as he did not see me any longer, he went into the dining room, sat alone at the table, ate a great plate of soup and cutlets, and drank two carafes of water. He heard knocking again at the street door, ran to open it, and saw Commissioner Chenu who, surprised by the horrible mess in which he saw my household, especially amazed at my wounded face, asked me what had happened.

"What happened, Monsieur, is a cowardly maniac entered here with the intention of dining with me, assaulted me in the face as soon as he set foot in my study, wanted to kill me with my own sword, then with his own. You see, Monsieur, that with the people around me, I could have torn him apart, but it would have been too good for him. His parents, charmed to be rid of him, might still have given me a hard time. I contained myself, and except for the hundred punches with which I repulsed the outrage he has done on my face and wig, I have stopped anyone from doing him harm."

The duke spoke and said he was supposed to fight at four o'clock with me in the presence of the Comte de La Tour-le-Pin but that he could not wait until the appointed hour.

"What do you think of this man, who after making a horrible

scandal in my house, himself divulges before a public official his guilty intention, compromising an officer by naming him as designated witness and destroying in a single word any possibility of executing his plan, which this cowardice proves he never seriously intended anyway?"

At these words, my maniac, brave at fisticuffs like an English sailor, launched himself on me a fifth time. I had dropped my fire tongs when the commissioner arrived. I defended myself as best I could before the assembly, who separated us a third time. M. Chenu asked me to stay in my salon and took away the duke, who wanted to break the mirrors. At this instant, my valet came back with a new sword; I took it and said to the commissioner:

"I do not have designs on a duel, I never will have. But if I do not accept a rendezvous with this man, I will have to go around the city with this sword constantly attached; if he comes to insult me (since the publicity he gives this horrible adventure proves that he is the aggressor), I swear that I will remove him, if I can, from the society that he dishonors with his cowardice."

The weapon I held commanding respect, the duke withdrew without a word to my dining room, where M. Chenu, having followed him, was also more surprised than frightened to see him punching himself in the face and tearing his hair with both hands out of rage for having failed to kill me. M. Chenu finally persuaded him to go home; he had the sang-froid to first have his hair combed by my valet, whom he had injured. I went back up to have my wounds dressed, and he threw himself into his carriage.

Beaumarchais could have (and perhaps should have) lodged a complaint on the spot against his aggressor. After all, he had Commissioner Chenu right there; the women of the house, frightened by what was happening, had sent for him by calling to the neighbors from the window. But Beaumarchais did not do so and did not authorize anyone else to. If the commissioner had questioned him and got depositions from witnesses, the duke being caught in flagrante, a criminal trial would have followed; the king alone could have spared him by sending him to some citadel. "I did not have him arrested this morning at the tribunal and I will never have him arrested at my home," Beaumarchais wrote. "Between men of honor, there is another way of proceeding, and this is the only one I will employ."

"Thus on that day," exclaimed Gudin, "Beaumarchais, insulted and provoked without cause by all sorts of oaths, saved the life and liberty of the person who had just attacked him and spared him a criminal trial." Dear Gudin, always so naïve! Always prompt to find the most generous motives in the actions of his friend! It is clear that Beaumarchais was only obeying the most elementary prudence, at all costs avoiding further enraging this man whose delirium equaled his power and who, with one stroke, was capable of turning the situation in his favor and making the victim appear to be the attacker. His vengeance might be feared: an assassination, a lettre de cachet,* calumnies still more awful than what he had already propagated. Beaumarchais knew better than anybody that a lord "does us rather good when he does not do us evil."

At the end of this crazy day, one might imagine that an exhausted Pierre-Augustin would want only to tend his wounds and rest quietly at home. But this devil of a man always surprises us. That very evening, as fresh as if nothing had happened, he went to his old friend M. Lopes, to whom he had promised a reading of *The Barber of Seville*. He arrived so late that he was no longer expected; some of the women accused him of forgetfulness, while others had been worried. Barely had he entered the salon when he was pressed with questions, and so he gaily recounted what had happened. Everybody thought that there was no longer a question of him reading the comedy. They did not know him: he was not going to spoil the pleasure of these ladies—or his own—on account of this country bumpkin! And so he read his play with verve, then played the harp and sang seguidillas for the rest of the evening and into the night.

Chaulnes' later deposition blackened his adversary's character: "I have never been known to a law-court, to the police, in Paris or any place, as a quarrelsome person, a gambler, or a madman; while the reputation of M. de Beaumarchais is far from being equally intact; for

*Imprisonment by royal order.

independently of his well-known insolence, and the most incredible rumors, *he is at this moment undergoing a criminal prosecution for forgery.*" Forty-eight hours later Commissioner Chenu sent a report to his superior, Chief of Police Sartine. With much less verve, it confirmed the tale we have just read.

All Paris was talking of the famous quarrel, all the more interesting in that it opposed two of the capital's most visible personalities, one for his extravagances, the other for his talents. Gazettes and broadsheets fed on it, and court and city alike were divided between partisans of the grand seigneur and the defenders of Caron. The topic became a political debate.

The Minister of the King's household, Duc de La Vrillière, kept Beaumarchais under house arrest, under guard, until he accounted to the marshals (who settled disputes between noblemen), for the quarrel with the Duc de Chaulnes, whom the king had just incarcerated by a lettre de cachet. Whether because of a misunderstanding over the terms of his release from house arrest, or because he published his account of the quarrel, or because La Vrillière thought it indecent to let Caron go while a nobleman was locked up because of him is not clear. But eight days later, on February 26, 1773, in execution of a lettre de cachet signed by Louis XV and countersigned by the minister of the king's household, Beaumarchais was sent to the prison of For-l'Évêque.

Seven

THE PRISONER OF
FOR-L'ÉVÊQUE

*Being right is always a crime in the eyes of power, which always
wants to punish and never to judge.*
—*Beaumarchais, Letter to Gudin*

*In this way I shall spend my life making mistakes and then beg-
ging to be forgiven, committing sins and inventing excuses:
deserving your sympathy and tolerance for the naïve good faith
with which I acknowledge the one and overwhelm you with the
other.* —*Beaumarchais, "Restrained Letter"*

For-l'Évêque was an ancient, cramped building, situated between the
quai de la Mégisserie and the rue Saint-Germain-l'Auxerrois, just
behind the current Châtelet Theater. It was a site of detention for
actors arrested for serious offenses: refusal to perform, insulting the
public, public indecency, chronic absenteeism, drunkenness, and so
on. Its walls were honored to shelter, ordinarily for short periods, the
greatest artists of the Paris theaters.

Barely arrived in the cell that he would share with another
detainee, Beaumarchais begged the tribunal to bring him quickly to
justice, for while he was spinning his wheels in jail, the appeal of the
Comte de La Blache was still in court and justice was following its
due course. He had to see his lawyers and visit his judges—but
instead he was condemned to immobility, hands and feet tied (figuratively, of course, but it amounted to the same thing), as he bitterly

complained to M. de Sartine, the chief of police and one of the few allies remaining to him.

Profiting from the prisoner's forced immobility, the Comte de La Blache mounted a veritable verbal lynching campaign. Every day, escorted by his lawyer, he went to the magistrates and discussed the trial. His goal was simple: to ruin the reputation of his adversary and present himself as the victim. After all, who was this Caron, so-called Beaumarchais? A shopkeeper's son, a vulgar arriviste, a forger, a jealous lout, full of gall, running after dowries and women! False rumors, bits of gossip—everything was passed along, and everything appeared true coming from the mouth of this minor nobleman, heir to one of the largest fortunes in France. The whippersnapper was worth more than a million and a half livres! Sire La Blache thought his case was won in advance.

Meanwhile the unfortunate prisoner begged in vain for authorization to be absent for a few hours a day to go solicit his judges, as was the custom. It was an execrable custom, true, but one deeply anchored in the judicial habits of the era, and a failure to engage in it might cost one dear. The granting of this authorization was exclusively the right of the minister of the king's household. Beaumarchais thus wrote to M. de La Vrillière a memo in which he explained his conduct day by day and argued for his innocence: on March 10, a response to the memo came to Police Chief Sartine, who communicated it on the spot to the prisoner. It was a refusal without appeal. What Beaumarchais was demanding, though, was by no means presumptuous: all the actors held in For-l'Évêque benefited from provisional liberty in order to perform. Why not he, who had such need to petition his judges? The answer is simple. M. de La Vrillière had not at all appreciated the terms of Beaumarchais's memo. What had he said? That he had done no wrong, that his conduct had been "a masterpiece of prudence and courage," and that he had been thrown in prison "to the great astonishment of the world, that is to say, of all honest people." In other words, the real guilty party was none other than M. de La Vrillière himself, who was unjustly persecuting him.*

---

*Bachaumont's *Miscellany*: "This very insolent individual, who has so much self-assurance, is not liked; and although in this quarrel it does not appear that there is anything to reproach him with, he is pitied less than another person would be for the vexations he has experienced."

Prevented from going to solicit the judges in person, Beaumarchais addressed his requests to them by means of his lawyer, explaining his present situation, hoping that the rigors he was unjustly enduring would make the court more favorably inclined to his cause. Sartine, for his part, pressed him to offer La Vrillière a full and entire submission, accompanied by sincere regrets, and present his request as humbly as possible, as if asking for grace: it was the only means to obtain his right to leave. What! Prostrate himself before this crusty old man? Implore his pardon? Repent faults he had not committed?

Things stayed there until Pierre-Augustin was offered help—unexpectedly, to say the least—from Mlle. Ménard. Freshly out of the convent where she had taken refuge after the scandal over her official lover, she came on her own to offer assistance to her beloved. Truly Beaumarchais ought to have declined her offer, for far from settling his affairs, her help might make everything capsize. He knew the lovable scatterbrain well enough to distrust her initiatives. Sartine had to be warned, to be put on guard against her intrigues. But Beaumarchais did so in a light and teasing tone:

> Mme. Ménard only told me yesterday, through one of my friends [probably Gudin], that you had indeed promised to make a new effort in my favor, on Sunday, with the Minister. But the mysterious fashion in which this announcement was made to me makes one almost doubt, for the good little girl put in the many gentle and puerile affectations with which her sex seasons the least good deed. To listen to her, it would take an express order to see me, witnesses to accompany her, permission to write to me, and even precautions to be able to correspond with me through a third party.

He had written a more serious and interesting letter to Gudin:

> By virtue of a *lettre sans cachet*, signed Louis, recommended by Sartine, executed by Buhot and suffered by Beaumarchais, I am lodged, my friend, in For-l'Évêque, in an uncarpeted chamber, at 2,160 livres of rent, where I am told that apart from the necessary, I will lack for nothing. Is it the family of the duke whom I saved from a criminal trial, life and liberty? Is it the minister

whom I have constantly obeyed or anticipated his orders? Is it the
dukes and peers, with whom I can never have anything to do? I
do not know. But the sacred name of the king is such a fine
thing . . . Thus it is that in any well-policed country authority
torments those who cannot be incriminated justly. What is to be
done? Everywhere there are men, odious things happen, and the
great mistake of being right is always a crime in the eyes of
power, which always wants to punish and never to judge. I wrote
to all the Marshals of France.

Matters were stuck there, with both parties fixed in their respective positions—one refusing to yield and the other to crawl—until
March 20. That day the prisoner received a long unsigned letter that
might be summarized as follows: *Under an absolute monarchy, one
must not plead one's case as an oppressed citizen but rather submit to the
strongest law and speak as a supplicant.* The next day Beaumarchais
signed his surrender. Apparently the minister had only been waiting
for that! The next day he sent Sartine the authorization to allow the
prisoner of For-l'Évêque to leave during the day, escorted by a sworn
police officer, "on condition that he will come back on time for his
meals and to sleep." Barely had he received his authorization than
Pierre-Augustin turned bravely to his task. But from the first visits, he
had to face the fact that it was too late. The Comte de La Blache had
preceded him, spreading harmful allegations, offering base flattery,
and giving small presents. Blinded by warnings about Beaumarchais,
most of the judges claimed to be absent when he arrived. Was the
reason distrust? Or contempt? A little of both perhaps.

On April 1 Beaumarchais learned that Louis-Valentin Goëzman
had officially been designated as the case's court assessor. Now his
fate and fortune depended on this man—and on him alone, since the
magistrates almost always followed the assessor's conclusions. The
choice could not have been worse! An obscure, docile, and disci-
plined jurist without convictions, bereft of personal ideas, Goëzman
was quite devoted to fulfilling the minister's orders.* And since bad

---

*Chancellor Maupeou had introduced Goëzman in 1771 into the suspect body with which he
had replaced the old parlement. Attempting to get rid of corruption by suppressing gratuities,
some new magistrates would now find other ways of being compensated.

news never comes singly, Beaumarchais learned the same day that judgment would be handed down on April 5. In four days! Such haste! Such a judge! Was it solely bad luck? Was some machination at work? Beaumarchais went several times to quai Saint-Paul, but Goëzman refused to receive him. The time was shrinking like a *peau de chagrin*, each minute counted. What to do?

On the evening of the second, while Beaumarchais was coming back from one of his harassed errands, he made a detour to Place Dauphine, where his sister Fanchon Lépine lived. He found her in the company of Antoine Bertrand d'Ariolles, a merchant from Marseilles, who was her lover. This man seemed quite particularly interested in the story of his tribulations. And luckily so, for he knew a publisher and bookseller named Le Jay who published Goëzman's law treatises. This Le Jay saw Mme. Goëzman regularly in his bookshop, when she came to collect her husband's copyright money. An avid and spendthrift coquette, she had imprudently declared one day before witnesses "that if a generous client presented himself whose cause was just and who demanded only honest things, it would not offend her delicacy to receive a present."* Le Jay went to find her straightaway. She told him that her husband was ready to grant an interview with Beaumarchais for the sum of 200 louis. Pierre-Augustin was shocked. Two hundred louis was 4,800 livres! They were trying to ruin him! He started to refuse, then thought better of it, bargaining as he well knew how, and he ended up reducing by half the lady's price. Le Jay would take the sum to Mme. Goëzman that evening. Everything happened as planned: a valet introduced Beaumarchais to the councilor, and a few minutes later M. Goëzman joined his visitor. Craggy-faced, with hunched shoulders and a shaggy beard, his left eye affected with a divergent squint, the man inspired a sort of repulsion. He contested certain items in the file, but his observations made Pierre-Augustin wonder whether he was sufficiently informed about the case to report on it in forty-eight hours? The response fell like a bombshell: he knew it sufficiently well to judge it; moreover it was cut and dried. Another detail intrigued

---

*In Mme. Goëzman's resounding phrase, "It would be impossible to live decently with what we get, but we know the art of plucking the fowl without making it cry out."

our petitioner and increased his unease. Throughout the interview, which lasted about a quarter hour, Goëzman shook with nervous laughter. This bizarre hiccup seemed a bad sign.

Sunday April 4. Only one day left. Beaumarchais had paid so dearly for the single favor of a short audience! Negotiations resumed. Yes, there existed a way—one only—to obtain a second audience: to make a second sacrifice. Mme. Goëzman had not finished gouging the petitioner. Short of money, Beaumarchais offered her a repeating watch set with diamonds. The lady examined the jewel a long time, then declared herself satisfied. However, an additional fifteen louis were required for her husband's secretary. They were brought to her. She locked the purse in her desk and promised an audience for that very evening at seven. Arriving promptly for the rendezvous, Beaumarchais was turned away as a beggar.

On Monday, April 5, Goëzman handed in his verdict: it was overwhelming and damning. The next day the parlement issued a decree condemning Beaumarchais—but it curiously abstained from giving any motive. Goëzman's report rested on evidence whose slightness shocked more than one contemporary, and not only Beaumarchais's partisans. According to Goëzman, Duverney's settlement of accounts was worth nothing because the sums had been written in numbers and not in letters, as the law required. But if you turned the sheet, the said sums appeared in letters on the recto side, and in numbers on the verso, a perfectly legal procedure. It would be overly fastidious to detail the magistrate's argument at length: it rested only on shaky or deceitful assertions and on bad-faith interpretations. For example, claimed Goëzman, Duverney had left blank checks lying around. Unlikely! The old financier was too exact, too prudent to have committed such negligence. But even if this allegation were true, how to explain his signature of fixed date on the verso of the large sheet of paper? Reading the file today, one is quite astounded: no piece of evidence casts suspicion on Beaumarchais. The judges of the Cour des Requêtes de l'Hôtel, the lower court, had found in his favor. How to explain such an iniquity in the appeal verdict?

La Blache had been chipping away at that verdict from the start. His frequent visits to Goëzman, attested to by the concierge's log, testify to an understanding between the two men. Finally, if La

Blache obtained from Goëzman a report in his favor, it was also, we cannot doubt, because he had paid a higher price than his adversary. Goëzman had sold himself to the highest bidder. He saw two choices: either Beaumarchais was a forger who had imitated Duverney's signature on a blank document (in which case he was liable to be sent to the galleys) or else he had profited from the senility of the financier to induce him to sign the account. In either case, there was dishonor, and La Blache triumphed.

There is also a political reason for this miscarriage of justice. Beaumarchais belonged to the faction of the Prince de Conti, Chancellor Maupeou's adversary, with whom he had been intimate for several years. Their first meeting was over a trifle (a garden wall that the prince had demolished to make way for his carriages). Gudin tells us that after this incident, Conti developed "the greatest affection" for the judge of the Varenne du Louvre, and Gudin adds: "This prince had a lot of spirit and—more rare in a man of this rank and rather absolute character—he had liberal ideas." The friendship of such a man was at the moment very compromising for Beaumarchais. Conti had been one of the first princes of the blood against Maupeou; he put himself in the lead to ask the King to recall the old parlements. It was also insinuated that Conti used Beaumarchais for his parties of debauchery. The gazette *L'Espion Anglais* intimated that there was familiarity between the two men: "We know that the rapprochement between a plebeian of the lowest class and such an elevated person can only operate through vice and debauchery."

The decree of April 6 condemned Beaumarchais to pay La Blache 56,300 livres plus court costs. Better still, these sums were demanded immediately. La Blache unleashed the bailiffs, seized Caron's country house, and confiscated his house at the rue de Condé. His old father was thrown in the street and had to ask friends for asylum; his sister Julie took refuge in a convent. A hundred other creditors came out of the woods, like wolves smelling carnage. "It seems that the happiness of ruining me is the only attraction that animates my adversary," sighed Beaumarchais, who was not exaggerating when he painted his situation in his *Memoranda Against Goëzman*: "Outraged in my person, deprived of my liberty, having lost fifty thousand écus, imprisoned, calumnied, ruined, without free revenue, without money, without credit, my family bereft, my fortune pillaged, and having for sustenance in prison only my pain and misery; I fell in two months time from the most agreeable state which an individual may enjoy, into abjection and despair; I was ashamed and pitiful to myself." Touched by his situation, Sartine pleaded his cause once more to the Duc de La Vrillière. The prisoner addressed a request to the king, begging him to have compassion on his situation and order his freedom so he could put his affairs in order. The minister was finally convinced and signed a release on May 5. Three days later Beaumarchais left For-l'Évêque after ten weeks' incarceration.

After the judgment Mme. Goëzman had duly paid back her bribe, except for the fifteen louis that she claimed to have paid to her husband's secretary. Interrogated a few days later, the honest young secretary denied having ever received them, adding that in any case he would have refused them. By all the evidence, the magistrate's wife had pocketed this sum. Seeing the advantage he could draw from this small mischief, Beaumarchais had written to her from prison:

> I do not have the honor, Madame, of being personally known to you and I would avoid importuning you if, after I lost my case, when you had returned the two rolls of louis, and the watch set with diamonds that was attached to them, you had also returned to me the fifteen louis d'or that our mutual friend who negotiated had left you as collateral. I have been so horribly treated in your husband's reports, and my defenses have been so demolished by someone who ought, according to you, to have a legitimate respect for them; it is not just that on top of the immense losses this report has cost me there is added that of fifteen louis d'or, which ought not to have strayed from your hands. The injustice should not be subsidized by the one who is suffering so cruelly. I hope that you will respect my request, to which you will add the justice to render me these fifteen louis.

Was it not risky to raise this issue, especially for such a ridiculously small sum? "It is not the sum that matters to me," replied Beaumarchais to his sister and friends, who advised him not to aggravate his case. "It is the proof of the iniquity that pursues me."

Beaumarchais was playing a delicate game. His friends, led by Gudin, had warned him against writing to Mme. Goëzman. In fact, Pierre-Augustin wanted to force Goëzman to attack him in court; the letter to his wife had no other goal. Double or quits: either he would be condemned for slandering a magistrate and receive banishment or even the pillory, or else said magistrate could be convicted of corruption, and Beaumarchais would obtain the quashing of the judgment. Meanwhile he gave a maximum of publicity to the affair of the fifteen louis—not without success. Soon people were talking only of that in the salons and theater lobbies. Once more Beaumarchais used public opinion to turn the situation in his favor. Through the person of Goëzman, he knew, he could challenge Chancellor Maupeou's legal reform and specifically the integrity of the new Maupeou judges. What a hubbub if tomorrow the public were told that these judges, who had suppressed gratuities in order to improve the morals of public life, instead received bribes by the intermediary of their wives! Suddenly this sordid story of baksheesh was becoming a real affair of state. And the Goëzman affair, grafted onto the La Blache affair, would soon reverse the roles played by Beaumarchais and his adversaries.*

Naturally Goëzman could not allow the allegations against his wife to stand, lest his own reputation and those of the chancellor and the parlement be imperiled. Yet a legal action was not without risk, for by sinking his adversary he might go down in the same shipwreck. His colleagues pressed him to act; he at first thought he was skillful enough to take the offensive against Beaumarchais. On May 30 he extorted a false confession from Le Jay (based on a draft that he had written himself) that exonerated his wife from all suspicion. The bookseller, basically an honest man but weak and impressionable, had acceded to intimidation.

Armed with this false testimony, Goëzman complained to La Vrillière and Sartine that Beaumarchais was slandering him after having

---

*Although there was no regulation of the press, a 1769 edict simply condemned to death every author of writings tending "to excite the public mind, with ironic results." As Lomenie explains, "All polemic writings published in the eighteenth century acquired from the very fact of their illegality an indecorousness and violence of style, which produced no astonishment and seemed almost excused by the prohibition itself."

tried to corrupt his justice. Beaumarchais responded to the accusation on June 5 to Sartine and profited nonchalantly from the occasion to entice the magistrate along the path to the court:

> About the complaints that M. Goëzman, assessor to the parlement, makes of me, saying I tried to bribe him by seducing Mme. Goëzman with proposals of money that she rejected, I declare that such an exposition is false, from whatever quarter it comes. I declare that I never tried to corrupt M. Goëzman's justice in order to win a trial that I have always believed I could not lose without error or injustice . . . If he has something to complain about, it is before a court that he should attack me. I have no fear of any light cast on my actions.

No doubt, but M. Goëzman did not see things this way at all. He wanted to avoid a lawsuit at all costs, for if the accusation of corruption proved to be founded (which it would be) the scandal would spread to the judicial body as a whole, perhaps the institution itself. No, the ideal thing would be a good lettre de cachet that would send Sire Beaumarchais to prison and put an end to his campaign of insinuations. But a lettre de cachet would be interpreted as a denial of justice; La Vrillière refused to issue one. Beaumarchais remained at liberty, while rumors swelled daily. Law President Bertier de Sauvigny summoned Beaumarchais to try to find out if the rumors running around, even in the corridors of the Palais de Justice, had any truth to them. It would be a fine occasion to plead anew for judicial action.

On June 21, 1773, Goëzman fell into the trap by deposing a complaint for calumny and attempted bribery. The parlement took the case and designated an assessor. Barely had the witnesses been summoned when Le Jay, trembling at the consequences of his false declaration, ran to a lawyer, told him the facts as they had happened, and received the advice to tell the truth in his deposition. Then he made the same confession to the premier president, repeated it to others, and finally told anyone who would listen, as if to assuage his conscience. Warned about this setback, Goëzman called him in, along with his wife, extracted from him the draft of the false testimony that was in his writing, bitterly reproached him for his successive refutations, and tried to negotiate. Promises, threats, blackmail—Goëzman exhausted all kinds of arguments to circumvent the Le Jay household. In vain. Called by the clerk, Le Jay revealed everything he knew. On July 10 he was arrested and imprisoned in the Conciergerie.

The interrogations were catastrophic for Goëzman, yet Beaumarchais was engaged in an impossible struggle against an adversary a hundred times more powerful than he. Prosecuted for corruption and calumny by a judge, before other judges who had an interest in finding him guilty in order not to acknowledge themselves as unworthy, Pierre-Augustin had little chance of escaping the punishments set by criminal procedure, the harshest short of the death penalty. The Maupeou parlement would strike as harshly as possible at someone accused of acts that imperiled the very existence of that judicial body. In the event of a conviction, he knew in advance that he could count on no one. The Prince de Conti, his most powerful protector, had warned him: "If you have the misfortune to be touched by the executioner, I will be forced to abandon you."

No certified lawyer dared to defend Beaumarchais against a judge, supported by all the members of this omnipotent tribunal. So he decided to plead his case himself. He would challenge the mystique that surrounded criminal procedures and expose the evidence to the light of day. Not hesitating to violate legal confidentiality, he wrote a series of *Memoranda Against Goëzman* to rally public opinion to obtain the justice that the institutions were obstinately refusing him. Once again he had to arouse that opinion, excite its curiosity, retain its attention, impassion it, move it, intrigue it, amuse it. Again he had to lend his self-defense all the dramatic interest one might find in reading a play or a novel. Again he had to manage his effects, portray milieux and manners, improvise dialogues—in short, he had to raise his legal brief to the rank of a work of literature. These were the combined qualities that Beaumarchais's genius put brilliantly to work in his four *Memoranda Against Goëzman*.

Living in temporary quarters since he had lost his house on the rue de Condé, he wrote, corrected, and rewrote each memorandum up to four times in a row, without lifting his head from the pages; with the help of friends and family, he cut, amended, and tightened.

Did he receive help from outside? Political assistance, for example, from those interested in seeing Louis XV's policy fail? Possibly; even on the Goëzman side the roles were clearly divided between the couple. While Madame fought in the front line, Monsieur was also writing memoranda and trying to blacken his victim's name with all the means at his disposal. But Beaumarchais was planning a great coup to destabilize Goëzman indefinitely. Launching an inquiry into the assessor's past, he discovered a well-guarded secret: Goëzman had once maintained illicit relations with a damsel of modest condition, by whom he had a child, to whom he had sent a pension for only five months. Beaumarchais made this accusation in a full courtroom, providing proof; it had the effect of a bombshell. People cried treason, dishonor, and called for the judge's dismissal. For Beaumarchais it was a victory. And then a few weeks later, at the beginning of October, he obtained a judgment that allowed him to reopen the La Blache case.

Today we have a hard time imagining the success of the *Memoranda Against Goëzman*. Rarely has a literary work, let alone a legal satire, had such a resounding impact among diverse publics. From the first one to the fourth, they all aroused public opinion in favor of their author. Voltaire followed the cause célèbre from his home in Ferney: "What a man!" Voltaire wrote to d'Alembert, "he unites everything—humor, seriousness, argument, gaiety, force, pathos, every kind of eloquence . . . and he gives lessons to his judges. His naivety enchants me. I forgive him his imprudence and his petulance." One reader of the *Memoranda* (probably unknown to his ministers), Louis XV, found them so funny that he suggested putting them on stage. Mme. du Barry took up the idea and had performed in her apartments a comic piece taken from Beaumarchais's confrontations with Mme. Goëzman.* In the middle of the performance Louis XV laughed so hard, he had to leave. Beaumarchais had won his wager. With his lampoons he had conquered opinion beyond all expectations. His name was on everybody's lips. A year before he had been "the horror of Paris." Today the world was crazy about him, and he was a hero.

---

*The role of Beaumarchais was taken by the actor Préville, who would later play Figaro.

Eight

VENGEANCE DOES NOT
ERASE A REPRIMAND

If you are merely taking advantage of a position of authority you have no right to in the first place, I find it even more disgusting! —Rosine, in **The Barber of Seville**

Beaumarchais was now the darling of Paris—everybody was talking about him and wishing him victory over his adversary Goëzman (and over the detested Maupeou parlement). Discreetly he resumed rehearsals for *The Barber of Seville*, which his quarrel with the Duc de Chaulnes had interrupted; now the public was clamoring for the play. The Comédiens-Français made haste, counting on public curiosity, if not taste for scandal, to bring a quick success. Still, the author had to submit his play once more to the censor. It was almost identical to the version that had been approved the previous year, but he could not resist slipping in topical allusions to the trial characters, whom the *Memoranda* had made popular. After asking for minor corrections, the censor approved the play on February 5, 1774, and Sartine soon delivered his authorization to the actors. The premiere was announced for Saturday the twelfth. Barely was the date announced in Paris than the ticket offices were mobbed. In one afternoon all the loges were sold out through the sixth performance. The dauphine, Marie-Antoinette, it was said, was burning to attend and was alleged to have intervened personally with the gentlemen of the chamber to have the last obstacles lifted.

Then suddenly, on the evening of the tenth, the Comédiens-Français received from the government an express ban on performing *The Barber of Seville*. For the theater the loss was total; it had invested enormously in the décor and costumes and had to reimburse the tickets sold. The public, "as respectful of its superiors as zealous for its equals, grumbled in low tones about this harshness, and its love for the author augmented," wrote the acerbic critic Baron Grimm.

> For me, who does not know M. de Beaumarchais, who has nei-ther hate nor enthusiasm for him, I prefer not to believe him guilty on any count, because that puts the soul at ease and because the troop of furies hovering at his steps have not been able to prove anything, nor even articulate anything against him; and I say that it is a shame that we have been deprived of the per-formance of his play. I have read it, and it appears to me worthy of the praise that has been prepared for it in advance . . . I do not doubt that *The Barber of Seville* would have had great success; but M. de Beaumarchais would have been more responsible for the interest it inspired than the play's merits, which would per-haps not have been felt until the fifth or sixth performance.

The interdiction was the result of a small war raging between Mme. du Barry and Marie-Antoinette. The dauphine had never been able to bear the king's favorite. More influential than the princess (at least for the time being), the royal mistress and her ally, the Duc d'Aiguillon—minister of foreign affairs, who could refuse her noth-ing—had asked the Duc de La Vrillière to use his authority to pre-vent the performance. The official reason was that the author had introduced into his play allusions injurious to the magistracy. In fact, those in power feared a popular reaction in favor of Beaumarchais and hostile to authority. When informed, Beaumarchais turned to Sartine and asked him to name a new censor so that a closer examina-tion of his play might expose the error of the allegations against him. Simultaneously, he deposited a copy with the palace clerk, so that anybody could read it and form an opinion. "It should be either played or judged!" he declared.

The author's enemies welcomed the news of the interdiction with relief. After such a snub, the tribunal could not decently absolve Beaumarchais. Goëzman and his band triumphed—but for only a few hours. On the evening of this same Thursday, February 10, while they were savoring their victory, the fourth *Memorandum*, which ends with an account of Beaumarchais's voyage in Spain, left the press. Six thousand copies were sold in forty-eight hours. The still-damp sheets were snatched at the printer's door. At court, in the city, in the salons, dance halls, cafés, and theater foyers, in the cabinets of ministers, in the galleries of the Palais, everyone talked of this last *Memorandum*. Readers exclaimed, guffawed, and applauded. Ah, that Caron! Never had he been so funny! Never had he pushed his charges so far! Never had he struck so hard!

It was to the *Memoranda*, and not to his theater work, that Beaumarchais owed his reputation as a writer. "Beaumarchais ought to give his lampoons to the theater and his dramas to the courts," a contemporary said. Voltaire admitted to d'Argental, "I was never so amused. I fear that this brilliant scatterbrain might be right in spite of everybody. Heavens, what roguery! What degradation in the nation! How disagreeable for Parlement!" Voltaire's admiration carried Beaumarchais's fame beyond the French borders and across Europe. At the court in Vienna the *Memoranda* were the event of the winter; Austrian Chancellor Kaunitz was delighted with them. In Frankfurt, Goethe attended a reading of the fourth and based a drama on it. In England, Horace Walpole thanked Mme. du Deffand for having procured the pamphlets for him.

So it was that at the start of 1774, a female admirer, transported by reading these writings, asked their author to lend her his harp. In fact, the woman—who was described to him as an orphan of Swiss origin—was burning to meet him and had found this pretext for obtaining a rendezvous. The charm of this twenty-two-year-old—her gaze, her voice, her face—was difficult to resist. Her big blue eyes radiated tenderness and intelligence. Cheerful and easygoing, she was educated in the spirit of the philosophes and endowed with their principles. According to Gudin, who witnessed their first meeting, "their hearts were united, from this moment, by a tie that no circumstance could break, which love, esteem, trust, and the law would render indissoluble." Marie-Thérèse Amélie de Willermaulaz became the companion of the great man twenty years her senior (she would marry him twelve years later, after giving him a daughter) and accompanied him throughout his adventurous destiny, sharing his victories and defeats, his dangers, joys, and tribulations, until his final moment. Cultured in the philosophical spirit, Marie-Thérèse was a talented letter writer and for sixteen years exchanged candid and vivacious letters with a childhood friend; for longer than that her "sweet letters" were a comfort to Pierre-Augustin. Undoubtedly she would be deceived less often than his two first wives, but her equanimity would allow her to accept what she could not prevent. "I have less need than others of drawing consolation and seeking support outside myself. Nature gave me strength, courage, and a gaiety of character and a sort of routine instinct that suffices all my needs, and finds me prepared for all sort of events that could spoil present and future. As regards hopes for another life, I admit that I do not think about it at all. I roll in my whirlpool and feel neither fear nor desire for it to stop."

Beaumarchais, accustomed to easy success with women, was more preoccupied with the judgment of the parlement in his case against Goëzman than with her pretty face. On February 26 at dawn he crossed the Seine toward the Palais de Justice to hear the verdict. The court went into session at six-thirty. He had spent the night putting his papers in order and preparing for the worst. In the event of conviction, he seemed decided to end his life; better death than the galleys or banishment. A curious crowd from all social ranks filled the galleries. Everybody wanted to glimpse Pierre-Augustin. When he crossed the Salle des Pas Perdus for a drink at the *buvette*, he was acclaimed.

Hours passed. The deliberations went on forever. The fifty-five magistrates debated in the greatest tumult; some had a thirst for vengeance, and others feared popular demonstrations in favor of the accused. Raised voices could be heard in the antechamber. Outside, the people grew impatient, voiced hostile cries, clapped their hands and stomped their feet. At the foot of the grand stairway called the May Stairs, two saddled horses stood ready to carry the verdict to Versailles. In order to avoid any incident, orders had been given that the judgment was not to be handed down until after the magistrates had left the Palais.

At eight-thirty in the evening the hearing was finally adjourned.

As the doors were opened, most of the fearful judges fled by the subterranean corridors. But the president, Bertier de Sauvigny, had to
pass through the great hall to return to his house. He appeared
around 8:45, surrounded by five or six colleagues. The cortège
plowed through the people waiting in almost religious silence for the
verdict. A whiff of rebellion wafted through the crowd. Finally a
magistrate revealed the verdict to one of his colleagues of the bar;
word spread like a trail of gunpowder, provoking an explosion of
anger. By thirty votes to twenty-five, the court had condemned
Pierre-Augustin Caron de Beaumarchais "to be remanded to the
Chamber to be reprimanded on his knees" and "condemned to pay
three livres in fines to the King, to be taken from his goods." The
four *Memoranda* printed in 1773 and 1774 were to be torn up and
burned at the foot of the great staircase of the Palais.

Gabrielle Goëzman was also reprimanded. The court imposed a
fine on her as well as her accomplices, Bertrand d'Airolles and Le Jay.
Her husband Goëzman was condemned to be "reprimanded,
stripped of his status, and declared incapable of ever holding an
office, as having been declared guilty and duly convicted of the crime
of falsehood." It was a compromise judgment, half and half, testify-
ing to the tribunal's immense embarrassment, caught between popular opinion and political power, hesitating to lean to one side for fear
of displeasing the other. The reprimands, distributed indiscriminately
to the Goëzmans and to Beaumarchais, were so contradictory that
they would be laughable if they did not indicate a deep malaise in the
justice system. Condorcet commented on the decision in a letter to
Voltaire: "Beaumarchais was reprimanded by the parlement. They say
that is to prevent those who have given them money from saying so
out loud. They declare him loathsome for the cases resulting from
the trial, as if it were not crime itself but the tribunal's opinion that
causes infamy. There is nothing simultaneously more absurd, more
cowardly, more insolent, and more maladroit than this verdict."

"At least I am avenged," as the Count says in *The Marriage of
Figaro*. But his revenge does not erase the reprimand, and Beaumarchais's defamatory punishment involved the loss of his civil rights.
Custom demanded that he be judged guilty on his knees before the
whole law court. Its president had to pronounce the words: "I repre-

mand you and I declare you unworthy." But the magistrates, fearing catcalls, renounced this ceremony. On the other hand, a week after the verdict, on Saturday, March 5, the four *Memoranda* were torn up and burned at the foot of the great staircase of Paris, by the executioner of high justice, in the presence of a criminal clerk of the court and two hussars. This execution was purely symbolic, it must be said, since copies of the *Memoranda* continued to circulate freely, and a collected edition would soon be available from the Ruault bookshop. The *Memoranda* did not attack religion or divine or royal authority; they contained neither political subversion nor a call to insurrection. Beaumarchais had indeed denounced Goëzman, but had he not been punished by the contradictory verdict? And so what was he being reproached for? Simply for exposing the turpitude and infamy of his judges, for giving his case too much publicity, for endangering the kingdom's government. "The corruption of his judge is evident," wrote Voltaire, and "they dishonor the one who dared make this manifest and complain about it. . . . Beaumarchais was right in everything and has been condemned."

Nevertheless, his triumph in public was total. People of all walks of life expressed their sympathy for the author of the *Memoranda*. The Duc d'Orléans, the Duc de Chartres, and the Prince de Conti, who were known to satirize royal power, were delighted. As Mme. du Barry, transported with admiration, remarked, "He lost the case before the court, but he won in the public tribunal." At the Comédie-Française the groundlings noisily manifested their esteem for the "reprimanded one."

If Beaumarchais appeared vindicated and drew real comfort from the support of princes and the populace, his reprimand nonetheless deeply wounded him. Banished from society, consigned to civil death, his career was ruined by two trials, one after the other. One trial had deprived him of his honor and fortune; the other had stripped him of his civil rights. But at age forty-two, he had no vocation for martyrdom. He wanted the king to quash the verdict, and by law he had six months to formulate his request, supported by a letter of appeal. But since Louis XV had forbidden him to write or publish anything at all, he was reduced to silence.

The king recognized the qualities of his mind (the *Memoranda*, we recall, had made him burst out laughing) but distrusted him, as did the royal entourage, who compared him to the British agitator John Wilkes, defender of liberty against the authoritarianism of George III. (Some went so far as to call him the "French Wilkes.") The parallel cast Beaumarchais as a political subversive, dangerous to temporal power. John Wilkes, a fierce adversary of his own king, was considered a rebel and had been arrested twenty times and then released; expelled from the House of Commons, he had been reelected. Forced to take refuge on the continent, the "hero Wilkes," as Mme. du Deffand called him, had spent several months in Paris in 1763–64. During his stay in the capital he associated with Holbach and Diderot ("your generous and patriotic principles will make your name immortal," the latter wrote to him), while Voltaire, who welcomed him at Ferney, sent him this simple message: "You set me aflame with your courage, and you charm me with your wit."

Somewhat inadvertently, then, Beaumarchais had become a symbol of political contestation; his four pamphlets were thought to be directed against Chancellor Maupeou; songs, epigrams, and broadsheets spontaneously associated his name with that of the execrated puppet parlement. A few days after his conviction a placard was found: "Miserable men, who themselves merit conviction, the galleys, the wheel." Echoes of the popular agitation reached Voltaire, who told one of his correspondents: "In truth, the public judges as a last resort, but its decrees are only executed in speech. The world speaks in vain, one must obey." To another he wrote on March 7, 1774: "As for Beaumarchais's conviction, I do not yet know precisely what it signifies. As for me, I blame only those who are boring me, and in this sense it is impossible to blame Beaumarchais. He should have his *The Barber of Seville* performed, and laugh by making you laugh."

Beaumarchais, champing at the bit to see his play performed, was secretly warned that an order for his arrest had been issued; he had to flee as quickly as possible, he had not a minute to lose. The Prince de Ligne helped him slip into England, later recounting in his memoirs that "the Prince de Conti asked me to save Beaumarchais the day he was arrested and then he gaily read us his *Barber*, although he had entered the salon with the air of the most unfortunate man. I went to the trouble of taking him to the first poste, giving him a carriage, and one of my men led him to Ostend, where I had him put on board ship."

Just before leaving Flanders, Beaumarchais secretly sent a letter to Louis XV by the intermediary of his friend La Borde, first gentleman-in-waiting to the king. The original has been lost, but its substance, according to its author,

> was to prove to His Majesty how little I had wanted to displease him. I was retiring to London, to a place and under a name known only to His Majesty, where I would live for five and a half months, silent and ignored as at the Bastille. I respectfully observed to the king that I was only seeming to remove myself from his authority so that my silence in a free country could be to him a proof beyond suspicion of my voluntary submission and my profound respect for his repugnance. I finished by saying that I hoped that the king, touched by so many sacrifices, would not oppose my soliciting his justice by a request to his council for a reversal of the verdict before the expiration of six months, past which an unfortunate man unjustly condemned no longer has the right to obtain one, if he has not acted before this fatal deadline.

This pseudonym "known to His Majesty alone," under which he would thenceforth travel incognito, was none other than an anagram of Caron: M. de Ronac. In fact, Sartine had discreetly asked the banished to perform secret missions in London in the king's name! The country of press freedom, Great Britain, was the paradise of pamphleteers. There one could write more or less what one wanted, and about whatever one wanted. Even scandalous anecdotes about the throne of France were not prosecuted; in fact, the British government actually protected their authors against any reprisal on the part of French authorities, sometimes even subsidizing them, and never acceding to demands for extradition. Let us not forget that the two countries remained rivals and enemies.

For almost two years, the highest courts in France had been trying in vain to prevent the publication of a satire against Mme. du Barry entitled *Secret Memoirs of a Public Lady, or Research on the*

Adventures of Mme the Comtesse du B*** from Cradle to the Bed of Honor. The author was Charles Théveneau de Morande, whose *Gazetier Cuirassé* (1771) had made all of Versailles tremble some years previously. The pamphlet's title says enough about its content: poisonous bits of gossip, misquotes, calumnies, and the usual smut under the cover of a pseudo-memoir. It described Louis XV as "making coffee for Chonchon [Mme. du Barry], who said to him throatily: 'Can people really believe that you are the master of twenty million subjects and that I am subject to you?' This same Chonchon when leaving her bed has her slippers put on by the Archbishop of Rheims, who kisses them like the pope's; dining at the Trianon with His Majesty, she lifts the wig of the chancellor and, putting it in curling papers, covers with her handkerchief this *head* of justice." How could the regime prevent such a scandalous work from appearing? Nothing simpler: it must pay the price. In several letters addressed to the chancellor and the Duc d'Aiguillon, Morande demanded 120,000 livres and a pension of 4,000 livres, payable to his wife and son!

The French secret services had tried to kidnap Morande, but in vain. They needed to send a new man. That was why Louis XV smiled after reading the letter that Beaumarchais sent him via La Borde. "Your friend claims to possess the highest degree of talent for negotiation," he said to La Borde. "Do you think that he might be used in strict secrecy to find out where all these libels stand and what must be done to stop them?" La Borde assured his master as to his talents and his zeal and hurried to convey the sovereign's statements; the man sentenced to civil death was about to become a secret agent.

Upon reading them in London, Beaumarchais could not suppress his optimism. Finally the horizon was clearing, and hope was being reborn. This mission not only offered him an unexpected chance to rehabilitate himself, it excited his imagination to a high degree. "La Borde gave me no order from the king," he later wrote. "It was a simple opinion. But he told me enough to inflame me." Without hesitation, he set about collecting information about the libels. Who were the authors? From what headquarters had they emanated? He learned that three thousand copies of the work had already been printed and were ready to be shipped to Holland and Germany, from whence they would be distributed in France, where the bookshops were impatiently awaiting them. Beaumarchais went to see Morande, who was distrustful and refused to open his door, alleging that he was surrounded by assassins. "Were I an angel of peace," recounted Beaumarchais back in France,

> it sufficed for me to say I was French for him to have no communication with me. Time was passing, I insisted, he was obstinate . . . Finally, by a ruse as interesting as extraordinary, but reserved for a grander memoir, I managed on the same day to stop everything, carrying away with me a copy of each pamphlet, which I had La Borde send to the king in the greatest secrecy, so he could judge for himself if these works which appeared infernally nasty to me, in fact merited the effort to effect their suppression.

Agreeably surprised by the rapidity of Beaumarchais's action, Louis XV conveyed his satisfaction and had him sent back to the Duc d'Aiguillon. He returned to London, but this time as "trusted commissioner" responsible for the total destruction of these satires by fire. Here then is Beaumarchais, or rather M. de Ronac, special envoy of His Majesty, charged with negotiating with Morande the auto-da-fé of the *Mémoires secrets d'une femme publique*. The king had fixed a price to pay to the blackmailer that should not exceed a certain sum. Naturally Beaumarchais was held to the most absolute silence on his mission, as it related to a state secret. He bore the king's signature in a gold locket around his neck. The Chevalier d'Éon, another king's agent we will meet, did not exaggerate when he painted an ironic portrait of Beaumarchais on the ship carrying him to the shores of England: "Soon the romantic and gigantic heart of Sieur Caron swelled and filled with the most chimerical ideas; his ambition rose as high as the sea waves that he had to cross; he conceived the hope of succeeding in the design to flatter the loves of his master, to abase his enemies, and to lift his fortune." But his major preoccupation was to achieve his rehabilitation. M. Caron de Beaumarchais left the Paris scene; the Chevalier de Ronac made his entry onto the world stage.

Nine

THE ADVENTURES OF
THE CHEVALIER DE RONAC

The government gave an affair that's secret
To Beaumarchais and they all said: "What!
Send to courts a wit to interpret?
An ambassador who jokes—how respectable is that?
The reply came: "Sometimes Mercury
Was picked by Jupiter to be crafty."
                                    —*Popular song*

A veritable colony of French people had sought and found protection in hospitable Albion, the only nation in Europe where freedom of opinion and expression reigned. Here there was no Bastille, no censorship, no *lettres de cachet*, and no absolute monarch; instead there was a free press, a climate of tolerance, and real parliamentary debates. The best welcomes were reserved for Frenchmen at loggerheads with the authorities of their own country. Among these émigrés were not only France's best but also its worst: corrupt aristocrats, libertines eluding their families, courtesans who lacked protectors, adventurers, shady financiers, professional informers, scandalous pamphleteers, pornographic chroniclers, blackmailers, bankrupts, thieves, prison escapees, rebels of all kinds, swindlers of all stripes . . . Everyone felt sheltered, even though these refugees knew that the French police kept them under surveillance from afar. Records were kept on all of them, for they were regarded as dangerous enemies of France. Most of these renegades had expatriated to escape either prosecution or a verdict already pronounced against them. Deserters from the military supplied an important contingent to French emigration.

But the leading lights within this little community were decidedly the satirists and writers. They were also the most feared, not because of their number but because of their potential to be nuisances. How many of them could boast of having troubled the sleep of ministers of the French kingdom, if not the king himself! Among the small group of pamphleteers and journalists who had taken refuge in London was the celebrated Théveneau de Morande, one of the era's most cynical blackmailers, as we have just seen.

Very quickly Beaumarchais wormed his way into the espionage network within the English capital. His proven political savoir-faire would now be put at the service of intrigue. But as Figaro would say, aren't intrigue and politics close relatives?

Beaumarchais had always known how to reconcile amusement and serious business, but no London siren (any more than a Madrid lady) could make him neglect his mission. In a hurry to achieve his rehabilitation by the king's hand, he acquitted himself with particular diligence. Morande was only asking to be paid off, it must be said, and his corrupter had the wherewithal to seduce him. After six weeks of laborious bargaining, the satirist came to terms for the sum of 32,000 livres, to which was added the pension of 4,000 livres, half payable to his wife. The honor of Mme. du Barry would be preserved—expensively. Once the deal was concluded, the three thousand copies of the lampoon, with engravings, were burned. The auto-da-fé took place a few miles from London in the presence of Morande and Beaumarchais. A single copy was saved from the flames, its sheets were cut in two, and each man kept half. Then Pierre-Augustin had the pamphleteer sign an act submitting himself to the full rigor of British law if he ever again wrote a word against France.

Morande was exultant. Now he was at ease, and would be given a pension by the French court, half of it payable to his wife. And that was not all! Beaumarchais proposed that he enter his service as an individual spy—a job that fit him like a glove and in which he could render inestimable services. The king's agent congratulated himself

on his new recruit. "This man has become for us of major usefulness," Beaumarchais wrote to Police Chief Sartine, "as much for his
zeal for pursuing and capturing pamphleteers even in the dens of
London printers as for the useful surveillance that he maintains on
that party, as having been linked with many members of the opposition, he is in a better situation than anybody to give us very recent
political news."

Now Pierre-Augustin, accompanied by his faithful Gudin, galloped to the coast, intending to board the first ship for France. In
forty-eight hours he would lay his victory at the feet of the monarch,
after which the sovereign would surely rehabilitate him in the fullness
of his civil rights, the only recompense to which he aspired. Setting
foot in Boulogne, unfortunately, he learned that Louis XV had been
stricken with smallpox and was on his deathbed. Three days later
came news of his death. It was a hard blow: not only did Beaumarchais's hopes for rehabilitation evaporate, but His Majesty had not
yet reimbursed his costs for the journey, which amounted to the
charming sum of 12,000 livres.

On May 10, 1774, the reign of Louis XVI opened. The new king
was not yet twenty years old, and the dauphine Marie-Antoinette was
only nineteen. Louis, whose virtuous manners were stressed by
everyone, had never manifested much sympathy for the author of *The
Barber of Seville*. Learning of his conviction during the Goëzman
affair, he had even declared: "This is well done! He is a vile and atro-
cious man, who is known only for his nastiness." So Beaumarchais
could not count on him to recompense his success. Eager, though, to
return to service, Pierre-Augustin turned to Sartine, who had always
treated him as a friend. "Anything that the King wants to know solely
and promptly," he wrote, "everything he wants to have done quickly
and secretly, here I am." Beaumarchais, who had several strings to his
bow, was now entering a unique "sphere," the only one where he
now felt useful: the secret service.

On June 20 he sent to Sartine a memo written for Louis XVI in
which he warned him against a pamphlet that directly challenged him
in the person of the queen. Called *Avis à la branche espagnole sur ses
pretensions à la couronne de France*, it contained outrageous statements. It advised the young queen to break off all contact with her

mother, Empress of Austria; it warned the king against his wife's ambition and coquetry; and it recommended that he take against her "all the precautions that prudence, religion, and love of justice ought to inspire." The libel continued on themes of the sovereign's impotence and the misconduct of the queen, raising still more serious suspicions about the latter's intentions: the heirs of the throne should be armed, it said, against "any criminal and infamous intrigue for which the queen is preparing."

Since Louis XVI could not personally see to the pamphlet's destruction, a secret operation was necessary, conducted by a skillful, vigilant, and discreet servant. "I proved myself under the reign of the dead king," Beaumarchais declared, "in having burned two satires already headed for the booksellers.

> The author of one of them is today working for me; he is established in London and signals to me any seditious writing that appears among our English neighbors. He is a clever poacher whom I managed to convert into an excellent gamekeeper . . . He has the mission to ascertain all the French persons who pass through London and communicate to me their names and reasons for their voyage. Thanks to his relations with the principal printers of the city, he can track down any manuscripts that reach them.

But how could Beaumarchais justify paying emoluments to Morande (for it was he)? Simple: the pamphleteer would do library research—on old charters relating to the respective rights of the two crowns, for example.

The author of the current pamphlet against the queen remains unknown, but its publication and dissemination were being conducted by Guillaume Angelucci, a Jew from Venice who was hiding in London under the name of William Hatkinson. As a precaution, Angelucci was having the pamphlet printed simultaneously in two editions, one near London and the other in Amsterdam, another paradise for the clandestine press. So Beaumarchais proposed establishing a secret correspondent in the Dutch capital. With the help of Lord Rochford (from Spain) he could pass information on subjects about which His Majesty would be instructed via confidential notes. In short, he wanted to show Louis XVI all the advantages of a parallel diplomacy, such as that which the late king had practiced under the rubric "the King's Secret," with himself holding the principal role.

That would be Beaumarchais's principal track. Yesterday, he was saving the reputation of a royal favorite. Today, he was fighting for the honor of a queen (as well as for his own much-desired rehabilitation!). This mission would give him his wings.

Impatient to enter the fray, he sailed for London ten days later.* Armed with an order from the king, he had only to find Angelucci and his frightful pamphlet. Using stakeouts, pursuits, and bribes, Pierre-Augustin managed to lay his hands on the pamphleteer and undertook to buy his opus. After another haggling effort, they finally concluded the bargain on July 23, 1774. The sum of 1,200 pounds sterling (or 28,000 French livres) would be payable, a third in London and the rest in Holland, under the terms of an official contract signed by both parties. The next day the manuscript and four thousand copies of the pamphlet were to be destroyed. But the Dutch edition remained at the printer's. A courier was dispatched, and forty-eight hours later Beaumarchais embarked for Amsterdam, where Angelucci met him. For a few florins more, the pretty octavo copies were set on fire. Beaumarchais sighed in relief and paid Angelucci part of the sum due, and promised to pay the rest the next day.

Finally it was done. The manuscript was destroyed, both editions were in cinders, and Angelucci was out of commission. The Chevalier de Ronac could boast of bringing the affair to a triumphant close. He savored his success and was thinking of resting a few days in Amsterdam. But the next day he learned that Angelucci had quit the Dutch capital during the night without even waiting for the rest of the money promised him. After absorbing the initial surprise, Beaumarchais realized that he had been fooled and this scoundrel had gone to have his pamphlet printed somewhere else. The resulting chase is recorded in his copious letters to Paris.

*He never overcame a propensity to seasickness or an aversion to learning English.

Mad with rage, Beaumarchais jumped into a post chaise to pursue the blackguard, who (according to his information) had left for Nuremberg. On Sunday, August 14, 1774, at three in the afternoon, while his carriage was crossing the forest of Neustadt, Beaumarchais caught sight of a silhouette on horseback trotting peacefully. Distinguishing a blue jacket, a round wig, and an English hat, he thought he recognized Angelucci, who heard the roll of the wheels, turned, and saw Beaumarchais poking his head out the carriage window. Panicked, he spurred his horse and fled at a gallop. On the verge of being caught, he swerved sharply to the right and plunged into a wood. Beaumarchais stopped his carriage on the pretext of nature's call, jumped down, called to the driver, "Keep going—I'll be back," and pursued the fugitive on foot, pistol in hand. He soon found Angelucci's horse tangled in the branches. Seizing the horseman by a boot, he pulled him to the ground and commanded him to turn out his pockets and empty his valise. At the bottom of the valise he found the two notes for a hundred louis he had given Angelucci in Amsterdam, as well as copies of the pamphlet that he had apparently sneaked out of the fire. Throwing himself on his knees, Angelucci begged Beaumarchais to spare his life. Magnanimously, the Frenchman sheathed his weapon, recovered his bank notes, slipped the pamphlets under his arm, and resumed his journey, abandoning the rascal to his fate.

Suddenly a horseman surged upon him, jumped down, and brandished a knife. He called an order in German, which Pierre-Augustin did not understand but whose apparent meaning was "Your purse or your life!" Beaumarchais plunged his hand into his pocket as if to get his purse, but he pulled out his pistol and pointed it at the attacker's nose while raising his cane in the other hand to avoid a knife thrust. Weapon in hand, he withdrew toward a big pine tree, hid behind it, and still walking backward, reached a second tree, then a third. When he reached the road, he heard a voice behind him. Glancing back, he perceived a strapping fellow in a sleeveless blue jerkin who jumped at him. Beaumarchais just had time to jump forward onto the first brigand, brandish his pistol at him, and pull the trigger . . . but the gun did not fire. Profiting from his confusion, the second man grabbed him by the shoulder and threw him backward, while his companion jumped on him. The two men rolled in the dirt, wrestling furiously. The King of France's envoy was stabbed in the right cheek. Stunned, his face bleeding, he managed to stand up. He seized his adversary, shoved him down, laid his knees onto his belly, and tore away his blade, receiving a gash on the palm of his left hand near the thumb. Seeing the affair turn to their disadvantage, the second bandit jumped on his horse and galloped off. Beaumarchais got up, knife still in hand, while his adversary prostrated himself at his feet, repeating "Mein Gott! Mein Gott!" Repressing an impulse to disembowel him, Beaumarchais decided to treat him as a prisoner.

Arriving in Nuremberg, he went to an inn called the Coq Rouge to have his wounds tended. The next day, August 15, he went to the burgomaster to file a complaint against his aggressors. But instead of trying to identify them, he thought it more useful to name Angelucci, whom he had been chasing for a week now.

Despite gashes to the right cheek and left hand, pains in his stomach, and repeated vomiting, Pierre-Augustin had enough strength to resume his journey. He pushed on to Vienna, where his mission now led him. He could not consider it accomplished as long as the grievous pamphlet still threatened Marie-Antoinette. Had Angelucci kept another copy? Was he going to try to negotiate with a German or Austrian bookseller? This blackguard, as long as he was free, was capable of anything. He had to be put under arrest and extradited to France. The thought of his denunciation of Angelucci to the German authorities made Beaumarchais burst with pride: this ruse had had a touch of genius. "This moment appears the masterpiece of my conduct in this whole affair," he boasted in his account to Louis XVI. (The fortunate Angelucci, however, was already far away, perhaps in Italy, or elsewhere. In any case, he had disappeared.)

Riding in his carriage, with his left arm in a sling and his head bandaged, the buffeting and jolting of the trip reopened Beaumarchais's wounds. He reached Vienna by boat from Ratisbon, and on the evening of August 20 he wrote a letter to a friend about the attempted "murder." Then without taking time to change, he went to the Baron de Neny, secretary to Empress Marie-Thérèse (and Marie-Antoinette's mother) to submit a request for an audience. Prudently he did not give the reason but insisted on the gravity, urgency, and secrecy of his mission. The baron hesitated to transmit the request of this slovenly foreigner, but struck by his determination and the gravity of his demeanor, he promised him an audience with Her Imperial Majesty at Schönbrunn.

Marie-Thérèse received Beaumarchais, listened, and took the pamphlet that he handed her. Back at his inn, he was congratulating himself on having done a capital job, when eight grenadiers erupted into his room. They told him he would be held in police custody until they had more information about his activities. Beaumarchais immediately wrote to Sartine, begging him to have himself conducted to the French border, even if tied up like a criminal. Instead he was detained under surveillance for thirty-one days (or "forty-four thousand six hundred forty minutes," noted the former watchmaker). Then he was set at liberty. He was presented with a thousand ducats (about 11,000 livres) from Marie-Thérèse, which he refused "without haughtiness but with firmness."

That evening he left Vienna and rushed toward Paris, where he arrived nine days later. Finally returning home, his first visit was to Sartine, newly named secretary of state for the navy, from whom he requested clarification. "What did you expect?" answered the minister. "The empress took you for an adventurer." An adventurer! Him? But did he not have an order signed in the king's hand? And could his good faith be doubted after the proofs he had given? Had he not paid Angelucci's price out of his own pocket and pursued the miscreant for hundreds of leagues? Had he not risked his life in the woods of Neustadt? And his injuries, his suffering, his desperate letters when he was in irons—were they those of an adventurer?

Of course, it was the very extremity of Beaumarchais's behavior that had triggered suspicion. So much ardor, so much money spent, so much danger run, all for a nasty brochure—how could he think it would not have raised eyebrows? Of course he would be suspected either of madness or of treachery. The first hypothesis had quickly been ruled out, but the second was plausible. His tale was full of improbabilities, and his peripatetic travels seemed lifted out of a picaresque novel; it is still not clear today how much of his account is based on fact and how much on imagination. His travel to Austria and his detention in Vienna from August 22 to September 23 could be verified, but the attempted murder in the forest seemed the stuff of fiction. His aggressors might have been inventions. His wounds might have been self-inflicted. That was what had emerged from the postilion's deposition before the bailiff of Neustadt on August 14. As for Empress Marie-Thérèse, regardless of whether she had believed Ronac's story, she had not ordered him arrested but was said to be "angry" about an initiative probably attributable to the Austrian Chancellor Kaunitz. Beaumarchais had said the empress received him with infinite grace, distinguishing him with a touching recognition of his zeal. However, the letter that she sent a few days later to her ambassador in France, the Comte de Marcy-Argenteau, gives quite another story. She wrote of her importunate visitor: "I am angry that someone has arrested this man. I had thought that he ought to be treated as a miserable imposter, sent off in two hours and even ejected from my country, showing him that one is not his dupe and that one is acting out of charity, not wanting to use him as he merited." Asked to investigate, Chancellor Kaunitz understood that Ronac was Beaumarchais—and concluded that the pamphlet was indeed penned by this man of intrigue, capable in his eyes of any villainy.

But Beaumarchais's subsequent treatment proves that he had not been dismissed as an imposter or a rogue. When a secret agent commits a grave fault yet eludes punishment, people at least cease to trust him afterward. But soon after his return from Vienna, Beaumarchais would be charged with new missions, still more delicate than the previous ones. (In the realm of the American affair, Foreign Minister Vergennes would entrust him with a task suited only to a reliable man.) On the other hand, Beaumarchais may have wanted to give a romantic tone to the story of his mission, enhancing it with intrigue, vivid incidents, and even an attempted assassination. He might have embroidered the Angelucci affair, even wholly invented the episode in the woods, dramatized his dialogue with the empress, and theatricalized his detention—in a word, he may have wanted to give himself a hero's role. One can indeed recognize here the creator of Figaro.

To the powerful (Marie-Thérèse, Kaunitz, Louis XVI), Beaumarchais appeared a brilliant person, whom it was pleasing to praise for his wit but who was too inconsequential to play a major political role.

They were amused by his adventures, whether true or false, but they gave no more credit to his actions than to his word. He remained in their eyes a watchmaker who had gone into business and was succeeding pretty well, a schemer who knew how to deploy his talents in the service of his ambitions: a "droll fellow," as Kaunitz said; a "madman," as Louis XVI characterized him, who amused others by his "sprightliness" and his "careless mistakes." He was regarded with a sort of derisive condescension. His experience in espionage certainly made him a precious auxiliary in unmasking the authors of libels and catching blackmailers, but that was the limit of his competence. His zealous excesses, his loud personality, his swaggering manner, the self-satisfaction that he proclaimed in every surrounding—he had the gift of entertaining some but annoying others. He possessed the wit to amuse, the calculation to get rich, and the shrewdness to survive, but not the springs to move the complicated machinery of government. In the coming years he would acquire such springs, to the extent that his activities as a secret agent became a part of France's foreign policy during the war in America. But let us not jump ahead.

Ten

"I WOULD PREFER TO BE A GOOD BARBER"

Rosine: *You're always blaming the poor age we live in!*
Bartholo: *Forgive the liberty! But I cannot see it has produced anything we should be grateful for, but every conceivable kind of idiocy: free-thinking, magnetism, electricity, religious tolerance, inoculation, quinine, Diderot's* Encyclopedia *and dramas . . .* —The Barber of Seville

He must have had the devil in him to succeed in his negotiations with d'Éon. —Louis XVI

Beaumarchais, we remember, had only six months to request the restoration of his civil rights, and since this deadline had long passed, the judgment against him had become irrevocable. He was told that he might obtain, with difficulty, "letters of abolition," that is to say, the equivalent of a simple pardon. But he did not want to settle for that: he was asking not for a pardon but for justice. That meant he sought the legal annulment of the infamous verdict by a royal action, through what was called a letter of civil request. Since it involved seeking a new verdict, it was a much slower-moving procedure. However, Beaumarchais was not overly worried about the outcome: the new ministers (the Maupeou government was gone) and the king himself had proved rather well disposed toward him since his journey to Vienna. So much zeal deployed in the service of Their Majesties well merited this recompense.

Beaumarchais actively prepared for his defense before the Grand Chamber. To assist him, he retained the services of the very popular lawyer Guy Target. It was a deliberate choice, for Target had refused to plead before the discredited Maupeou parlement and enjoyed a certain favor at the court. But another part of his defense was to gain the favor of public opinion, whose power Beaumarchais knew better than anyone, and so he increased his public statements and witticisms. His brilliant retorts circulated around the capital within an hour of their utterance, annoying more than one person.

The court proceedings were under way. After Target's summation, the advocate-general Séguier decided in favor of Beaumarchais's rehabilitation. On September 6, 1776, a solemn decree from the Grand Chamber assembly annulled the previous verdict. Thus Pierre-Augustin was absolved of all blame, and his civil rights were restored. He was returned to his previous office, notably that of lieutenant-general of the Varenne du Louvre, from which he had been suspended. At the announcement of the judgment, the crowd in the courtroom applauded and bore him in triumph to his carriage. His victory was marred only by the recent death of his protector, the libertine Prince de Conti.

Meanwhile Beaumarchais always had several irons in the fire—a nightmare for a biographer, who is condemned by his profession to follow chronology. "A multiplicity and diversity of affairs did not bother him," observed Gudin; "the most disparate occupations were equally suitable to this wide-ranging genius—firm, energetic and untiring." Thus while he was working on his rehabilitation, he was also sending arms to the insurgents in America, opening a business establishment, defending authors against the rapacity of actors, and preparing his return to the Comédie-Française. Having regained favor among the powerful as well as in public opinion, he undertook to have his *Barber of Seville,* which had been sleeping in a drawer for more than two years, produced. The interdiction still hung over the play, which contained allusions to his troubles with the authorities. Beaumarchais solicited that the interdiction be lifted. A censor was appointed to examine it: Claude Crébillon, himself author of libertine novels, was charged with the task. On December 29, 1774, he approved *Barber,* and the confirmation was signed by the new chief of police, Lenoir, who had succeeded Sartine.

The simple plot was summarized in Beaumarchais's preface: "An old man in love means to marry his ward the following day. A young lover, cleverer than he is, prevents him from doing so, and that same day makes the woman his wife, under her guardian's nose and in his house. That is the basic material, from which it would have been possible to construct, with just as much success, a tragedy, a comedy, a drama, and an opera." The latter Rossini would create much later.

On Thursday, February 23, 1775, the curtain of the Comédie-Française rose for the first act of *The Barber of Seville, or All That Trouble for Nothing*, which had been anticipated so many times and had been so many times postponed. All the conditions seemed right for a triumphant premiere. Alas, Beaumarchais's disappointment was equal to his hopes: immense. The first act was applauded, but the second unfolded to commotion from an angry audience that amplified throughout the three remaining acts. The finale was received with whistles. Beaumarchais recalled this woeful evening a few weeks later, with a good dose of bitterness behind his habitual humor: "This is how men are: if you have success, they welcome you, support you, caress you, honor you; but beware of ever stumbling in this career, or else at the least setback, my friends, remember that you will have no more friends."

All the gazettes took note of the rout. The *Correspondance Littéraire Secrète* panned the play in two lines of rare cruelty, effectively wounding the author with a particularly odious image: "Here is Beaumarchais well stripped of his reputation, and people can now believe that if his peacock's plumes are plucked, there will be nothing left but a hideous black crow with a brazen and greedy beak." Beaumarchais answered this review in his "Restrained Letter on the Failure of *The Barber of Seville* and Its Critics": "Since I have indeed been *brazen* enough to write this comedy, so that the prophecy may be fulfilled in its entirety, I will be so *greedy* as to entreat you, dear Reader, to judge me for yourself, and not be influenced by critics, past, present or future; for you know that by their very position journalists are often hostile to men of letters."

Three days later, on Sunday, February 26, a second performance took place to a full house. The white-hot audience openly placed bets. A rumor ran through the theater that the author had reduced his play to four acts, with many cuts. After the three customary strokes, the curtain rose. Silence. The actor Bellecour as Count Almaviva entered the stage enveloped in an ample black cape, his hat down over his eyes. He began mezza voce: "Earlier than I thought— still hours before the time she usually appears at the window. It can't be helped . . ." The dialogue flowed. Préville vehemently portrayed Figaro, in whose adventures the audience saw allusions to the author's life. The second act provoked ripples of laughter. While the action went on, the tension continued to rise, both in the theater and backstage. When the curtain finally fell after the final line, the applause was thunderous. Spectators stamped their feet in a frenzy. It was not only a success but a triumph. The bomb of the first performance had become an ovation at the second. It is unique in the annals of the theater.

What had happened? Beaumarchais tells us in a parody of epic style:

> The day of the combat, seeing the ferocious enemies, the undulating spectators, agitated, a rumbling from afar like waves, and being certain that this was the precursor of a tempest that produces a shipwreck, I reflected that many plays in five acts (like mine), all very well made (like mine), would have gone to the devil (like mine) if the author had not taken a risky wager (like mine). "The god of the cabals is irritated!" I said to the actors. "Children, a sacrifice is necessary!" So tearing up my manuscript, I offered the devil the fourth act to appease his fury.

In forty-eight hours, in effect, Beaumarchais had cut the fourth act, transposed a scene, cut a longueur here, a useless scene there, trivialities elsewhere; in short, he gave his play the rhythm and vivacity it had previously lacked. The reduction of the customary five acts to four excited the verve of the gazetteers.

One reviewer accused the author of having filled the parterre with the best claque in the city: "The *battoirs* (huge mitts), as Sir Caron himself calls them in his play, served him very well. By this burlesque nickname he refers to those flunkeys who earn their parterre seats by prompted applause and the perpetual clapping of hands." The argument smells of bad faith: the use of claques was common practice, and the best authors had no scruple about it. Moreover, the best judges have recognized that Beaumarchais's changes acted on his play like a riding crop on a restive horse, giving it the nerve and vigor it was lacking. The faithful Gudin de La Brenellerie, friend through thick and thin, summarized it best, I think: "Beaumarchais gave his play an even and lively pace that sustained the attention and let people savor the charm of the details. People noted that Figaro was a fresh character, as was Bazile; that the plot was lively and gay; the imbroglio easy to follow and well-plotted; the dialogue natural and full of wit; that Bazile's situation in the third act is without comic parallel . . . People laughed and applauded from start to finish of the play. The parterre revoked its prior verdict, and the trial was completely won."

In act I the author explains through the character of Figaro why he had left Madrid:

> Having formed the impression that the literary world in Madrid was largely inhabited by wolves, hunting each other in packs, and as you would expect, given all the ridiculous tipping and tearing that goes on, all the swarms of miserable insects, mosquitoes, midges, critics, horseflies, mean-minded little hacks, journalists, publishers, censors and all the other bloodsuckers that attach themselves to writers, God help them, had done lacerating them and sucked them dry of any last drop of red blood they might ever have possessed; sick of writing, boring even myself, disgusted by everyone else, up to the eyes in debt and not a sniff of any money; in the end, coming to the conclusion that a steady income from pulling a razor is preferable to the unpaid distinction of pushing a pen, I left Madrid, slung my bag over my shoulder, and tramped very happily through every province in the country . . . In one place they greeted me with open arms, the next they locked me up; wherever I went I rose above it; praised by some, condemned by others, taking risks when I was on a winning streak, cutting my losses when I wasn't. Paying no attention to fools and not afraid of villains; no money, no worries, and shaving anybody; here I am finally, setting up in Seville and ready once again to serve you in whatever way Your Excellency requires.

This brilliant success was contested by very few, and the Comédie-Française was the first to recognize it. When Beaumarchais asked them to perform his play "on the big days" (Mondays, Wednesdays, and Saturdays), they complied without argument. On Tuesday, March 14, the day after the seventh performance, Queen Marie-Antoinette brought the troupe to Versailles to perform *The Barber of Seville* before the court, along with Molière's *Les précieuses ridicules* as a curtain-raiser. In Paris the play had twenty-five public performances before the end of 1775, and ticket sales remained constant.

Naturally, this degree of success could only amplify the animosity of the playwright's less fortunate rivals. Some went so far as to write anonymous malicious letters against the author of *Barber*. Even apart from the envious ones who wanted him to fail, however, it has to be admitted that *The Barber of Seville* did not win unanimous approval— far from it!—even among persons kindly disposed to him personally. Countess Berkeley, a young English aristocrat passing through Paris, disliked it, to put it mildly. What shocked her most was a barber interfering in an aristocratic family.

> A barber should never be the hero of a play, although he can fig-
> ure on stage . . . A comedy that was titled *The Tailor of London*
> would give by its very title such a disadvantageous idea of the
> subject that the taste of the public would not fail to be offended
> even before the performance. M. Figaro, the barber around
> whom the whole plot turns, and who is always joking, is a very
> bad joker; his character is false from start to finish: sometimes he
> rises above the situation and sometimes he descends below his
> calling. Such an intrigue is not worth three hours in a theater lis-
> tening to the foolishness of an author who breaks all the theatri-
> cal rules.

The countess was only twenty-five, with little knowledge of the French repertoire and all the prejudices of her class, but her criticism deserves to be cited for it epitomizes, ten years in advance, the political and social controversy over *The Marriage of Figaro*.

Among the malcontents was a certain species that may raise a smile; the guild of Paris barbers. They sent a petition to the chief of police to denounce the disloyal competition from this colleague Figaro who had emigrated from Spain. But the petition has the flavor of a hoax.

> Monseigneur, We learn with pain that the barber of Seville has arrived in Paris, and since he announces he is going to trim everyone's beard, we beg you that actors be forbidden from releasing his talents. What would become of us, we who have paid dearly for our positions, if this foreigner had the exclusive privilege, as he pretends, of doing everyone's hair? You know, Sir, that any exclusive privilege is banned. But this is not all. Did you know that all Paris is running to this newcomer? His figure is so droll and he makes everyone laugh so much that he is taking away our customers. He has even dared to shave gratis. By Saint Barbe, what have we come to? How many people he wins over. We are going to unmask his conduct. How many people he wants to seduce! He prefers big shots, wigged heads . . . our lords of Parlement, all the sailors. But he ignores that in the latter band there is someone against him: he scalped him so hard that he is plotting to teach this universal barber that one should not despise little enemies. He joins us in lodging this complaint. We also have consulted our lawyers and they will establish our rights. May we be permitted, while waiting for the question to be decided, to trim the beards of Jews, monks, hermits, and other people who hide from us.

As the petition is far from unfavorable to Beaumarchais, we can unhesitatingly attribute it to him, for this kind of joke was very much to his taste—and in his style.

In his "Restrained Letter on the Failure of *The Barber of Seville*," Beaumarchais's privileged target had been a widely circulated periodical, highly thought of in literary circles, called the *Journal Encyclopédique*. This bimonthly, printed in Belgium, had taken a stand against him during the Goëzman affair. And in its issue of April 1775 it was virulent in criticizing *The Barber of Seville*. While recognizing the success of this "carnival farce" reduced to four acts, the editor (who posed as a rival) complained of not being able to follow the plot, for the scenes were "linked almost by chance." Beaumarchais understood that this journal could hurt him with the public, much more than the confidential gazettes; therefore he concentrated his attacks on it. The *Journal Encyclopédique* was one of those most prized by the philosophes, whose writings it published and whose ideas it defended. We know that Beaumarchais had very ambiguous relations with his colleagues in the philosophical sect. Not only was he never considered one of them, but in their eyes he represented what intellectuals have always despised: wealth and luxury. The occasion was too fine not to ridicule them by taking gibes at their press organ!

Finally and most especially, Beaumarchais took revenge on the execrated mob of journalists. To those "page people" (*gens de feuilles*), as he called them—pretentious pedants, the natural enemies of "people of letters"—he wrote:

> I would most of all like to persuade our brothers the journalists to abandon the didactic and authoritarian tone with which they thrash artists, the sons of Apollo, and make fools laugh at the expense of men of wit. Open a newspaper and you might think you were in the presence of a martinet, a cane or rod raised over negligent schoolchildren, treating them like slaves for the smallest mistake in their schoolwork. Ah, my brothers, this isn't work here! Literature is a way out of weariness and sweet recreation.

At the same time Beaumarchais was keenly aware that the press might render services when one knew how to manipulate it: a newspaper is a double-edged sword, and he would not disdain collaborating with the *Courrier de l'Europe*, for everyone understood its exceptional importance during the American War of Independence. He would justify this contradiction in a letter to Minister Vergennes: "[Journalists] were so given to odious liberties at my expense during the course of my affairs that it is quite just that the same route now serves me just as well as it hurt me in the past."

With his *Barber of Seville* a success, in April 1775 Beaumarchais embarked for London. Chancellor Maurepas sent him on a mission to seize more flourishing pamphlets against Louis XVI and the queen before they could cross the Channel. As we have seen, particularly defamatory satirical prints were easily available on the city streets. A defrocked monk named Vignoles was publishing a kind of scandal sheet taken from material, true or false, that arrived from Paris in manuscript form; he sent it back a few days later in print. Beaumarchais sent the fifteen first sheets to Sartine; one could read all that was brewing in Paris against the government. One sheet contained a pretended edict of the king in verse, in which it is said that Louis cannot claim to be king "except in appearance." Let us recall that the young sovereign had reigned for less than a year. Beaumarchais denounced these writings to the police and declared himself ready to destroy the "viper's nest" that produced them.

A few days after his arrival in London, one of the most extravagant personages of his century—a century that certainly had no shortage of them—came to visit. This was the Chevalier d'Éon de Beaumont, whose life would furnish material for several books. In 1755 this jurist, descended from an ancient Burgundian family, had been recruited by the King's Secret, Louis XV's unofficial agency that existed in parallel to official diplomacy. After the end of the Seven Years' War in 1763, its main agenda was to prepare for revenge against England by planning a French invasion across the Channel. Agents recruited for this purpose, about thirty in number, were known only to the sovereign and a few initiates; the minister in charge did not know their names or even of their existence. They worked in the shadows and communicated with their master, the king, by encoded correspondence; in order to avoid discovery, their expenses were taken from the king's privy purse or from the Treasury with the note: *for the king*.

Of medium height, with the slim waist of a woman and magnificent blond hair carefully curled, smooth cheeks, delicate features, and great laughing eyes, Charles-Geneviève d'Éon still appeared young and was welcomed into the best society everywhere. But in this century when libertinage was the favorite sport of any gentleman, he was not suspected of any amorous adventures. His ambiguous gender and his effeminate manners had launched him into the strangest diplomatic negotiations of his time.

In May 1762 d'Éon was sent to London as embassy secretary, charged with assisting the Duc de Nivernais in the peace negotiations. He succeeded so well in the English court that after the departure of this duke, Louis XV made him a Chevalier de Saint-Louis and named him interim plenipotentiary minister pending the arrival of the new ambassador, the Comte de Guines. But when the latter arrived, he and d'Éon became immediately and mercilessly embattled, ending up fighting a duel. The principal reason was d'Éon's refusal to surrender Guines the ultrasecret documents in his possession, which included the plans for a French invasion of the English coast. Possessing this compromising evidence, d'Éon undertook a scarcely disguised attempt to blackmail the court at Versailles, demanding money and increasing his extravagant expenditures.

Strange rumors circulated in London about the sex of the Chevalier of Golden Square. Some said that his fine uniform of a dragoon officer, gray with red decorations, was only cross-dressing! In the salons, clubs, and pubs, and even in popular circles, the prattle proliferated: was the chevalier a man or a woman or androgynous? Bets were placed, and the odds were posted in public places, as if for a cockfight or a horse race; the stakes rose to extravagant sums. At the same time caricatures circulated publicly. One showed d'Éon half-man, half-woman, deliberating if he should reveal the secret of his nature; in another, he was proclaimed queen of the Amazons; another anonymous drawing represented a captain in the dragoons giving birth to twins.

But the affair quickly took a less pleasant turn. The gamblers who had bet significant sums were burning to have the enigma finally resolved. Warned that a group of major bettors had conceived the project of kidnapping him to submit him to a physical examination, d'Éon was departing to travel abroad—until he was warned that seals were being posted on his domicile. He raced back to his apartment in Golden Square, for that was where his secret archives were hidden, notably the plan for the invasion of England.

On May 13, 1774, three days after the death of Louis XV, the Comte de Broglie sent Louis XVI a report telling him about the correspondence his father had maintained with a number of secret agents. He begged him to get hold of papers that were in the hands of various persons faithful to the King's Secret; the Chevalier d'Éon held the most compromising papers.

Louis XVI decided to shut down the secret office. The agents, deprived of employment, were rewarded with pensions according to their grade and level of service. But the Chevalier d'Éon considered his pension unworthy compensation for his services—and summoned public opinion to his aid.

Harassed by his creditors, and even less convinced that the French court would yield to his blackmail, d'Éon decided that the only way he could get out of trouble was to wager his most precious treasure, the papers concerning the invasion of Great Britain, the restoration of the Stuarts, and his talks with Wilkes. He placed them all in a carefully sealed iron casket that he deposited with his friend Lord Ferrers against an advance of 100,000 livres, which allowed him to pay his most pressing debts. Not despairing of reaching a deal, he continued to inform Minister Vergennes as to what was happening in London political circles, as did Beaumarchais himself—no doubt on the basis of the same sources and informants.

Vergennes paid homage to the chevalier's patriotism but seemed in no hurry to reach an agreement with him. His strategy was to let the situation stagnate, persuaded that the d'Éon papers would only lose value as time went by. This prolonged silence got on d'Éon's nerves: he had to find a way to resume negotiations without putting himself in the position of supplicant. At this moment, at age fifty, he decided to live in the clothing and identity of a woman. His new condition might help: a member of the fair sex might willingly be granted what was refused to a man, he thought. But he had to find an intermediary who enjoyed some royal consideration and was ready to plead his cause with the authorities.

Then along came the perfect person, whose renown would serve a hundred times better than anyone else's and who seemed in great favor at the court. The intrepid and witty adversary of Goëzman, the man who had negotiated with Morande over the pamphlet against Mme. du Barry, the glorious destroyer of Angelucci, the author of *The Barber of Seville*, feted in all the courts of Europe—in short, Beaumarchais in the flesh. As our chevalier would later write: "Like a drowning man whom the dead king and his minister had abandoned to the torrent of a poisoned river, I tried to hang on to the ship of *Caron*."

Alerted to his presence in London, the chevalier took hope: Beaumarchais would certainly make him a new offer from the French government. No doubt he had been sent just for that purpose. This time d'Éon would not miss his chance—perhaps the last one! In any case, this man would be his best advocate with Vergennes. A week, then ten days passed. He heard no news, received not the least invitation. On April 20, 1775, at the end of his patience, d'Éon suddenly arrived one day at Beaumarchais's quarters with no appointment. He tried to get the playwright to pity his fate, crying that he was only a poor defenseless woman, and to give proof of his trust, he told him the story of the state papers he had deposited. Beaumarchais listened and played along.

As soon as he got back to France that June, Beaumarchais proposed to Vergennes that he resume talks. After informing the king, the minister said that he was ready to agree to pay d'Éon his pension of 12,000 livres and to convert it into a lifetime annuity. But the debts were too high to be repaid by the crown.

Returning to London, Beaumarchais easily convinced d'Éon to accept these terms; d'Éon knew that this negotiation would be the last. Either he must definitively adopt female attire, or else he could never set foot in his homeland: a cruel dilemma. Aware that he could not resist any longer without arousing suspicions about his true sexual status, he ended up conceding, a victim of his own hoax. Once this transvestite affair was settled, they moved on to the essential thing: the restitution of the secret documents. After new digressions, Beaumarchais obtained the strongbox. He brought it to Vergennes, who complimented him and discharged him with a veritable *satisfecit* from Louis XVI. D'Éon would return to Paris in 1777—first as a dragoon and then in female attire.

And here the chevalier's sex surreptitiously returns to the agenda. In the *Morning Post* of Saturday, November 11, 1775, one reads the following snippet: "The City is preparing a new investigation of the sex of the Chevalier d'Éon, the wagers are seven to four for a woman as against man, and a gentleman well acquainted with this sort of business has promised to have the matter clearly elucidated within two weeks." D'Éon had no trouble recognizing this "gentleman" as his former suitor, Beaumarchais in person, who had just left London.

Beaumarchais was a cold negotiator, insensitive to tears and reproaches, preoccupied only with applying the terms of the transaction. Since he held the purse strings and could open or close them at will, according to the lady's disposition, he did not despair of making her see reason. Meanwhile other more urgent tasks were awaiting Beaumarchais—first of all, his initiatives in favor of the Americans. For him, the d'Éon business was already in the past.

Eleven

THE CAUSE OF AMERICA

The cause of America is in many respects the cause of humanity.
　　　　　　　　　　　　　　　　　　　　—Beaumarchais

In Beaumarchais's case, a stated mission could always conceal a covert one. For example, people thought he was in London to recuperate the papers from d'Éon. That was true, but not exclusively. Moreover, the task was so beneath his abilities that he would never have accepted it if it had not led to a more promising project. At forty-three he aspired to great affairs, to official diplomacy, to international conflicts. He had sufficiently proved his talent as a negotiator to qualify for the highest missions. Knowing that a man of his caliber shows his true mettle in troubled periods, the crisis that Great Britain was traversing appeared to be an unexpected occasion for him to realize his political ambitions. He would not let it pass.

The crisis had begun ten years earlier in 1763, with the disappearance of the French colonial empire in North America. It was then that the American colonists began to manifest some desire for independence from the mother country; they refused to participate financially in the debts Britain incurred in the Seven Years' War and objected to the parliamentary votes in London where they had no representatives. "No taxation without representation" became their now famous motto. London resisted, which provoked violent reactions: after the Boston "massacre" (March 5, 1770), the inhabitants of that great New England port destroyed the cargoes of tea from ships of the British East India Company in what became known as the Boston Tea Party (December 16, 1773). The British government replied by passing repressive laws that ruined Boston's commerce and suppressed liberties in Massachusetts (1774). But repression succeeded only in solidifying the unity of the American colonies: in September 1774, at the instigation of Benjamin Franklin, delegates gathered in Philadelphia in a first Continental Congress. In England itself the political party of the prime minister, Lord North, manifested vehement impatience with the rebels, while that of his opponent, William Pitt, ardently supported them.

Just as Beaumarchais set foot in London in April 1775, a fusillade in Lexington precipitated the opening of hostilities between the rebellious colonists and the Crown of England. He told himself that France had a role to play, or at least revenge to take against the Treaty of Paris (February 10, 1763), which had sealed France's defeat in the Seven Years' War. Nobody, he thought, was better placed than he to persuade the French government to support the insurgents in their struggle against perfidious Albion.

On April 27, 1775, in a report to Louis XVI on a secondary matter, he turned quickly to what was dear to him: what side would France take in the Anglo-American conflict? This capital question could not be decided without knowing beforehand and in depth the balance of forces in England. Hence Beaumarchais solicited the role of an information agent: "I have devoted myself to more noble and more satisfying research. As my name alone has made me welcome among people of various parties, I was able to find out from the proper sources about everything that relates to the government and the current situation in England. I am in a position to put before Your Majesty's eyes very faithful and instructive portraits, highly detailed or succinct, of men and the state of things."

> I can give the clearest notions about the king [George III], his family, Lord Bute [his favorite], his ministers of the first and second orders. I know who is of the king's party in the House of Lords, in the House of Commons. I know the current state of what is called in England the opposition, which party has the majority in Parliament; the state, name, rank, character, credit

and intrigues of all those who are influential in public affairs in both parties; the effects of the metropolis on its colonies; the effect of their disorder upon England; what should result on both sides; the extreme importance of all these events for the interests of France; what we can hope or fear for our sugar islands [in the West Indies]; what might give us peace or else necessitate war. Finally, I might put things so certainly and so clearly that Your Majesty, without any other effort other than rather amusing reading, will know what is happening in England, its currency, its maritime forces, the genius of those who govern it; in such a way that as every political event occurs, Your Majesty, glancing at my work, may be *au fait* with the motives of everything that happens and the interests of those who cause it.

Your Majesty can indeed decide between a succinct summary or a much more detailed examination of all the subjects I have mentioned. The only recompense I dare desire, in giving fresh proof of my zeal for the service of my master, would be that Your Majesty deign never to abandon me to resentment, to the hatred of minister or courtiers who will certainly make every effort to ruin me if they ever learned that anything came from me to Your Majesty without passing through their channels.

A few weeks later he made a second appeal, insisting particularly on his "perfect knowledge of England, of its forces, resources, banking, and most intimate liaison with everyone who has power and influence on public life." And he added something that reflected his reputation for immodesty: "Possessing the language* and knowing English laws better than the scholars of the country, full of genius, courage and vigor, and especially having bought experience and wisdom at the cost of mistakes and long misfortune—the only true tutors to educate a man—I believed, Sire, it was my duty to bring this important opinion to Your Majesty."

Beaumarchais was unequaled in building himself up while flattering a prince's pride, as this offer of service testifies abundantly. But he also (whatever that pest d'Éon said) possessed the highest intuition

---

*In fact, Beaumarchais could not speak English, and the language barrier would aggravate misunderstandings with both colonists and the British.

of public affairs; he had shown it on many occasions, and he proved it again now in his analysis of the situation. His various trips to England had persuaded him that a domestic revolution was on the point of breaking out, that major upheavals were in store, and that, helped by the uprising of the colonies, France could assert its power over its rival. His correspondents were closer to English public feeling and confirmed that Great Britain was facing a serious crisis. Posterity, he thought, would condemn France if she did not profit from it.

What then should she do? Make war against England? Beaumarchais may have wished for it, but he did not openly say so, for French public opinion was not prepared to embrace it. The question of war was nowhere near the top of the French king's agenda, so Beaumarchais recommended vigilance: "[England] is very occupied with its colonies in America, and although I do not believe they will ever get along with the metropolis, nevertheless some political act might present to the English people a war with us as a remedy for present evils. I therefore think that we should bring all our attention to the preparations to be made and the most useful precautions to take in concert to avoid war."

In this climate of distrust, an informer well versed in the British political world, particularly in its opposition circles, could be of use to the American insurgents. Beaumarchais had close relations with John Wilkes, head of the parliamentary opposition and Lord Mayor of London, who had embraced the colonies' cause and enjoyed immense credit with the populace. At his London home, Beaumarchais met many Americans who came to plead the cause of the insurgents; by this channel, he could inform Louis XVI's government about everything the rebels and their allies said or did. His correspondents in Versailles (Sartine, Maurepas, and Vergennes), attached great value to his information, corroborated via diplomatic routes. For them, the resolutions of George III and his cabinet were gravely compromising British supremacy.*

---

*Vergennes had revived Choiseul's policy of debasing Britain at all costs—even if it meant supporting the democratic ideology of the American rebels. As he wrote to Louis XVI: "The separation of her northern American colonies, her shrunken and diminished trade, her more encumbered finances, will proportionately reduce her power and make her less worrisome and less proud."

Beaumarchais threw so much energy into this role not only because the Anglo-American crisis appeared as a capital advantage in France's favor but also because it was a sure means of serving his own interests—to which, as we know, he was not insensible. If his missives outstripped the tone of a simple observer and assumed the style of diplomatic memoranda, and if he never passed up an opportunity to denounce the French ambassador in London, it was because he secretly coveted the post currently occupied by the Comte de Guines (a flashy but inconsistent character).

On September 11, 1775, in the course of a reception given by Wilkes at Mansion House, Beaumarchais met a young American named Arthur Lee, an agent from Massachusetts. Lee gave Beaumarchais an overview of the most urgent needs of his fellow citizens to continue the struggle. They lacked everything: money, arms, munitions. They needed around a million livres immediately. Beaumarchais promised to intercede in their favor, but at that time he had no mandate from the French government. At the end of the evening Wilkes said off the record: "For a long time the King of England has done me the honor of hating me. For my part, I have always done him the justice of despising him. The time has come to decide which of us has better judged the other, and on which side the wind will make heads fall!"

A week later, on the pretext of visiting the countryside, Beaumarchais secretly went to Versailles to confer with Sartine and Vergennes "on subjects too important and too delicate to be confided to any courier." On September 21 he wrote a memo to the king on the current feeling in Britain, in which he pleaded heatedly in favor of the American insurgents. They were resolved, he said, "to suffer anything rather than bend, and [were] full of that enthusiasm for freedom that has for so long made the small nation of Corsica redoubtable for Genoa." As for the situation in the metropolis, he painted a dramatic portrait. "The open warfare happening in America," he wrote, "is much less disastrous for England than the internal war that must shortly break out in London. The bitterness between the parties has risen to the highest extreme since the king of England's proclamation declaring that the Americans are rebels. This ineptitude, this madness on the part of the government, has renewed the energy of all the opponents and united them against him." Then he asked the essential question: What should France do? "It seems to me," he added, "that there exists a strange inaction in the conduct of France's minister. At a time that all the skill of the most transcendent genius would be barely sufficient to watch over France's interests in England, they appear absolutely abandoned to a combination of negligence and incapacity."

And who was responsible for such inertia? The Comte de Guines, of course, whom Beaumarchais took evident pleasure in demeaning to the king:

> Do I dare say this to Your Majesty? I have reason to believe that your ministers, Sire, do not receive daily from your ambassador on this great subject anything but trivial news and very inaccurate notions. I am neither the friend nor enemy of the Comte de Guines. But independently of the known indolence of his character, it cannot be disguised that the consequences of his lawsuit against English negotiators over public funds have excessively circumscribed his useful relations in England, leaving clouds over him that make everyone stay away. . . . If considerations beyond my knowledge make the stay of this ambassador in London indispensable, it appears to me just as necessary to the interest of Your Majesty that he be supplemented by a capable man who is charged with state secrets.

Beaumarchais offered his services as plenipotentiary in the interim.

> While I may be wrong to believe that I have all the qualities necessary for a man charged with the weighty affairs of France and England (while waiting for Your Majesty to make a more worthy choice), the hazard of my good fortune having made me welcomed by some of the leaders of the opposition, I can certify to Your Majesty that I am well enough informed on the secret disposition of the party leaders to respond to you—not to prevent war, but at least to delay it for as long as it takes our minister and our navy to get themselves ready to forestall it or sustain it, if it becomes indispensable.

Sire, these are the powerful motives of my secret mission in France. Whatever use Your Majesty makes of this work, I count on the virtue and goodness of my master not to turn these proofs of my zeal against me by confiding them to anybody, increasing the number of my enemies, who will never stop me as long as I am certain of the discretion and protection of Your Majesty.

Impatient to return to London, Beaumarchais questioned Vergennes on the king's intentions the next day, September 22.

Must I wait for His response, or should I leave without having any? Have I done well or ill to broach an approach to minds whose dispositions have become so important to us? Should I in future abort confidences, and reject men instead of welcoming any opening that might influence the current revolution? Finally, am I an agent useful to my country or only a deaf and dumb traveler? I am not asking for new employment, I have too much that is serious to finish in France with regard to my personal business; but I thought I would be doing a disservice to the king and to you and to my duty as a good Frenchman if I left aside the good that I can do, or the evil that I might prevent. I would await your reply to this letter before leaving.

Vergennes asked him to postpone his departure until the following day and obtained the same day an audience for him with the king, who granted Beaumarchais a mandate to pursue his work in England and gave his approval to the intrigues and plans sketched— on the condition that all of it be dealt with verbally, without any indication that would allow it to be traced back to the monarch or his minister. One can easily imagine Beaumarchais's comfort and joy upon learning of the royal decision. At last his dream was realized. He was charged with a mission up to his measure, no longer chasing after libelers but weighing on the destiny of nations. From now on relations between France and Great Britain would depend on his influence and intelligence; peace or war between the two rival powers would rest on his zeal in defending one against the other. But what mattered to him above all was his new power to help the Americans in their struggle, which carried the promise of everything the men of the Enlightenment had dreamed of: the creation of a republic, the hope of incarnating an ideal of democracy and freedom, and the prospect of a vast commercial and industrial market. The author of *Les deux amis* had great faith in economic exchange, to which he owed his own social and political status, his fortune, his influence, and even his noble title. The nation not yet called the United States of America symbolized to Beaumarchais all the values that were venerated by the "men of talent" who would guide the France of tomorrow. American society essentially belonged to the bourgeois or laboring classes, and its elite was composed of the self-made men with whom Beaumarchais felt natural solidarity.

Defending the American cause in France required a man endowed with a rare combination of virtues: a spirit of enterprise, political intelligence, a sensitivity to human relations, a taste for risk, tenacity, enthusiasm, and especially an unshakable optimism. In entrusting the responsibility to Beaumarchais, Louis XVI and Vergennes could not have made a better choice. Not only did the author of *The Barber of Seville* possess all these qualities, but he also manifested a force of conviction, a confidence in himself, and an ability to retain his drive in adversity. Such qualities were not common in the Republic of Letters. "It has rightly been said, Monsieur le Comte," he wrote to Vergennes, "that a little exaltation in the heart of an honest man, far from ruining his actions, vivifies everything he touches and makes him do more than he would have dared promise in his natural capacity. I feel that exaltation: it is my prudence to direct it such that it gives the King's affairs a good outcome." This same exaltation, however, would ultimately blind him to the reality of the American situation, to the point that he failed to perceive the grave divisions between the rebels and the loyalists. Instead he preserved the naïve vision, widespread in Europe, of an America unanimous in its struggle against the oppressor.

Twelve

"THE AMERICANS MUST BE HELPED"

I would consolidate our liaison with America in all its forms.
—Beaumarchais to Louis XVI

As he was leaving Paris for London on the evening of September 23, Beaumarchais tried to reassure Vergennes: he would prove worthy on all counts of the heavy task awaiting him, and he would respect its secrecy.

> Monsieur le Comte,
>
> I am leaving, well informed of the king's and your intentions. Your Excellency should be calm; it would be unpardonable stupidity in such an affair to compromise in any way the dignity of the Master and his ministry. To do one's best is nothing in politics, any blunderer can do as much. To do things as well as possible is what distinguishes common servants from the one whom His Majesty and you have honored with your confidence on so delicate a matter. Pledges will be necessary, but it is my concern that in no case may they be traced back to you or the king. I will find in Boulogne a way of extending the previous passport that I happen to have on me, in the hope that you will say nothing to M. le Comte de La Blache, who would use this against me in the lawsuit he must lose, for he is a terrible arguer, this count.

I have the profoundest respect, Monsieur le Comte, for you.
Your very humble and obedient servant,
Beaumarchais

Upon his arrival in London, Beaumarchais reflected on his major business—which preoccupied him much more than d'Éon, the captain in skirts—and outlined a plan for Louis XVI, adapting it as much as possible to his recipient. Beaumarchais knew the sovereign personally; he was a young man of twenty-one, with a good general culture (and a clear predilection for geography) but no education in economics. So he tried to present this aspect of his program in a simple and intelligible form.

He began by stating a major principle: France must extend a helping hand to the insurgents without it becoming a bone of contention with England. The funds destined to support the Americans could not appear to come from the French state, and so transactions had to be arranged between the dispensing hand and the receiving hand, the capital increasing along the way. So a million livres would double, as if the Americans were receiving them twice. This aid, wisely administered, would serve to maintain and feed the war between England and its colonies, leading to the ruin of France's hereditary enemy. Each time France invested a million in helping the rebels, the British would spend a hundred million to cross the Atlantic to attack them, two thousand leagues from their base. The essential thing was for the king of France not to be implicated in these operations, so that it would seem that a private company were financing the Americans, counting on reimbursement in Virginia tobacco. Secrecy was the soul of the enterprise. That was the theory, but let us look at the practice.

France would pay in currency, and in the greatest secrecy, a million livres to Beaumarchais, who would found an agency in Paris (called the Roderigue Hortalez Company). Half the million would be converted into Portuguese gold pieces, the only non-British currency recognized in America, where they were to be immediately sent to procure American paper currency, which was on the verge of collapse: "It is a little yeast that has to be put into the dough to make it rise and usefully ferment." Against this half-million, Congress would promise to supply Virginia tobacco to the Hortalez company, which would already have sold it at a good price in France. With the other half-million, Roderigue Hortalez would buy gunpowder and send it to the Americans. But instead of paying 20 to 30 sols to the livre in Holland or France, Hortalez would secretly buy it from the French controllers of powder and saltpeter (with His Majesty's blessing, of course) at the price of 5 sols, which it would sell back at 20 sols to Congress, which would in turn be paid back from the tobacco sold in advance. The total profit from the operation was to be 3 million livres, which would then be recirculated in the same manner: a million and a half in Portuguese gold coins to support American paper money, and 60,000 hundredweight of powder for cannons and mortars. Hence 9 million would be owed by America, and so on by arithmetic progression. But Beaumarchais did not want to bother his young pupil with any more figures: "And that is enough to show Your Majesty how the product of this affair, treated under the greatest commercial principles, should grow in circulating, not by doubling (1, 2, 4, 8, etc.) but by tripling (1, 3, 9, 27, etc.) . . . Your Majesty will not be afraid of the complicated air this operation assumes under my pen, when He knows that any commercial speculation works or succeeds by any means as simple and natural as this one."

Most political historians consider French support for the American rebellion as motivated by a simple desire for vengeance after the humiliation of 1763. For Beaumarchais, though, the stakes were quite different: he wished to establish across the Atlantic the bases for economic expansion; he foresaw vertiginous growth. The power of a nation, he knew, depended not on its territorial expansion or domestic resources but on its capacity to dominate its neighbors on the international market. His approach to Louis XVI must be read from this perspective, and its audacity might legitimately rival that of Figaro addressing the nobility. Perhaps Beaumarchais went even farther than his barber when he tried to persuade his young sovereign as to the benefits of liberal economics, which he contrasted with the injustices of domestic speculation. His arguments, not limited to strategic considerations, aimed to force France into modernity. Paradoxically, he took Britain as model, for alone in Europe, Britain had realized its economic and industrial revolution; but he was careful not to say that. In fact, Beaumarchais's thinking was close to the Physiocrats, when they defined the "philosopher king" as an "economist prince" who should know and respect the "laws of economics" for the welfare of his subjects.

> Sire, I have treated the affair as a major negotiation, and if I have explained the unique secret of how large-scale commerce, drawing its profit abroad by the advantageous exchange of goods, increases the prosperity of all States that have the good sense to protect it, this is how superior it is to the art of the financier who, gaining his profit only from domestic speculations against other subjects, cannot increase tax revenue except at the expense of the universal existence of all subjects. Instead of the real sturdiness given by commerce, this destructive art produces in the State only a monstrous *confissure* [*sic*], with a swelling of the head caused by the penury, pain, and general strangulation of all the other parts of this suffering body.

Knowing of Louis XVI's almost pathological indecisiveness, the indefatigable agent asked Vergennes to intervene to obtain for him a short interview:

> Would you approve of writing to him anew that I am here, that you find me worried that over such an affair (as easy as it is necessary—perhaps the most important that the king may ever have to decide)? His Majesty might choose the negative. Whatever the motives, I beg Him to take no decision until he has heard me for a quarter hour, to show Him respectfully the need to undertake it, the facility of doing so, the certainty of succeeding; and the immense harvest of glory and peace that would be given to his reign by the paltry seeding proposed. May the guardian angel of this State make the king's heart favorably disposed and give us such a desirable success.

The "guardian angel" would be deaf to this appeal. Louis XVI, as an absolute sovereign, understandably hesitated to support a rebellion against a fellow monarch. Moreover, the plan seemed to him contrary to morality; it repelled him to use roundabout means, even against a rival power. He said via Vergennes: "His Majesty believes it is in the interest of his justice not to adopt the proposed expedient." Beaumarchais hastened to justify his strategy, writing a "Very Important Address to the King Alone" that he secretly sent under Vergennes's seal.

Again, it was as a teacher that he addressed the young king, attempting to shake his indolence as one would an inattentive student's. His statements run close to insolence, suggesting that the sovereign had not understood his memo of November 25. "Some projects are so overwhelmingly important for the well-being of your kingdom that a zealous servant might believe it proper to present them more than once, lest they be not grasped the first time in the best light." Later on, he vigorously contested the king's narrow conception of justice and subjected him to a veritable lesson in public law: "The policy of States is in no way like the morality of citizens," he explained.

> An individual may not do his neighbor wrong, whatever benefit he might draw from it, because all men live under the rule of a civil and common law, which has provided for the security of all. But a kingdom is a large and isolated body, more separated from its neighbors by the diversity of interests than by the seas, citadels, and frontiers that enclose it. A kingdom has no common law for those who guarantee its security, for their only relations are those of natural law, that is to say, those imposed by the safeguarding, well-being, and prosperity of each citizen; these relations are modified in various ways under the name *right of peoples*, whose principle, according to Montesquieu himself, is *to make its own welfare* the first law; *with the least possible harm to other States* as the second.

Hence it follows that "the national policy that maintains States differs in almost every respect from the civic morality that governs individuals."

In the name of principle, Beaumarchais urged the young prince to show the greatest firmness toward Britain, the "natural enemy":

"You will always be dealing with this audacious, reckless and shame-less nation. My plan is aimed at it alone. It is Britain, Sire, that you should humiliate and weaken, if you do not wish her to weaken and humiliate you at every opportunity." He spoke of the "state of weak-ness and disorder in which the dead king handed over his kingdom." At certain moments, we hear the accusing accents of Figaro: "How can you permit your merchant vessels to be seized by force and see shackled in chains black men whom Nature made free, and who are wretched only because you are powerful? How can you suffer three rival powers to wickedly carve up the spoils of Poland in front of your eyes, Sire, when your mediation should have such weight in Europe?" Naturally, he pleaded for his project as the only way to reduce England to powerlessness: "An indefatigable and zealous ser-vant manages to put in your hands the most redoubtable weapon with which you might, without commitment or opposition, pull down your natural enemies and keep them from hurting you for a long time, and yet you think your just interest is to reject an unex-pected fortune such as will not present itself twice in your whole reign, should you live as long as we desire!"

The conclusion must be read through the prism of history. The jest aimed at Louis's naïve optimism demonstrates Beaumarchais's perfect understanding of his character. It also carries the shadow of a threat—or premonition—in the final words:

> If men were angels, no doubt we should despise or even detest politics. But if men *were* angels, they would not need religion to enlighten them, law to govern them, magistrates to restrain them, or soldiers to subdue them; and the earth, instead of being the living image of hell, would be a heavenly place. But, in the end, one must take men as they are, and the most just king can-not go farther than the legislator Solon, who said "*I have not given the Athenians the best possible laws, but merely those most appropriate for the place, time, and men for whom I am working.*" Hence it follows that any politics is founded on very imperfect principles, but it is indeed founded, and a king who wants to be the only just person amidst the wicked and remain good among wolves, will soon see himself devoured, him and his flock.

Only a week after he wrote this "Very Important Address," Beaumarchais subjected Louis XVI to the questionnaire below. After asking about the d'Éon affair, which was then on its way to being solved, he abruptly switched the subject to America. The king replied in the margins in his fine writing, evidently trying not to get involved. His laconic and prudent marginalia become even more evasive on the American issue:

> *Beaumarchais:* Will His Majesty grant the Demoiselle d'Éon permission to wear the Cross of Saint-Louis on his woman's clothing?
>
> *Louis XVI:* Only in the provinces.
>
> *Beaumarchais:* Will His Majesty approve the present of 2,000 écus that I gave this lady for her trousseau?
>
> *Louis XVI:* Yes.
>
> *Beaumarchais:* Will he leave her the total disposition of all her manly attire?
>
> *Louis XVI:* She has to sell it.
>
> *Beaumarchais:* As these favors must be subordinated to certain mental dispositions to which I desire to bind the lady forever, will His Majesty allow me to be the master of granting or refusing, according to whether I believe it useful to him?
>
> *Louis XVI:* Yes.
>
> *Beaumarchais:* The king having given me by his minister of foreign affairs due acknowledgement of all the papers that I had brought back to him from England, I desired M. le Comte de Vergennes to beg His Majesty to add, at the bottom of this acknowledgement, *in his hand,* a few words of satisfaction on the way I fulfilled my mission. This recompense, dear to my heart, might moreover become of great use to me. If some powerful enemy ever wanted me to account for my conduct in this affair, with one hand I would show the king's order and with the other I would offer my master's attestation that I fulfilled his orders satisfactorily. All the intermediary operations would then become a deep pit that everyone could fill as suits him, and I would not be obliged to speak of them or ever be embarrassed by all that I could say about them.

Louis XVI: Good.

Beaumarchais: Since the first person I will see in England is Milord Rochford, and since I do not doubt that this lord will ask me in secret the response of the King of France to the request that the King of England made to him through me, what will I answer on behalf of the king?

Louis XVI: That you did not find any.

Beaumarchais: If this lord (who certainly has close relations with the King of England) wants secretly to engage me in seeing this monarch, will I accept or not? This question is not pointless and well merits being weighed before giving me orders.

Louis XVI: That may be.

Beaumarchais: In the event this minister were to engage me in the secrets of a particular policy, if he wanted today to link me to other ministers, or if, in whatever fashion, the opportunity is offered me, will I accept or not?

Louis XVI: [No reply.]

Beaumarchais: I have the honor of warning the king that M. le Comte de Guines has tried to make me suspect among British ministers. May I be allowed to tell him so in a few words, or does His Majesty wish that, in continuing to serve him, I pretend to be ignorant of all the rumors used to blacken my reputation, my operations, and consequently harm His good service?

Louis XVI: He should ignore them.

Beaumarchais: Finally, I ask before leaving for a positive response to my last memo. If ever an issue was important, it must be agreed that this one is. On my oath, after having well reflected on it, I answer for the most glorious success of this operation in the entire reign of my master—without his person or that of his ministers or his interests ever being compromised. Would any opponent ever dare to be equally answerable to the king, on his oath, for any evil that must infallibly happen to France for having rejected it?

In case we are so unfortunate that the king should constantly refuse to adopt so simple and wise a plan, we beg His Majesty at least to allow me to remind him of the time when

> I brought him this superb resource, so as to prove one day
> the rightness of my views, when he will be able only to regret
> bitterly not having followed them.

To this last question—essential to his agent's heart—Louis XVI did not reply. Nor did he reply to Beaumarchais's dispatch of January 1, 1776, when the rebels' friend—without being discouraged (it would take more than that!)—came back to the charge. "Our great affair goes somewhat astray while we battle over the incidentals," he warned. "I assure you that people are profiting as much as possible from our indolence in starting things; the enemies of the administration and those of the State make equal efforts to extinguish in our friends any hope of the utility they expect from us. I see with pain that in a few weeks, it will be past the time to remedy things." Vergennes, bearing the message, confined himself to communicating this warning to the king and begged him to enlighten him on the course to take. One senses that the minister was shaken by his agent's arguments. "What appears most important to me," Vergennes declared to Louis XVI,

> is the portrait of the actual state of affairs and the consequences
> that might result. England is on the verge of despair. I easily
> believe, as Sire de Beaumarchais insinuates, that the revolution in
> the ministry may not be far off; there perhaps is still some time
> before the storm for it to escape the danger that threatens the
> heads of individuals and desperate parties. This foresight seems to
> require all the same of Your Majesty. But perhaps it is easier to
> imagine what might be done than to indicate the means to exe-
> cute it. As it would be only after Your Majesty's orders that I
> could respond to Sire de Beaumarchais, I beg you very humbly
> to give me orders as to when I might come receive them.

But the king lent his minister only a distracted ear; the situation in England and the fate of the rebels obviously interested him only halfheartedly.

Seeing that he was gradually winning over Vergennes, Beaumarchais stepped up his initiatives, opposing to the sovereign's indifference his own overwhelming activity. Without involving Ambassador

de Guines, whose inadequacy and detriment to the cause he ceaselessly denounced, he established new relationships, arranged plans,
organized collaborators, opened contacts with the suppliers of the
English colonies, passed writing around in the taverns, introduced
himself into the secret society of the Friends of America, always in
search of information, and prepared with Arthur Lee for France's
participation in the coming revolt. In short, he did not stay still and
spent money without counting—and not without results. Thanks to
his tenacious ingenuity and indiscreet insistence, he broke down people's resistances. His incessant comings and goings—all that febrile
agitation—did not pass unnoticed, especially since Beaumarchais was
well known. His success in the theater had made him popular; far
from disdaining this notoriety, he avidly sought it. "Sire de Beaumarchais is still in England," noted the *Mémoires Secrets* chronicler,

> and has already made several trips there on government orders
> without the politicians being able to fathom the motives for so
> many mysterious errands. One presumes, though, that given the
> state of crisis of our neighbors, given the character of the man,
> his genius for intrigue, his activity, his impudence, his flexibility,
> he has gone to fulfill one of those firebrand roles that a known
> agent cannot perform, which are given to a man without a title
> who can be disavowed if needed and even left to hang if neces-
> sary.

From Paris, Lord Stormont, the British ambassador, had him followed at all times. The British espionage services kept an eye on him
and watched his every act. But this could not be helped, at least at
the start, and he avowed to his minister: "Despite the danger I am
running in writing you from London, I feel myself once again more
French here than in Paris. The patriotism of these people revives my
own. It even seems that the precarious and dangerous state in which
I find myself, due to the suspicions and severe inquisition over everything I undertake, makes my zeal more ardent." But as his credit
grew at the French court, the British spying became more threatening. In the following weeks the vise tightened so much that he
begged Vergennes to guarantee his safety: "Do not neglect, Mon-

sieur le Comte, to press M. Sartine on the subject of my safety. It is the least of what is owed me."

At the same time Beaumarchais tried to push his advantage with foreign affairs. By turns insinuating and threatening, enthusiastic and prophetic, insistent and harassing, he overwhelmed Vergennes with memos, ever more pressing, that seem to have made a rather vivid impression on the minister's mind. And as he could not explain himself freely by mail, he increased his channel crossings between London and Versailles, where he met the minister almost every day; the chances of preserving peace with England were rapidly diminishing. Aiding the rebels was becoming urgent: it was now 3 million that was necessary, without delay, to cover their immediate needs.

In the course of one of his lightning trips to Paris, Beaumarchais addressed to Louis XVI a third memo, sent under Vergennes's seal on February 29, 1776. This text (titled "Peace or War") pointed out the king's responsibilities bluntly, without vain flourishes or mincing words. "Today, as the moment of violent crisis advances, I am obliged to warn Your Majesty that the safeguarding of our possessions in America and the peace that we appear to desire both depend solely on this single proposition: *The Americans must be helped*." If France persisted in refusing its help to the insurgents, Beaumarchais went on, she condemned herself to becoming the victim of Britain and the laughingstock of Europe. If, on the contrary, she brought help, France would profit from all the economic advantages previously reserved for Great Britain, which would last for several years after the peace. Congress had sent two emissaries to the Madrid court to submit the same proposal, and they were well received there. "Will France's Council today have the glorious prerogative of being the only one blind to the king's glory and the interests of his kingdom? . . . You will maintain the peace you so desire, Sire, only by thwarting peace between Britain and America at all costs, and preventing the complete triumph of either. And the only means of achieving this is to give enough aid to the Americans to put their forces in balance with Britain's, but no more. Believe me, Sire, saving a few millions today may cost much blood and money to France before long."

Vergennes was losing faith that peace could be saved, especially because of Great Britain's offensive attitude toward France. The cabinet in London claimed the right to board French ships, to pursue American vessels right under the cannons of French forts, and to interfere with her commerce by obliging her to punish merchants who traded with the rebels. Naturally, Beaumarchais exploited fully these vexations with Albion for the benefit of his grand design. He recounted to Vergennes a rather lively discussion with Lord Rochford about an American vessel: the Continental Congress had entrusted the ship with letters of credit and merchandise destined for a Nantes merchant named Montaudin, with the order to exchange them against war munitions. A captain faithful to King George had turned the ship back to Bristol, and the correspondence seized on board showed that this traffic was taking place with the consent of the French government. Rochford queried Beaumarchais:

"A few badly informed people have even tried to make suspicions over this connivance fall on you," added Lord Rochford. "But the King is so little convinced, that it is with his knowledge that I am talking to you. What do you think of all that? I know that you are here to end this business with d'Éon, and on this, I take your word alone, for which I have answered to the King, as you know."

"Before answering you, Milord, as regards myself, allow me to begin with the subject of the American vessel, not according to any order received from our ministry but according to my natural lights. The insurgents have need of munitions and have no money to buy any in Europe; thus they have to risk sending raw merchandise to exchange for them, and all the ports where munitions can be found should be absolutely equal to them."

"But, Monsieur, has France not given orders to its ports about this? And have we not the right to hope that the Nantes merchants will be punished?"

"Milord, you have allowed me to speak frankly to you; I will do so all the more freely because having no commission here, my statements do not compromise anybody. Why would you want our administration to be harsh with Nantes? Are we at war with someone? And in peacetime, aren't our ports open to all the world's merchants? Over a particular quarrel with the English, into which we have not and do not want to enter, does England have the right to restrain our commerce? And what treaties oblige us to close our ports to merchant vessels according to the desires of the British nation?"

"But, Monsieur, the Americans are rebels, our declared enemies!"

"Milord, they are not ours."

"And when we are at peace with France, should she favor them?"

"Favor them! By God, Milord, that is what you might say if we prevented you from boarding all the insurgents' vessels at sea because they are supposed to be loaded with merchandise bound for our ports or coming from our ports. What prevents you from sending supplies against them? Cruise all over the place, seize them everywhere (except under the cannons of our forts), and we say nothing. But to demand that we disturb merchants because they have commercial relations with people with whom we are at peace—in truth, this is a bit much! I do not know what our administration would think of such a demand, but I know that I would find it much more than out of order."

"I see that, Monsieur, for you are red with anger."

"Milord, you who are English and a patriot, you should not find it wrong that a good Frenchman has pride in his country. Now, I will account for my stay here. The d'Éon affair no longer occupies me; whether he returns to France or not is his affair. Nobody in France is interested anymore. You are going to ask me, then, what attracts me here?"

"No, for I know your answer."

"I gather, Milord, someone has opened my letters."

"My friend, we are too experienced in politics, you and I, to ignore that people may write anything at all."

Beaumarchais concluded the account of this dialogue: "I am a little like Figaro, Monsieur le Comte, and I do not lose my head over a little rumor."

The conversation with Rochford won Beaumarchais the congratulations of his minister and the king himself:

I placed under the king's eyes, Monsieur, the letter that you did me the honor to write on Tuesday the 16th (and not the 12th of this month). I have the satisfaction of telling you that His Majesty has much approved of the noble and frank manner in which you repulsed the attack that Lord Rochford made on the subject of this American vessel, destined, they say, for Nantes and conducted to Bristol. You said nothing that His Majesty would have forbidden you from saying, if he had been able to predict that you would be in a situation to explain yourself on a subject so foreign to the concerns with which you have been commissioned.

He concluded with these words: "Accept all my compliments, Monsieur. After having assured you of the king's approval, mine may not appear to you very interesting. However, I cannot forbear the satisfaction of applauding the wisdom and firmness of your conduct, and conveying all my esteem."

By all evidence, the Beaumarchais plan had made great strides toward acceptance in the minds of the king and his minister. Louis XVI appeared more than ever the plaything of contrary influences. Vergennes was now convinced that France's duty and interest lay in being engaged on the American side, even at the price of war with England. But Turgot, the comptroller-general of finances, was less concerned with the American situation than with reforming France's social economy; he was worried primarily about his budget. Despite his militant anticolonialist outlook (heralding in many respects the coming revolutions in attitude), he was very removed from current ideas; Turgot privileged the necessity of internal reform over the hazards of armed intervention. Turgot prophesied (with a pedantic and sententious dogmatism that irritated his colleagues) that the colonial system was doomed eventually; all nations would renounce it one day or another, willingly or not. Therefore France should beware of engaging today in a war that was as uncertain as it was pointless and ruinous.

One month later, Vergennes won the argument.

Thirteen

"THE DESIRE
OF ALL NATIONS"

M. de Beaumarchais . . . has merited so well of us, and . . . has excited our greatest veneration by his affection for the true rights of man, his genius, his literary reputation. —*Thomas Jefferson*

The balance was finally shifting toward intervention, although whether the sovereign's final decision arose from personal reflection or from Beaumarchais's eloquence, as relayed by Vergennes, will never be certain. Irresolute by nature, inexperienced in public affairs, and incapable of forming an opinion, Louis XVI did suffer more than embrace the power he had inherited. He performed his tasks conscientiously and with unfailing probity, but he was ever gloomy, worrying about the pertinence of his choices. As much as he appeared firm on the great theocratic principles of the monarchy (which would cost him his throne and his head), so he appeared inadequate in the daily exercise of his duties. The dilemma posed by America undoubtedly caused him more torment than any event since the start of his reign. Apart from Turgot, most of his advisers told him that France had everything to lose by remaining neutral in Great Britain's colonial conflict. He dared not reject their advice or even delay for reflection. After all, at the first sign of aggression on England's part would be the time to act. Instead he took as currency Beaumarchais's castles in Spain and Vergennes's sophisms, for he had no other sources of information with which to test their arguments and so form a personal opinion. He did not even perceive Beaumarchais's flagrant and deliberate contradictions. How could the Americans say that in the event France abandoned them, they were ready to ask for aid from any other nation, and yet declare that they depended on France alone for the support they needed? If that support was lacking, they threatened to submit to Mother England, thereby imperiling the French colonies in the West Indies. How could Louis XVI not sense the absurdity of this reasoning? How did he not see that Beaumarchais's discourse on "Peace or War" did not stand up? For whether England succeeded or failed in subduing her colonies, the struggle would cost such economic and military sacrifices that the country would emerge battered and thus absolutely unable to sustain armed conflict with France. Fortunately for the Americans, Louis XVI was weak enough to finally cede to the pressure of his entourage, for without French intervention, the colonies would most likely have eventually gone back under British domination.

Beaumarchais knew very well, as did the cabinet, that by encouraging the rebellion of the subjects of King George, the French government was ineluctably going down the road to war, which was their ultimate goal. Their strategy never varied by an inch, and their speeches to the king had no other object. Under cover of preserving French colonies in the West Indies, they dreamed of satisfying their desire for vengeance and erasing France's humiliation in the Seven Years' War. The American Revolution offered them an unexpected opportunity to shrink Britain's merchant fleet and its Caribbean possessions and to reduce their eternal enemy to second-rank status. So Beaumarchais would argue in a pamphlet dedicated to Benjamin Franklin with the eloquent title *The Desire of All Nations and the Interests of All Powers in the Abasement and Humiliation of Great Britain*. Here are a few extracts:

> For a century, Great Britain has tried to conceal from the whole world's eyes the irregularity of its conduct and the perfidy of its procedures. For a century it has imposed itself on Europe, on all nations, on all powers, by false declamations spread in its writings. Great Britain cannot wash away the reproach of having for a century troubled the general calm. Its hateful conduct revolts any

thinking man. Its infractions of treaties, its innumerable attempts against all nations, against all powers, demonstrate its boundless pride, greed, and ambition . . . The Englishman wanted to have establishments on every sea; he has appropriated them by right of conquest. He wanted to conquer the New World and put it in irons . . . What blindness! What pride! Posterity will not believe that in the course of a century, an isolated people tried to impose its yoke on the rest of the earth's inhabitants, while always announcing that it does not want to increase its power. A faithful portrait of the progress of its forces, the circumspect gradation with which it made use of them, its deceitful intrigues to reach its ends, announce better to all nations and all powers what they must prevent than the most far-fetched arguments and flattering eloquence . . . Fortunately for the glory of powers and the welfare of peoples, a great revolution was starting, and it is already achieved. For a century, Europe was impatiently awaiting this revolution. Europe naturally did not believe its liberty was guaranteed until it saw cruising the oceans a flag that did not tremble before the flag of Great Britain. The desire of all nations and the interest of all powers, at this moment, demand that all nations and all powers defend themselves against the blatant pretensions of a single people, a single power with universal monarchy of the seas. The political system in equilibrium demands that all nations and all maritime powers augment their naval forces in concert, that they share their influence, and finally make themselves feared by the one nation and power that for a century has been trying to disturb Europe's harmony, to invade all branches of commerce, to predominate on all seas, so as to make laws for the whole world.

For once, Gudin de La Brenellerie was in total disagreement with Beaumarchais on the American question. "We both loved the glory of France," he wrote in his memoir, "but I did not want the weakening of the British. I wanted us to be great by raising ourselves up without pulling any other nation down. If one of these nations were to crush the other, [I] said to Pierre-Augustin, the victor would feel more misery than Rome from the loss of Carthage, its emulator."

There were endless discussions, sometimes very agitated, between the two friends. This divergence is worth stressing, for Pierre-Augustin ordinarily followed the opinion of his faithful companion, knowing it was dictated by common sense and friendship. If, on this occasion, he set it aside, it was because his conviction was strongly anchored, not only with respect to his own interests, but also—and especially— with respect to his patriotic feelings. If he used cunning, especially in his memos to Louis XVI, and exaggerated in describing the situation fallaciously, even to deliberately deceive, it was always with a view to avenging the honor of his country. Did he have an ulterior motive that was ideological? Did the watchmaker of the rue Saint-Denis, whom the court always mocked for his common origins, perceive as personal revenge the birth of a young republic, brought into being by an absolute monarch? Did his adherence to the American Revolution foreshadow his engagement in the French Revolution fifteen years later? It is possible. Was he guided by the idea of profit? Did he hope to achieve the financial deal of the century? He never hid his taste for money and found it perfectly moral to get rich through business. But undoubtedly he would have given up his project on the spot if he had thought it contrary to the superior interests of France.

Having decided to assist the Americans, Louis XVI and Vergennes had to take one step more and move from simple plotting to actually providing aid. In May 1776 the minister promised Beaumarchais that a million livres would be placed in his hands. For his part, Charles III of Spain joined the king of France in supporting the insurgents and promised to spend the same sum so as to "reciprocally weaken the British in order to destroy them and put the colonists in a position to achieve their independence." Since it was important to make the British, and even the insurgents, believe that their investments were purely private, the funds would be gathered in the greatest secrecy, according to means planned by Vergennes. "With these two millions and the cooperation of individuals who want to be associated with your enterprise," he told Beaumarchais,

> you will found a major company, and at your own risk you will
> provision America with arms, munitions, equipment, and all the
> other objects that it will need to sustain the war. Our arsenals will

deliver to you the arms and munitions, but you will replace them and you will pay for them. Do not ask for any money from the Americans, since they don't have any, but you will ask them for payment in goods, the delivery of which you will facilitate throughout the kingdom, and on your side you will grant them all possible facilities.

In other words, the enterprise, first subsidized by France and Spain, would achieve self-sufficiency on the model of a company with mixed financing. And since the two commissioning states would be able to foster or hinder its evolution according to their policies, Beaumarchais would be held to an exact accounting for his profits and losses. With an eye on results, governments would then decide either to lend him new funds or else to draw the line. Thus it was a matter, as Beaumarchais put it, of a *political and commercial affair*. The essential point was that neither France nor Spain be exposed and that absolute secrecy be kept. In case of an information leak, the French government would not hesitate to *release* its agent, even publicly condemn him. He was warned.

On June 10, 1776, Beaumarchais signed a receipt for a million livres over to Duvergier, France's public treasurer, "in line with the orders of M. le Comte de Vergennes dated the fifth." Two weeks later, on June 27, the Spanish government sent a letter of credit for the same amount to its ambassador in Paris, Comte d'Aranda. In order to guarantee the secrecy of the transaction, d'Aranda deposited the Spanish million into the French public treasury in return for a cashier's check that he sent to Vergennes, who in turn gave it to Beaumarchais, who delivered a receipt:

> Versailles, August 11, 1776
>
> I have received from His Excellency the Comte de Vergennes the acknowledgement of a million livres that M. Duvergier had given to the Ambassador of Spain, with which acknowledgement I will withdraw from the Royal Treasury the said sum of a million, and for the use of which I will account to his Excellency, M. le Comte de Vergennes.
>
> Caron de Beaumarchais

His two million in his pocket, Pierre-Augustin founded an import-export company located in his home while awaiting more suitable headquarters. Since Spain had already brought him luck, he baptized his company Roderigue Hortalez. Under this name, designed to fool the London authorities, he performed his activities as a ship owner discreetly supported by the French court. Adding to the initial capital would quickly come the financial support of various associates: small shareholders of 15,000 or 20,000 livres, rich arms manufacturers from Lorient and Bordeaux, merchants established in ports, and even some nobles. As for the company's founder, he put all his holdings into the business, even though he was seriously squeezed by the La Blache suit, by his own sumptuous expenditures, by his love affairs, and by the reacquisition of his house in the rue de Condé, where he kept his father and the two of his sisters who had remained at home, as well as two nephews and a niece who had been orphaned at an early age and whom he also took charge of. His sister Julie, who had renounced marriage to devote herself to her dear Pierrot, kept house. Happily, he enjoyed immense credit on the Paris stock market. Once the Franco-Spanish millions were gone, private investors would respond en masse to his appeal for funds, while he expected the French government to grant him a new advance. The expenses for which he would claim reimbursement from the American Congress during 1777, after a year of operation, would exceed 5 million livres! His associates gave him enormous sums as loans for the duration of the campaign, with a view to repayment augmented by eventual dividends. Capital flowed in, and Beaumarchais soon found himself at the head of a veritable financial empire. Naturally, such sudden wealth caused gossip: people wondered about the source of his fortune, and he was invited everywhere. He was soon forced to explain things to his mistress, Mme. de Godeville, when refusing her a loan from the company account:

> Two years ago I had malaise about my means. I did not suddenly become wealthy but only a major administrator of funds for a company that honors me with its perfect trust, which I merit. But I cannot permit myself to tap the funds in this account for the benefit of my friends in need, because I imposed on myself the

law of being pure as a virgin on the use of these funds, and not accepting into the account anything but notes from the high bank, which always take the place of money. All this means that I can indeed sometimes oblige a friend for 10, 12 or 20 louis, but always by drawing from my personal account, which is not suddenly swollen by some miracle.

The British were not duped for long by this operation. On November 6 their ambassador in Paris, Lord Stormont, who kept a spy network, sent the Foreign Office a confidential note denouncing the French government's trickery, revealing Beaumarchais's role in this affair, and exhorting his government to counter his scheme.

Meanwhile on July 4 the delegates of the thirteen British colonies adopted the Declaration of Independence, proclaiming their desire to separate from Great Britain and to constitute a United States of America. Almost entirely written by Thomas Jefferson, the declaration rested on the political theory of natural rights. It was not content to recall the grievances of the colonies against Britain: for the first time in the world, thirteen years before France's Declaration of the Rights of Man and the Citizen, a nation asserted:

We hold these truths to be self-evident, that all men are created equal, that they are endowed by their Creator with certain inalienable rights; that among these are life, liberty, and the pursuit of happiness. That to secure these rights, governments are instituted among men deriving their just power from the consent of the governed; that whenever any form of government becomes destructive of these ends, it is the right of the people to alter or to abolish it, and to institute a new government.

The Declaration of Independence would constitute the basis of the political philosophy of the American people, while exercising a profound influence on the actors of the French Revolution of 1789. "Never has Rome or Greece or any people of the Old Continent expounded the reasons for its independence with such noble simplicity, or based them on more evident truths. I believe that there is nobody in the United States who does not learn the preamble by heart in childhood or regard it under the aegis of liberty." The author of these lines, Gudin de La Brenellerie, Beaumarchais's friend and confidant, shared his enthusiasm when the news reached Europe.

In London, however, this act proclaiming the foundation of the American Republic was secondary to the resistance of the "rebels" and produced no visible emotion. The chargé d'affaires at the French embassy in London communicated the information in his report of August 13 without any wonderment:

> General Howe informs us that Congress has declared the inde-
> pendence of the united colonies. It is also known that Congress
> has formally declared war on Great Britain and that this declara-
> tion is justified in twenty-three articles giving the reasons that
> have determined it to take this stance. But the government has
> not believed it ought to recognize this; and in fact I do not see
> why this hue and cry should be any sensational news here, either.

Shortly before the Declaration of Independence, the American Congress had sent to France an official ambassador in the person of Silas Deane, furnished with full power to negotiate supplies. He was a rich merchant from Connecticut, rather educated, with lavish tastes and zeal but little judgment. As the French government was reluctant to make public the presence in Paris of a colonial representative, he had to travel incognito as a simple merchant. Before his departure he had received very precise instructions from Franklin himself on which attitude to take on every occasion. Each minute act and word had been prescribed. Franklin could not resist warning Deane about the seductions of Parisian life: "There will be no question of satisfy-ing the curiosity that leads everybody to visit this famous city."

Under Franklin's influence, one Dr. Jacques Barbeu-Dubourg had become a fiery partisan of the American cause. Gaining special entrée into the minister's cabinet, he learned with joy that the French gov-ernment was getting ready to encourage the export of military matériel to the insurgents by discreetly subsidizing the exporters; the ulterior motivation for his joy was that he intended to make a profit from the operation, since his love of botany had not stifled his taste for money. Lured by the prospect of enormous profits, Barbeu-

Dubourg surrounded himself with friends and businessmen, of whom the most important was none other than Le Ray de Chaumont, the former associate of Pâris-Duverney, who in 1764 had commissioned Beaumarchais's mission to Spain.

Silas Deane's arrival would furnish Dubourg with the ideal occasion to finally deploy his business talents on a large scale. To get the American into his clutches, he lodged him nearby and promised to present him to the French authorities at the first opportunity. He made Deane believe that the ministers would not receive him in the present circumstances for fear that Lord Stormont would accuse them over it. Meanwhile he advised him to avoid any contact with the outside: it would even be better for him to change his name. Dubourg had excellent relations with Vergennes, seeing him and writing to him freely; he corresponded with Arthur Lee and his agents; and he had access to the highest war officials. So Dubourg regarded himself as the ideal intermediary between the American Congress and the French government. When Silas Deane gave him Franklin's letter, it amounted to patent recognition, making him absolutely certain that the Americans had designated him to negotiate with France for the sale of military supplies. So Dubourg went alone to Versailles to tell Vergennes, very eloquently, that he would set up a supply syndicate offering every guarantee to the interested governments.

The minister's answer came like a bolt from the blue. It was too late: the arrangements had already been made with Beaumarchais, to whom Dubourg should speak about all these matters. Dubourg's disappointment was as great as his hopes had been. On the carriage ride back to Paris, he tried to take comfort. It was not possible! Vergennes could not have entrusted such great responsibility to a public entertainer! The author of *The Barber of Seville* could furnish information on English policy, at most, but to organize help to the Americans! No, he must have misunderstood! Without losing an instant, he set up a rendezvous with Beaumarchais, who received him on July 13.

What a cold shower! His host confirmed that he had been "entrusted to take charge of all details and all commercial operations, regarding what was sent out and back, whether war munitions or ordinary merchandise, from France to the colonies and from the colonies to France, to direct all affairs, fix prices, conclude deals, make all arrangements, recover payments, settle debts, etc."

Dubourg then told him that "in running off with this immense trade, and absolutely excluding the people who had put up so much money at the cost of so much effort and run all the dangers for a year, for the service and by order of Congress, this would give them reason to decry a monopoly and would do them real wrong when they merited a different fate." Returning home, trembling with impotent rage, Dubourg wrote Vergennes this hateful—and almost defamatory—letter:

> Monseigneur,
>
> I saw M. de Beaumarchais this morning and as expressly authorized by you, I confided unreservedly in him. Everybody knows his mind, his talents, and nobody renders more justice than I to his honesty, his discretion, his zeal for everything that is great and good. I think him one of the most able men for political negotiations, but perhaps at the same time one of the least suited to mercantile business. He likes pomp, it is certain he keeps ladies, and he is a glutton for money, and in France there is neither merchant nor manufacturer who does not have this opinion of him and who would not greatly hesitate to make the least commercial deal with him . . . I admit that these particular motives might not suffice to balance that of the necessary secrecy in such a critical conjuncture. But what allows me to suspect that there are other means, that there are indeed better means to guarantee this important secret, is assuredly that M. de Beaumarchais, with all the resources of his genius, cannot avoid employing many subordinates, always less discreet than the merchants, whose capital goal is to hide their speculations and to continually distrust everybody. But I come back to my first and principal thought, and beg you, Monseigneur, to think again. Perhaps there are a hundred, perhaps a thousand, people in France who, with talents much inferior to those of M. de Beaumarchais, would better satisfy your wishes and yet inspire more confidence in all those with whom they would have to deal.

Vergennes, although perhaps not in a playful mood, was so amused by this diatribe that he took pleasure in communicating it to the interested party. Beaumarchais smiled, shrugged his shoulders, and struck back at his unfortunate competitor in a riposte that earned him an implacable enemy—yet another!

> And what difference does it make if I like gadding about and keeping girls? The girls I have kept for twenty years, Monsieur, are indeed your very humble servants. There used to be five of them, four sisters and a niece. Over the past three years, two of the kept girls have died, to my great sorrow. Now I only have to keep three: two sisters and my niece, which is not extravagant for an individual like me. But what would you have thought, if, knowing me better, you had realized that I pushed scandal to the point of keeping men as well, two very young and handsome nephews and even the very unhappy father who gave birth to this scandalous pimp? And my ostentation is even worse! For the past three years, finding lace and embroidered coats too petty for my vanity, I have even affected the arrogance of having my cuffs decorated with the finest muslin! A superb black serge is not too fine for me. At times I have even been seen to extend my foppishness to silk, when the weather is very hot. But I beg you, Monsieur, not to describe these things to M. le Comte de Vergennes—or you will end up destroying me in his eyes.

This letter was written on July 16. Two days later Beaumarchais reported to Vergennes his amusing quarrel with Dr. Barbeu-Dubourg, demonstrating that the old scholar inspired more malice than resentment:

> I want to instruct you tomorrow morning about my conferences with the doctor. He began with hostility but ended up with trust, and as I make it a law to move always under your watch, I send you, for a moment's laughter, the copy of what I sent in response to his invitation to dine, when he wrote to you that I keep girls. The good doctor, seeing he was not able to anger me, took the tack of confiding in me. Thus it is that Turkish women, being

unable to deceive their husbands, amuse themselves by loving
them, for lack of anything better.

The comedy amused the minister and wounded the doctor, who
had no recourse other than to await the arrival of his friend Benjamin
Franklin. When the latter set foot in Paris on December 27, 1776,
Dubourg rushed to retail to him a thousand horrors about Beaumarchais. A ferocious friend of virtue, Franklin felt the strongest repugnance for the "ostentatious pimp" and caused him many difficulties
later. Dr. Dubourg, supplanted in the great operation that he had
wanted to direct, was not beaten and tried to export munitions to the
insurgents on his own account, but the small vessel that carried them
a few weeks later was inspected by the British, who confiscated the
cargo.

In Paris for more than a week now, Silas Deane was starting to
wonder if the meeting with Vergennes would ever happen. The minister, for his part, knew of the American's presence in the capital and
manifested just as much impatience to meet him. Little did he realize
that Dr. Dubourg had literally sequestered Congress's emissary in his
hotel. Deane finally realized that the doctor was by no means the
trustworthy man Franklin had described. He asked for an audience
on his own, which happened at Versailles on July 15.

The meeting between Deane and Vergennes lasted two hours;
Gérard de Rayneval of the Foreign Ministry acted as interpreter.

Congress's ambassador at once explained his mission: Congress
had sent him to solicit the help of a European power.

> If we thought first of France, it was because its friendship will be
> more useful to us than any other, in the event of definitive rup-
> ture with Great Britain. But it is also because France will profit
> the most from trade with the colonies, to which England owes a
> part of its wealth. America needs equipment and war matériel for
> 25,000 men and a hundred cannons. Its repayment in stages will
> be all the more sure if its commerce is protected by itself or its
> allies. It could also buy cloth, woolens, and other articles, for
> which it would not need credit. All this would form a cargo ship
> escorted by two or three warships.

Silas Deane then pointed out that the most elementary resources were lacking to his fellow citizens, and that their want was each day more aggravated. "Many questions were asked," Deane told Philadelphia, "and many explanations given."

Congress had recommended that Deane "not be discouraged by possible coldness or reserve on the part of the Minister; if necessary, he should withdraw and ask M. de Vergennes to reflect, telling him that he remained in Paris for a little time and that he would await orders." This was a sage precaution, for the minister listened to his visitor with interest but left him no hope of obtaining official support. He responded to his demands with a formal refusal but vigorously advised him to seek out Beaumarchais, who might come to his aid at advantageous conditions.

As soon as he was back in Paris, Deane requested a rendezvous. Beaumarchais answered the next day:

> Paris, July 18, 1776
>
> I do not know, Monsieur, if you have near you someone trustworthy on whom you can count enough to have him translate French letters dealing with serious affairs; for my part, I cannot freely do so with English letters until the arrival of someone whom I am expecting from England at this moment, who will serve us as interpreter. I may have the honor of alerting you, though, that I have long been occupied with the desire to aid the brave Americans to shake off the British yoke, and have already tried in various ways to start a sure and secret commerce between Congress and a company that I formed for this purpose. By means of our islands or else directly, I could manage to provide the continent with what the Americans need and can no longer get from England. I am open about this with somebody in London who says he is very attached to the interests of America [Arthur Lee]; but our correspondence since my return has been difficult and in code, and I have not received an answer to my last letter in which I tried to establish the conditions of the great affair.
>
> Since you have a character that allows perfect confidence in you, I could not ask for better than to recommence in a more

sure and continuous way the negotiations that I regard as sketched out with the other. My means are not yet considerable, but they may be infinitely increased if we manage to lay together the foundations of a treaty that is presentable as to its conditions and exact as to its execution.

I cannot accord either M. du Bourg nor anyone except you, Monsieur, the trust to speak freely of my commercial plan. But when you have compared the nature of the offers that will come to you from elsewhere, with the disinterested zeal that attaches me to the cause of America, you will feel the difference there is between dealing with ordinary businessmen in the harshest terms, and the pleasure of meeting a generous friend who will take pleasure in proving to your nation and to you, its secret representative, with what devotion, Monsieur, I am your very humble and obedient servant.

Caron de Beaumarchais

This letter is crucial, for it marks the debut of Franco-American commercial relations and of an uninterrupted correspondence that would last until 1778. On Friday, July 19, the founder of Hortalez and Congress's agent met for the first time. Prior to any negotiation, Beaumarchais had asked to see Deane's credentials, as was customary when dealing with the representative of a foreign nation. Deane sent him the next day a copy of his commission and an extract from his instructions, which called upon him to go first to ministers, so as to obtain from them by means of purchase or loan the supplies the Americans needed. If this failed, he should try to procure them by any other means; hence his approach to the Hortalez Company.

It remained to solve the thorny problem of credit. Silas Deane took a written promise that the value of the exchange in tobacco from Virginia and Maryland, as well as other products, would be shipped to France as soon as maritime navigation was possible: a year from then at the latest. After this deadline the sums due would rise according to interest calculated at the current rates. In his response of July 22 Beaumarchais agreed to all these conditions and left it to Congress to choose between two methods of fixing the sale price of the merchandise to be shipped to him. This simple exchange of correspondence would take the place of a contract between the two parties. After having defined the general ways and particular conditions of these Franco-American exchanges, Beaumarchais concluded his contract-letter with these words:

> As I think I am dealing with a virtuous nation, it will suffice for me to have in my possession an exact account of all my loans. Congress will decide either to pay for the merchandise based on their usual value at the time of their arrival on the continent, or else receive them according to the purchase price, plus delays and insurance, with a commission proportionate to the trouble taken, which it is impossible to fix today. I intend to serve your country as if it were my own, and I hope to find in the friendship of a generous nation the true recompense for the labors that I devote to it with pleasure.

Naturally, Congress's agent was overjoyed to see their cooperation begin under such favorable auspices and told Beaumarchais so:

> The generous confidence that you place in the virtue and justice of my constituents inspires the greatest joy in me, gives me the most flattering hopes for the success of the enterprise, to their satisfaction but also to yours, and allows me to assure you anew that the united colonies will take the most effective measures to send you repayment and to justify in all respects the sentiments that animate you on their behalf.

But Beaumarchais's letter had ended with a warning (in English): "I ask for all the discretion you sense we need in order not to excite the attention of the British ambassador and not to alarm our ministers by complaints from that ambassador, which would gravely embarrass us. Our sole affair, you and I, is to slip between everyone's fingers and not to cause anyone to squeal while we do our business." Spies were in fact hovering around the operation; Deane felt he was constantly under surveillance and shared his fears with Beaumarchais: "You know that the British ambassador attends to everything I do, that his spies watch all my movements and probably even watch all the movements of those with whom I am in touch."

In this case how can we explain the fact that Deane took as a confidant a personality as nefarious as Dr. Edward Bancroft? True, this man of science, a physicist and a naturalist (like Dr. Barbeu-Dubourg) and the author of highly regarded books, appeared to be above all suspicion; Benjamin Franklin maintained a scientific correspondence with him and sometimes used him as a secretary to write pamphlets supporting the colonies and articles for the English papers, in particular the *Monthly Review*. Better still, he had recommended that Deane make contact with him before his departure for France and attract him to Paris so as to benefit from his experience and contacts. Such marks of American confidence were of enough value to Bancroft to pass as proof to the Foreign Office, who soon directed him to Paris, where he arrived the same day as Deane. Received by Vergennes a few days before Congress's envoy, he received the confidences of both and hurried to communicate them to the London cabinet. It was also he who served as interpreter during the first meetings between Deane and Beaumarchais. Nobody—neither the Americans, the French, Franklin, nor Lord Stormont himself—suspected that he was a double agent. Later Beaumarchais did perceive abnormal information leaks, but he didn't manage to identify the traitor. "The King of England knows, I do not know how, everything that happens in your great assemblies," he wrote to members of Congress. "Some indiscreet or perfidious citizen is giving the Palace of St. James an exact account of your deliberations."

Today Edward Bancroft is considered one of the mythical figures of British espionage—for good reason. During the five most critical years for Great Britain, from 1776 to 1781, the Foreign Office and King George III—who shared with Louis XV an immoderate taste for information—were much better informed about the international relations of the United States than was George Washington himself. Astonishingly, Bancroft recruited his informants even among the American circle in Passy, among the intimates of Benjamin Franklin. Having gained the trust of the principal actors in the Franco-American alliance, he sent regular information to Lord Suffolk, head of the secret service, who gave him 500 pounds and assured him of an annual fee of 400 pounds. Thanks to him, the Foreign Office was informed daily of all the transactions between Deane and Beaumarchais, the latter being designated in this correspondence by the number 26. On August 14, 1776, Bancroft sent to Suffolk a detailed report on Deane's conversations with Vergennes, which the American deputy had repeated to him verbatim. All this information was then transmitted to Lord Stormont, the ambassador in Paris, who could thus match it with that supplied by his own networks.

In addition to Bancroft, Lord Suffolk had sent to France one of his American friends, Paul Wentworth, who had once lived in the West Indies, then in England, and spoke French fluently. Wentworth was asked to set up a spy network in Paris whose aim was to spoil the Franco-American negotiations. According to Beaumarchais, Wentworth was "one of the most adroit men of England." He lodged at the Hôtel Vauban, on the rue de Richelieu—not by chance, for other tenants there were Americans and patriots. There one met Samuel Nicholson, commander of a corsair ship in Lorient; William Carmichael, secretary to three American commissioners in Paris; and Jonathan Austin, secretary to the war council of Massachusetts. Miraculous fishing waters for an informer!

Despite the quality of Suffolk's agents, notably Edward Bancroft, the information that they supplied to the British services was often contradictory, incomplete, and approximate. So the real usefulness of that supposed information is questionable. Lord Stormont might consider the sale of arms to the American rebels as a gesture inimical to Great Britain, and he might interrogate the ministers about it, but he certainly could not prevent a French enterprise from doing business with the countries it chose. He knew well that this enterprise was commissioned by the Spanish and French governments, but he had no means of opposing it; he had to be content with making official protests to the ministers, which had the sole result of strengthening the clandestine French system. Despite his remonstrances and his spies, France and America would avidly pursue their collaboration, to the great satisfaction of both parties.

Fourteen

"A NOBLE AND FREE PEOPLE!"

From Frenchman that I was, I made myself American, business-man, politician, shipowner, writer.
—Beaumarchais to Congress, July 14, 1783

Having founded his company, Pierre-Augustin looked for lodgings big enough to house his offices, his warehouses, and his household. For the sake of economy, he preferred the Marais quarter, where prices had been falling. The aristocracy had once made it a privileged district, then little by little deserted it in favor of the Faubourg Saint-Germain (the "noble Faubourg," as it was called), and its magnificent *hôtels* were transformed into residential rentals. A Parisian guide of 1763 vaunted the agreeableness of these dwellings and their gardens but noted also their moderate rents, a revealing sign of disaffection: "One finds in the Marais many fine houses all the more agreeable in that almost all have ornate gardens and the rents are less expensive in this quarter." On October 9, 1776, Beaumarchais leased from Louis Letellier, master mason, one of the finest Marais hôtels, at 47, rue Vieille-du-Temple, ordinarily called the Hôtel de Hollande, for the relatively modest rent of 6,600 livres. "Sieur de Beaumarchais develops his vast projects of fortune," commented the editor of the *Mémoires Secrets* with his habitual perfidy. "He has taken a very grand hôtel on the rue du Temple; he sets up offices and establishes a considerable house of commerce; he has many funds at his disposal."

The general appearance of the building had not changed since 1660, when Jean-Baptiste Amelot de Bisseuil built it, or rather renovated the original work of the architect Pierre Cottard. Despite many transformations (not always wholesome) it remains one of the jewels of seventeenth-century Parisian architecture, as well as a treasure trove of sculpture and painting.

Its decor was more austere under Beaumarchais's ownership. The company offices can be easily imagined: maps of the North Atlantic and ephemera on the walls. Beaumarchais's office probably had inlaid paneling—and almost surely secret hiding places. Down the length of the main room stood five or six mahogany tables with pewter inkwells and quill pens sticking out of them, and heaps of papers: mail, invoices and delivery slips, bills of lading, French and foreign gazettes. At its inception Roderigue Hortalez had only five or six employees, but soon the personnel grew. "This politico-commercial affair will become immense," predicted Beaumarchais, "and I would be drowning in details, me and the handful of staff I have employed up to now, if I did not promptly hire more. Some will travel, others reside in the ports, the manufactories, etc."

The key posts were occupied by men he could trust. The foremost was none other than the younger brother of his dear alter ego, Philippe-Jean Gudin de La Ferlière, who assumed the role of chief accountant, and whose office was on the mezzanine, just above the front door. The second, Théveneau de Francy, was the young brother of Théveneau de Morande (the former libelist) but very different with respect to morality; he worked in a room adjoining the director's office, where he managed freight and shipping, and supervised the mail and office work. Beaumarchais treated him like a son and considered him another version of himself: "You and I are the same thing," he would one day write. For three years Francy hardly occupied his office, since his missions sent him along the coast, from Dunkirk to Le Havre to Lorient, to Nantes, Bordeaux, and Marseilles. During a long stay in America, he represented the interests of his employer. He stopped traveling only during the last year of the war, when tuberculosis rendered him immobile, at which point Beaumarchais gave him the job of managing the office while he himself toured the ports.

The team would soon be completed by a vast network of correspondents in France and abroad. They were businessmen who exploited varying ships' tonnage. They were consignees of ships and merchandise as well as maritime suppliers, ship handlers, warehouse owners, and managers of dockers and stevedores. Moreover, they controlled the correspondence sent to the crews (it was to them that Beaumarchais and Francy sent mail) and helped the captains, representing their client in case of litigation. On the other side of the Atlantic, in addition to his deputy Théveneau de Francy, Beaumarchais had two other agents.

Beaumarchais was Figaro himself in the role of Roderigue Hortalez: Spanish businessman, merchant, importer of rice and tobacco and cod-liver oil, smuggler, shipowner, naval strategist, and minister of his own navy. Since nothing in his past had predisposed him to this career, he had his apprenticeship from Carrier de Monthieu, the great Nantes shipowner, whose methods he severely criticized once his initiation was complete (not long after). The details of the work being less familiar to him than its principles, at least at the start he took advice from everybody but later relied on his own judgment. His strict observation of this rule, combined with his steady memory, his exceptional facility to assimilate facts, and his indomitable energy, would soon transform the author of *The Barber of Seville* into an expert on the merchant navy.*

In the daytime his offices were like a beehive. The staff bustled about, verifying arsenal lists, making orders to private industry, dividing the matériel among the ports nearest the suppliers, requesting transfers, sending them to local agents charged with taking delivery of the matériel and dealing with cartage companies, drawing up waybills, handling complaints if necessary, managing the stock, verifying invoices, and sending them to the cashier. The American insurgents had to be sent hundreds of cannons, mortars, bombs, and cannonballs and thousands of muskets, uniforms, and camp equipment for 30,000 men—all without arousing the least suspicion from local

---

*Gudin: "In every circumstance of his life, he was entirely devoted to whatever occupied his attention, without being turned away from it either by what had taken place or by what was to follow, so sure was he of his own faculties and his presence of mind. He never needed preparation on any point; his intelligence was at his command at all times, and his principles were never faulty."

authorities. The laws of the kingdom formally prohibited the export of arms, and the watchful British ambassador bounded off to Versailles to report the first suspect movement. The operation would have been impossible without the tacit complicity of French authorities—which could occur only in the greatest secrecy. At the least leak or diplomatic snag, the ministry would turn against Beaumarchais without pity. This political pusillanimity, desired by Louis XVI, exasperated all French supporters of America, not only Roderigue Hortalez's boss. The Marquis de Lafayette strongly criticized it in his memoirs, maintaining that the French government was slavishly obeying Lord Stormont's orders: one word from him "was sufficient to have arrested, discharged, or sometimes imprisoned, those Americans admitted to our ports. Versailles lost itself in a maze of precautions, weaknesses, and denials." To elude Stormont's spies, Beaumarchais had to split his cargo into separate lots and smuggle them toward three or four different embarkation points—hence the incredible complexity of the operations. "To help America," he remembered later, "I was obliged to mask and disguise my work in France: the shipments, ships, the name of suppliers—right up to my reason for being in commerce, which was a mask like all the rest."

But his life was a perpetual combat, as he loved to repeat. The more the difficulties accumulated, the more he felt compelled to try to overcome them. His schedule was frantic: he was everywhere, thinking of a thousand things at once: buying 12,000 cubic feet of marine lumber in London, 40,000 infantry muskets in Saint-Étienne, artillery pieces from the Château-Trompette arsenal; in Paris, he rounded up from a draper the wherewithal to clothe 30,000 men. On September 11, 1776, his memo to the courts of France and Spain stated total purchases of 300,000 units of cannon powder, 30,000 muskets, 3,000 tents, and 200 cannons, plus gun carriages and front axles, 27 mortars, 100,000 shells, and 13,000 bombs. To which must be added 95,000 measures of cloth for soldiers' uniforms (plus 30,000 "for officers") and 42,000 measures to line the trousers, plus material for shirts and caps, 120,000 dozen buttons, linens, handkerchiefs, pairs of shoes, garter buckles, and 600 tinplate coffers.

Once the obstacles were removed, the deals made, and the formalities completed, the supplies would be transported to the various French ports, ready to go to sea. Silas Deane had promised, a little rashly, to have them loaded onto American ships. When these ships did not arrive, and the insurgents were waiting agonizingly for the arms for the 1777 campaign, Beaumarchais tried hard to find the necessary tonnage to send them. As there was no question, at least for the moment, of constructing or even buying ships, he had to charter them. With the help of the Nantes shipowner Carrier de Monthieu he chartered ten ships in October 1776: nine cargo ships and a frigate, the *Amphytritus.* To avoid concentrating his squadron (which would have alerted British attention), he dispersed the ships among various coastal ports: Le Havre, Lorient, Nantes, Rochefort, La Rochelle, and Bordeaux. To these first ten vessels would later be added others that Beaumarchais chartered, bought, or had built. Finally Beaumarchais had refitted the *Hippopotame*, an old three-deck vessel of the line, and transformed it into the *Fier-Roderigue*, named after his company. It was the jewel of his fleet, with a capacity of 1,000 tons, 60 bronze cannons, and 350 crew. So close was this ship to his heart that when it was finally unable to take to sea, he had a new one built, armed as a warship. He also bought four Bermudan vessels, basically brigantines with lateen rigs, to transport from Santo Domingo to North America the merchandise stored in Cap Français. At the end of 1778 he joined with Monthieu to arm eleven other cargo ships and three smaller courier boats.

So it was with legitimate pride that Beaumarchais could boast of a flotilla of forty ships. But can we believe his claim that they were all sailing at the same time? His abundant commercial correspondence reveals that in fact he never put to sea more than a dozen ships simultaneously. As they fell out of use, sank, or were captured by the British, which was most frequently the case, he replaced them. He also needed good-quality sailing personnel. From his first steps in shipping, he explained his views on this crucial question with the assurance of an experienced navigator. "It is not enough to choose brave naval captains," he said. "They must also be endowed with prudence, intelligence, and proper conduct, to which is added knowledge about commerce, since they must be entrusted with the management of their cargoes." But a captain, however perfect, will do no good unless his ship is worthy of all the artillery that is compatible with its tonnage and unless he has around him "a complete crew sufficient to maneuver it and for combat, which it must not sustain except in retreat." A plentiful crew is also necessary to prevent, in case of boarding, any arrest on board. During the smuggling period Beaumarchais instructed his captains in the delicate art of fabricating false papers for their return to France. To escape any accusation of carrying contraband, they had to disguise the real destination of their voyage west. A ship intended for, say, Boston had "to go via Saint-Pierre and Miquelon; and when for [South Georgia or Carolina] to go via the Mississippi; but on the return, the ship should be in a state during the crossing to prove that it is coming from a French possession or from Spanish Louisiana."

The Americans needed more than supplies and ammunition—they needed men to train their troops. Silas Deane insisted that the French send officers, especially artillerymen and engineers. Beaumarchais got the ministry to close its eyes to this new operation. Starting in 1776, he and Deane recruited fifty French and foreign instructors, and at their head as lieutenant-colonel of artillery he placed Jean-Baptiste Tronson de Coudray, brother of a famous lawyer, former teacher of the Comte d'Artois and then of the Duc de Chartres; he had found him at a garrison in Metz in 1774. Coudray initially seemed adroit and a good soldier: dreaming of a brilliant military career in America, he had adopted all the mannerisms. But Figaro could not have made a worse choice, for Coudray was actually fatuous. Barely in possession of his command, he fomented discontent among the ranks. He alienated officers whose control he feared and replaced them with men in his own pay. He encouraged complaints and complained himself. He confided to indiscreet ears the secret of his mission and attributed to Beaumarchais the rumors he was spreading. Once in America he continued to undermine the reputation of his employer by all sorts of intrigues and calumnies, which would eventually sow doubt even within Congress. The officers he signed up idled in the public places of Paris and in the ports, wasting their time, bragging and making demands, awaiting an embarkation too long in coming. Still, among them were the Poles Casimir Pulawski and Andrej Koscinszko, the German Baron Steuben, the Irishman Thomas Conway, and the French Marquis de La Rouërie. And a few months later, on June 13, 1777, Lafayette, aged twenty, disembarked in Georgetown to defend the cause of the insurgents. In 1780, when France formally entered the conflict, 6,000 men of the expeditionary forces placed under the command of Rochambeau joined all these volunteers.

On December 13, 1776, the *Amphytritus*, commanded by Captain Fautrel, was waiting in the port of Le Havre to take on powder. On board was a convoy of forty-nine soldiers of all ranks commanded by Coudray, and in its holds was a formidable arsenal. But the frigate had almost failed to raise anchor—on account of Beaumarchais's own vanity. On December 12 Beaumarchais, traveling under the pseudonym "Durand," had arrived in Le Havre; that same day Benjamin Franklin had set foot in Nantes. The double event was recorded in a police report for that day: "The arrival of Dr. Franklin in Nantes has caused a sensation, and the departure of M. de Beaumarchais, who is said to have gone to Le Havre, no less so." But Beaumarchais was supposed to be using a pseudonym—how could the police have got wind of his presence in Le Havre? Well, because the theater there had programmed for that day *The Barber of Seville*! The effect on Beaumarchais was such that he forgot "Durand" and rushed to the theater, rehearsed the actors, and that very evening attended the performance, accepting ovations from the audience. Discreetly, of course.

The same day Stormont's spies reported that Beaumarchais had been seen in Le Havre, that the *Amphytritus* was at the quay loaded to the gills with war matériel, and that the officers had just embarked. Pushed by an east-southeast wind that was "small, fresh and favorable," the *Amphytritus* got under way. The British ambassador stormed. Sharply summoned, Navy Minister Sartine visited all the vessels of the Hortalez flotilla. The *Amphytritus*, already launched, escaped the search, but the others were disarmed and placed under French sequestration. Beaumarchais protested, but Vergennes demanded that in future all his vessels were to land at French islands and not on the continent. Even this, however, was a ruse to calm the ambassador. Thenceforth the captains would travel with two sets of instructions concerning the route to take, one official and the other secret.

Whatever else he undertook, Beaumarchais remained above all a man of the theater. Yesterday he had been pleading against Goëzman in pamphlets that seemed written for the stage. Today he was a shipowner, in the role of Roderigue Hortalez, using his genius for intrigue to trick the "Stormont inquisition." To play a part, to out-smart, to play upon someone: this was his creed, and he created a new scenario in order to deliver the cargo of the *Fier-Roderigue* without attracting the enemy's attention. It was a crazy invention, about false pirates and real smugglers, operating under the nose of the British martinets! Here is how he described his plan to his friend Francy:

> I must keep the word I have given to M. de Maurepas, that my ship can serve only to carry to Santo Domingo seven or eight hundred militiamen and come back without touching the continent. However, the cargo of our ship is very interesting to Congress and to me. . . . Thinking about this, I thought you might arrange secretly with Congress's secret committee for them to send one or two American corsairs right away to Santo Domingo. One of them will send its launch to Cap Français, or else make the signal agreed long ago for all American ships who come to the Cap, to put up a white flame, raise a Dutch flag on the main mast, and fire three cannon shots. Then M. Carabasse will go aboard with M. de Montaut, captain of my ship the *Fier-Roderigue*. They will arrange that when my ship leaves, the American corsair will seize it under some pretext and make off with it. My captain will protest violently and make a statement of complaints and threats to Congress. The ship will be escorted to where you are. Congress will haughtily disavow the brutal corsair and free the ship, with obliging excuses to the French flag. During this time, you will unload the cargo on land, fill it with tobacco, and send it back to me quickly, with all those you will have been able to find. By this means, M. de Maurepas will be extricated from the word he gave to others, and my operation will be successful despite all the obstacles put in my path.

Avoiding traps, surmounting obstacles, thwarting ruses, Beaumarchais almost always managed to deceive the vigilant enemy. His three first ships eluded British cruisers and unloaded more than 5 million livres in matériel in the Portsmouth, New Hampshire, harbor just before the campaign of 1777. It was the first time that the American people had received from Europe such a cargo of cannons, powder, muskets, and uniforms. The crowd rushed to the shore to welcome it with explosions of joy. Shortly afterward two more vessels arrived in port to unload further weapons and munitions. When Silas Deane told Congress about the success of his mission on November 29, 1777, he gave all the credit to Beaumarchais: "I should never have completed what I have," he said with honorable modesty,

> but for the generous, indefatigable, and spirited exertions of Monsieur Beaumarchais, to whom the United States are on every account greatly indebted, more so than to any other person on this side of the water; he is largely ahead in stores, clothing, and the like, and therefore I am confident you will make him the earliest and most ample remittances . . . I cannot in a letter render full justice to M. de Beaumarchais for his skill and zeal in sustaining our cause. All that I can say is that in this operation, he conducted himself by the greatest and most liberal principles, and that he made our affair his very own. His influence and his reputation are great and have been entirely employed in serving our interests, and I hope the results will be equal to his hopes.

Alas, Silas Deane's "confidence" must be placed in the category of pious wishes, or pious lies, for those remittances of Virginia tobacco designed to reimburse the Roderigue Hortalez Company for its trouble and its arms, which were supposed to be sent within six months, never appeared on the horizon; the docks would remain desperately empty, the French ships return home empty, and Beaumarchais's complaints would go unanswered. Over two years he received only two cargoes valued at 150,000 livres each, of which one was composed exclusively of indigo and rice instead of the Virginia tobacco that he was impatiently expecting. In effect, the insurgents disagreed as to the nature of the French shipments. Were the arms being sold to them by Hortalez? Was it a trade, as Deane thought, or a free gift from the French government, as Arthur Lee claimed?* Lee even

---

*Lee's malicious assertions were inadvertently substantiated by Beaumarchais's florid enthusiasm for the cause, from which anyone might conclude that his support was ideologically based.

wrote a confidential note to the congressional committee: "M. de Vergennes, the Minister, and his secretary have repeatedly assured us that no return was expected for the cargoes sent by Beaumarchais. This gentleman is not a businessman; he is known to be a political agent employed by the court of France." This shameless lie was rebutted in Vergennes's correspondence. A few days later Lee compounded the fraudulent claim: "The Minister has often given us to understand that we have nothing to pay for these cargoes from Beaumarchais. However the latter persists in his demands." While the ambiguity (carefully maintained by Franklin himself) served the ministries, attached as they were to secrecy, it plunged Beaumarchais into frightful financial difficulties. Between May and July 1777 Vergennes had given him more than a million additional livres in compensation and to commit him to continuing, which raised the subsidy Beaumarchais had received from the French and Spanish governments to a total of 3 million. But this sum was a mere drop in the bucket: the advances Hortalez had made to Congress already exceeded 5 million. In short, bankruptcy was around the corner. "I have exhausted my money and my credit," Pierre-Augustin wrote to Congress in December 1777.* "Counting on the return from goods so often promised, I have greatly exceeded my funds and those of my friends. I have even exhausted other powerful help that I had secured to begin with under the express promise to pay them back before long." This appeal went unanswered.

What was happening on the other side of the Atlantic? Why were the Americans silent? Why were they showing such hostility to so faithful a friend? Why delay the reimbursement of his cargoes? The reasons were several. A dispute between Deane and Lee had been brewing for some time, and when it burst forth, Beaumarchais was its first victim. Franklin, warned by Dr. Barbeu-Dubourg, had abstained from intervening in Beaumarchais's favor to Congress; he had even had 150,000 livres' worth of rice and indigo seized from the *Amphytritus* (which would be restored shortly after). The slander

---

*December 1777 saw the surrender of General Burgoyne's force at Saratoga and a stock market collapse in London. The French had a popular song about the success of the insurgents: "To finish the job one day / Send your children to dance / On the ruins of England."

spread by Coudray had had its effect in Congress. Finally, people were muttering that the arms and munitions sent by Hortalez were not the latest models. And since the orders he had received from Maurepas and Sartine were perfectly contradictory, Beaumarchais could not understand the situation. "I am losing myself, my mind wandering in an ocean with no shore," he confessed to Vergennes. "All I see seems one of those dreams that makes those who are ill delirious, and what I should do to effect the most implicit submission seems quite as difficult to divine. Whatever the king's will, the pros and cons cannot both tend toward the execution of his orders. This is breaking my head."

To sound out Congress's intentions, and especially to obtain payment (either in money or in kind) of the sums due to him, Beaumarchais sent his dear Théveneau de Francy, who crossed aboard the *Flamand*, which docked at Portsmouth on December 1, 1777. On the twentieth, after Saratoga, he sent instructions to his young proxy:

> I am fighting against obstacles of all kinds, but I am fighting with all my strength, and I hope to win with patience, courage and money . . . Upon the arrival of the *Amphytritus*, which finally unloaded in Lorient a feeble load of rice and indigo, they had the injustice to make off with the cargo, saying that it was sent to them and not to me; but as M. de Voltaire says so well: "Injustice has ended up producing independence." People probably took my patience for weakness and my generosity for stupidity. As much as I am attached to the interests of America, I am just as much offended by the barely honest advantage that the Passy deputies have tried to take of me.
>
> Amid all these annoyances, the news from America overwhelms me with joy. Brave, brave people! Their military conduct justifies my esteem and the enthusiasm we French have for them. Finally, my friend, I want repayment only so as to be in a position to serve them anew, and meet my commitments in order to be able to contract others in their favor.

However, the young Francy had a difficult trip to the United States. Upon his arrival he saw that Beaumarchais's reputation had suffered from the perfidious insinuations of Coudray, the deliberate falsehoods of Arthur Lee, and the hostile silence of Benjamin Franklin, who did not expend one word to defend him despite their cordial relations in the past. Persuaded that Silas Deane was mistaken about Beaumarchais, the Americans gave more credit to the slanderers than to those, truly too few, who treated him as the sincere friend of their nation that he was. "I will be happy if I can avenge you," wrote Francy, "and prove that I have great obligations to you. I keenly feel them, and my gratitude equals your generosity." He describes his difficulty in getting the rights of his benefactor recognized: "The true Americans here," he observes,

> are infinitely more rare than in Paris, and I am indeed persuaded that there is not one whose zeal approaches yours . . . My trip had been announced by both Coudray and Lee, and people were scarcely disposed to listen to me, since at first sight the welcome I received made me fear having to undergo so many difficulties. I would never finish this letter if I gave you a detailed account of all the feeble and futile objections that have been made to me and of all I have been obliged to reply. I would have to write volumes to prove the simplest and most evident things. Ten times at least I have been asked to explain all that you have done, etc. Without being disheartened, I continually repeated the same thing. Finally, after three months of effort and constancy, I managed to convince those who opinion influences others, and I have succeeded in having drawn up the attached contract.

This contract was made on April 16, 1778, and signed May 18, between members of Congress's commercial committee and Francy, acting in Beaumarchais's name. It recognized that the financial claims of Roderigue Hortalez, which everybody had previously contested, amounted to 5 million livres. The company promised to continue its shipments of arms and supplies and opened to the United States credit worth 24 million; the latter had the right to inspect the arms and munitions before accepting them. But Beaumarchais refused to execute the contract because of the difficulties raised by Congress over payment of the previous deliveries; it was never put into effect.

Fifteen

"THE MOST PATIENT
OF AMERICA'S CREDITORS"

> *The nation is not seated on the benches of those who will pronounce judgment, but its majestic eye surveys the assembly. It is always a good thing to instruct it, for if the nation is never the judge of individuals, it is at all times the judge of the judges.*
> —Beaumarchais, Fourth Memorandum

On February 6, 1778, after a long hesitation, Louis XVI finally signed a treaty of commerce and friendship with the United States of America. Politically, Beaumarchais had triumphed, but he still had not recouped his costs. Prodigious in their testimonies of gratitude, the American authorities were in no great hurry to reimburse him for his services, either in money or in merchandise. On March 13 France recognized American independence and accredited a plenipotentiary minister to Congress with the mission of concluding a treaty of alliance. Gérard de Rayneval, commonly called M. Gérard, assumed his duties in August 1778. Britain, as soon as it was notified of the Franco-American agreement, withdrew its own ambassador to France. After two years the covert conflict was now officially a war between two powers. But the hostilities would commence only three months after French recognition, with British aggression against a French vessel.

On June 17, 1778, the French frigate *Belle-Poule* came upon a flotilla of twenty British ships cruising off the Breton coast. Its commander, Chadeau de la Clocheterie, tried to head back to Brest but was caught by the British frigate *Arethusa* under Captain Marshall. Hailed to surrender, the captain refused, and the *Arethusa* opened fire with its twenty-eight cannons; the *Belle-Poule* riposted with its twenty-six. After five hours of violent combat, the *Arethusa* was put out of action, to be carried back to its squadron by wind, while the *Belle-Poule,* seriously damaged, headed toward Brest with forty dead and fifty-seven wounded on board. So began the armed conflict between France and England, in which the navy would play an essential role and which quickly turned to French advantage. The combat would end five years later, on September 3, 1783, with the signing of the Treaty of Paris, in which England recognized the independence of the thirteen American colonies, while victorious France took back the island of Tobago, all its possessions in Senegal, and Saint-Pierre and Miquelon, lost twenty years earlier.

France's official engagement in a war with Britain should have put a virtual end to Beaumarchais's commercial activity. The French government no longer had any reason to hide its arms deliveries to the United States, and so the Roderigue Hortalez Company lost its raison d'être, and its patron could come out into the open. He could retire from business and devote himself to writing, under the tender gaze of his "housekeeper" Marie Thérèse. But that was not Beaumarchais's way: what would become of him if he was deprived of all that made life spicy: adventure, struggle, and intrigue? In addition, the enormous liabilities of his company obliged him to continue in business, even to expand and diversify. Continuing to deliver war matériel to Congress, he launched into the export of raw materials and consumer products to various southern states, especially the Carolinas and Virginia, which offered particularly advantageous outlets. "Merchandise is commonly sold at 300 percent profit," he assured, "and is paid for in paper money." Unfortunately, the paper suffered an enormous depreciation before he could use it. Among the most sought-after products was brandy in barrels circled with iron; lead ingots, laminated and loaded as ballast; then came woolen coverings, textiles from Elbeuf, cotton velvet, various fabrics and canvases, stockings, second-quality rope, tinplate, lead shot for hunting, window glass, bottles, goblets, glass carafes, charcoal, and haberdashery notions.

To reduce the risks, Beaumarchais deposited all this merchandise in the French casks in which the return goods would be stored: Carolina's rice and indigo; furs, whale oil, cod oil, baleen, and whalebone; and in Virginia tobacco but also furs. These returns were supposed to come directly back to France from the continent, but it was more lucrative to stop either at Santo Domingo or at Martinique and substitute for indigo and tobacco a cargo of construction beams and salt cod for Martinique, "where that comestible, serving to feed negroes, is very sought after; but little cod is wanted in Santo Domingo, where the blacks have another kind of food."

This trade was so fruitful that it bailed out the company's financial difficulties for a while. But the ships now had trouble leaving Europe, for England had set up a maritime blockade that had to be crossed under cannon shot. In order to ensure an escort for his merchant flotilla, Beaumarchais now transformed the *Fier-Roderigue* into a warship, armed with sixty cannons and carrying a crew of 350. "I am going to cruise the ocean in convoy, to attack, burn or seize pirate ships," he wrote to Minister Sartine.

But instead the *Fier-Roderigue* became caught up in a naval battle and lost its captain. The ship was conducted to the port of Grenada in a pitiful condition, its sides pierced, the rigging and masts useless. The ships it was convoying almost all disappeared with their cargoes, some sunk under fire, others captured by English corsairs; those that managed to flee were dispersed in mid-ocean. "Oh, the disastrous campaign! The taking of Grenada about which I was so delighted has cost me dear!" Beaumarchais told Francy. At the edge of ruin, his credit exhausted, his coffers empty, he urgently needed 400,000 livres for a debt settlement due at the end of September. He sent an anguished appeal to Louis XVI:

> Sire, war is a game of kings that crushes individuals and sweeps them away like dust. The *Fier-Roderigue* was convoying ten other ships destined for commercial operations (just as useful to the state). The death of my prime captain, thirty-five men out of service, the damage to my vessel, the most mistreated in the squadron (having three cannonballs in its sides, four at the waterline, of which two have pierced all the way through, five in the masts and spars, which are very damaged, and the rest of the rig-

ging that they had to cut down); the exhaustion of all the sailors put into other vessels on their arrival in Fort-Royal to complete the crewing of the squadron—all that has ruined me.

Beaumarchais would receive this advance of 400,000 livres against a much more substantial indemnity, the amount of which would be set later by three tax inspectors named by the ministry. After long debates, the shipowner's losses were estimated at 2 million livres, which were paid to him in several stages, of which the last was not until 1785. As for his financial claims of 5 million livres against the United States, Congress had evident ill-will about honoring the debt. Citing the deplorable state of its finances, it was content to send him 2,544,000 livres in letters of credit—payable three years thence! This was a mockery! No commercial company could support such a delay without risking bankruptcy. Finance minister Robert Morris had imagined this device as a means of getting rid of the creditor, but Franklin made him see that this plan did not stand up, since the bills were already in circulation.

Despite all this trouble and disappointment, Beaumarchais persisted in wanting to maintain commercial relations with the United States. "If one never saw a French flag on any coast," he wrote to Francy,

> the American people would regard the commercial treaty with France as an illusion, and the need to draw from Europe indispensable objects would gradually lead them back to England and we would be stuck with the cost. This is what makes me so keen to encourage, both by my advice and my associations and by my example, all those whom I believe have enough soul and courage to profit from it (or at least to serve the country) . . . Despite the bad dealings of the Americans with me, I am working seriously to procure them a loan in Europe with French collateral.

In truth, his generosity was not exempt from ulterior motives; he saw the creation of an economic partnership with the United States as highly advantageous for his country. Thinking more lucidly than most of his contemporaries, and better inspired than even certain ministers, he perceived in the young American Republic the potential to become a great world power.

In 1780 Silas Deane came back to France to settle the accounts. Having been a part of the original transactions with the Roderigue Hortalez Company, he was better placed than anyone to untangle the affair's complicated web. On April 6 he fixed the credit due to his supplier at the sum of 3.6 million livres. This amount took into account both the advances already spent and the overdue interest. Armed with this document, Beaumarchais claimed reimbursement from the Americans. Two years later he still did not have a reply. Meanwhile, Deane's own reputation met with serious reversals. Arthur Lee, Thomas Paine, John Adams (who had replaced him in Paris in 1778), and others regarded him with suspicion. His conduct was considered indelicate, and some went to far as to speak of corruption; Congress therefore declared his arrangement with Beaumarchais null and void. Beyond that the American authorities were silent, leaving Beaumarchais in desperate straits.

In November 1782 the onset of peace negotiations with Britain delighted the patriot but afflicted the shipowner. "I laugh with one eye and cry with the other," Beaumarchais wrote to Vergennes. Two days later the British took three of his frigates, using "infernal grapeshot," in the Gulf of Gascony. It was a debacle. On January 20, 1783, just when the peace preliminaries were being signed in Paris, Beaumarchais launched an appeal to the king: "I am only pressing you because I am dying. My respectful patience for almost six years proves to you that it is in the last extremity that I demand justice of the King, as anyone would demand a favor." In July a new United States agent, Barclay, arrived in Paris as consul-general, with the mission to proceed to a new examination of the accounts. Beaumarchais told him they had already been verified by Silas Deane, but Barclay insisted, adding that Congress would not pay the Frenchman a cent if he objected. After a year the unhappy creditor ended up ceding, but he also raised an official protest to Congress. The complaint sent on July 14, 1783, displays his bitterness:

> Recall, Messieurs, those unhappy days when, overcome with war
> and British persecution, you sent secret emissaries to all the pow-

ers of Europe, when you implored the great commercial houses of various Nations, without being able to obtain help. I alone, Messieurs, subject of a monarchical state and without any other stimulus than my love for the good of mankind and my respect for the virtuous efforts that you were promising, I worked for two years to make you friends in Europe and to warm hearts and minds in your favor . . . I spread gold everywhere to remove the obstacles that I found everywhere. And believing it would hurt the nation I was serving if I doubted that it would put into its gratitude the generous sentiment that made me act, I regarded as straw the gold I spread for it, happy to be able at this price to procure it prompt help. And when your agent [Silas Deane], Messieurs, admired and encouraged these sacrifices, vaunting to me the gratitude his country would forever have, I was very far from imagining that this nation, one day becoming free, far from settling its debts with me, as had been promised on its behalf, would send new agents to dissect my messages with a fine-toothed comb, and demand to inspect anew all my already inspected accounts; and subject me, after seven years of waiting and suffering, to an injurious debate, and minutely calculate each item in my advances; and that, forgetting my character and my services, it would treat me as a base merchant tailor—who is too graciously given the commission and money to buy rags in Europe.

He concluded with this flight of oratory: "Noble and free people today, rival of the proudest sovereigns, friend and ally of my king! You will feel that it is just, honorable and without danger to your glory, to recall that an individual in Europe had the courage to espouse your interests when everyone else disdained them, and who dared to send you—at the peril of his health, his fortune, and his life—the first generous help that you received from our continent."

Before Congress made any decision concerning Beaumarchais, an incident occurred that added to the confusion and postponed indefinitely any settlement of the debt. On February 25, 1783, Franklin and Vergennes signed a memorandum recapitulating the sums that the French government had advanced to the United States, in which figured 3 million livres spent before the Treaty of Alliance of 1778. At the time there had been no objection. Only three years later Franklin, returning to the United States, remembered having received only 2 million from the French government and another million advanced by the tax farmers, part of which the Americans had repaid in tobacco worth 153,229 livres. The banker Georges Grand was charged with finding out from Vergennes whether, among the 3 million mentioned in the memo, 1 million did not come from the tax farmers—an embarrassing question, for the million in question, delivered by the Royal Treasury on June 10, 1776, had been literally handed to Beaumarchais in the greatest secrecy. Even at this late date Vergennes did not want to divulge that he had subsidized the Roderigue Hortalez Company to supply military equipment to America while France was still at peace with Britain; he had many times assured the latter of its perfect neutrality. On the other hand, he did not want to embarrass Beaumarchais, who had had so much trouble settling his accounts with the United States. Pushing his advantage, Grand asked for a copy of the June 10 receipt, but the French government refused to furnish it. From the refusal, Congress concluded that it was Beaumarchais who had received this million, which he ought therefore to restitute to Congress, which therefore had nothing to pay until this mystery was cleared up.

What did they want to prove—that Beaumarchais hoped to make money from his commerce with the Americans? That was obvious. That he had neglected to credit the sums spent by the French and Spanish governments? Probably. Should we forget, though, that he had continued to supply the United States even though they were already his debtors? Or that the millions that had come from his pocket were never reimbursed? Should we forget the perils he ran after the declaration of war against Great Britain? What shipowner would have hazarded sending his cargoes through full naval battle, under enemy fire, at the risk of being sunk or captured, when even in the best case he was unloading merchandise that would never be paid for? What better proof that Beaumarchais had placed the American cause above his private interest?

While the negotiating between Vergennes and the United States' bank trundled on, Beaumarchais pressed Congress to liquidate his claim, proposing if necessary the arbitration of Vergennes and accepting in advance any arbitrator named by the other party, except Arthur Lee, whom he considered his personal enemy. On July 12, 1787, at the end of his patience, he wrote to the president of the Congress:

> The most zealous and oldest (and I daresay the most patient) of America's creditors, has the honor today to call for your justice, and the overly tardy justice of the honorable Congress of which you are president. The constitutional form of assemblies of this Congress, giving each of its members perpetual removability, is as contrary to the interests of foreigners who have claims against it as it is advantageous to a country governed by such an assembly. The result of the perpetual change of members is that affairs that cannot be finished in six months, forced by new members to whom they are unknown, languish and are delayed long enough to be often forgotten; and this is what has happened to mine for a dozen years. This painful situation has been so long prolonged that all honest and enlightened men of the Republic might be afflicted on its account and suffer for me from the injustice I have been experiencing with unrivaled patience for the almost twelve years now that I have been the State's creditor, that is to say its creditor long before it was certain it would one day be a State.
>
> The person entrusted to present you this letter will put before you the important services that I rendered your country, my generous agreements with your agent in Europe in 1776 to secure arms and munitions, clothing and dry goods for a virtuous people who lacked everything. I do not speak of my zeal, although no other man in Europe would have devoted such to you; and at a time when fear and uncertainty froze the hearts of everybody and closed all purses to you.
>
> I attest before you that none of the conditions to which M. Silas Deane, your agent, committed his country to me in 1776 has been accomplished. No, not one! My merchandise, my vessels, my weapons, and my munitions arrived on the continent or at their agreed depots on our islands, starting in 1777. Abundant and very prompt returns were solemnly promised me; a perpetual and uninterrupted circulation ought to have fed the

commerce established on my sole confidence in these virtuous Insurgents, sustained by the most active and the most generous zeal of which any individual has ever furnished an example. But penury and disorder were so great then among you, Monsieur, than in three years I have barely received a single response to my pressing letters; recently an employee of your ports has acknowledged the receipt of immense cargoes, without any return being made to me to continue my services.

At the end of 1777, tired of waiting and seeing nothing coming, I had the honor of sending you a general agent for my affairs, M. de Francy, entrusted with my power to terminate things. He remained three years in America. In all this period he was barely able during the second year to pass me an account in letters of exchange due in three years, which would then make a credit of six years on the remittances that I had been assured would be settled within the year.

Finally, in 1778, M. Silas Deane, your sole commercial agent, settled all my accounts with you. It remained only to give them the sanction of his legal signature as agent of the United States. My house was occupied with writing triple copies, one for you, one for him, and the third in my hands serving as authentic copy, when his mysterious departure from Europe . . . suspended the sole formality that remained to give us all our settlement of accounts.

All these promises have resulted in making me lose a year and a half, making me await his return with more than impatience. He came back in 1780, with no other mission, he tells me, than settling for the supplies from Europe for which he had been the agent, so they might be then paid by the State.

In effect, he reviewed our accounts and the only thing lacking was his signature; he applied it to all the accounts as *Agent of the United States for all Commercial Supplies*. Nobody then came to dispute this title. No letter from the Continent, from any authority, came to me to cast doubt that the sole person with whom I had been dealing in the interests of America, who alone had the mission and the power of his country to obtain help on credit from the businessmen of our Europe, who alone had followed and shared my long labors to furnish supplies, had not conserved the right to settle the account . . . Approved by him in 1781, I solicited Congress for the help I needed to fulfill my commitments in Europe. That help was indeed due me, since six years ago those goods I had furnished that nation, for which I was asking for return, had been received and consumed by it, during its great distress, and had much contributed to acquiring its precious liberty.

Who can doubt that at least a down payment, so necessary and long solicited, on debts so sacred, ought to have been sent to me earlier, if Congress's difficulties prevented it from settling the lot? I vainly awaited this help from 1781 to 1783. Then, in response to and as payment of my financial claim, I saw arrive from America a new agent charged, he says, with powers to discuss, solve, decree and settle all accounts from the great suppliers of Europe— M. Barclay. I observed to him that my accounts had been discussed, audited, and decreed in 1781 by Silas Deane, your first agent, and that it remained only to wind them up, and that after the old inspection, I had settled with my collaborators in Europe.

M. Barclay declared to me that he could not recognize M. Deane's decisions, but I did not consent to lose the sole document that I had between my hands about the advances I made in 1776 to the American insurgents, approved in 1781 by the sole agent with whom I dealt. I consented for M. Barclay to check them but he wanted to destroy them. After a long fight, I finally agreed with him that I would send to Congress a duplicate of the accounts approved by Deane and all this correspondence, with proof duly notarized, that the sovereign himself knew the basis of this discussion. I did so. Two years passed, and in response to a grand and prideful letter (I attach a copy), I received in 1785 from the same Barclay, the short and harsh declaration that "Congress undertakes nothing, sends nothing, pays nothing until he, Barclay, has approved my accounts." Then I saw clearly (I ask your pardon) that people were trying to gain time and that any pretext was fine as long as I was not paid.

Beaumarchais then cited the testimony of the highest American authorities on his courage and his disinterestedness. First he quoted Silas Deane, who in March 1778, when leaving France, had rendered vibrant homage: "I hope that your agent [in Philadelphia] will make considerable returns and that Congress will defer no longer recognizing the great and important services that you have rendered the cause of American freedom." A year later, when Beaumarchais complained to Congress about not having received payments for his invoices, John Jay, its president, responded:

> The Congress of the United States, recognizing the great efforts that you have made in their favor, presents to you its thanks and the assurance of its esteem. It bemoans the adversity you have suffered for the support of these States. Unfortunate circumstances have prevented the execution of its desires, but it will take the promptest measures to acquit the debt it has contracted with you. The generous sentiments and the breadth of view that alone could dictate a conduct such as yours, are the eulogy of your actions and the ornament of your character. While by your rare talents you have made yourself useful to your country, you have gained the esteem of this nascent Republic, and merited the applause of the New World.

Finally, Thomas Jefferson, governor of Virginia and future president, had celebrated the noble conduct of Beaumarchais in a letter to Francy dated December 1779:

> I am indeed mortified that the unhappy depreciation of paper money, of which nobody, I think, had the least idea during the contract made between the commissioner of the Fier Roderigue and this State, has enveloped in the common loss M. de Beaumarchais, who has merited so much from us, and who has excited our greatest veneration by his affection for the true rights of man, his genius, and his literary reputation, etc.

After invoking these witnesses, Beaumarchais returned to his argument:

> Deign to compare the past with the present, and the actual conduct of the United States to mine throughout this time. In 1776,

you asked for and obtained help from me, and you consumed my shipments in 1777. You were then only an insurgent nation. In 1787, I could not obtain from you either settlement or payment or response—and now you are sovereign! Such an incredible oblivion (too known in Europe) has served as pretext for wicked people to torment me in Paris. Vile rascals in my country have pushed the horror as far as to speak and print libels, among other insults, that I sent the American insurgents spoiled munitions, very bad weapons, defective merchandise, since I had not been paid, after ten years' waiting, by a nation that had become free. Others, even viler, have dared to affirm this. The casual public has believed them. I could refute the insult and prove authentically with evidence that in 1776, when my shipments were departing, some intriguer fabricated this issue: that if by misfortune my shipments were of poor quality, there would be no time for me to remedy this when they were on the Continent. I could demonstrate that Silas Deane reported this talk to me, but only as a statement to which none of his colleagues lent any credence, but I was indignant and stopped the departure of my vessels and wanted the two American commissioners, M. Williams, the nephew of M. Franklin, and M. Carmichael, today your minister in Spain, to be sent to Nantes and Le Havre, to break the seals and open the cases. I could prove, from the state they were in and the samples sent to Paris, that all were of excellent quality, and I was showered with apologies and with praise . . .

But how long must I wait for the American nation, having become free and sovereign, to acquit itself toward an individual in Europe who not only has devoted his time and fortune to it, but by his zeal and labors has contributed more than any other to stir France in its favor and position it on its side . . . Reflect, sir, I beg you, how unjust it is to leave me asking for eleven years for the payment of this sacred debt, not even wanting to find a solution to such legitimate demands. What do you want people here to think of the vicious circle in which it appears I am caught? We will make no reimbursement to M. de Beaumarchais before his accounts are checked by us, and we will not check his accounts so as not to have to reimburse him! A nation that has become powerful and sovereign might indeed regard gratitude, people will say, as an individual virtue above its politics, but nothing absolves a State of being just or of paying its debts.

I dare to hope that, touched with the importance of this affair and the force of my argument, you will honor me with an official response about what the honorable Congress will decide, whether to pay me promptly and settle things as an equitable and sovereign power, or else to choose arbitrators in Europe to judge these points in debate, with insurance and commissions, as M. Barclay had the honor of proposing to you in 1785, or else to write to me forthrightly that the sovereign American people, forgetting my past services, refuse me any justice. Then I will adopt the position suitable to my despised interests, my wounded honor, without abandoning the profound respect with which I am, of Congress and of you its President, the very humble servant.

Judging this letter inappropriate, if not unseemly, Congress resolved to teach its author a lesson in manners and confided the examination of accounts to the sole man whom Beaumarchais had always refused as an arbitrator: Arthur Lee. In several rounds of sleight-of-hand, the latter managed to establish that not only did Congress owe nothing to Beaumarchais, but that it was Beaumarchais who owed 1.8 million livres to the United States. Where did this result come from? All the equipment transited by the Hortalez Company was, said Lee, a free gift from the French government; on the other hand, all the merchandise furnished by the United States to said company (tobacco, rice, indigo, etc.) had to be invoiced to him. The upshot was that the company owed almost 2 million livres!

Despite repeated protests from Beaumarchais, the affair dragged on, or rather was made to drag on, four long years more. Then in 1793 Congress called on Alexander Hamilton, secretary of the United States Treasury, hoping that with his expertise and stature, he would morally guarantee Arthur Lee's conclusion. Hamilton carefully studied the files, then declared that Lee's conclusion had no foundation, and that Beaumarchais was legitimately a creditor of the United States for the sum of 2.28 million francs. He added, however, that no settlement could take place until the still-open question of the million that the French government had paid to the Hortalez Company had been elucidated. This affair would drag on until Beaumarchais's death—and beyond. We must return to literary—and happier—matters.

Sixteen

THE REVOLUTION
OF DRAMATIC AUTHORS

*Why should the son of Apollo, lover of the Muses, be constantly
forced to deal with his baker, yet neglect to deal with actors?*
—*Beaumarchais, "Account of the Dramatic Authors Affair"*

*I would enjoy a triumph that would be all the sweeter if not for
some crafty actor filching three-quarters of it.*
—*Beaumarchais, "Restrained Letter"*

"What characterized him perfectly," noted Beaumarchais's friend
Gudin de La Brenellerie, "was the ability to change his occupation
unexpectedly and to turn his attention as intensely and exclusively to
the new activity as he had felt for the one it replaced; neither fatigue
nor preoccupations distracted him. He called that *closing the drawer
on an affair.*"

It's no surprise, then, that during his years of struggle to aid
American independence, Beaumarchais also struggled to uphold the
rights of dramatic authors; he led both efforts with the same fire,
energy, and conviction. And as it turned out, actors made tougher
adversaries than those Roderigue Hortalez confronted on the seas,
considering the length of the conflict and its bitterness. It took Beaumarchais no less than twenty years to defeat the theatrical entrepre-
neurs and to consecrate the rights of authors who had been unjustly
despoiled; twenty years of cold war, marked by all sorts of contradic-

tory debates, petitions, memoranda, legal briefs, judgments, decrees, appeals to public opinion, and even a strike by writers—undoubtedly the first of its kind! The upshot of this struggle was the creation of a labor union that would become famous and still thrives today as the Society of Dramatic Authors and Composers.

In 1776 a dramatic author was still at the mercy of a corporation of actors and actresses that was directed in principle by four gentlemen of the king's chamber but in reality was left to its own devices. Since the middle of the seventeenth century actors had given a portion of their receipts to a dramatic author after their expenses had been deducted. But the moment the actors' receipts fell below the sum of 800 livres in the summer and 1,200 in the winter, the play was removed from the repertory. It thereafter belonged definitively to the troupe of actors, who reserved the right to revive it without having to pay anything to the author. Authors were thus reduced to servitude by actors and dared not say anything against them for fear of reprisal. For a long time playwrights had suffered without complaining about their meager living; actors got rich at their expense, while they themselves got only tiny royalties. In the previous century writers had taken pride in their independence and were even vain about being destitute. In Beaumarchais's day, however, a writer owed his independence and dignity to fair compensation for his writings. For a dramatist, maintaining independence meant getting free of the stringent constraints imposed by actors and theatrical managers.

In a general process of professionalization, men of letters were finally winning economic emancipation. They secured this victory only after waging an interminable struggle against governing powers. The most paradoxical thing about this revolt was that it was led by a man who was not only the richest among them but the least "professional," with the least personal interest in the triumph of the cause. He was a man of finance more than of letters, who by his own admission wrote for the theater only to divert himself. Beaumarchais led the fight for an equitable remuneration of authors for their intellectual property. His argument was effective because it stuck to authors' immediate and real needs, reducing them to basic necessities—not forgetting that while actors paid a writer in money, the public paid him in laurels: both offered compensation, as he acknowledged in the half-serious, half-comic prologue to the *Compte rendu de l'affaire des auteurs dramatiques*:

> They say in theater lobbies that it is not noble of authors to plead for base interest, then to pride themselves on claiming glory. They are right: glory is attractive. But they forget that in order to enjoy only one year, Nature condemns us to dine three hundred and sixty-five times; and if a warrior-statesman does not blush to collect the noble pension due his services by soliciting the promotion that might be worth more, why should the son of Apollo, the lover of the Muses, who is constantly forced to deal with his baker, yet neglect to deal with actors? We believe in giving each person what is his due when we ask for the laurels of Comedy from the public that grants them, and money paid by the public to the Comédie that withholds it.

Aware of risking failure if they fought in isolation, several authors advocated union and solidarity and appealed to Beaumarchais to take their affairs in hand. He was rich, powerful, influential, skillful, and enjoyed powerful relations—in short he was better placed than anyone to become their spokesman. However, Beaumarchais had much to lose in this adventure, notably his friendship with actors, from whom he had never asked for a cent. But he agreed to take up the cudgels, and from the moment he asked the actors for their accounts, he knew that he was putting their backs up forever—not to mention antagonizing actresses, to whose charms he was not insensible. Not only would he get no personal benefit from this cause, but his involvement would gain him new enemies—and he was not lacking enemies already. Was it not imprudent to open another fight when he was still working toward his own rehabilitation, negotiating with d'Éon, fighting La Blache in court, creating his Hortalez Company, and sending arms to the Americans? Making war against England was not sufficient—he had to make war against ham actors too?

The demon that pushed Beaumarchais toward this new enterprise was his immoderate passion for challenge: the irresistible desire to win the impossible wager, to succeed where others had failed, to move beyond braggadocio. In this struggle he would spend incalculable time, money, and energy, until achieving final victory. It would take no fewer than eighteen years of exhausting warfare—and a revolution—for the idea of an author's copyright to ultimately triumph and become standard practice.

Not until the thirty-second performance of *The Barber of Seville* did Beaumarchais realize that he should ask the Comédiens-Français for an exact account of what was owed him. The members of the troupe were stupefied by this unexpected request and more than a little worried. In the past Beaumarchais had always given them his works gratis. They sent the jovial Des Essart, an illustrious member of the company whose enormous girth destined him to play the "round part" of Bartholo, to negotiate. On Monday, January 6, 1777, Des Essart went to the Hôtel de Hollande with 4,506 livres in his pocket, which he assured Beaumarchais was the correct author's royalty for thirty-two performances. But to his great surprise Beaumarchais refused the money and persisted in demanding the accounts: "What I ask for from the Comédie is much more than money; it is a detailed account that can be used as a model for all future statements and so bring peace between actors and authors."

Three days later Beaumarchais requested in writing a precise enumeration of his account. After two weeks he received a simple statement with no signature. He sent it back to the Comédiens, demanding in a long letter that it be signed and certified accurate. The troupe decided to confer with their lawyers and named four commissioners to decide what path to take. But days passed, then weeks, then months, and Beaumarchais received no account. *The Barber of Seville* was no longer being performed. Beaumarchais got impatient but did not want to show it. Finally the Duc de Duras, a gentleman of the chamber who was inclined to favor the actors (and especially the actresses), invited Beaumarchais to discuss their differences with him, so as "to prevent the outburst that affair might produce." Beaumarchais was a little wounded that the actors, rather than organizing a conversation with him, preferred to take their complaints to the duke and invoke his protection, but he accepted the latter's invitation. The two men spoke of establishing a new regulation that would replace arbitrary accounts and badly drawn estimates with accounting that was equitable to both parties. Duras suggested that

Beaumarchais consult his writing colleagues and then submit their proposal; he promised his visitor prompt justice. The two men parted in hopes of reaching a negotiated peace with the histrionic guild.

But men of letters are exceedingly individualistic; the very idea of being part of a group terrifies them. Corporatism is so contrary to a writer's nature that he would prefer to renounce his rights rather than form a union to defend them. Occupational federations would not flourish until the very end of the century. Beaumarchais had no illusions about the difficulty of the task of organizing his fellow authors; he knew the weight of the inertia that he would have to overcome to mobilize them.

On July 3 invitees bustled to his home. Many of the authors (especially the older ones) felt an incurable repugnance at the notion of defending their rights; the younger ones were clearly more receptive. Diderot, the creator of bourgeois drama (as we have seen), had been invited by his former disciple, but he excused himself due to his age (sixty-four) and his aspiration to live peacefully. He had never felt much sympathy for his junior colleague Beaumarchais, whom he considered an arriviste, a jack-of-all-trades, and a money-grubber. Diderot was the first to pen the term *insurgence* in a mocking allusion to Beaumarchais's political and mercantile activity. From the insurgence of the Americans to the insurgence of authors, he provided enough to make the editor of the *Encyclopédie*'s head spin.

And so on July 3, 1777, the "Estates General" of the dramatic art took place for the first time at Beaumarchais's home at the Hôtel de Hollande. Beaumarchais's enterprise was generally well received, even among those who did not participate directly. As was his wont, Beaumarchais had brought the debate to the public forum and appealed to the whole nation as his witness. All France now knew that dramatic writers were meeting to join in a corporation and free themselves from the Comédiens-Français, with the author of *The Barber of Seville* at their head. This media frenzy around the affair would exacerbate passions in both camps.

At the Hôtel de Hollande twenty-three writers (including three members of the Académie Française) sat down in the paneled Psyche Gallery before a plate of soup to decide on the creation of a society of authors to be called the Office of Dramatic Legislation. The Estates

General of the dramatic art was representative in character, not unlike the Constituent Assembly that would result from the national Estates General of 1789. Minutes were taken, noting that only authors having one or more plays performed at the Comédie-Française would be eligible to debate within the society.

Presenting the appearance of concord, the union of authors in fact rested on no collective will; the quibbling that studded their early debates says a lot about the forced character of their association. These gentlemen had always placed their personal vanity above the common interest. What could mutual help and solidarity mean when one regarded one's colleagues as so many rivals? Only a few days after the official birth of what would become the Society of Dramatic Authors, Beaumarchais noted bitterly: "The liaisons with actresses, the divisions over principles, and I do not know how many pretensions, how many deaf malcontents, and how many hidden interests could add up to anything but a company of crazy people that is disunited, full of animosity and sour reproaches."

While they sought a solution to their tangled situation, and as long as no reform in their favor had been adopted, the authors did agree not to bring any manuscript to the Théâtre-Français. In other words, they declared an unlimited strike. But some of their younger colleagues, eager to do anything to get their plays performed, refused to join the movement. For their part, the actors had a very simple means of breaking the strike: it sufficed to put a novice author's play into the repertoire. Thus in 1780 they rehearsed an Oriental tragedy of uncommon mediocrity entitled *Nadir or Thamas-Kouli-Kan*, on the express condition that its author, Pierre-Ulric Dubuisson, openly take issue with his fellow writers. In this way the actors compensated him for his treachery and incited others to imitate him.

Beaumarchais, always in the thick of things, bore the brunt of this combat single-handedly. While scurrying around France in search of weapons for the insurgent Americans, he crossed swords ceaselessly with the internal insurgents, carrying on a quarrelsome correspondence with their lawyers, spending whole days planning strategy, holding conferences and endless discussions, and performing vain errands. He struggled when the other commissioners decided not to lift a finger. Gossip about Beaumarchais was close to defamation.

Rumor even had it that Beaumarchais had made a secret arrangement with the actors. Ordinarily calm and a master of his nerves, Beaumarchais was now hardened to calumny (his old and grimacing enemy), yet this time he could not suppress a violent explosion of anger.

The commissioners of dramatic authors and the representatives of actors negotiated for a seemingly endless stretch. Then in 1784 Beaumarchais triumphed with *The Marriage of Figaro* and made an appeal to Louis XVI: "Is not the foremost of all honors, Sire, to assure to dramatic authors, by a law, the ownership of their work and the just fruit of their labors?"

The word had been spoken: *law*. Not honor, not compromise, but *law*, the extension of legal protection to a personal right, of the kind that would figure so prominently in the celebrated Declaration of the Rights of Man. In 1791, after the Revolution, the National Assembly would recognize the legitimacy of an author's copyright on his intellectual property and its regulation. As Beaumarchais would state in a petition to that Assembly to extend the legislation to apply to provincial theaters:

> It is very strange that it has taken an express law to attest to all of France that the property of a dramatic author belongs to him and nobody has the right to run off with it! This principle, taken from the first rights of man, went so much without saying for all the other property of people acquired through labor, gifts, sale, or even heredity, that it was believed derisory for it to be established in law. My sole property, as a dramatic author, is more sacred than all other kinds because it comes to me from nobody else and is subject to no contestation for fraud or seduction. The work coming from my brain, like Minerva fully armed with the work of the gods, my property alone had need of a law to pronounce that it belongs to me!

Seventeen

"WHAT KIND OF MAN
HAVE I BECOME?"

You only know how to make love on a bed; sometimes it is charm-
ing on a piece of paper.
　　　　　　　—*Beaumarchais, Letter to Mme. de Godeville*

The years 1775 to 1780 were very full for Beaumarchais, encompass-
ing his rehabilitation process, the première of *The Barber of Seville*,
the foundation of the Roderigue Hortalez Company and support for
the Americans, the creation of the Office of Dramatic Legislation, the
composition of *The Marriage of Figaro*, the publication of Voltaire's
complete works, and an avalanche of *Memoranda*. These years also
saw the birth of his daughter Eugénie and the intense financial and
commercial activity that was the backdrop of his daily life. Well liked
at court, popular in town, rich—with several millions, immense
credit, and a legion of the envious—Beaumarchais approached fifty
years of age (he reached it in 1782) with serenity. But serenity was
not his goal. Serenity suits people of measured energies who know
how, once victory is won, to rest from the fatigues of war in order to
savor the triumph. But people of Beaumarchais's character disdain
sweet quietude in the shadow of trophies; they do not bask in the
aura of esteem and the fortunes they have erected. Never satisfied,
they pounce at perils to get a taste of risk, for the sheer pleasure of
defying their own destiny, again and again, endlessly. Beaumarchais
was the kind of gambler who plays, not to win, but to skirt the abyss.

By a decree of the Paris parlement in September 1776 that annulled the judgment of 1774, Beaumarchais was acquitted of his guilt and reestablished in all his civil rights. But nothing had been settled in the civil suit that opposed him to the Comte de La Blache, the great-grand-nephew of Pâris-Duverney and his exclusive heir. Thus the confidential agent of the minister of foreign affairs, a man entrusted with a mission by the king of France, the illustrious author of *The Barber of Seville*, whom all of Europe praised—that man was paradoxically under a sentence that indirectly declared him a counterfeiter and threatened to transfer his wealth to an enemy. The affair had been referred to the Provence parlement, a jurisdiction where in principle neither party had relatives or allies.

The judges examined the affair with the most scrupulous attention for no fewer than fifty-nine sessions. On July 21, after a series of exhausting debates, they acquitted Beaumarchais unanimously and accepted all his pleas without exception. The tribunal ordered the execution without delay of the deed that Pâris-Duverney had signed long ago, denied the heir his claims, condemned him to pay Beaumarchais 12,000 livres in damages and fines for his calumnies, and had La Blache's *Memoranda* suppressed. Some judges admitted that they would have awarded higher sums to Beaumarchais if he had not damaged himself by the vehemence of his own writings.

On the evening after the verdict was announced, the whole town of Aix wanted to share in the victor's joy: fires were lit on street corners: people sang, drank, and danced until the wee hours, as at a public festival. Workmen of Aix serenaded him with dialect song. When Beaumarchais asked the reason for this popular license, he was told that the parlement of Provence was essentially composed of magistrates issuing from the old nobility and that this was the first time they had ever condemned one of their own. In appreciation for these signs of sympathy, he offered a dowry of 3,000 livres to two poor girls. He became the idol of the best society in Aix: ladies fought for the honor of seating him at their tables; everybody wanted to speak to him, to touch him, and to make certain that this Parisian, famous for his *Memoranda*, his comedies, his verve and his songs, was celebrated in Provençal society, too.

On his return to Paris, Beaumarchais received many congratulations on the outcome of his lawsuit, some verbal and others in writing. Gudin, who had saluted him verbally, sang his glory in a letter of rhymed verse worthy of a Provençal epic, beginning with the lines:

> Thus by Parlement a severe justice
> Has confounded your enemies' malice
> Yet they flatter themselves that their dark skill
> Which of a profane senate in unhappy days
> Had tipped the venal balance scales
> Suspending the prudence of our true magistrates.

Gudin's well-intended but incriminating alexandrines ("profane senate") crossed the Channel and were published in the *Courrier de l'Europe*. A few days later, when Gudin was lunching at home with his mother and his niece, he received a note from Voltaire's niece, Mme. Denis, of whom he was fond. He read with stupor: "It has just been decreed you be seized by the Grand Council; you are going to be arrested for those verses printed in *Courrier de l'Europe*! You don't have a moment to lose."

Gathering a few things, he rushed from home without saying anything to his family. Beaumarchais was then traveling from Nantes to La Rochelle, so Gudin ran to take refuge in the Temple. He warned his mother that she might receive a visit from the Grand Council's envoys and that she should not worry about him, as he was hiding in a safe place. If anyone asked, she should reply: "I do not know where he is, no doubt a hundred leagues from Paris, with Beaumarchais." That done, he went incognito to a lawyer who advised him to not let himself be taken: "Those messieurs of the Grand Council hate Beaumarchais," he told Gudin. "They might well take vengeance for his *Memoranda* on his friend and be quick about condemning you, since they put you under arrest without informing you, which violates every law." Gudin returned to the Temple, escorted by two or three friends.

Originally built for the Knights Templar, the Temple, with its square donjon and pepper-pot towers, would be transformed into a state prison during the Revolution; here Louis XVI and his family would be lodged. Inside the Temple, which Philip IV had taken from the Templars to give to the Order of Malta, was a veritable town within a town, even a state within the state, since it had special privileges, its own justice, police, and maintenance systems. Four thousand inhabitants were crowded into an inextricable web of alleys, courtyards, and insalubrious buildings, in the midst of which were a few fine edifices: the square tower of Caesar, the former dwelling of pilgrims bound for Jerusalem, the ruins of a convent, the commander's residence, the Gothic pavilions of the hospital, the grand prior's palace, shops of artisans, and finally the church of Sainte-Marie du Temple, whose four clocktowers chimed for festivals and curfews.

The Temple enjoyed territorial freedom and especially the right of asylum, offering an inviolable refuge to certain people. Naturally, it did not grant this favor to anyone—it notably excluded major criminals, convicts, fraudulent bankrupts, the dangerously insane, and so on. On the other hand, the Order of Malta welcomed inside its walls certain insolvent debtors and citizens who had been placed arbitrarily under arrest. Before being inscribed on the register, any applicant for asylum had to undergo an interrogation by the bailiff. When Gudin underwent this, they asked him why he wanted to be admitted and where he wanted to live. "In the small apartment of Mme. de Godeville, who inhabits these confines and who wants me to share her chamber and her table during my stay." "You will not do badly there; she is a very beautiful and spirited woman." And indeed Gudin found in the company of his elected hostess "the sweetest asylum that ever a man under arrest could find in the world." Beaumarchais's former mistress was in the Temple for her debts.

What happens between a man and woman together day and night under the same roof is not very difficult to guess. But Gudin could not ignore that for two years his companion had had amorous relations with the man dearest to his heart: Beaumarchais. To sleep with Mme. de Godeville would be to betray his trust, and he was the most loyal of friends. Then again, maybe Beaumarchais was pushing his mistress into the arms of his friend, as he wrote magnanimously to her:

> If something, my dear friend, could console the poor shut-away
> for being in a private prison, it would be to meet there a pussy as
> deprived as you are. Why not eat and drink, do the sweet thing,

and then sleep together and do it again? . . . If you can both get in one or four good ones for the love of me, I promise to take part and to come as if I was myself ejaculating . . . Let's go, my lovely friend! A little spermatic gaiety embellishes the thighs of a woman and delights the heart of a prisoner. This would be my recipe, if I were with you.

Born in Bordeaux in 1740, Marie-Madeleine Levassor de La Touche came from a family of naval officers. Among her close relatives was the famous admiral La Touche-Tréville, who commanded the frigate *Hermione* at the start of the American War before becoming illustrious at Yorktown. We do not know when she married Robert-Nicolas-David de Godeville, a navy officer in Rochefort and probably allied to her family. In any case, it was under the name Godeville that she acquired her reputation for flightiness, if not ribaldry, which was echoed in the gazettes. Bachaumont in *Mémoires secrets* speaks of her as a "woman famous for her affairs and her swindles." Her physique was described by Beaumarchais: "You are one of the most seductive women I have known, and the pleasure of knowing you has erased in my mind every bad thing that others have pleased to make me think about you." Elsewhere he speaks of her "beautiful eyes" and declares that "you have the most beautiful body in the world." But in one of his last letters to this beauty, he states, "You need to get a little fatter because you are tall and slender." In the absence of any portrait, we must settle for these vague sketches.

"She played in Paris a grand role among our gallant women," one reads in *La Bastille dévoilée* (The Bastille Revealed).

> She was one of the most sought-after lays in the capital. The kindliness of her mind and her occasional piques kept her in vogue a long time. It is said her tongue was as sharp as a monkey's claw. There was no seigneur who would not strive for the pleasure of dining with her. M. Le Noir [the police chief], whom she had pleased, put her under his protection. Thanks to this kind of woman, the police knew a share of what was happening in Paris. Her insouciance was equal to her mind, but her fortunes were in a shambles. No order in her affairs nor in her loves, today

living in a fine apartment, tomorrow in a hovel. One day three or four lackeys are under her orders, and the next day she is deprived of everything, no chambermaid, serving herself.

Beaumarchais had made the acquaintance of Marie-Madeleine in the course of his mission to buy back Morande's libel and had a violently capricious infatuation with her. (The word *caprice* describes it better than *pleasurable liaison*, which he used himself in speaking of the relationship between a libertine and a courtesan.) We know about this adventure from a correspondence that was found and published in 1928—what a miraculous discovery, not only for the biography of a hero whose reputation as a seducer is already made, but for erotic literature, to which it offers one of the finest jewels. Reading these letters, one regrets that a man so inclined to the pleasures of the flesh never gave himself to a genre so much in favor in his day. This omission was strangely modest for someone whose audacity was never the least of his virtues—unless the stupid nineteenth century judged it better to suppress writing considered prejudicial to his memory, forgetting in its haste some sheets that were providentially taken from the flames or the trash. Whatever the case, the *Letters to Madame de Godeville*, 106 in number stretching over two years (February 24, 1777, to February 21, 1779) display the most delicate, free, burning, true, and most abandoned imaginations ever inspired by sensual libertinage in epistolary literature. "You only know how to make love on a bed," Pierre-Augustin wrote to his mistress, "sometimes it is charming on a piece of paper"—of which this collection gives us majestic proof.

"I am fickle by principle in order to be as happy as possible," he wrote to Marie-Madeleine, adding that "if constancy is a virtue, this is apparently because it is a sacrifice, for there is no virtue without sacrifice; but these grave words *sacrifice* and *duty* are so far from the childish banter of happy love that as soon as they appear, it is forced to blush and run away, hide, or vanish." In his inner self this "principle" of fickleness was accompanied by an invincible sentiment of guilt.

As if to prove the absence of any cynicism in his way of acting, he admits to his mistress what it sometimes costs him to betray his dear

Marie-Thérèse for her. His infidelity haunts him; he returns to the subject constantly, not to minimize his faults or to plead attenuating circumstances, but to express his repentance toward his unhappy companion. Although he had not yet thought of marrying Marie-Thérèse, he still considered her his legitimate wife. His "housekeeper," as he sometimes called her, had in 1777 become the mother of his child, little Eugénie, whom he adored. In spite of a want of passion, he felt toward her a real tenderness, mixed with gratitude and respect. Nothing appears more sincere than his remorse when he beats his breast writing to his mistress: "Ah, what blasphemy I have to dare write to one woman when I belong entirely to another! To offer one the attention that is showered on me by the other, and to belong to neither one nor the other, by the stupidity of wanting to belong to them both!" A week later, in response to a remark in his correspondence, he comes back to the double life of a forty-five-year-old man in the grasp of the midday demon:

> Twenty years ago I was a lovable young man—meaning conceited. If I made women unhappy in those days, it was because each of them wanted to be exclusively happy, and because it appeared to me that in this immense garden called the world, each flower had the right to a glance from the lover. Alas! This happy time of mischief is long gone! Forced to have a housekeeper rather than a mistress, the woman who wears the white apron at home, who handles the visitors and the laundrywoman—she has a right to my gratitude. This is neither passion nor ecstasy, it is the sweet affinity that the most austere and honest person can only approve, and which one cannot forfeit without unless one has as many faults as difficulties. Study this commentary and add to it that the man who made an honest and modest young woman the mother of his son [*sic* for daughter] without marrying her, owes her a lot, a very lot . . . And at my age, with my principles, these sorts of commitments entail more than the dearest passions of the heart.

As sensuality pushed him into the arms of Mme. de Godeville more than into those of his "housekeeper," his conscience shuddered:

> Study me since the first moment, and you have always seen my pleasures troubled by I know not what importunate ray of honesty that illuminates them in a sad light. Love is a cult. To enjoy it you have to give yourself without distraction. I have neither the time nor power to do so. That is my secret. And it is to draw you, and myself too, away from this painful state that I renounce these great pleasures, very great ones!

From time to time his mind forms an uncertain and fleeting plan to break with Marie-Madeleine. Why? Out of the simple desire to find himself, to revive the feeling of his own integrity:

> See what a difference between us! When you speak to me of your regrets, I am forced to reply about my remorse. Dear woman, or rather, cruel woman! Give me back my repose and I will have lost only my pleasures, the great happiness of loving you and being loved by you, but I will have found again that unity between moving and feeling that is so necessary in my situation . . . or if you do not want to, consent to see at your feet this bizarre and dishonest being who reproaches himself for loving you too much and for not loving you enough.

But another obstacle opposed his desires, something harder to deceive than poor Marie-Thérèse—and much more tyrannical. This implacable despot was his work. He was its most servile and consenting of subjects, but he was also well rewarded for it. In addition to gold and power, Beaumarchais received from it the only wealth that mattered to him, the only kind that gave meaning to existence: the whirlwind of business, the anguish of the gambler, the vertigo of victory alternating with defeat, the exhilaration of peril vanquished, of shipwreck barely averted. This left time only for furtive embraces and titillating notes: for love "on a piece of paper," as he put it, of "the spermatic style." How many times, and with what raging impatience (more performed than real), did Beaumarchais tell his mistress of his office invaded by importunate visitors, of an urgent meeting in Versailles, a letter to dictate, a burning deadline, obliging him to postpone the hour or day of the rendezvous.

Beaumarchais described his relationship to work as the inflexible but voluntary servitude of a slave to a master. He makes excuses to Mme. de Godeville:

> Fie, Madame. What you demand is nonsense, without meaning or taste! You, from the leisure of an alcove, whose whole business is to turn me away from mine, nothing prevents you from giving yourself over to gentleness of mind.
>
> If you could see on what a stack of papers I write this little note, far from finding it dry and short, you would say: "Alas how can he manage to finish it with all these people around him?"
>
> If it was possible for me this evening to go give you the most positive assurances of a tenderness that is somewhat slighted in your letters, I would do so, but it is also possible that I cannot, since this week is so encumbered with business relating to the departure of vessels ready to set sail.
>
> The demon of business is unleashed against me. Its worries have rocked me disagreeably for forty-eight hours. I don't know what to listen to, and today is the third day that I see myself exist in so strange and turbulent a fashion that I am quite ready to flee. Ah, if I could flee to your retreat and keep myself far from austere or bothersome ideas! And how much I need to see you again, to give myself to feelings that you alone have the power to render so lively and so delicious! Unfortunately, again it is not for this evening!
>
> My office is not emptying at all, and any ideas of pleasure have evaporated.
>
> My disquiet, my dear, has not been calmed, but it has been covered by occupations so exacting and multitudinous that for four days I have had time only to read my business letters. I was in Versailles the day before yesterday. Yesterday, tonight and this morning I have not stopped writing or dictating and my head, much more encumbered than yours, is boiling.
>
> For the last two weeks I have a thousand times cursed love, women, jealousy, and my foolishness in letting myself be torn between two women when I need all my wits for the only occupations that are suitable for a man of my age. In honor, I am ashamed of myself and all that is happening to me.

In a word, business was the real rival of desire, the only thing capable of deferring, blurring, or even abolishing it:

> When, exhausted by work, I cannot see or even write to you, don't think me ill willed. When excessive fatigue makes us need to take care of ourselves, how can we claim the happiness of amusing somebody? Well, for five days that is the life I have been leading. Shut in, working on things that cannot be delayed, my beard like a Jew's, and forced to throw myself in bed at eight o'clock like a packet useless to the world. When my head is at the end of its tether, it becomes incontinent and my disparate ideas roll in a tiring wave. Then only sleep can repair things. Ah, meanwhile what happens to poor love? Shriveled up, humbled and null, it does not even know what use it is. It is dead. When the brain attracts for its use all that gave life to that rascal, its existence is reduced to zero. But instead of railing bitterly about my love, my attentions, the happiness of loving me on credit, be good, be indulgent, and summon pleasure by the picture of desire . . . Speak to my senses, awaken them, and since you are happy enough to have a brazier in your heart, a burning lake in your belly, and a volcano in your head, not counting the leisure it takes to communicate all that by means of the pen, be good, be indulgent. Tell me what you feel, what you want, what you desire, what you hope, what you are doing, and what I ought to do to you. Show me my poor mistress trying to replace me with a sweet effort of her big finger, tiring of taking trouble over pleasure she would prefer to leave to me. It is never in vain that you speak to my senses; this is a sick man who has to be comforted, reanimated; give me back the desire that I am losing along with my strength. You want a lover—make him! Or else do not worry any more about him, be content with the tranquil friendship that I offer you and which in me is the widow's mite.

This "widow's mite," as he prettily calls it, serves at best to dissimulate his indifference or disaffection:

> Friendship is only an austere feeling and made for people of the same sex, or those who no longer have one. Everything that

comes from there is only double twaddle, in which the author
does not believe himself any more than do those to whom he is
speaking. If each examines himself in good faith, he will feel in
his friendship for a woman an aftertaste of love, something spermatic that animates intercourse and vivifies it.

Feelings, whether called love or friendship, are almost never in accord
with the philosophy of the libertine, and Beaumarchais will never
stop claiming himself to be one: "I am *libertine*. Partisan of freedom,
put crudely and positively, this is how I am *libertine* . . . When one
has got a bad reputation, what remains but to enjoy it?"

For him as for all the libertines of his century and his caliber, love
was confused with desire. Everything that remotely related to the
emotions of the heart awakened his skepticism, to say the least.

> I am too carnal a lover to be delicate. I have a rather spermatic
> style; is it my fault I am like that? At least I did not deceive you,
> and so I am not false. To sleep with a mistress is to enjoy her, is
> to . . . (you understand me) her every morning, while to receive
> her libertine emanation by means of her pen, this is what I love;
> some day I will read you the letters of a woman to me and mine
> to a woman. Over them you will blush and quiver, but you will
> also f—k.
>
> Friendship is the intercourse of the spirits; love is the inter-
> course of bodies, and what are called sentiments of the heart are
> a combination of all that, including the spirit in absence and the
> body in presence. And isn't your satin skin a fine sentiment, and
> your tender profusion another? The great question is no longer
> knowing if we f—k because we love, or if we love because we
> f—k—a subject for endless noisy debate. Thus the person who
> said, "To love without screwing is something, but to screw with-
> out loving is nothing" has no more decided the issue than if he
> had said the contrary.

When his occupations or business trips kept him apart from his
desired object, Beaumarchais made up for it by writing. In his letters
the erotic imagination flows in incandescent prose, traversed with lascivious visions that could be described as masturbatory, since the

prose seems to obey the impulses of the body and to inflame its own excitation to the point of a liberating spasm. The words renounce signification to be pure incantation, with no other purpose than to electrify the nerves.

Far from attenuating his ardor, the notorious gallantry of Mme. de Godeville and the perfume of scandal trailing after her name made her all the more desirable in his eyes. Unlike Valmont in *Les liaisons dangereuses*, Beaumarchais did not court virtuous ladies for the simple pleasure of subjecting them to vice. In love as in business, he acted pragmatically; more instinctive than cerebral, more a gambler than a strategist, and little inclined to perversity, he found his most intoxicating sensations in the caresses of expert women (with no marked preference for prostitutes) and in the greatest secrecy, for he detested publicity in matters of sex; the voyeurism to which it necessarily led due to the scandal gazettes inspired in him a distaste that did not belie his pursuit of pleasure. Quite the contrary, "To climax happily, let's climax hidden" might have been his motto, for the drunkenness of the senses was only deployed freely in the secrecy of the alcove bed: "Is it so important to sacrifice reputation or esteem to pleasure that one can only climax by making a very scandalous noise? Our scatterbrains and roués say you have to blare it, and I say you have to screw and keep quiet." Had Figaro become the disciple of Tartuffe?

"Screw and keep quiet" is what dear Marie-Madeleine could not do, nor could ever resign herself to. Keeping quiet did not suit her temperament, insofar as this one-sided correspondence allows us to discern. Although her letters have never been found, we can reconstruct them through those of Pierre-Augustin. They say a lot about the responses he received; silence was not a major virtue of this unpredictable and tempestuous woman, whose epistolary squalls had a great effect on her lover.

The first of her demands—the most legitimate, no doubt, and also the most painful—was her desire for maternity. Marie-Madeleine wanted a child by Pierre-Augustin, but he had just become a father and did not want to repeat the experience with another woman. Her railing on so sensitive a subject could only sour the relations between the two lovers, relations that deteriorated day by day.

Quarrelsome by nature to say the least, Godeville scolded the unhappy Pierre-Augustin constantly. Any subject was suitable, starting with jealousy, of course. But in this respect she had nothing much to fear, for since his installation in the rue Vieille-du-Temple Beaumarchais's amorous activity had slowed markedly, and paid-for gallantries were not to his taste. Although still a bachelor, he led the life of a head of household, joining his mistress almost every evening and corresponding with her almost every day. Far from resigned to this domestic situation, Marie-Thérèse de Willermaulaz fought to keep the inconstant man at home, but her supplication and tears only pushed him farther away. She did not see (or would not see) that his love was crumbling daily from the effects of boredom and habit, while desire gradually gave way to tenderness and compassion. Moreover, this current liaison was not a passing one, like before, when his heart wondered after the first petticoat but quickly came back, contrite and more loving than ever, to the sweetness of conjugal intimacy. This liaison was a furious conflagration of the senses, a passionate earthquake that annihilates in a few seconds the achievements of half a lifetime. Like many men of his age, Pierre-Augustin was a victim of that sexual frenzy whose violence exorcised, at least for a while, the anguish of impotence, vulgarly called the "midday demon." For her part, Marie-Madeleine, who increasingly disliked sharing her lover with a wife, caused scenes more frequently. Torn between these two women, obliged to justify himself to one and then the other, and especially to himself, it remained only for Pierre-Augustin to write a gloss on his torment, which he did without excessive shame: "It is not you whom I have deceived, it is not you whom I sacrifice to another, but rather the tranquillity I am chasing without being able to catch. I have to have peace, without which I can neither work nor think nor write nor live in my house."

But the "sullen belle" objected mightily, driving Beaumarchais to make pronouncements that were as cruel to his daily companion as they were painful for himself:

> What you write me has just been said to me word for word by my housekeeper, and if I could believe impossible things, I would imagine that she saw you writing, or else you heard her speaking.

I am no longer the same man, she says. Absorbed in my office, I profit from no occasion to have fun. I no longer love anything, she says, and the ice of the last age is as cold as my senses. I lack confidence in her whose tenderness is so well known! Never an outpouring of affection. I do not love her anymore, her face is covered in tears. And what kind of man have I become, my dears? The organic molecule that nourishes the brain and the one that pricks the membranes of pleasure are apparently of the same kind, and what happens above spoils what would benefit down below.

In the course of his letters to Mme. de Godeville, Beaumarchais reveals a new face of himself, one that even his most faithful admirers did not know. Here melancholy and gravity emerge from behind the deceiving mask of inalterable gaiety. "To complain of troubles, you have to know them," he writes to his mistress, "and my own system is to shut them all away and only share around me what is happy in the course of my life." Between his two erotic caprices he becomes prey to the most somber thoughts, as if a gulf of anguish and doubts had suddenly opened before him. Far from easing somberness, the whining love of Marie-Madeleine only increased it.

Disappointed in each other, tired of seeking their lost intoxication, the two lovers felt in a confused way (that they did not like to admit to themselves) that a rupture between them was not far off. As always in these circumstances, it happened as stupidly as possible, over nothing: a rather lively letter from Pierre-Augustin that might have shocked a prude but certainly not a woman like her. No doubt something besides a wound to her amour propre was the real cause of the separation. Pierre-Augustin had no serious grievances against his mistress, but the ones she produced against her lover were unceasing, starting with the desired child that he refused to give her. Already thirty-seven at the start of their liaison, her time was running out; hence her impatience and irritation, added to which her obsessive jealousy caused almost daily scenes that poisoned their existence together. Curiously this flighty woman discovered tardily that she had a shopgirl's soul: she dreamed of great love, of torrid declarations, wedding vows—in short, of everything that Pierre-Augustin, libertine that he was, in thrall to independence and pleasure, detested. This fundamental misunderstanding, often debated in their correspondence, may well have finally defeated their mutual attachment. Beaumarchais's last letter bears the date February 21, 1779, dealing with a little puppy baptized Lisette that Marie-Madeleine had given him. We will never know if the break had already taken place or happened soon after. What is certain is that from that day Beaumarchais removed her from his heart, if not totally from his mind—not yet.

The documents in *La Bastille dévoilée* reveal that, having exhausted the generosity of her friends and the service of the police, to whom she supplied information, Mme. de Godeville left for the Netherlands, where she became the correspondent of her former lover. For his part, he got her family to pay her an annual pension and with his own generosity advanced her the sum. Established in The Hague, capital of the clandestine press, she opened an office and launched into the confection of libelous pamphlets that would disturb those in power. Armed with a good dose of cynicism and experienced in techniques of blackmailing by pamphlet, she could cause a lot of trouble to men and women in society—all the more because her incessant needs for money led her to increase her defamatory writings and to raise her blackmail prices. This could not last; everybody ended up feeling threatened. After an attack on Sartine, a decision was made to get rid of this Morande-in-skirts. She spent a year in the Bastille.

Eighteen

"AND VOLTAIRE WILL NEVER DIE"

Kings in life with pomp provided
Death will throw their altars down
Voltaire wears the immortal's crown.
—*Figaro, in* The Marriage of Figaro

Even those who did not attend the performance of Voltaire's *Irène* at the Comédie-Française on March 30, 1778 read the gazettes' accounts of that memorable evening. The audience had been delirious, a bust of the author stood on the set, the ovations were unending, and the frail old man in his loge, teary-eyed, stammered: "You want to make me die with pleasure?!" He did die barely two months later, at the age of eighty-four, and ever since has been a national hero. Whether loved or hated, he soared above any aesthetic, political, or philosophical criticism: adulated, deified, fetishized, totemized, and soon to be elevated to the Pantheon, he belongs to the national mythology.

Three months after his hasty burial in the Abbey of Scellières (because the Church refused to bury his remains), his niece and heir Mme. Denis, who wanted to take advantage of the popular fervor to render a brilliant homage to her uncle, asked the Marquis de Condorcet to manage a publication of his complete works. To take charge of the printing, she proposed Charles-Joseph Panckoucke, the head of one of the largest publishing houses. The latter, scion of a dynasty of publisher-booksellers from Lille, would today be described as a press magnate. In August or September 1778, at the invitation of Mme. Denis, he went to the Voltaire home in Switzerland, Ferney, to gather from Wagnière, Voltaire's last secretary, the precious "packets of literature" that had been sorted and set aside during the arrangement of his library, which had just been acquired by Catherine II of Russia: they amounted to "several packets and three or four volumes." At the end of the summer Mme. Denis also gave him the manuscripts remaining in Paris. Among the "chaos of papers" piled into chests at Panckoucke's premises were many folders spilling over with letters, minutes, and copies, some dealing with business and some more private ones dealing with friends and relations. With the assembling of these primary materials, the integration of the complete correspondence—which would be the great novelty of the new edition—could begin. Unknown at the time was that Panckoucke had taken the trouble to have copied all the original letters that Frederick II of Prussia and Catherine II of Russia had addressed to Voltaire, foreseeing (not without reason) that these monarchs would oppose their publication. Panckoucke had at first accepted as an honor the mission entrusted to him, but upon reflection he began to assess the difficulties. Publication would require enormous investment at a time when his finances were parlous, and the profitability of the operation appeared more than uncertain. A good half of the oeuvre had been banned and remained so throughout French territory. The clergy, which had the power to prevent a universally adulated genius from being entombed in his sepulcher, would never tolerate a simple bookshop publishing his works inside the kingdom. Clandestine publication was out of the question; it would be impossible for all the required personnel to keep quiet. One gaffe, one slip, one jealous colleague, and Panckoucke could end up in the jails of the Châtelet.

Catherine II, whose veneration for the philosopher was known throughout Europe, was aware of the situation. She offered Panckoucke the possibility of setting up his presses in St. Petersburg and even advanced him 110,000 livres by means of her factotum Grimm. Not inclined to this solution, which he regarded as a stopgap, Panckoucke appealed to Beaumarchais. The author of *The Barber* was a notable personality, a financier with enormous capital who was supplying weapons to the American insurgents, and thus possessed the complete confidence of the government. As we have seen, Beaumarchais had received many encouragements and marks of friendship from the philosopher, notably during the Goëzman trial. Likewise, Beaumarchais had a long-standing admiration for his illustrious elder; Voltaire had always been his model. Would he see to the work's publication?

Before committing himself, Beaumarchais wanted assurances. He went to Versailles to convince the old Voltairean and minister of state Maurepas that it would be a disgrace for France to let the Muscovites print "the works of the most illustrious man in French literature." The minister agreed, though he apprehended grousing from the parlement and the clergy, and he promised the king's protection for the distribution of the volumes. It was a daring promise, for Louis XVI had always detested Voltaire and had not changed his mind.

Assured of ministerial support, Beaumarchais founded a company that he pompously called the Philosophical, Literary, and Typographic Society but whose sole shareholder was himself, and in which he took the modest function of "general correspondent." The project testifies once more to his *folie de grandeur*: he foresaw two editions, a deluxe one in octavo would have no less than seventy volumes (the *Encyclopedia* had only thirty-five), and the other in the smaller duodecimo format would have ninety-two. The correspondence alone would take up the last quarter of the set's volumes. A print run of 15,000 each was projected.

Nothing was too fine or too expensive to honor the author of *Candide*. "Our intention is to raise to his memory the most beautiful literary and typographic monument of this century," Beaumarchais wrote to the Marquis de Bièvre. Negotiations were fierce, for Panckoucke was as hard a businessman as he. But on February 25, 1779, he bought from Panckoucke the editorial and publishing rights, as well as all Voltaire's manuscripts and correspondence, for the sum of 300,000 livres.

Now when the editors announced their intention to publish the letters of Catherine II to Voltaire, the empress was furious and cried outrage, sacrilege, and theft. Did these miserable men have copies? She had bought the philosopher's library after his death and paid three times the asking price on the assurance she had got the lot. Basically, his library books did not interest her; she had bought them only to take possession of his letters. And now they were in the hands of booksellers! How had they got there?

Horrified at the idea of seeing her prose fed to journalists, the empress ordered Grimm to "let none of these letters be printed by Sir Figaro"—not that they contained the least thing that might be shocking, but he "deserves to be punished for having wronged me." In buying these copies, he had made himself the accomplice of an indelicacy, she accused. "I am not to blame," Beaumarchais defended himself. "I am a businessman, I buy and sell. Blame those who sold them to me . . . How would I have the stupidity to pay 300,000 livres for works of Voltaire that have been printed for forty years all over Europe?" But he chivalrously promised to submit to Her Majesty's order—a pure hoax, since one relevant volume (number 67) was already printed! But now there was no question of her being the patron of this edition, as she had promised. The "Figaro-ized Voltaire" inspired her defiance, as did its initiator, who, not content with publishing her letters against her will, audaciously used them to boost sales.

Beaumarchais had not thought of publishing Voltaire's oeuvre in France: he knew too well the vicissitudes of the court and the instability of human affairs to base his enterprise on the word of the eighty-year-old Minister Maurepas. He preferred to listen to the voice of caution, which advised him to go abroad. His ideal destination would be a small state, neutral and independent, not too far from France. The Margrave of Baden, Charles-Frederick, had an empty fortress near Strasbourg in Kehl. There Beaumarchais obtained authorization to set up a printing factory without difficulty for a reasonable rent. It was understood that the workers, largely recruited in France, would spend their salaries in Baden and thus contribute to the grand duchy's economic development.

Soon an unexpected difficulty arose. It was funny at first, but it risked making everything capsize: the margrave, or rather his courtiers, denounced the novel *Candide*. Voltaire had openly mocked the châteaux of Westphalia and the Leibnitzian philosophy of Pangloss: a sister of Baron Thunder-ten-tronckh refuses to marry a gentleman who can only prove seventy-one degrees of nobility. How could one dare to publish this infamous firebrand on German soil? The margrave also feared appearing to connive in Voltaire's insolence toward these petty German princes. After a series of half-serious, half-comic debates, Beaumarchais thought it necessary to settle things with the margrave. His enterprise, he reminded him, obeyed rigorous principles that brooked neither discussion nor compromise. He had promised to publish the *complete* works of Voltaire and would accept neither amendment nor censorship under any pretext. (Beaumarchais later swore to the gods that no censorship was ever performed on the texts published in Kehl, but some testimony proves the contrary. We know today, irrefutably, that entire passages were suppressed in the edition because they risked displeasing one institution or another.)

To further enrich his edition, Beaumarchais posted an announcement in *Le Courrier de l'Europe* asking any person who possessed "individual writings, missing pieces or letters from M. de Voltaire," to make contact with him. Aiming to reconstruct the most exhaustive and exact corpus as possible, he also sought a technical realization of the "monument" that was equally irreproachable. With his characteristic pride and feigned humility, he proclaimed himself now "Voltaire's compositor." "I will not be content with offering something mediocre," he said, "which I cannot bear in anything, but in this much less than all the rest." Privileging his perfectionism over his anti-British sentiments (France and Britain were still at war), he asked an agency in Birmingham to negotiate on his behalf for the acquisition of the famous fonts of John Baskerville (6,100 pieces of type), wholly fashioned by their creator and in perfect condition; they made up the most complete printing press in Europe and were one of the masterpieces of the typographic art. The matter of transporting the Baskerville fonts from Birmingham to Kehl was formidable: the cargo amounted to sixty-eight cases, the war was at its height, and ships that were armed to the gills worried about exceeding their tonnage with printing fonts. Instead of putting the fonts on a neutral ship, Beaumarchais's agent had them loaded onto the British *King George*. Leaving at the end of December 1780, they only arrived at their destination in May 1781 after a crossing of five months!

Once Beaumarchais had cleared up the issues of type and paper and got down to editing Voltaire, he was submerged by other tasks:

managing Roderigue Hortalez, arming the Americans, steering the Office of Dramatic Legislation, and making many trips to ports and arsenals. Whatever his powers of work—and we know it was enormous—he could not be everywhere at once nor direct everything himself. Moreover, the publishing venture called upon him to master various new techniques quickly—bookselling, paper-making, typography, casting. Hence he needed to delegate; he had always done well by surrounding himself with diligent and devoted collaborators. To manage the Kehl workshops, he called on an intelligent and dynamic young man who claimed to have some experience in these things, Jean-François Le Tellier.

Not content with making Le Tellier the manager of his business, Beaumarchais proposed to make him half-partner. He required no capital investment of the man, only "his time and his industry." But from that day onward, problems developed for the unfortunate editor. Le Tellier, although he was involved in political circles and possessed an ample information network across Europe, was, it turned out, a disastrous manager. Curt, rough, and contemptuous, he behaved like a despot, treated the workers like slaves, paid them badly, and subjected them to infernal work rhythms, to the point that some preferred to quit their jobs rather than suffer his regime. In fifteen months there was a fourfold personnel turnover! In the workshops he was called the "tyrant of Kehl." At the same time Le Tellier's financial management was leading the enterprise slowly but infallibly to the verge of bankruptcy.

Undertaken with enthusiasm, the Voltaire edition gradually turned into a nightmare. After more than two years the truth finally became manifest, and Beaumarchais decided to replace Le Tellier. At the start of January 1785 he designated his successor: a former captain of dragoons and formerly the king's commissioner in Santo Domingo. Jacques-Gilbert de La Hogue by his own admission had never set foot in a printing works.

Barely had Beaumarchais put his "great enterprise" into action than he launched into a grand publicity campaign. Of course he could not solicit the French newspapers, which had no right to print it. On the other hand, *Le Courrier de l'Europe*, printed in London but cheerfully smuggled across borders, did enjoy freedom of the

press. Beaumarchais had friends at the *Courrier* and himself contributed from time to time, so he made it the principal promotional
outlet for his enterprise. A first article announced the Kehl edition of
Voltaire's complete works on January 28, 1780.

The prospectus caused a lot of ink to be spilled, both servile and
vicious. But naturally the announcement insisted on the splendor of
the monument to Voltaire's memory and on the advantageous conditions for subscribers. Although sales were forbidden on French soil,
Beaumarchais played the traveling salesman during the course of his
many trips to provincial ports and arsenals. In some cases he was the
agent of the Hortalez Company, and in others, the representative of
the Philosophical, Literary, and Typographic Society. Apparently the
arms merchant made a fine bookseller: his aplomb, his loquacity, his
personal charm, and especially his fame assured him lively success
among the clientele. Passing through Bordeaux in the summer of
1781, he came back with a notebook full of orders.

In November 1781 the Comte de Maurepas died at age eighty,
depriving Beaumarchais of his main ally at the moment he most
needed one. Subscription solicitations were inundating the major
cities of the kingdom, causing a stir. Despite the discretion with
which the operation was conducted, nothing could prevent the
clergy and the parlements from being alerted. The clergy complained
to the king about the ministry's tolerance of a declared adversary of
the Church. The parlement did not prosecute Beaumarchais but circulated a pamphlet of rare vehemence denouncing Voltaire's oeuvre
as destructive of religion, morals, and authority. The pamphlet's
author was a particularly boisterous parlementarian called Duval
d'Eprémesnil, who pressed the parlement of Paris to deploy against
the new edition "all the rigor and power that the Prince has confided
in it." Pastoral letters, subpoenas, lampoons, and clerical decrees
descended like locusts on the unfortunate enterprise, lumping
together the diabolical Voltaire and his editor, consigning them
together (or one after the other) to flames of hell.

Nevertheless, the politicians would gradually jettison their religious convictions and balk at taking such unpopular measures. To
condemn the Kehl enterprise would not only reap public disapproval
but transform Beaumarchais into the victim of absolutism and intol-

erance. The risk of suppressing the edition was greater than the Voltairean menace. Throughout the operation Beaumarchais would benefit from the tacit but effective complicity of the government. Thus, although the Kehl edition was officially banned on French territory, bundles of sheets crossed the Rhine and arrived in Paris in tens of hundredweights, thanks to highly placed protection and favors.

Publication continued from 1783 to 1790 at the cost of enormous financial sacrifices. Of all Beaumarchais's enterprises, the Voltaire edition would be by far the most disastrous financially. The events of 1789 lifted the constraint of censorship and the last volumes finally left the presses, but buyers were more and more rare, subscribers were slow to take delivery of their copies, and the gazettes and bookshops spread critiques; and most of all, a political earthquake was not conducive to bookselling. The result was that the Philosophical, Literary, and Typographic Society's deficit deepened each day, while Beaumarchais exhausted himself refloating it. After the shipwreck he would try to give new life to the business by publishing the works of Jean-Jacques Rousseau and a few others, but without success. In the end he repatriated his type fonts, thus putting at the disposal of French printers the complete Baskerville fonts, for which he had paid dearly, at "a moderate price." Meanwhile European bookshops remaindered the Voltaire edition. Many copies were in Beaumarchais's mansion when it was sacked during the Revolution.

If the Voltaire edition was a stinging commercial failure, however, nobody could contest its success on the literary level. "The difficulty of succeeding only adds to the necessity of undertaking it," declares Figaro in *The Barber of Seville*. This was Beaumarchais's philosophy: courage and optimism. Making a thousand sacrifices, overcoming a thousand obstacles, setting aside fatigue and disgust a hundred times, he brought the enterprise to a conclusion. He did his oeuvre. The Kehl *Voltaire* is not only a "beautiful monument to the greatest man that literature has produced," it is also the victory of tenacity over defeat and abandonment.*

---

*The Kehl edition of Voltaire's work is still available from a handful of rare-book dealers.

Nineteen

"THE CRAZIEST REVERIE IN MY NIGHTCAP"

The Bastille would have to be destroyed for the performance of this play not to be of dangerous inconsequence.

—Louis XVI

What happened to the characters in *The Barber of Seville* once the curtain came down? What were the fates of Figaro, Rosine, Bartholo, and Bazile? This proto-Pirandellian question was posed by Beaumarchais as early as the preface to his first comedy. Giving free rein to his fantasy, he had imagined a follow-up to his play:

> If instead of staying within the simple world of comedy, I had wanted to complicate, extend, and elaborate my plot into a tragedy or a drama, do you seriously think I would have been short of material? I have after all shown only the least astonishing episodes of the story on stage! Indeed, there can be no one today who doesn't know that at the historic moment when I portrayed the tale as ending happily, the quarrel—behind the scenes, as you might say—between the Doctor and Figaro about the hundred écus really heated up. Mutual abuse gave way to blows. The Doctor, who was being punched and kicked by Figaro, happened, in the struggle, to pull off the Spanish hairnet the Barber had on his head, at which those present espied (not without some surprise) the outline of a hot spoon, or doctor's spatula, branded on his

shaven scalp . . . At the sight of this, the Doctor shouts ecstatically, "My son! Heavens, my son". . . . Figaro, who until that moment has had no family in the world other than his mother, is Bartholo's natural son. The physician, in his youth, has had a child by a lady in service, who, as a result of her misdemeanor, has been hounded out of her employment and left entirely destitute. However, before he abandoned them, Bartholo, in floods of tears, and then still only a student, heated his spatula and used it to stamp his son upon the occiput, so that he would recognize him again if one day fate should ever reunite them. Mother and child had spent six years in respectable penury, begging, when a gypsy chief traveling through Andalusia with his troupe, consulted by the mother as to her son's future destiny, furtively stole the child away, leaving in his place this horoscope:

> After he once his mother's blood hath shed
> Thy son shall smite his cursèd father's head
> Then, turning on himself the fatal blade
> See him legitimate and happy made.

Unwittingly, the young man has changed his status in society, unwillingly he has changed his name: he has grown up as Figaro, and as such he has lived. His mother is Marceline, grown an old woman and become governess in the doctor's house, her son's dreadful horoscope her only consolation in her loss. But today all is to be fulfilled . . . At that moment the most touching reconciliation occurs between the Doctor, the old woman, and Figaro: "It's you, it's him, it's you, it's me . . ." What a moment in the theater! But the son, in despair at what his own innocent enthusiasm has driven him to, bursts into tears, and taking out his razor, has a very close shave indeed, in the sense of the third verse:

> Then, turning on himself the fatal blade

What a tableau! In not revealing whether he uses the razor to cut his throat or simply the stubble on his chin, it may be observed that I could, had I so chosen, have ended my play on the most elevated note of pathos. But the Doctor marries the old woman, and Figaro, in accordance with the last part of our quatrain, is seen "legitimate and happy made." What a curtain! All I would have needed was a new act VI!

At the time Beaumarchais was not thinking of a sixth act, and still less of a sequel. Yet any reader will recognize in this scenario, intended to cock a snook at melodrama, the original canvas of *The Marriage of Figaro*. Why and how did he shift from parody of melodrama to a new form of comedy? This is how he explained it:

The deceased Prince de Conti challenged me in public to dramatize my preface to *The Barber* as being more gay, he said, than the play, and to show the Figaro family I had sketched there. "Monsieur," I replied, "if I put this character a second time on the stage, since I would show him older and knowing somewhat more, it would be another din, and who knows if it would see the light of day." But out of respect, I accepted the challenge and I composed this play *Une folle journée* [*One Mad Day*], which today causes so much rumor.

Protector and friend of Beaumarchais, the Prince de Conti died in August 1776, without having been able to read or see the result, which would only be finished, according to the author, in 1778. For the three years following, which could rightly pass as the most active of our hero's life, *The Marriage of Figaro* rested in its boxes. Circumstances did not lend themselves to its getting out, and his relations with the Comédiens-Français had never been as bad. Only after 1781 did his play begin to be known, through readings at his or friends' homes. Before submitting a play to the official censors, he usually asked for the advice of colleagues. A reading aloud, by the author himself in chosen company, played an essential role in the work's launching; its purpose was to arouse a response that would influence the censors or the future actors and audiences by exposing them to honest judgments and fine-tuning. A past master of the art of reading his works in society, Beaumarchais had no equal in filling the salons, mingling the nobility, the monied, and fine minds among those most predisposed in his favor. Knowing that flattery works but is bearable only in moderation, and that unlike the groundlings a Parisian salon is not duped by a claque, he took care to measure the effects, to seduce without forcing. He repressed flights of passion and never pleaded an argument—in short, he nuanced the excessive confidence that he normally exuded with a smattering of timidity.

Thus, from salon to salon, from the Duchesse de Villeroi to the Prince de Conti to the Princesse de Lamballe, Beaumarchais promenaded for three years "his grave person and his crazy work," offering or declining to read it "with all the devices of a refined coquette," enrolling all of Paris in a conspiracy of curiosity, and eventually of fever. An expert in communication, he knew how to tame his listeners, preparing them for the daring bits and forestalling hostile reactions. Before each reading he pronounced a sort of *captatio benevolentiae*, of playful and rather gallant inspiration, suitable to defuse the scabrous and risqué dialogues that the ladies would hear from behind their fans. The readings followed an unvarying ritual: so many people gathered around the platform that they had to stand on tiptoe "so as to catch everything."

On Saturday, September 29, 1781, at ten o'clock, the reading committee of the Comédiens-Français met to rule on *The Marriage of Figaro*. Setting aside their quarrel with the founder of the Office of Dramatic Legislation, the committee members accepted the new play unanimously—"by acclamation," as was said in those days. Convinced that it would be a success, they were counting on it to recoup some previous financial losses.

As soon as his play was accepted, Beaumarchais pressed the lieutenant of police Lenoir to designate a censor and asked, as a particular favor, that the censor read it alone. The magistrate promised that nobody else (clerk or secretary) could poke his nose into the manuscript and that the censor could work in his own office. He delegated the task to Coqueley de Chaussepierre, one of the most picturesque figures in the theater world. A poet in his leisure time, he was not indulgent toward his colleagues. Rather ill disposed toward Beaumarchais, he gave his approval, although at the cost of a few minor alterations, stressing that the gaiety of the play, "although approaching

what is now called slap-and-tickle, does not go as far as indecency."
Moreover, the play appeared to him very well written and "suitable
to attract to the Comédie, which badly needs it, many spectators, and
consequently income."

Incredibly, Coqueley seems not to have paid attention to Figaro's
seditious monologue in act V. Indeed it was much more provocative
than the amended version we know today:

> Just because you're a great nobleman, you think you're a great
> genius! Being an aristocrat, having money, a position in society,
> holding public office—all that makes a man so arrogant! What
> have you ever done for all this wealth? You took the trouble to be
> born and nothing else! Apart from that you're rather an ordinary
> man. And me, God damn it, a nobody, one of the crowd, and
> I've had to use more skill and ingenuity simply to stay alive than
> they've expended in a hundred years in governing the whole of
> Spain! And you dare challenge me!

In fact, the original setting was not Spain but France, and the famous
monologue was markedly longer. Instead of calling the Bastille the
"fortress on entering which I abandoned hope and liberty," Figaro
mentioned it by name, saying he had been "well received there
thanks to the recommendation that it attracted" and joking about
the "economical retreat" from which he benefited. Not content to
make fun of the state prisons, the ecclesiastical authorities, and the
press, he insisted on Count Almaviva's libertinage, put his vassals in
league against him, and featured angry, threatening murmurs, like
the foretaste of a riot. But Beaumarchais was not a revolutionary, as
his first biographer, Loménie, explains: "Disposed to censure vanities,
privileges, and abuses from which he had suffered more than once,
he was certainly far from being disposed to push things to extremes";
he was continuing "the mission of Moliere to make the small laugh
at the expense of the great and amuse the great themselves, while
interesting their self-love, so that they should not recognize themselves in a somewhat exaggerated picture of the abuses of rank and
fortune."

Soon *The Marriage of Figaro* became the subject of a lively debate in the capital's salons. Even at court, coteries formed, for or against the play. Mme. de Polignac and the Baron de Breteuil, minister of the king's household, lobbied openly in its favor, in the hope that Louis XVI would soon grant authorization for public performances, while the hostile cabal gathered around the king's brother. At first enchanted by these debates, which offered him free and unexpected publicity, Beaumarchais now feared that prolonging them might challenge the censor's conclusions and delay the play's premiere.

But the readings continued to roll along, in Versailles as in Paris, instigating more debates: clans were formed, passions were irritated, partisans and detractors were aroused. At the court, in town, in salons, circles, cafés, and promenades, in all corners of the capital, everyone talked of *The Marriage of Figaro*—which nobody had ever seen, pending the king's permission to perform it.

Louis XVI, who detested the buzz and found the nagging about Figaro unbearable, decided he had to form his own opinion and asked for a reading of the comedy. Beaumarchais sent the manuscript to the lieutenant of police, and Mme. Campan, the principal lady-in-waiting to the queen, was entrusted to read it aloud. Campan has left a lively story of the scene:

> When I arrived in the interior cabinet of Her Majesty, I found her alone with the king; a seat and a small table were already placed opposite them and on the table was an enormous manuscript in several folders; the king said to me, "It's Beaumarchais's comedy, you have to read it to us; there are some difficult places because of crossings out and transfers; I have already skimmed it but I want the queen to know this work. You will speak to nobody about the reading you are doing." I started. The king interrupted me often with ever judicious exclamations, either of praise or of blame. "That was in bad taste; this man constantly brings Italian conceits into the scene." At Figaro's monologue, which attacks various parts of the administration but is essentially a tirade about the state prisons, the king arose abruptly and said: "This is detestable and will never be performed; the Bastille would have to be destroyed for the performance of this play not to be of dangerous inconsequence. This man mocks everything that should

be respected in a government." Of course the king had arrived at
a judgment to which experience must bring all the enthusiasts of
this bizarre production. "So it will never be performed?" said the
queen. "Certainly not," replied Louis XVI, "you may be sure of
that."

This ban was confirmed in the most official form, a letter from the
king to the keeper of the seals, M. de Miromesnil: "I send back to
you, Monsieur, Beaumarchais's comedy. I read it and had it read
aloud; the censor cannot permit either its performance or its
printing."

Faced with what he called "the court's proscription," Beaumarchais made some changes to his play, switching the setting to near
Seville and softening the monologue. Then he put the manuscript in
rose petals in his drawer, swearing that he would never take it out; he
claimed he was too afraid of displeasing the king to promote a play of
which the monarch disapproved. At the same time he coquettishly
continued his public readings, while giving the impression of depre-
cating them. One cannot help admiring the rather perverse talent
with which he knew how to make his work desired. Everybody in the
city was singing Chérubin's romantic song—on the melody "*Marl-
brough s'en va-t-en guerre*"—even the queen found it charming. But
he obstinately refused to read his comedy in the salons. To obtain the
favor of hearing it, one had to make several requests, produce warm
recommendations, and insist, beg, and implore. "Each day," writes
Mme. Campan, "one hears it said 'I went or I will go to a reading of
Beaumarchais's play.'" Thus did he make the readings appear a privilege. The desire to see it performed became universal. And Beaumarchais skillfully inserted into his work a new line: Figaro says that
"only little men are afraid of little jokes." That change made all the
great lords and powerful people aim at the honor of being placed
among the superior minds. He also drew benefit from the minor
scandal caused by the reading of a banned work; he offered his audience the delicious shiver of rare and forbidden fruit. But prudence
obliged him to consent to perform only before persons whose birth
or rank would shelter him from royal sanctions.

Barely had the Parisian salons discovered the play than Cather-

ine II of Russia asked for a reading, through the intermediary of
Prince Bibikov. Three months later, in May 1782, the Russian grand
duke, her son, passing through Paris accompanied by his wife, expressed a desire to host a reading of *The Marriage of Figaro*. This
reading for the Comte du Nord (as the czarevich was known when
he traveled incognito) would allow Beaumarchais to press his advantage. Strengthened by the grand duke's approval, he made an approach to the keeper of the seal, who shut his door to him. Then the
grand duke asked to take the manuscript to his mother, the empress.
Beaumarchais implored the police lieutenant Lenoir to assign him a
second censor. Lenoir did so, but the censor he got was one of his
worst enemies, the academician Jean-Baptiste Suard, an unhappy
choice that may have been imposed from on high. Suard's report
concluded by interdicting the play. The manuscript was sent back to
the author, who thus lost all hope of ever seeing it performed on the
French stage.

One year later, in April 1783, the Comédiens-Français received
from the first gentleman of the chamber an order to study *The Marriage of Figaro* "for the service of the Court." How to explain this
turnaround? Later Beaumarchais wrote to the Baron de Breteuil:
"People whose requests I respect, having desired to give a party for
one of the king's brothers, wanted absolutely that *The Marriage of
Figaro* be performed. Despite my deference, I prayed that the play,
difficult to perform, be entrusted only to the Comédiens-Français.
The rest I left up to the will of the demanders."

The little conspiracy consisted of Mme. de Polignac, the Comte
de Vaudreuil, the Duc de Fronsac, and other partisans of Beaumarchais; at its head was the Comte d'Artois, younger brother of
Louis XVI and a frivolous libertine. Artois had managed to obtain
the permission that had been vainly solicited for three years! The performance, exceptional in all respects, was to take place in the small
apartments of Versailles, but that plan had to be changed; successive
sites were the Trianon, Choisy, Bagatelle, Brunoy, and Maisons.
Beaumarchais even thought of the hôtel of the Duchesse de Polignac, but that idea went nowhere. The small hall of Menus-Plaisirs,
in the rue Bergère in Versailles, was the final choice.

Despite the secrecy surrounding the performance, the news soon

toured court and city, arousing joy among Beaumarchais's friends
and fury among his adversaries. Following the author's wish, the
troupe of the Théâtre Français was asked to perform the work
(except for the young ingénue to play Chérubin, who was borrowed
from the Comédie-Italienne). Throughout May and in the first week
of June 1783, more than thirty rehearsals took place in Menus-
Plaisirs under the author's vigilant eye. The first rehearsals were conducted in the greatest secrecy, but as days went by, more and more
privileged invitees managed to slip into the hall. Beaumarchais
watched over everything and was particularly exacting with the
actors. As always, he left nothing to chance and was even involved in
printing the invitations, which he addressed to the whole court, setting the performance for June 13, 1783.

That day, about two hours before the curtain rose, the actors were
putting on the final touches when a breathless courier arrived with
a paper sealed with red wax: it was a lettre de cachet banning them
from performing the play. The king's order! General consternation
erupted. The carriages would soon be arriving at the rue Bergère; the
crowd was pressing at the doors. Then the announcement was made
that the performance would not take place: disappointment was succeeded by muffled fury. "The King's ban appeared to be an attack on
public freedom," Mme. de Campan later wrote. "All the disappointed hopes aroused such discontent that the words *oppression* and
tyranny were never pronounced with as much passion and vehemence as they would be in the days preceding the fall of the throne.
Anger carried Beaumarchais so far as to say: 'Well, messieurs, he does
not want it performed here, but I swear that it will be played, perhaps
in the choir of Notre-Dame!' " It was a great blunder, badly compromising the future of his own play.

Shaken by the affront, and much needing a change of scene,
Beaumarchais embarked for London, where business called him. In
his absence his partisans continued, against all the odds, to try to get
Figaro performed. Finally the queen obtained permission from her
husband; undoubtedly she had yielded to the wishes of her circle of
intimates, notably Mme. de Polignac and the Comte de Vaudreuil.
At the latter's home a party was planned: there would be a hunt, followed by a supper attended by many women of the court, and to

close it, they would watch *The Marriage of Figaro*. Such was the plan. The Duc de Fronsac, who had succeeded his father as first gentleman of the chamber, promised to help arrange the evening's events. The king's agreement having been obtained, they lacked only that of Beaumarchais; the author was asked to let his play be performed in Gennevilliers. Vaudreuil awaited his reply with impatience and anxiety, for he knew the man was unpredictable. On the pretext that the accusation of immorality was still weighing on the play, Beaumarchais requested a third censor to cleanse it of any suspicion. The censor was appointed; he suppressed two insignificant sentences and gave his approval. The performance was scheduled to take place on September 26, 1783.

Relieved, the Comte de Vaudreuil hurried to express his gratitude to Beaumarchais. The almost obsequious deference of his note says much about the evolution of the nobility's attitude toward writers:

> The Comte de Vaudreuil had the honor of passing by Monsieur de Beaumarchais's house to thank him for his kindness in allowing his play to be performed in Gennevilliers. The Comte de Vaudreuil has seized this occasion to render to the public the masterpiece that if awaits with impatience. The presence of Mgr. the Comte d'Artois, and the real merit of this charming play, will finally destroy all the obstacles that have delayed its performance and consequently its success. The Comte de Vaudreuil desires to be able soon to extend the same thanks to Monsieur de Beaumarchais.

Constructed by Giovanni Servandoni in 1752 for the Duc de Richelieu, the Château de Gennevilliers offered "hunting grounds" where the usual circle of the Comte d'Artois met. "The house was furnished in the best taste, although without magnificence," remembers the painter Elisabeth Vigée-Lebrun.

> There was a small but charming theater . . . The first spectacle that was given was a performance of *The Marriage of Figaro* by the actors of the Comédie-Française. I recall that Mlle. Saint-Val played the countess and Mlle. Olivier the page, and that Mlle.

> Contat was charming in the role of Suzanne. Nevertheless Beau-
> marchais must have cruelly harassed M. de Vaudreuil to have per-
> formed a play so unsuitable in all respects. The dialogue, the
> couplets—everything was directed against the court, of which a
> large part was present, not to mention our excellent prince
> [Artois]. All suffered from this lack of propriety, but Beaumar-
> chais was drunk with pleasure; he ran around like a man beyond
> himself. When some complained of the heat, he did not open the
> windows but broke all the panes with his cane, which made peo-
> ple say after the play that he broke the windows twice over.

According to Mme. Vigée-Lebrun, some in the audience were
shocked by certain daring things, including Figaro's famous monologue ("without the liberty to criticize no praise has any value, and
only little men are scared of little jokes"), which would be suppressed
for the public performances. Nonetheless the party was a great success, according to other witnesses. The day after the memorable Gennevilliers performance, Louis XVI asked his brother Artois what he
thought of it, no doubt hoping for a negative reaction. The prince
whispered in his brother's ear: "Should I tell you in two words? The
expression, the plot, the ending, the dialogue, the ensemble, the
details, from the first scene to the last, was f*** and then more
f***." It seems the king laughed a lot. The witty Sophie Arnould,
who reported this scene, remarked delicately: "How can a comedy
with that basis not be a work of genius?"

Three months later this *Marriage of Figaro*, which Louis XVI had
declared "detestable" and "unplayable," was openly performed by
"the king's actors" before the fine flower of his court, in the presence
of his brother, with the blessing of the queen. Louis XVI had no illusions about his influence in secondary matters, and the remark attributed to him—"you see that Beaumarchais has more credit than the
keeper of the seal"—proves that he judged the situation rightly. His
sole fault—one with heavy consequences—had been precisely to treat
the theater as a frivolous thing.

So it seems the Comédiens-Français did not replay *Figaro* before
the premiere at their own theater. However two friends of the Comte
de Vaudreuil mounted it abroad: the Prince de Ligne in his château
of Beloeil and the Prince de Nassau-Siegen near Warsaw. But the per-

formance of September 26 at Gennevilliers, before a court audience, passes for historic. From that day Beaumarchais's unloved comedy was on its way to redemption. The Gennevilliers evening now appears as the dress rehearsal for the grand premiere that would soon take place in the new hall of the Théâtre Français.

Beaumarchais became the man of the day: his name was on everyone's lips, people spoke only of his *Marriage of Figaro* and the royal opposition; he had the wind in his sails, and knew and used it. He now formally requested from the police permission to have the play performed before the general public. The magistrate responded that the king's interdiction for the Menus-Plaisirs was still in force, so the playwright had to defer to His Majesty. But why refuse to the general audience what had just been granted to high society? To understand this apparent contradiction, it must be remembered that in the eighteenth century, private performances enjoyed a freedom of language of which public performances were cruelly deprived. The best society could welcome licentious *parades*, parodies, and spoofs in the salons of the Faubourg Saint-Germain, but the general public had no chance of seeing them.

Tired of waiting, Beaumarchais announced that he was giving up. "Fifty times I have traveled from the Marais to your hôtel," he wrote to the lieutenant of police, ". . . to obtain a simple thing: a decision about a frivolous work . . ."

> If it is gall they are asking you to give me, I have drunk it to the dregs. If there is to be an absolute ban on anything I write, why make me wait for the decree? . . . I beg you, monsieur, to give me back my manuscript; this bagatelle has become important to me only for the relentlessness with which I am accused of committing a public wrong, without allowing the public to judge for itself. I am sure that you . . . have some regrets about the disagreeable things you are obliged to do to me, but it is time they end. Never has any serious business caused me so much upset as the craziest reverie in my nightcap that is this play.

This was a little bit of blackmail—for the court did not intend to go so far as a rupture. A fourth royal censor had to be found. Lenoir charged François Foucques-Deshayes, called Desfontaines, with the thankless task. The former secretary of a duke, then librarian to a count, Desfontaines had written alone or in collaboration some small comedies mixed with vaudeville; they had been nimbly mounted, nimbly played, and forgotten. A modest dramaturge, he could recognize the genius of a more talented colleague. Indeed, he had the honesty and virtue to praise the play in a panegyric that compared it to the works of Molière. One could dream of no higher—nor more sincere—praise.

Yet no authorization was on the horizon: *Marriage of Figaro* remained under royal veto. Not knowing what saint (or censor) to appeal to, Beaumarchais asked for an audience with the Baron de Breteuil, minister of the king's household, and framed his request in these terms:

> Not knowing if there remain obstacles to the performance of a gaiety that has become for me so sad and so contrary, I await your final orders by assuring you that no affair, as grave as it may be, has cost me so much trouble and effort as this, the slightest work that has ever come from my pen. And if it is true that there is no good marriage in this country without great opposition, you will admit that if one judges the goodness of a marriage by the obstacles it overcomes, none has suffered so many as *The Marriage of Figaro*.

A sixth (and final) censor was named. Again a dramatic author, Antoine Bret approved the play without correction, but that was still not sufficient. Beaumarchais demanded and obtained permission to hold a reading at the home of the Baron de Breteuil, before "a kind of tribunal composed of French academicians, censors, men of letters, men of the world, and persons of the court (just as enlightened) who discussed in the presence of the minister the principle, the basis, the form and diction of this play, scene by scene, phrase by phrase, and word by word."

Breteuil was predisposed against the work, the actor Fleury tells us, "yet it was this minister that Beaumarchais would turn in his favor. He had already calculated what benefit he could draw from the character and position of the baron. Devoted to the queen and to the Comte d'Artois, he was very amenable, in his lovely blue office, to worldly seduction. So Beaumarchais had him solicited by the prettiest girls, perhaps including some who gave the appearance of being flexible." Do we deduce what overcame the minister's hesitations? Whatever the case, the brilliant committee met in March 1784, as Fleury described:

> We sat down and listened. Beaumarchais began by announcing that he would submit to any cuts without reservation, to all corrections these gentlemen (and even ladies) found his work needed; he read, they stopped him, made observations, discussed it; at each interruption he gave way, then going back, he ended up defending the slightest details with such skill, verve, force of reason, seduction of wit and reasoning that he shut the mouths of his censors; people laughed, were amused, and applauded: "It is a unique work!"

Everyone wanted to add something: Mme. de Matignon put in the color of the page's ribbon. This time the game was well and truly won! Louis XVI had to yield. He had been persuaded that the committee would reject the play and that he would be finally rid of the author—and he had believed it! The date of the premiere was decreed: April 27, 1784.

That date merits being inscribed among the great moments of French history. Symbolically it marks a decisive turning point in the visible decomposition of the old order and in the constitution, at first subterranean, of the new. Every journal, chronicle, news sheet, correspondence, and memoir describes a vertigo of curiosity, passion, and argument, sharpened by the blunders of authority. It pushed people that day from the court and the city to the Théâtre Français, which for a few hours was the nerve center of the capital.

Ten hours before the opening, the crowd started to gather at the box office. People chatted, speculated, even made bets on the triumph or failure of the new play. They commented on the heroic struggle of its author, the obstinacy of the sovereign, the intervention of the queen, the affair of Menus-Plaisirs two years before, the Gennevilliers party the previous September—the gazettes had been feeding the public with it all for months. Princes and princesses of the blood, duchesses and blue-sashed aristocrats, stood elbow to elbow with clerks, artisans, and savoyards, all scrambling to buy scalper's tickets at fifteen to twenty times their regular price. People made sacrifices to obtain a corner, even parterre. The Duchesse de Bourbon sent her valet to the ticket office to await the distribution of tickets, set for four o'clock. Mme. de Talleyrand paid for a triple loge. More than three hundred women were in the loges of actresses, hoping to be the first to enter; the fat Marquise de Montmorin barely fit into the cubbyhole of Mlle. Olivier, who was playing Chérubin. Beaumarchais received in an hour more than forty letters asking for complimentary tickets "to serve as big mitts."

When the doors finally opened, the hall was assaulted. The guards dispersed, the iron grille was broken, and three unlucky people were suffocated in the shuffle. Barely half the spectators found seats; most of them entered by force, throwing their money at the porters. Fights erupted, cries of scandal: Beaumarchais had triumphed. The receipts totaled 5,698 livres, an unprecedented figure. In the prime loges sat the members of the queen's circle at Le Petit-Trianon. "All of them shone, chattered, greeted each other; there were soft arms, white shoulders, manicured fingers, swans' necks, moving rainbows, prettily animated, crossing and flapping their wings, impatient to applaud, impatient to denigrate—all that for Beaumarchais and by Beaumarchais!"

At five o'clock the curtain finally rose: Dazincourt and Mlle. Contat entered on stage. Beaumarchais had taken a place at the back of a grilled loge, between two ecclesiastics: the Abbé Sabatier de Cabre and the Abbé de Calonne, whom he had invited to dine and to accompany him "in order to administer, in case of death, very spiritual help." After years of struggle, he had arrived at the fateful moment, so awaited and also so feared, when the public would give its verdict. The era just passed must have seemed sweet, when "holding my manuscript in reserve like the coquette who often refuses what she always burns to grant, I made some greedy lecture to preferred people, who believed they ought to pay me the compliment of pompous praise for my work . . . No more evasion, no trickery, coquetry, inflections of the voice, theatrical illusion, nothing. It was my naked virtue that people were going to judge."

In the theater world failure or success is measured in coin. Beaumarchais knew this well enough that he trembled before the parterre of princes and great lords, come to attend their own roasting. But then the incredible thing happened. The nobility laughed at the raillery, was amused by the satire, and even welcomed joyously the mockery of ministers, the Bastille, the press, the police, the censors. The aristocracy laughed at everything, first of all at itself. When the curtain fell, the entire hall, parterre and loges, erupted in thunderous applause. It was a spectacle that Beaumarchais could not have dared imagine: "There is one thing crazier than my play—its success!" The critic Jean-François de La Harpe was amazed when he heard the whole hall, essentially composed of men and women who merely "had taken the trouble to be born," exult in Figaro's monologue. "The more they clapped," he remembered, "the more I was stupefied. Finally I concluded the author was not wrong, that truly the play, there where it was placed, was a comprehensible absurdity, but that the tolerance of a government that let itself be demeaned on stage was still more so, and that after all Beaumarchais was right to speak thus in the theater, à propos no matter what, since it was found à propos to let him say it." But the final word belongs to the Jesuit Joseph Cerutti, who wrote to the Marquise de Boufflers in London: "*The Marriage of Figaro* is the maddest comedy, the gayest, the most impertinent, the most ingenious thing in the world. If I were not sick, I would return there again to laugh, to whistle, to applaud. The prodigious movement caused by this play does not make that of magnetism fall: madness is at its height." Begun at five o'clock, the spectacle finished only at ten-thirty because almost every line was applauded, which was unprecedented.

Was it a triumph of Figaro or of Beaumarchais? Contemporaries generally refused to distinguish the hero from his creator. If the success of *The Marriage of Figaro* largely exceeded the framework of dramatic literature or Parisian events, if its repercussions soon spilled over the borders of the kingdom, it indeed constituted a political event in all its dimensions—and the public of the day well understood it as such. For a long time the theater had served as a tribune for the diffusion of new ideas. But never had criticism of a regime found such direct or powerful expression; never had a critic dealt so bravely with the powerful, their manners, and their privileges. To proclaim, as the author Charles Nodier did, that after *The Marriage of Figaro* the Revolution was made would be to exaggerate its influence, but clearly Beaumarchais gave the French an early lesson in shaking off the respect for servitude that absolutism had imprinted on the whole nation. The nation dared to approve of satire because it was trying to despise authority. "Figaro killed the aristocracy," Danton would say in 1789.

Twenty

THE LEGENDARY SPANKING

Whoever is happy, or appears so, should be constantly on his knees to ask pardon, and won't even always obtain it thereby, especially if he came from afar to arrive where he is now.   **—La Harpe**

Never had the Théâtre Français had a success comparable to that of *The Marriage of Figaro*—at least not in ticket sales, and the actors were sensitive to those. The controversy aroused by the moral and political implications of the work helped, of course. Epigrams from the play appeared in gazettes. Broadsheets were even launched from the third-story balcony of the theater during the fourth performance, provoking a joyous brouhaha in the hall and whistles down below. Excited by the claques, to which Beaumarchais may have lent a secret hand, the audiences poured in. Far from ruining the play, the scandal fed its triumph. In the space of eight months, from April 1784 to January 1785, it had an unprecedented sixty-eight performances.

For the fiftieth the author, claiming there was a slump in ticket sales, launched into a vast campaign, once again putting to use his genius for publicity. Persuaded that nothing pleased the popular consciousness like a charity for the most disfavored, he chose as his theme assistance to destitute nursing mothers. For the first time, a public figure would use humanitarianism for self-promotion—and the precedent would not be forgotten. In a letter to the *Journal de Paris* dated August 12, 1784, Beaumarchais promised to donate a portion of his royalties to the creation of a charitable organization to help needy breastfeeding mothers: "When I am meant to be treated as a vain man, I will put all my Figaro into it: this is money that belongs to me, which I have earned by my labor, through torrents of insults, printed or epistolary. So when the actors have 200,000 francs, my nursing mothers will have 28,000; with 30,000 from my friends, we'll have a regiment of kids stuffed with mother's milk; all that is well worth the insults." Better still, he invited spectators to make their own contributions at the box office, which the Comédie-Française would pass along. He expected his offer to soften tender hearts because a great majority of the French favored maternal breastfeeding. The Enlightenment philosophes, led by Rousseau, had agitated for years against the practice of sending babies out to wet nurses and urged women to give their own breasts to their newborns: they invoked the ancients, the idea of Mother Nature, and pseudo-medical considerations. The philosophes ended up persuading young mothers, and the better-off had already returned to the practice of nursing, so Beaumarchais intended the profits of his subscription to go to the more deprived.

Readers of the *Journal de Paris* were not all duped by this apparent generosity. Many denounced his operation as a cynical ruse. At the fiftieth performance of *The Marriage of Figaro*, whose ticket sales were supposed to go to nursing mothers, attendance was as numerous as at the premiere. Prince Henri of Prussia, brother of Frederick II, who was traveling incognito, gave the box office 300 livres. But his example was not followed, and Beaumarchais's appeal met with almost no effect. The public came to the show to be entertained, not to relieve the misery of the world. Fought by some and praised by others, the nursing mothers' foundation did not last in Paris, although the idea caught on in the provinces.

Meanwhile we remember that Jean-Baptiste Suard, a royal censor, had categorically refused to give his approval to *The Marriage of Figaro*. Since then he had been pursuing his overly fortunate rival with tenacious rancor. Now overseeing the *Journal de Paris*, he spread negative rumors about the play and its author. Beaumarchais responded to these attacks with his customary irony, calling Suard "a good man who only lacks a little wit to be a mediocre writer." An academician, Suard was supremely disdainful about the popular, even vulgar, success of *Figaro*; as he put in an anonymous letter: "The name of Figaro has become immortal in people's mouths, like that of Tartuffe in the mouths of high society. But the latter is confined to designating a hypocrite, while the former applies to all kinds of bad subjects: it is even given to dogs, cats, and fiacre horses. The other day I heard a sedan chair carrier say of a dog in the street barking at passersby: 'Let's kill this lousy Figaro!' "

This was too much, and with righteous anger Beaumarchais wrote a letter of protest to the editors of the *Journal*. Carried away by passion, he seems to have lost control of his pen and allowed himself to make unfortunate inferences: "Messieurs, what is your purpose in publishing these foolish remarks? When I had to vanquish lions and tigers to get my comedy produced, did you think, after its success, you could reduce me to beating the carpets against the vile night insect, like a Dutch chambermaid?" By "lions and tigers" he naturally meant the leaders of the claques who had persecuted and slandered him for three years, seething with hatred and envy, to prevent the performances, and all those who had torn his work and his character to shreds. As for "vile night insect," he was clearly referring to Jean-Baptiste Suard: this reedy man, always dressed in black, recognized himself in this phrase. Pierre-Augustin's remark appeared so insulting that Guidi, the royal censor of the paper, initially refused to let it pass, but an order higher up forced him to publish it: "Beaumarchais is spiking himself, and we have to let him do it."

On the morning of March 6, 1785, the *Journal de Paris* containing Beaumarchais's reply was sent to the Comte de Provence, the king's other brother, who had strong ties to Suard and was another ferocious opponent of *The Marriage of Figaro*. He had even helped the academician write the incriminating letter, as Beaumarchais certainly suspected; otherwise he would never have been so imprudent. Suard in his resentment now tried to make it seem as if Beaumarchais were insulting His Highness: "Has this man not been insolent enough? Treating an august person in that manner!" Not unhappy to see Beaumarchais fall into the trap, the Comte went to the king, where he found the Comte d'Artois, Beaumarchais's strong friend (and future Charles X), who had no part in this base intrigue. "Is there something new here?" Louis XVI asked the Compte de Provence. "Yes, Sire, there is something new in the *Journal de Paris*. The impudent Beaumarchais insults you in a signed letter. Here, listen, these words, 'lions and tigers' . . . !" Piqued by the triumph of a comedy that had been performed against his will, scandalized by Figaro's tirades against the aristocracy, worried about the possible political fallout of a subversive work, and warned on all sides against its author, Louis XVI did not doubt for an instant that these insults were aimed at him in particular. He reacted, not as a lion or tiger, but as an angry sheep. On the spot he ordered Beaumarchais arrested and conducted—not to some noble fortress like the Bastille, nor to the donjon of Vincennes (which Diderot had honored with a stay but which had just been closed), nor to the For-l'Évêque (which Pierre-Augustin had already seen from the inside), nor to any other prison of state—but to Saint-Lazare, a house of correction for depraved young men. Louis XVI thus added an affront to the severity of the punishment. Since the king had been playing cards when his brother came in, he wrote these angry words on the back of the seven of spades: "Beaumarchais to Saint-Lazare."

The police lieutenant Lenoir received the card at two o'clock in the afternoon. Recognizing the king's writing, he was astonished at this unusual procedure; he flew to Versailles to obtain an official confirmation. Meanwhile, the king confirmed his decision to the Baron de Breteuil in more or less these terms: "As soon as the letter is received, you will give the order to lead Sieur de Beaumarchais to Saint-Lazare. This man has become too insolent by far; he is a badly brought up boy who must be taught a lesson." Returning to Paris at nine o'clock at night, Lenoir asked Commissioner Chénon, who had ties to Beaumarchais, to execute His Majesty's order. An hour later the honest functionary and a police inspector went to his friend's house in Rue Vieille-du-Temple. Beaumarchais was dining *en famille*, with Marie-Thérèse; his editor Nicolas Ruault and his wife; Gudin; M. de Serionne; and Abbé Sabatier, counselor to the parlement. They were all still at table when the evidently embarrassed Chénon asked Beaumarchais for a tête-à-tête and then gave him the lettre de cachet; when he went to put his seal on the safe Beaumarchais said the measure would prevent him from meeting his financial deadlines and would hurt his creditors. Consulted on the spot, Lenoir dispensed the commissioner from taking this formal measure. After about an hour the master of the house excused himself from his guests, asked his "housekeeper" to prepare his sleeping cap, two shirts, and a dressing gown, and left with his visitor. "I will not sleep at home this night, by order of the king," he told her.

Led under escort to Saint-Lazare, Beaumarchais entered this juvenile detention house—so feared by wayward adolescents that merely threatening them with it was sufficient to correct their behavior. According to an editor of *Politique Errant*, he was lodged not in an individual room but in the dormitory amid "lost children," obliged to eat his meals with them in the refectory, to read from scripture, to go to mass and make confession, and so on. But Gudin's testimony contradicts the editor:

> In informing us of the place where Beaumarchais was detained, we were told that courtesies were taken for him that were unheard of in this desolate place. He had found a great fire and good bed in the room, a servant to wait on him, an antechamber he could use. M. Lenoir, lieutenant of police, came less to interrogate him than to console him, for he posed no questions. He even deigned to take charge of three letters that the prisoner had written, one to the Minister, the other to the Marquis de Lafayette, and the third to Madame de Beaumarchais.

In the early hours of Tuesday, March 8, 1785, rumors of the arrest spread across Paris. People at first refused to believe it. It had been so often announced and then denied! But as the day wore on, the evidence had to be acknowledged: Beaumarchais was indeed detained at Saint-Lazare. In a few hours the news had toured the capital, producing in turn incredulity, stupefaction, indignation, and finally anger. It was a powder keg. In all public places—at the Palais-Royal, on the boulevards, and in the faubourgs—people gathered to talk about the event, as if it were a naval battle or the disgrace of a minister. In bourgeois homes, in artisans' dwellings, in aristocratic salons, no other topic was discussed. At Versailles people at first laughed. Beaumarchais at Saint-Lazare, like a street urchin—how funny! Would he get a spanking twice a day, they asked, as was the custom there? It seems that the authorities no longer used this infamous practice.

Nonetheless the next day the songsters and cartoonists made the rounds, scoffing at the misfortunes of M. Figaro and especially at the spanking. He never received a spanking, and yet it went into legend, thanks to the Comte de Provence, due to the patronage of the Suard coterie; his many enemies, envious and jealous, were overjoyed by his humiliation.

Beaumarchais's detractors produced not only songs and epigrams, but also satirical prints, even more vicious, representing the (fictional) scene of the flagellation. In one of them the police commissioner presents the order of the king to the director of the Lazarists, while the condemned man "appears modestly dressed and bent over." Three brothers of the monastery, armed with whips and canes, escort him; his pants are at his heels and his bottom is exposed, ready to receive the strap. The caption says: "Monsieur, the general has said that we should administer a spanking and, if you resist, that we should double it." Another caricature shows Beaumarchais, ass in the air, head hidden between the legs of a young Lazarist with cherubic features who is getting ready to beat him with a fistful of sticks. On the right the Countess Almaviva witnesses the scene, her eyes fixed on the patient's behind; at her side, Chérubin hides his face with one hand and lifts the other to heaven.

Beaumarchais never received the cane, there or anywhere else. But the public believed it; song and image alike popularized the scene, which thereafter stuck to him like the most caustic wound his pride had ever suffered. Far from inspiring compassion for him, this punishment had the sad effect of placing those who laughed on the side of his enemies. He would never forget it. No future reparation could ever erase Saint-Lazare. A stay in the Bastille or some other state prison would have been less infamous and even flattering, since many men of letters (including illustrious ones) had inhabited these prisons—there was nothing vexing about figuring on the list. But a penitentiary for juvenile delinquents who were thrashed by monks— nothing could have been more humiliating! It would leave deeper traces on its victim's heart than anyone would have thought.

Michelet's *Histoire de France* states that "henceforward he did not laugh; the blow from Louis XVI took away his laughter forever."

What crime had Pierre-Augustin committed to have deserved such severe punishment? Today most agree that his letter to the *Journal de Paris* was only a pretext. A more serious reason was the satiric verses he had let fly against the Archbishop of Paris, who forbade his diocesans to see *The Marriage of Figaro* (but did permit them to eat eggs during Lent). This innocent banter had profoundly shocked His Majesty. Louis received the archbishop's complaint piously, as a son of the Church, but he was too debonair to be ruthless. Beaumarchais's insolence, his very person, had always inspired a kind of muted irritation, until then without repercussion, but the affair of the newspaper, thin as it was, exasperated him: it was the straw that broke the camel's back. This "amuser" had too long teased the powerful and divided the court between partisans and adversaries; too long had he mocked the established order; too long had he involved public opinion in his ordeals and publicly denounced arbitrary power. Had he not gone so far as to shout down the aristocracy, scorn privileges, offend religion, and scoff at the government? And in the theater! He had to be taught a lesson.

But Beaumarchais was a man whose fame extended to all the capitals of Europe; he was admired in France as one of the most brilliant writers of his generation and enjoyed relationships with men highly placed in the worlds of finance, politics, and diplomacy. To treat such a man like a depraved youth was to dishonor the king's own power. To throw into the Saint-Lazare the author of *The Marriage of Figaro*, the editor of Voltaire, the secret agent of the King of France, the founder of the Society of Authors, the defender of American independence—this was a blunder by the French monarchy.

Public opinion saw this attack on individual freedom as something more serious than a simple matter of censoring caricatures or satiric songs. Indignant about the pettiness of the royal reaction, people denounced the perverse effects of power uncontrolled by laws, and they began to be afraid. If Beaumarchais had undergone this punishment despite his celebrity, his talents, and his services, then anyone might be sacrificed to the pleasure of the prince. No monarch was less tempted by despotism than Louis XVI, but like all weak people, he was sometimes seized by brusque attacks of authoritarianism. His bad humor, although fleeting, had unhappy consequences for the designated victims, but in the case of Beaumarchais, it would prove disastrous for the sovereign—a boomerang effect. Very quickly the affair took on a political character, and most contemporaries stressed its gravity.

By sending Beaumarchais to Saint-Lazare, Louis XVI had intended to win the sympathy of those who were laughing, and at first he seemed to succeed. The flagellation had an enormous comic success: copies of the print sold like hotcakes. The public amuser was being caned like an urchin! But two days after its release, the police banned its sale. Suddenly the public became aware that this saucy devil whose ass was offered to the priest was in fact themselves; that Figaro incarnated the people. And so Parisians stopped laughing and took the victim's part; through him they felt humiliated, betrayed, and threatened in their fundamental liberties. We are in March 1785. Five months later the Affair of the Diamond Necklace broke out, another, more tragic farce that would resonate like an amplified echo of this one. Figaro in Saint-Lazare heralds the consequent imprisonment of Cardinal de Rohan in the Bastille. Beaumarchais would be told of the incarceration of the prelate in these words: "Your ridiculous adventure has just been buried under a red cap." If the two affairs were not at the same level, they posed the same issues.

On Sunday, March 13, at midnight, on the king's order, Beaumarchais left Saint-Lazare after five days in detention. His forced stay had not only humiliated him as a citizen and a private man; it delivered the coup de grâce to his credit as a businessman. While it may not have been the cause of his new money difficulties, it contributed to aggravating them. The day after his liberation Beaumarchais begged Calonne, the comptroller-general of finances, to advance him 50,000 écus (or 150,000 livres) on the indemnities that he was owed for the requisitioning of his merchant fleet in 1778 and 1779. He returned to the offensive on September 1, then on December 30, noting bitterly: "Since the wrath of the crown struck my person and my credit, buried in retreat, I have swallowed my losses, and have lived only with sources of grief. One of the most painful for me is the horrible ingratitude of these Americans I have so well served." In the same letter he told the minister of his intention to go to the United States to plead his case: "Thus with my fortune and the fruit of all my labors reduced to interminable accounts owing by America and debts due in Europe, I am forced to expatriate myself for a while and make the painful voyage to the other continent." And he concluded on these disillusioned terms: "My bad health leaves me little hope of seeing my country again after my embarkation, since seasickness has always put me close to death even during the very short trip from France to England." In fact Beaumarchais had no intention of crossing the Atlantic (two months of navigation would have been intolerable even to someone less ocean-phobic than he); his remark about nausea had no other purpose than to make his correspondent feel pity. But it did not produce the desired effect. Twelve days later he issued a new call for help: "Still nothing!" Pierre-Augustin decided to go directly to the king. After all, it was because of him that he was in this horrible mess. Here is his letter:

> Sire,
>
> Too unhappy to ask for favors, from the depth of the retreat I am living since the wrath of the King struck me, I ask of Your Majesty only the rigorous justice I am refused in person. A creditor of the King for eight years, after having sacrificed everything for his service, I am going to perish dishonored if he does not order my legitimate reimbursement. Sire, all that is seriously due me, under the laws of commerce and honor, has been harshly refused me.
>
> May I add, Sire, that by the instigation of my enemies, on the sole suspicion of a fault that I was far from committing, in taking away my freedom you have destroyed my repose, my esteem, and my credit. From that moment, shut up at home, I have lived with only losses and pains. The perfidious Americans, whom I so warmly served, learning of my disgrace and believing me lost in my own country, have thought they could deny me justice with impunity. They have just sent me 5,000 livres on an account of 9 million that they owe me. I must perish!
>
> But if, for lack of help, I miss the sacred engagements of a businessman, and am forced to show publicly the reasons why to

all the commercial cities of Europe, then my work for the last fifteen years, the letters to ministers and generals, the prime statesmen who have sustained me in my efforts, will all attest to my country that I was worthy of a better fate. And the King, better informed, will perhaps regret (in his goodness) having reduced to despair a man of honor who has always encouraged patriotism, commerce, and the arts by his example: who has never ceased being a good Frenchman, a laborious citizen, and a very patient creditor and faithful subject of Your Majesty.

Caron de Beaumarchais

Not a word came in reply, not the least sign of encouragement. Meanwhile the Baron de Sainte-James, one of the richest bankers of the time, wanted to loan him 350,000 livres for a short period; Beaumarchais would have to reimburse the loan very soon. Hence this distressed appeal to Calonne of January 27, 1786: "It is a sick man in agony who asks the King for justice, crying out for pity!" Fifteen days later, on February 12, Beaumarchais finally received the indemnity so long awaited, fixed at 800,000 livres "to settle all accounts." If one adds this sum to the first two payments (905,400 livres and then 570,627, paid three months before the first performance of *The Marriage of Figaro*), one reaches a total of 2,276,027 livres. Had it arrived forty-eight hours later, Beaumarchais would have faced bankruptcy. He also received from Calonne "an infinitely honorable letter by which this minister declares that the services rendered to the state in the last war having been put before the eyes of the king, His Majesty has charged him to tell him of his satisfaction and assure him he will seize with pleasure occasions to give him the marks of his benevolence."

Another moral compensation that Beaumarchais received must have gone right to his heart, for it emanated spontaneously from the public. At the Comédie-Française, where *The Marriage of Figaro* was still pursuing its brilliant career, the parterre applauded at the famous words of the monologue: "When they see the spirit will not bend, they persecute it simply from vindictiveness." The seventy-second performance attracted no less of an audience than the premiere— even the presence of several ministers. Were they expressing their repentance?

Knowing that the offended party was particularly sensitive about his amour propre, the court deployed the red carpet: on August 19, 1785, *The Barber of Seville* was performed in the queen's little theater at the Petit-Trianon. Marie-Antoinette herself played the role of Rosine, while the Comte d'Artois played Figaro, the Comte de Vaudreuil played Almaviva, the Duc de Guich interpreted Bartholo, and the bailiff of Crussol played Bazile. As a notable honor, the author was invited to join the small circle of intimates who watched. He could not have received a more delicate or flattering reparation for the affront he had suffered. For this occasion he consented to leave his self-imposed retreat, which had embarrassed the king and the Baron de Breteuil. The voluntary prisoner stopped sulking: no more did he talk of going into exile. The queen's charm offensive had succeeded.

No doubt he would have joyfully accepted the Order of Cincinnatus, established by George Washington in 1783 to recompense the heroes of the War of Independence, but unfortunately, it was not bestowed on him. On May 10, 1785, during the general assembly of the Cincinnati to designate future members, eleven Frenchmen were chosen, among whom were the Maréchal-Prince de Beauvau and his wife; the Duc d'Harcourt; the Duc de La Rochefoucauld-Liancourt; the Comtesse d'Houdetot; the Comte de Jarnac; the Marquis de Condorcet; and others. A New Haven journalist commented acidly:

> The ridiculous thing about this list is that there is not one of these persons who is known to us other than by name, and all these titles (marshal, prince, duke, marquis, count), far from being titles of adoption, ought to be titles of exclusion, unless they have really done services. But the enormous ingratitude is in having preferred these sumptuous titles to our real benefactors, to Chaumont, Monthieu, Beaumarchais, and other principal businessmen of Bordeaux, Nantes, and other ports of France, who were the first and true authors of our glory and our freedom by furnishing us with help and with weapons to fight the British and free us from their tyranny.

Beaumarchais was assuredly disappointed, more than was understood at the time and more than has been said later. It would have cost the American authorities nothing to receive him into the glorious legion. Had he not earned it more than others? Perhaps they feared that recognizing his services would also mean recognizing the debt of several millions. He could at least console himself that he had emerged once more the victor in a rude combat—and against what enemies! Decidedly, age does not seem to have harmed him.

Twenty-One

THE (THIRD) MARRIAGE
OF FIGARO

Even in the most exalted circles, women receive only the most contemptible treatment, trapped with the appearance of respect and love into a slavery that's all too real! Treated as children in property, punished as adults for our faults.
—*Marceline, in* **The Marriage of Figaro**

At fifty-four, Beaumarchais still fought like a young man. But then another duelist—a redoubtable and mercenary man, a gallows bird—challenged him. He was called Honoré Gabriel Riqueti, the Comte de Mirabeau; at thirty-five, he had spent seven years in prison.

When Mirabeau came to see Beaumarchais, he was still known only for his love affairs, his trials, his debts, and his *Essay on Despotism*. The conversation, as one might imagine, was lively, animated, witty. As he took his leave, Mirabeau, with the lightness that belongs only to cadgers of quality, asked his host to lend him 12,000 francs. With a big smile Beaumarchais refused. Mirabeau protested, "But it would be easy for you to lend me this sum." "No doubt," Beaumarchais replied, "but since I would have to quarrel with you when repayment was due, I would like it to be today, saving myself the twelve thousand." Mirabeau soon took revenge. A fire pump would furnish the occasion.

In 1769 the Chevalier d'Auxiron had proposed that the government provide Paris with water through the establishment of a pumping engine, a steam machine such as he had seen working in England. The government refused. In 1777 two skilled mechanics from Vizille, the Périer brothers, obtained an authorization to build a fire pump that would take up water from the Seine and fill a reservoir on the Chaillot hill, so as to distribute running water to the various quarters of the capital. Technically the enterprise was so well conceived that the pump would work until the Second Empire, but as they did not have the necessary funds to realize the project, the Périer brothers founded the following year a company that took the name Compagnie des Eaux de Paris.

The former watchmaker Caron always had a weakness for new technologies; this passion induced him to finance the Périer brothers' steam pump. Later he would be interested in Baron Scott's "aeronautical ship" and the digging of a canal in Nicaragua; since the businessman was often lurking inside the mechanic in the industrial era, Beaumarchais was lying in wait for lucrative operations. He soon became one of the principal sponsors and administrators of the water enterprise. In this capacity he wrote the prospectus for subscriptions, in which he insisted on the public interest of such a project. *Patrie, Progrès, Profit* (Country, Progress, Profit) could have been his motto. The first pump, supplied in 1779 by the British mechanic James Watt, was installed in 1781 on the Chaillot hill, and the second would be inaugurated in 1788 at Gros Caillou.

The Compagnie des Eaux had a meteoric start; its launch coincided with the establishment of fire insurance, which already existed in England; the company obtained authorization from the King's Council and quickly registered three hundred subscriptions for it. The joint stock company was taking off and seemed to have a bright future, when it came up against one of the most powerful banking groups of the era, directed by the financier Étienne Clavière. Of Swiss origin, a democratic Genevan, Clavière was linked to Mirabeau, whose talents as a writer and polemicist he appreciated. He had spent two years in London, the country of liberalism, where he absorbed the theories of the economist Adam Smith; he quickly assimilated the principles of insurance as well. Having decided to offer life, maritime, and fire insurance to France, Clavière settled in Paris in 1784. At fifty, he had enough financial capital and political support to make him one of France's three or four main economic actors. He created a bond market partially backed by the government, and when the bubble burst, he commissioned Mirabeau to sink his competitor, the Périers' water company, causing its shares to tumble. Pushed by speculators, Finance Minister Calonne tried to stop the hemorrhage and gave Beaumarchais the task of responding to the attacks of their common enemy, sure that he would crush Mirabeau with a flick of the pen.

Pierre-Augustin took up the challenge eagerly—he had a large portfolio of shares. Moreover, the boasting of this show-off from the provinces annoyed him—it was time to teach him a lesson. The prospect of a duel between these two jousters piqued the public's curiosity. The combat was very unequal: Beaumarchais had the advantage of fortune, celebrity, and success, while Mirabeau was of noble birth and family name, but his adventures had been painful, and clandestine writings of debatable taste did not help his bad reputation. People expected from Beaumarchais a fireworks of witticisms and caustic insults, but instead he delivered a catalog of sagely aligned arguments, with considerations taken from accounting, mechanics, and hydrology that would be worthy of any minister of urban development. The letter he wrote to the water board administrators discusses the price of barrels of water per day, the rates of annual subscription, and the costs of mains and conduits in wood and iron; the amount of water it took to wash the streets, for emergency pipes in case of fires, and for distribution in fountains; the time it took the water carriers to supply their recipients, and so on. All this data was solidly supported by columns of figures. Beaumarchais did not entirely efface himself behind the technocrat; he slipped into a panegyric on the future of indoor plumbing, a facile pun typical of the pamphleteering style. "In thirty years, everyone will laugh at the critics of our day, as today we laugh at the critics of those days. When they were bitter, we called them *Philippics*. Perhaps one day, some bad joker will call today's by the pretty name of '*Mirabelles*' (plums) from the Comte de Mirabeau, *qui mirabilia fecit*."

This innocent joke might have simply amused the interested party, but Beaumarchais followed it by telling harsh truths about Mirabeau's venality and his collusion with the bankers whose servile instrument he was. Enraged, Mirabeau replied with a hail of insults bordering on hatred. His irony was heavy and did not miss its target. Mirabeau tried to kill his adversary with words.

After this violent assault, the author of *The Marriage of Figaro* remained voiceless. For the first time in his life, he refused to respond. Was it laziness? The effect of aging? Had he made a prudent retreat? Today the silence that gravely harmed his reputation remains unexplained. Whatever the reason for it, Beaumarchais's silence was interpreted as a sign of weakness: he was thought to be vulnerable, which was enough to encourage new adversaries to confront him. Mirabeau's first memo against the Périer brothers had caused irreparable damage to the company; the second was the coup de grâce. In 1788 the bankrupt company was taken over by the city.*

Something had decidedly changed with Pierre-Augustin. Had these last years taught him wisdom? Certainly they had not spared him; his business worries and harassing struggles had been compounded by emotional duress. In 1782 the Marquis d'Argenson, whose château he had visited when he went to the Atlantic ports, died. Two years later, in May 1784, his young protégé, Théveneau de Francy, succumbed to lung disease. Around the same time he lost two of his nephews, sons of his sister in Spain, in their prime: a cruel loss, given his attachment to his relatives.

His favorite sister, Julie, still a spinster and increasingly turning to religion, begged him to regularize his situation with Marie-Thérèse and give Eugénie, now almost seven years old, a father. Pierre-Augustin had thought of it many times. Once in August 1782 he had gathered his family members and soberly confessed to all his escapades, adding that he sincerely repented the scandalous life he had led. He wanted to put an end to it, he said in conclusion, and to redeem his wrongs with honest and proper conduct. Consequently he had decided to marry his mistress, Mlle. de Willermaulaz, with whom he had been living for twelve years; he reassured his relatives that he would provide for them. "They left very edified by the vows and repentance of this famous libertine," reported the journalist to whom we owe this infor-

---

*Four years later, when Mirabeau had become famous as a Convention orator, he and Beaumarchais were reconciled.

mation. But the scene, worthy of Diderot's pen or Greuze's brush, had no consequent marriage. Had Pierre-Augustin simply given himself the pleasure of playing the scene without meaning it?

Only four years later did he seriously envisage marrying the woman he usually called his housekeeper, who deserved better than that humiliating description. No doubt this young woman's image suffered from Pierre-Augustin's renown: his genius pushed her into the shadows, and his amorous conquests relegated her to the background. But nothing justifies this oblivion. When they finally married in 1786, Marie-Thérèse de Willermaulaz was only thirty-five; she was twenty years younger than her husband. Slender, with chestnut brown hair and deep blue eyes, she was considered a beautiful woman. Gudin, who had witnessed her first meeting with the author of *The Barber of Seville*, said, "It was difficult to resist the charm of her gaze, her voice, her bearing, and her speech." Gudin, who would outlive Beaumarchais by thirteen years and publish seven volumes of his papers, remembered:

> His house was embellished with the charms of a wife of whom I would perhaps hazard a portrait here, if the mind and graces were not more easily hidden from the writer's pen than beauty from the brush and palette of the artist, and if the historian were not more suspect than the painter when he sketches something out of the ordinary. Moreover, she is still alive, occupied with the happiness of her family and consequently she does not yet belong to the domain of history. I will say only that those who knew her were not surprised that she had captivated the heart of the man who knew best how to appreciate her merit.

Marie-Thérèse was in fact a more extraordinary person than one might expect. Yes, she was a domestic woman, an excellent mother, a docile wife, suffering patiently her husband's infidelities. But her letters reveal her to be a woman who, without indulging in coquetry (which she abhorred), preferred the company of men to that of her own sex but also knew how to keep her distance. "My vivacity, my gaiety," she once told her friend Mme. Dujard, "are given to whatever people want to make of them. With young people, I strive to do my best; with thinkers, I meditate; with the madcap, I laugh till I cry; with the boring, I try to forget them if I can." As a letter writer, she is enchanting: such a variety of impressions and nuances, such a prodigious richness of colorful language and an impulsive vivacity, are not often combined in correspondence. She wrote some pages that Pierre-Augustin would certainly not have disavowed. For example, she wrote to her same friend:

> If I had at my disposition one of those aerial "velocifers," the time and the season would not stop me and you would see me in your room, as you see M . . . After having reassured you, embraced and cajoled you, I would place myself between you two, in front of your hearth, and I would make cracks quite at my ease! . . . The tongue is the only tool that can make them; the pen does not succeed. If it is blunt, the result is only flat banter; if on the contrary it is sharp, well honed, it goes galloping along, grazing one person and running down another.

She clearly took intense pleasure in writing the letters. Most were composed after the death of her husband; they give the impression of someone enjoying a new freedom that she could never have had during his lifetime. She is visibly enchanted to discover her talent for writing; dazed by the flow of thoughts rushing from her pen, she casts them without deletions into elegant and easy prose. There are felicitous turns of phrase, tender and teasing terms, fantastic ideas, and a mocking tone—in short, all the marks of an intelligent, sensitive, loving, and skeptical woman, careful never to be duped. Her friends nicknamed her "the new Madame de Sévigné,"* the critics publicly praised her style, and her letters circulated in salons. The literary critic La Harpe devoted a paragraph to the gracefulness of her prose. She writes to her friend, "Twenty women in my place would be puffed up to find themselves in the work of a famous man intended for posterity. Ah well, my sweet, I had forgotten it so well that I was quite taken aback when you spoke of it, because I know no more about what he said about me than what I heard at your house.

*Mme. de Sévigné's correspondence is a jewel of seventeenth-century literature.

There is not much feminine amour propre here." With her intimates, she speaks without reserve or constraint and tries "to translate [my] soul to their eyes, to make them read it there as [I] do myself." But to do that, she adds, "you have to have tranquility, contemplation, solitude—and I daresay, mystery."

Perhaps this rich and delicate soul remained unknown to Pierre-Augustin. Had he discerned her fantasy, humor, caprice, and critical sense? Did he ever know to what extent she despised convention, how far her thoughts ranged, her aversion to the false and sanctimonious? How could he have missed her many traits that should have made him closer to her? Why did he not consider as a kindred spirit this nature so full of enthusiasm, resources, and gaiety? Like Figaro, she regarded boredom as her principal enemy and every weapon was used to combat it. "It is not your situation that bores you," she wrote to Mme. Dujard. "It is your mind and your imagination that are languishing for want of pasturage. Take a gamble, even be a devotee if you can. There is nothing more distressing than boredom!" Last but not least, Marie-Thérèse gave to the only man in her life a tenderness that survived his death. The humiliations that she had suffered all those years did not change her love for Pierre-Augustin, which remained as intact as on the first day.

Such was the Suzanne that Figaro consented to take as his wife after twelve years of cohabitation. Probably he would never have done so without his daughter Eugénie, whom he adored: she had just had her ninth birthday and it was time to give her a father. On March 8, 1786, the curé of Saint-Paul blessed the union with Marie-Thérèse, who had wanted a discreet ceremony, given that for her it was simply a regularization and for him a third marriage. But she did not count on Pierre-Augustin's immoderate taste for publicity. As if he had to cry from the rooftops that he had gotten married secretly, he published in the press a letter that he had supposedly written to his wife before leaving for Kehl. This singular document testifies to a real obsession with self-promotion. In any case, this boorishness wounded the bride's delicate feelings and did nothing to enhance his own image:

> I do not want, my dear friend, to deprive you of the joyous state
> that belongs to you. You are my wife; you were previously only

the mother of my daughter. Nothing has changed in your prior state, but I desire from this moment of my first absence that you represent me honorably in my house and that you take my name that has become yours.

Embrace our daughter tenderly and make her understand, if you can, the cause of your joy. I have fulfilled all my duties to her, to you. My absence is without the bitterness that followed me on my other trips. It always seemed that an accident might kill all three of us at once; now I am calm and at peace with myself and I can die without remorse.

Do not gather our friends to celebrate this, but let each learn from you of the justice I have rendered you. Keep, I beg you, the modest air and tone that I asked as the only recompense, so that your enemies and mine do not find anything to censure in the most serious and considered act that I have done in my life.

Go see my two sisters, ask them for their good and frank friendship. They owe me this sweet and honorable deference; they owe their attachment to my daughter and her mother; and my benevolence will be proportionate to the respect that you will be shown.

Openly assume the reins of your house. May M. Gudin, my clerk, deal with you as with myself. Dress our people for my return with modesty but as you please. Give your daughter to the good priest of Saint-Paul who showed you such tender respect when he married us.

Always be what you are, my dear; honor the name you are going to bear; it is that of a man who loves you and who signs it with joy, your friend and husband—

Caron de Beaumarchais

Beaumarchais must be blamed for this shameless effort; he perpetually needed to be talked about for any reason. Indeed, he spread in the public square the most intimate acts of his life, even though his marriage was less suitable than anything for such publicity. A phrase in his letter claims our attention, however, because it expresses an unexpected awareness on his part: "Embrace our daughter tenderly and make her understand, *if you can*, the cause of your joy." For the first time the birth of their child outside marriage appears to him as a matter of scruple; he is now realizing the embarrassment of Marie-Thérèse might have felt with respect to Eugénie and is worried about its effects. A child born out of wedlock features in every single one of his theatrical pieces.

Twenty-Two

THE ADULTEROUS WOMAN

This affair, although quite particular, would suffice to convince you that everything is to be reformed in the immense system of your laws.
                                                              —*Bergasse*

On an October day in 1781 Beaumarchais was lunching at the home of the Princesse de Nassau-Siegen with many other guests, when the conversation turned to the detention of Mme. Kornman. The chronicles had been featuring this affair for weeks. The young woman, a rich orphan, had been married at fifteen to another Protestant, an Alsatian banker; now seven years later she was pregnant but also incarcerated by him for adultery, alongside prostitutes, in inhumane conditions. Moved by her story, the prince and princess appeared particularly touched by her cruel fate; they said they would help her regain her freedom; Pierre-Augustin encouraged them. They asked him to join their effort, adding that such a service would be worthy of his courage and his sensitivity. He resisted, alleging that he had never undertaken a generous action that had not brought him trouble.

Then a magistrate who was present took out of his pocket a memorandum that Mme. Kornman had composed in prison and had passed to the president of the parlement; he gave it to Beaumarchais to read. After a quick glance, the father of Figaro stood up and declared to the assembly: "Messieurs, I think as you do; this is not the writing of a nasty woman, and the husband who torments her is mistaken about her, or else nasty himself, unless there are things we do not know. Despite the interest she inspires, it would be imprudent to take action on her behalf until we are better informed."

One of her most zealous defenders then rose and held out a packet of letters from the woman's husband, dated July, August, and September 1780. M. Kornman had written them in Spa or in Paris to his presumed worst enemy, the art critic and chief magistrate of Strasbourg, Daudet de Jossan, Mme. Kornman's lover. Beaumarchais withdrew onto the terrace, read them avidly, and discovered that M. Kornman had offered his rival the most sincere friendship and the warmest confidence, not skimping on "affectionate compliments," "sincere attachments," or "inviolable sentiments." "I embrace you," he wrote to this man he suspected of criminal designs. But what jumped out at Pierre-Augustin were his incredible phrases about Mme. Kornman. "Since she does not have the experience to behave herself," he wrote from Spa, "so prevent her, dear sir, from making a major mistake." The husband was asking his wife's lover to watch over her virtue! This might be a comedy! Or else it was a ménage à trois, complete with ambiguities. In another letter, also from Spa, five days after the preceding one:

> If we could make the trip to Alsace together, it would be more gay . . . You cannot doubt the pleasure I would have in finding myself in Alsace with you. My wife can decide to be in the party— but then I must not make the trip with continual disagreement; my health will not bear it. I think I have done everything that was reasonable, but everyone has his limits; I cannot say anything more to her. She is no longer a child and it is up to her to make herself esteemed by the public and by her husband. For the rest, she will be her own mistress and do what she wants; I have never had the mania to injure the taste and inclination of anybody, finding that of all tyrannies, the most absurd is that of wanting to be loved out of duty. Apart from the fact this is impossible, one cannot command the sweetest sentiment. On this principle, one can well live together, not loving but esteeming each other, with good manners that always prove the reciprocity on the part of an

honest soul. I believe that what I require is neither unjust nor difficult, and I submit it to your reflection.

All these letters were signed "Guillaume Kornman," postmarked and
addressed to "M. Daudet de Jossan, syndic-royal of the city of Strasbourg, at la Chaussée d'Antin in Paris."

When he had read the letters, Pierre-Augustin rejoined the company and blustered:

> You can count on me, Messieurs. And Princess, I am ready to
> accompany you to M. Lenoir to plead avidly for the cause of an
> unfortunate woman punished for the crime of someone else.
> Make use of me. I know of the husband only by the disorder of
> his affairs. I have never seen his unhappy wife, but after what I
> have just read, I would think myself as cowardly as the author of
> these letters if I did not assist with all my power in the generous
> action that you want to undertake.

He accompanied the Princesse de Nassau to see police chief Lenoir,
where he pleaded heatedly the cause of "our prisoner," as he now
called her; then he went to Versailles, saw the ministers involved in
the affair, and showed them Kornman's letters to Daudet (which he
still had) and demanded justice for his presumably unseen protégée.
He obtained a commitment that the "unfortunate woman will not
give birth nor die in the house of detention where intrigue has
thrown her." He then wrote to Maître Turpin, Kornman's legal
adviser, in an urgent and imperious tone, telling him that he was now
taking Mme. Kornman under his protection; if by the king's order
she had been arrested and put into a secure place, "this order displeased him," and if his conditions were not met, he would employ
his pen and his credit to ruin her husband.

It took uncommon aplomb to oppose the royal will and to set
oneself up as an agent of justice in a public affair, without credentials
or mandate. By what right did Beaumarchais threaten a citizen with
his pen? In the name of what authority did he dare brandish his credibility as a power before which people should bow? But that was
Beaumarchais, whom we know well enough not to be astonished

either by his audacity or his outbursts. We have already seen at work in the Goëzman and La Blache trials his talent for turning public opinion to his advantage. But on those occasions he was defending his own interests; what did the Kornman affair have to do with him? His adversaries imagined that he had had a guilty liaison with the charming wife. Pure calumny, he protested: when he went on a crusade to defend her, he had never met her. He would meet her only after her exit from prison, and their correspondence never offered the least reason for suspicion: he would help her with his advice as a friend, nothing more. For the rest, she only ever called him in her letters "My dear papa": is that what a woman calls a lover?

Bergasse, another of Kornman's lawyers, told another story. "Sire de Beaumarchais frequently saw Dame Kornman before her detention," he declared in his client's name.

> I even know that there are new witnesses who depose that Sire de Beaumarchais, again before her detention, came to find her once in my home, at two o'clock in the morning, and took her away in his carriage to Nouvelle-France to a house where Sire Daudet was waiting for them. Moreover, everybody knows that Sires Beaumarchais and Daudet habitually frequent the Prince de Nassau, and many others know that Dame Kornman was frequently there. With such facts, how does Sire de Beaumarchais dare to say that he did not know Dame Kornman, even by sight, until the moment of her deliverance, and what opinion must be formed of his good faith?

This testimony is confirmed by a letter from Gudin de La Brenellerie to Marie-Thérèse in 1782, advising her to privilege love over jealousy. Reading between the lines, we may surmise that Daudet, learning that Camille Kornman had become Beaumarchais's mistress, had revealed it to Marie-Thérèse—not so much to make her suffer (she was used to infidelity) as to cause difficulties for his rival. One thing is certain: Beaumarchais was indeed the lover of the beautiful Camille, as we know from one of his closest friends, a man whom he esteemed so much that he confided in him about his love affairs, and whose literary genius he admired. I refer to the writer Restif de La

Bretonne, who noted in his journal on February 28, 1789 (seven years later): "Was at Beaumarchais's at midday: he proposed writing two letters, as if to his wife, to make her believe that his erotic letters to La Cornman [*sic*] are not authentic; they were stolen from him. A devilish intrigue!"

Some might suppose that Beaumarchais took up the defense of Mme. Kornman because he had always loved women. He would answer them:

> And why would I blush at having loved them? I still cherish them. I once loved them for myself, for their delicious intercourse; today I love them for themselves, out of rightful recognition. The frightful men who have troubled my life! A few good-hearted women have delighted it. And should I be so ungrateful as to refuse in my old age my help to the beloved sex who made my youth so happy? Never does a woman cry than my heart feels a pang. They are alas so mistreated both by the law and by men! I have a daughter who is dear to me; she will become a woman one day; but I would die in an instant if she should not be happy! Yes, I feel that I would smother the man who would make her miserable! Here I am pouring my heart onto paper.

But this outpouring was disingenuous. If he pleaded the case of Mme. Kornman, it was not only because she was his mistress but because he took pleasure in playing on the public stage the role of the valiant knight fighting injustice and defending the oppressed.

Learning that Beaumarchais had taken up his wife's defense, Kornman rushed to Lenoir for an explanation. Why was this intriguer meddling? The police lieutenant asked Kornman to worry only about his own interests. Kornman was persuaded to set aside his resentment of Beaumarchais. But of Daudet—never! Especially since the latter continued to scheme in the shadows. Kornman then explained the situation to Maurepas: threatened by the homicidal plots of his adversary, he would already have dragged Daudet before the courts had he not feared compromising his wife and their legitimate children. Condemned to silence, he asked that Sire Daudet be at least detained. Maurepas assured him that he would order his arrest.

But Lenoir opposed this procedure: Kornman, he said, was on the point of reaching an agreement with his wife, and the arrest of Daudet risked jettisoning it. Of course, Daudet merited punishment, if only for his abuse of authority. But severely punishing someone for a liaison was no longer the custom. If one were to arrest all the men who slept with another man's wife, the prisons would soon be full! Maurepas agreed to show more leniency, and Daudet kept his freedom.

Time passed. Maurepas died at eighty years of age. But no truce between the spouses seemed forthcoming. The unfaithful woman continued to have relations not only with her lover but with Beaumarchais. Kornman complained to Lenoir, demanding once again that his wife be sent back to her family in Basel. Lenoir objected that one could not transport a future mother without her consent, and moreover that nothing would be achieved by violence.

Almost assured of her impunity, Camille then asked for a legal separation, due to her unjust detention. At the same time, on the advice of Daudet and Beaumarchais, she announced her intention to sue in Basel to have her marriage annulled and get a divorce. Daudet had an ulterior motive: by obtaining the Kornman divorce, he could make himself absolute master of the woman and of her fortune. Kornman had invested her dowry in a bank that he managed with his brother; rumor had it that Mme. Kornman, in case of divorce, could withdraw her fortune, seriously disrupting the bank's financial equilibrium. A public request for an inventory of the property of the Kornman brothers sowed panic in business circles.

On December 28, 1781, Mme. Kornman was freed to be taken to Le Page, an obstetrician. In a great scene our hero came to rescue the victim from the hands of her tormentors. Beaumarchais depicted it as pathetic and tearful:

> When she appeared at the window, I was waiting, and she cried out, "Ah, if I am not mistaken, I see M. de Beaumarchais!"
>
> "Yes, Madame, it is he whom fate makes happy by contributing to take you out of here."
>
> She was at my knees, sobbing, raising her arms to heaven, *It is you, It is you, Monsieur!* She fell to the ground in a faint.
>
> And I, almost as overcome as she, could barely help her, as I

was crying with compassion, joy, and pain. I saw it, this tableau!
I was in it myself: I will never forget it. I told her, handing her to
the doctor who would deliver the baby, as the magistrate had
ordered: "This service, Madame, is not personal. I did not know
you. But seeing your gratitude, I swear that never will an unfortunate person implore me in vain in such circumstances!"

And Beaumarchais concluded with this childish remark: "I left her,
content with myself." Curtain!

The woman who left the prison appears to have been not a tearful
victim, but a radiant young person, proud of her sin, who did not
despise the pleasures of the flesh—quite the contrary. At least this
image emerges from an open letter she supposedly addressed to her
savior the day after her liberation:

> Without you, I would have been lost, shamed, despised, and
> why? For a peccadillo that honors so many women and gives
> relief to so many husbands . . . I have been reproached for having
> taken Daudet as a lover. I could no doubt have chosen better for
> the public, but for the tête-à-tête . . . Ah! My blushing says the
> rest . . . I pardon Bergasse gaily for having exposed me to the
> light in an indecent posture; he brought me everyone's gaze by
> painting me in the aspect of a woman unfaithful to her husband,
> which has only increased the number of both my adorers and my
> slaves.

Obviously dear Camille would clearly never have had the audacity
to publish such a statement, and one must attribute this epistolary
libel to her husband's "anonymous lawyers." The ambitious young
Bergasse was going to use this sordid case to make his reputation.

For five years following this theatrical coup, Kornman tried a hundred times to reach an accommodation with his wife, less out of sentiment than self-interest, and a hundred times he failed. On her side,
Camille pushed her suit for a separation of goods, for her husband's
business affairs were deteriorating. Its repayment deadlines unmet,
his bank was soon in bankruptcy. Concerned to save her dowry from
the debacle, Mme. Kornman turned to her savior, who would not

refuse her his further services, and so Beaumarchais was obliged to undertake proceedings against the banker.

Kornman was surrounded by the antiestablishment swells of the day, men from various backgrounds who would soon play a role in the revolutionary drama: Pétion, Brissot, Robespierre, and others who simultaneously aspired to nobility and pretended to equality. Lafayette paraded at Kornman's home his young republican glory, haloed with American laurels. Duval d'Eprémesnil dreamed of de-Bourbonizing France (his term) in favor of a parliament; the journalists Jean-Louis Carr and Antonio-Joseph Gorsas took notes for the next day's chronicle. Nicolas Bergasse, Kornman's lawyer, client, and lodger, a partisan of constitutional monarchy, pedantically spoke in truisms solidly built on the firm soil of principles: his ideas were the kind that were taught but not debated. Bergasse transformed everything, as if by magic, into a political subject—and he managed to politicize Camille Kornman's sleeping around. In this singular period of French history, any act of private life, even the caprices of an unfaithful woman, was grist for the national attention. With its rampant ideologies and its fixed objects of hatred, the year 1788 seemed like the night before a battle, the interminable wait before an assault —a kind of "phony revolution," analogous to a "phony war."

Returning to our adulterous spouse: she was a miserable sinner to some and a martyr to conjugal tyranny to others. The lawyer Bergasse saw an opportunity to make a name for himself by seeming to help a friend. Himself desperately in love with Mme. Kornman, who curtly rejected him, Bergasse's thirst for vengeance doubled when he learned that Beaumarchais, his fortunate rival for her heart, had taken her to the obstetrician. The lawyer thought at first that the simplest thing would be to obtain a second lettre de cachet: it would defend Kornman without scandal, while reserving the possibility of a future reconciliation. But to use an arbitrary act would go against the principles he had tirelessly propagated in speech and writing. No, he had to find another way—something that did not mean running to the police or using force against those defending criminals. He had to demand justice by making a public accusation of adultery against Mme. Kornman. Not only would this procedure have the guaranteed approval of the public, but it would compromise all the protectors of the unfaithful wife, who would now be cast as accomplices. And what accomplices! The Prince de Nassau-Siegen was a corrupt and debt-ridden aristocrat who thought he was allowed to play with the virtue of women. Daudet de Jossan was a plotter and scoundrel, without beliefs or respect for the law, living off the prince as his confidence man. And the "frightful blackguard" Beaumarchais, then at the height of his glory—the incarnation of delinquent intelligence, a master at flattering vice, and a genius for those who needed to procure license and those who allowed it—would be denounced as the kingpin of an abominable plot against all laws divine and human. Finally, there was Lenoir, expert at playing a double game and at trafficking in influence, always prompt to confuse his authority with arbitrary power, and who was also suspected of being the lover of the adulteress.

On the advice of Bergasse, Kornman lodged criminal complaints at the Châtelet court: one for adultery against his wife, and the other for defamation and complicity in adultery against Daudet, Beaumarchais, and Lenoir. He did not do so gladly: bringing his conjugal misadventure before the courts meant giving up the secrecy surrounding it and exposing himself to publicly playing the cuckold. But what did that matter, if he won a victory? Naturally, he asked Bergasse to take the case and was accepted with enthusiasm. Considering the personalities involved, Bergasse thought, this trial should win him fame as well as a forum to spread his ideas. The heart of Bergasse's strategy was to use a vulgar story of cuckoldry to publicize his political views. In the debate that was now launched, the unhappy Kornman spouses would become accessories, almost secondary figures, in an affair of law and the state.

Once the battle was joined, the pamphlets flew with unaccustomed furor, at least from Bergasse, who called Beaumarchais an "imposter," a "monster," a "corrupter," "an insipid compiler of obscure libels," and "the excrement of literature and taste." Read one of his vehement prosopopeias:

> I know your whole life, and it is execrable! Ambitious for any
> kind of success, you did not find in yourself, in your natural abil-
> ity, any resource to succeed, since you are audacious, vain, and
> indifferent to the means you had to employ, because you know

neither pity nor the deep feeling of justice that it breeds. And so
you used in turn intrigue, baseness, lies, calumnies, and assaults
to lift yourself to the degree of reputation, wealth, and power
you have reached. And now you will have to descend.

Not content with denouncing Beaumarchais as "a man whose sacrile-
gious existence attests flagrantly to the degree of depravity we have
reached," he ranted, "You sweat crime." Undoubtedly Beaumarchais's silence during the conflict with Mirabeau encouraged Bergasse to increase his virulence; he admitted as much in one of his
memos, calling the author of *The Marriage of Figaro* "a man who,
publicly dragged through the mud by a famous writer whom he had
the impudence to insult, has not dared to confront him and who by
his guilty silence has justified the opprobrium that covers him."

If the public followed the pamphlet war with bated breath, its
interest was reinforced by the questions of morality and politics into
which Bergasse folded the story of the adultery. After a few weeks
this petty private conflict became a war over despotism; the lawyer
made himself into a militant, and his memoranda increasingly resembled manifestoes. Lenoir's abuse of authority supplied him with good
pretexts to criticize the functioning of the police, whom he blamed
for instilling a climate of terror and suspicion.

All the major questions that agitated public opinion found echoes
in the Kornman affair. The consensus was that Bergasse was winning—indeed, to arouse the crowd in favor of a deceived husband, in
whatever circumstances, should have been almost impossible! Along
with championing the moral cause, he was defending public freedom,
and doing so with a fieriness, conviction, and vehemence unequaled
by his opponents, which won him massive adherence. All those
opposed to tyranny applauded his philippics, and his popularity
reached a sort of apogee.

After the king restored the parlements (the regional courts he had
exiled) the hearings for the Kornman trial could begin in December
of 1788; the raucous audience witnessed a legal cast who would all
play roles in the coming Revolution. By a verdict on April 2, 1789,
the criminal chamber rejected Kornman's complaint against his wife
and Daudet for adultery. It condemned him to restore her dowry,

acquitted Beaumarchais and the Prince de Nassau of complicity, and quashed the complaint against former police chief Lenoir. It ordered the suppression of Bergasse and Kornman's pamphlets as "false, injurious and calumnious," forbidding them to publish any more, "under the pertinent penalties"; it fined them a thousand livres in damages due to Beaumarchais and the prince, as well as court costs.

When this judgment was rendered, such protests erupted in the courtroom that the president was twice forced to interrupt the reading. Public opinion, at first favorable to Beaumarchais, had been so won over by the political arguments of his adversary that it had ended up sympathetic to Kornman and wishing him victory. By contrast, the author of *The Marriage of Figaro* was subjected to a growing hostility that would be transformed into a real hatred. He was assailed each day by vicious anonymous letters and was once attacked in the street; he could not even leave his home unless armed and accompanied. In Strasbourg, former fiefdom of Guillaume Kornman, he was even said to be involved in an attempt to assassinate the latter, with the complicity of Daudet.

How can we explain this abrupt turnaround? Despite his former tirades against privilege, Beaumarchais now passed as a courtier. Protected by the queen, well thought of by ministers, sought after by the nobility, and showered with gold, he had little in common with those victims of arbitrary power whose fate Bergasse deplored. Was he not one of those recently ennobled arrivistes whom the aristocracy scorned as intruders, and whom the Third Estate repulsed as vain ingrates, but who had left their own class behind, never to return? Of course, he too condemned injustice and the arrogance of the nobility. Quite recently, in his opera *Tarare*, he had advocated new ideas. But his personal situation undermined his formal positions on all counts, and the distance between the character of Figaro and his inventor was now very great, at least as regards fortune, and his very credibility suffered on that account. Beaumarchais was never able to place himself under a banner (and never wanted to) and therefore he remained unclassifiable. At a moment when each Frenchman was summoned to choose his camp, this was an unforgivable fault.

Far from representing public opinion, Beaumarchais now symbolized everything it execrated. It didn't help him to invoke his past, for every argument was drawn against him. No one believed that this incorrigible libertine was disinterested in Mme. Kornman, the women less than the men. And if he had succeeded in lifting the lettre de cachet, it was for the benefit of an aristocrat (Daudet de Jossan) against a commoner and because his friends at court could refuse him nothing. Finally, if he had won his lawsuit, it was no doubt because he had paid off the judges. A clever man, once adulated for his witticisms and sharp rejoinders, Beaumarchais had never possessed the fiber of an orator.

For some time and especially as the Estates General approached, a curious mutation was taking place in public opinion: the writer was becoming suspect, the philosopher was being replaced by the legislator, speaking was supplanting writing, and journalists and orators shared popular favor. Lofty dogmas fired people's brains; the person who talked loudest was taken as the spokesman of the multitude. High-spirited rhetoric triumphed in the newspapers and brochures, where formerly reigned the dry arguments of literature and the bar. In the great name of freedom, every disappointed ambition sought vengeance. Nothing was more natural or sweet than to justify one's passion by theory, to believe oneself a patriot, to envelop the interests of one's own career in the general political interest. Bergasse incarnated to perfection this mob spirit, but he was more dangerous than others, for he carried the magistery of words. Thus the verdict of April 1789 should be interpreted as one of the last victories of monarchical power over the "founders of liberty." It is not coincidental that this victory seemed like that of a courtesan and a notorious libertine defeating the defenders of virtue. Nevertheless, Beaumarchais and his allies welcomed the verdict with relief. As for Bergasse, rejoicing at the public reaction in his favor, he tried to appeal the judgment by alleging that the fourteen councilors who had presided, led by the aristocratic young attorney general whose eloquent summing up for the prosecution had influenced their decision, had deliberated under constraints and had not been impartial. Bergasse's friends even claimed that his adversary had bought the court. The campaign was long but resulted in no further review.

Beaumarchais had won his case in the court of law, but this time he had lost in the court of public opinion—and despite himself, he made Bergasse's fortune. Thanks to this affair, and his dazzling reputation as an orator and political writer, Bergasse won election to the Estates General in Lyons. He ultimately proved to be one of the guarantors of the old order. Sitting in the center right, linked to the monarchical party, Bergasse would stop coming to the Assembly after his transfer to Paris and would publish pamphlets against the Constitution of 1791; he barely escaped the Terror.

Twenty-Three

"A LYRIC MONSTER"

The least malicious ones wrote "Philosophy even in the Opera!
This writer is mocking us!" They laughed in my face, and I said
"Let's hope." —Beaumarchais, Preface to Tartare *(1790)*

On May 1, 1786, an event took place in Vienna that had almost no impact in France and that Beaumarchais seems to have ignored, but its repercussions would carry his work and his name to the ends of the earth. On that day the Burgtheater gave the first performance of *Le Nozze di Figaro*, an opera buffa by Wolfgang Amadeus Mozart with a libretto by Lorenzo Da Ponte.

Even before the German translation appeared, Beaumarchais's play circulated in manuscript copies in Viennese intellectual circles, most notably in the Masonic lodges of *Aufklärung* (Enlightenment) tendencies. It was spread by illustrious "brothers," such as Ignaz von Born, the mineralogist, and Josef von Sonnenfels, Mozart's friend and inspirer of the "Viennese Jacobins." Like many of his fellow citizens Mozart knew French sufficiently well to have read *Figaro* in the original text.

On February 2, 1785, a Viennese newspaper reported that Johann Rautenstrauch had translated Beaumarchais's comedy "with the most extreme rapidity" (two months after the French edition!) and announced its production in German at the Kärntnertortheater. Unfortunately, this tour de force never happened; although Joseph II had

authorized its publication, he formally opposed any public performance. And so Mozart decided to make the play into an opera.

This was not the first time he had set a Beaumarchais work to
music. In 1778 he had composed twelve variations for piano in E flat
major on the air "I am Lindor" (K. 354); Antoine-Laurent Baudron
had written the air to accompany the words of Almaviva in *The Barber of Seville* when he pretends to be a young commoner to woo
Rosine. We have no way of knowing whether the two men met then,
or if they ever did; we can only say that occasions for meeting were
not lacking. No doubt Mozart often heard Beaumarchais spoken of:
when he stayed in Paris in 1764, 1766, and 1778; regarding
Goethe's *Clavigo*, successfully performed in 1774 by a cast that
included Beaumarchais; or that same year when the former agent of
the King of France was the empress's prisoner and his quarrels
with the Viennese court were reported in the chronicles. No doubt,
too, the scandal caused by *The Marriage of Figaro* in Paris, and its triumph on the stage of the Théâtre Français, had focused Mozart's
attention on the work if not on its author. Mozart also had personal
reasons for the fascination he felt when he read it. Certain letters to
his father, written before Beaumarchais's comedy, contain strange
analogies between his reactions and those of Figaro. Mozart had
written: "We are not of high extraction, nor gentlemen, nor rich, but
rather of low birth, common and poor . . . Our wealth dies with us,
since we have it in our head, and that nobody can take away from us,
unless they cut off our head—and then we need nothing else." Seven
years later Figaro echoed: "Just because you're a great nobleman,
you think you're a great genius! . . . You took the trouble to be born
and nothing else!" Mozart, who never forgot the humiliation he had
suffered in the service of the Archbishop-Prince of Salzburg, Col-
loredo, who treated him like a servant ("I did not know I was only a
valet," he wrote in 1781, "and that is what broke my neck"), rediscovered in the character of Figaro all the bitterness and desire for
revenge that he had accumulated against his old master. What a comfort to encounter a similar revolt in the writing of another, and what
joy to adopt it as his own! The deep sympathy that he felt on the spot
for Beaumarchais's play, and the fact that he himself commissioned
the libretto from Lorenzo Da Ponte, are not surprising.

Mozart and Da Ponte had met for the first time in 1783 at the home of Baron Wezlar. They got along famously and promised to work together. A Venetian, defrocked priest, libertine, and adventurer—much like Casanova, with whom he was friends—Da Ponte was chased out of Venice in 1779 for adultery. Thanks to the protection of Salieri, among others, he was later named official poet of the Imperial Theaters of Vienna. He was one of the rare authors in Austria capable of adapting Beaumarchais's comedy into Italian. Mozart had chosen this language because lovers of the lyric art wanted no other; German diction appeared too harsh for opera. Moreover, *Il Barbiere di Siviglia*, written by his friend Paisiello, had triumphed in Vienna the preceding year, and Da Ponte could count on the *Le Nozze*, which formed the sequel, winning at least as enthusiastic a reception. Once the two collaborators made an agreement, they set to work in a kind of effervescence that is marvelously expressed in the feverish tempo of the overture. "As I was writing the words, he was making the music," remembered Da Ponte, "and in six months, everything was done." Begun in October 1785, the completed opera was dated by Mozart on April 29, 1786. The premiere took place forty-eight hours later.

It took audacity to compose under the nose of the emperor an opera drawn from a play he had just banned. Happily, Mozart did not lack support. We recall that, in order to disarm the censorship of Versailles, Beaumarchais had consented to a certain number of cuts; it took more cuts to disarm the Viennese censor. Mozart and Da Ponte bowed willingly because they could not include the authorial witty asides that are woven into the dialogue of the play; the sacrifices were minor, even derisory, given that the essential spirit was preserved. If Da Ponte suppressed Figaro's long monologue in act V, he kept all his subversive force in the cavatina: "Se vuol ballare, signor contino, il chitarrino le suonerò. Se vuol venire nella mia scuola, la capriola le insegnerò." (If, my dear Count, you feel like dancing, it's I who'll call the tune. If you'll come to my school, I'll teach you how to caper.) Borrowing the cadence of a minuet, the aristocratic dance par excellence, Figaro weighs it down angrily, while the pizzicati of the chords, imitating the guitar, sharpen the sarcastic edge. For this cavatina, Mozart supplied the exact reply in the aria of the third act, entirely invented by Da Ponte, when a furious Almaviva sees that Susanna and Figaro are teaching him a cabriolet of their own fashioning: "Vedrò, mentr'io sospiro felice un servo mio? E un ben, ch' invan desio, ei posseder dovrà?" (Must I see a servant of mine made happy, while I am left to sigh? And him possess a treasure which I desire in vain?) The musical writing—with the mocking trills from the orchestra and the Count's bare aria (running through great arpeggios succeeded by the wild rhythm of vengeance)—enriches with a thousand nuances and expressive hints this duel between master and servant, between the old world and the new. Even more than Beaumarchais's comedy, Mozart's opera announced the great social fractures to come.

In addition to class struggle, the composer also preserved—especially—the rivalry of hearts, the ambiguity of meaning, the games of love, and their primal excitement. The great Amadeus did not betray Beaumarchais's intentions. His music expresses so well all the nuances that it seems sometimes to transcend them; it is as if the musician took over from the poet just at the moment when the latter reached the frontier of verbal communication. Mozart took over Beaumarchais's intention and led it beyond what could be spoken, to those regions of the soul where language loses all power, which singing alone proves capable of expression.

The Marriage of Figaro would not be performed at the Opéra of Paris until the spring of 1793, in the middle of the Terror; even then it would run for five performances only, the first under the title of *Figaro*, and the following ones as *The Marriage of Figaro*. In that context, the event did not seem very important; nor was the name Mozart (as *Mansard, Mozard,* or *Mozzart*) well known enough to attract crowds. Invited to the premiere, Beaumarchais did not attend because it was imprudent for him to show himself at the theater in those days. Pressed by the director of the Opéra, he did attend the second performance, incognito, hidden at the back of a loge. He gave his impressions on April 3, in a letter to the actors of the Opéra, which does no honor to his musical taste. He did not even mention Mozart's music. By this time he suffered from almost total deafness, to the point of using an ear trumpet. In a letter of August 1797 he joked about his infirmity: "I am deaf as a sepulchral urn, what the people call *deaf as a post*." But then how did he hear the voices of the performers, on which he did comment—and quite distinctly, to judge from his remarks on their delivery and intonation?

Of all the activities that he exercised in the course of his life—and they were indeed numerous—Beaumarchais regarded music as the most precocious and durable, and it was the only one he never tired of. "I have always loved music: unwaveringly, never once unfaithful," he proclaimed in his preface to *The Barber of Seville*, and his theater plays, full of music, testify to it. He wrote no drama or comedy without songs. No play of his had a set without a clavichord. There would be no Figaro without his guitar, no Chérubin without romantic tunes. Every entr'acte had an orchestra. A musician to his fingertips, he had until then practiced only the lighter genres: ariettas, romances, comic operas. But about the noble genre of opera he had very clear ideas that he would employ both in theory and in practice: the preface of his own lyrical drama *Tarare* was addressed ironically "To Opera Subscribers Who Would Like to Love Opera."

When this letter "to subscribers" appeared, French opera was undergoing the most severe crisis in its history: librettos were no more than worthless canvases, mocked and usually forgotten in favor of the music. When the link between score and libretto was broken, the music mattered only for itself, and the story was either ignored or incomprehensible. For the lover of lyric arts in the 1750s and 1760s, dance took the front rank (the coquetry of the dancers had something to do with this fact); then came music, then singing, and in last place plot. It was this order that Beaumarchais intended to invert. He would represent opera as a total art that could and should combine all the others. "The real hierarchy of these arts," he wrote,

> ought to form a parade in the minds of spectators: first, the play or invention of the subject that embraces and carries most of the interest; then the beauty of the poem or the fluid manner of relating events; then, the charm of the music, which is only a new expression added to the charm of the verse. Finally, the agreeableness of the dance, whose gaiety and gentility embellishes certain cold scenes. In order of pleasure, such is the rank of all these arts.

This concept developed and extended his thinking about music as expressed in the preface to *The Barber of Seville*:

> Our music in the theater is still too much like our concert music ever to have any real effect, or energy to entertain. We shall only begin to make serious use of music on the stage when people come to understand that you can only sing if you have something to say: when our composers come closer to imitating reality, and above all stop insisting on the absurd custom of always going back to the first part of a tune after they have played the second. Do you have repeats and rondos in a drama? The repetition is agony: it is death to the dramatic interest and only indicates an intolerable absence of ideas.

These same arguments were reused and theorized in the preface to *Tarare* that Beaumarchais now called his "doctrine."

Nothing more fully contradicts these ideas than Mozart's 1781 statement "In an opera, poetry should ultimately be the obedient daughter of the music. Why do Italian comic operas please people everywhere, despite their miserable librettos? Even in Paris, I have witnessed this. It's because the music dominates them and people forget everything else." To the composer Gluck's monumental dismissal that French opera "reeks of music," Mozart responded with complex and mobile human beings, concisely and without emphasis. To the sacred shiver sought by his elder, he replied with the variations and intermittences of the heart. Gluck tended toward the epic, whereas Mozart tended toward lyrical expression of the modern sensibility.

As the French school had done since Lully, Beaumarchais advocated the idea that music is to opera what verse is to tragedy, "a more figurative expression, merely a stronger manner of representing sentiment and thought." But opera is neither tragedy nor comedy, and so he preferred to try the "sung drama," or "melodrama" as he called it in the preface to *The Barber*, midway between the marvelous and the historical genres. To this category his own opera *Tarare* indisputably belongs, as much for the setting and characters as for the situations. He justified in his preface the choice for *Tarare* of an imaginary Orient: "I perceived that very civilized manners were too methodical to appear theatrical. Oriental manners, more disparate and less well known, leave the mind freer and seem very suitable to fulfill this goal. Everywhere that despotism reigns, manners are very sharp. There, slavery is close to grandeur; there, love touches ferocity; the grandest passions are uncontrolled." Moreover, Beaumarchais was following the fashion for "Turkeries," very much to the public taste. Set in a fantastic Orient, *Tarare*'s characters seem drawn from a bourgeois drama: Astasie, the hero Tarare's wife, is "a spouse as tender as pious"; Atar, King of Ormus, is a "ferocious and uncontrolled man"; Calpigi, head of the eunuchs, is a vile castrato "out of the Italian cliques"; and Spinette is a "European slave, wife of Calpigi, a Neapolitan singer, intriguer and coquette." And with Arthénée, "grand priest of Brahma, a miscreant devoured with pride and ambition," who ends up converting to Christianity (for censorship!), Beaumarchais gave free rein to his visceral anticlericalism.

What could be more boring than aesthetic theories applied on the stage? What could be more contrary to creative freedom than a kind of theater called "engaged"? What more annoying than an opera at the service of an ideological or political thesis? These were the serious weaknesses that make *Tarare* an unformed mass, barely identifiable, which some people characterized as "a dramatic and lyrical monster." It is hard to believe it came from the same pen as *The Barber of Seville* and *The Marriage of Figaro*!

Very freely adapted from a story by Antoine Hamilton, "Fleur d'Épine," combined with an old Persian story titled "Sadak and Kalasrade," Beaumarchais's opera features a sort of fairground Spartacus crossed with a Pangloss-like philosopher. Tarare is a freethinker, an encyclopédiste, a physicist, and a big boaster, but not much of a singer, heavily planted amid a spectacle that wants to be total and in which we do find everything: rhetoric, science, politics, fairy enchantment, metaphysics—everything but music. Or rather, the music is so discreet, transparent, evanescent, impalpable, and insipid that it seems barely to exist. In order not to lose a single word of his text, the author required "a music that was not music," as a contemporary said, so it was his own choice. Of its score, only a vaudeville timbre remains in the mind, the tune for the couplets the eunuch Calpigi sings in the third act, "Ahi povero Calpigi!"

In his "Letter to Opera Subscribers," Beaumarchais asked the audience for "three hours of honest attention" for "the work of three years," which would mean composition of *Tarare* began in 1784. On May 10 of that year, only thirteen days after the premiere of *The Marriage of Figaro*, the bookseller Nicolas Ruault announced to his brother: "The other evening before dining, Beaumarchais read us an opera of his making in four acts, preceded by a prologue of an extraordinary genre, which did not resemble at all those of Quinault. This tragic-comedy was called *Tarare*, and Salieri, a student of Gluck's, will do the music." He added: "I will tell you nothing today about this *Tarare*, for one sole reading is not sufficient to give an account of it, but I can tell you in advance that while it should shine or interest by the invention of the fable, it will not shine or interest people for the poetry. Those rhymes appeared to me below the mediocre." We know today that Beaumarchais had first asked Gluck himself to do the music, giving him the libretto to read. Probably judging the place reserved for the music insufficient, the old master excused himself on account of his advanced age and state of health (he had had a stroke in 1781). He recommended one of his former disciples, then aged forty-five, Antonio Salieri, official composer to the court of Joseph II, with whom he had just written *The Danaïdes*, performed at the Opéra on April 26, 1784, the eve of the triumph of *The Marriage of Figaro* at the Comédie-Française.

So Beaumarchais brought Salieri to Paris and offered him and his German servant hospitality on the second floor of his hôtel. At the same time he obtained from the Royal Academy of Music a subsidy of a thousand livres a month until the work was finished, "which is the real means of exciting the directors to get rid of this expense by putting this masterpiece quickly into the lights." Despite some moments of annoyance (Beaumarchais was in the midst of the Kornman affair), Salieri was enchanted by his stay in Paris; he would evoke the memory twenty years later to Beaumarchais's daughter, Eugénie. Meanwhile, Beaumarchais employed diplomacy and seduction to maintain Salieri's participation. Adulated, flattered, and cajoled by his host's small family, well paid by the Opéra, Salieri acceded to all that was wished. "Make me music that obeys and does not command, that subordinates all its effects to the pace of my dialogue and the interest of my dramatic plot," Pierre-Augustin asked him. In other words, "Make me music without music." And Salieri did so, reducing the notes to a minimum, confining himself to underlining a dramatic effect here or there, keeping the music in the background, and always leaving the place of honor to the dialogue. Beaumarchais forbade Salieri to use singing and ensemble bits (for fear that the obligatory refrains would slow the pace of the action), so the composer found himself restricted almost exclusively to recitative, which had the serious disadvantage of monotony. To vary his score, he increased the choruses, marches, and dance airs. Salieri's self-abnegation (a capitulation that others would find excessive) nevertheless won him dithyrambs of praise from the poet-commissioner. The critics would judge otherwise. Even Gudin had serious reservations:

> The vaster the concept became, the more it became necessary for the dialogue to be up to it; it would have demanded the brilliant style of Voltaire and the harmonious melody of Racine. Beaumarchais, who had never written a single play in grand verse, did not possess enough skill at versification to render in a happy manner such strong and elevated ideas, which would be difficult enough to express elegantly in prose. I did not hide from him that it seemed to be impossible to put his prologue into music. Salieri, from a school able to overcome the difficulties, did manage . . . This opera would have certainly triumphed with the critics if the verses had been equal to the grandeur of the subject.

Everything touching Beaumarchais, near and far, interested the public. Whatever he did, whatever he said was discussed, favorably or not. When Parisians learned that an opera of his composition was to be performed, their curiosity knew no bounds. *Tarare* became a distraction from public affairs. This peculiar name intrigued and amused people, for in the popular imagination it meant *taratata* (an interjection of contempt in an argument) or *tarare pom-pom* (a sound made by a trumpet)! Was it a farce or a *parade* or a vaudeville?

According to his custom, Beaumarchais preceded the public presentation of his opera with many private readings. Beaumarchais and Salieri, sitting side by side with a pianoforte "and all the necessary paraphernalia," performed chosen pieces from their opera in the homes of great lords and bourgeois clubs: they resembled, said the chronicle, little Savoyards (itinerant entertainers who go from house to house to perform their magic lantern show).

When *Tarare* began to arouse interest, Beaumarchais judged it appropriate to refuse any more invitations. He accepted one from the Comte d'Artois only on condition that several personalities attend. And King Gustav III of Sweden, one of his most illustrious admirers, who was traveling in France incognito, could not be refused. The reading took place on July 16, 1784, at the home of the Comtesse de Boufflers.

When *Tarare* went into rehearsal in April 1786 under the eyes of the author—flanked by the inseparable Salieri (who observed, acquiesced, and said not a word)—it became a major subject of conversation. But the euphoria soon gave way to cruel embarrassment. By this time the Kornman affair had become as serious as the old battles with Goëzman and La Blache. In the midst of preparations for *Tarare*, a few days before the dress rehearsal, Bergasse, Kornman's lawyer, issued an odiously defamatory pamphlet. Beaumarchais had to make an immediate complaint and suspend the rehearsal. The premiere had been set for June 5, and so he went to the Baron de Breteuil, the minister of the king's household and in charge of the Opéra, to request a postponement, but the latter refused.

The first performance would take place on June 8, 1787 (three days later than planned), but a full dress rehearsal was given on the fourth, in the author's presence. Contrary to custom, the Opéra administration decided to make the public pay for attending, but that did not discourage the *amateurs*, who were more numerous than for any other dress rehearsal. They were also much less passive than other audiences. Having acquired with their tickets the right to manifest their bad humor, they whistled at certain passages, especially in the fifth act, which they widely and noisily spurned. Accustomed to thunder, Beaumarchais let the storm pass; standing in his loge, he asked for silence. It was despite his wishes that they had had to pay for entry, he said, and he was opposed to this innovation, and they were right to whistle at his fifth act, for it was not finished and he would set about making it worthy of the rest. The spectators fell silent, apparently reassured by these fine words. Certain connois-

seurs, however, were persuaded that he would not change anything—
and they were right.

Such a premiere had not been seen since *The Marriage of Figaro*.
The approaches to the Opéra were besieged, the crowd crushed
against the barriers, and four hundred guards were mobilized to contain them. There were cries, fainting fits, laughs, heckles, and a few
punches. When the doors finally opened, the excitement was high.
The Comte de Provence and the Comte d'Artois occupied the royal
loge. It was said that the queen longed to be there, "but Her Majesty
was told that this work, like most of the author's productions, despite
the gravity of the subject, was infected with smut, that it would not
be suitable for her to confer authority with her presence." The curtain went up on the prologue, showing a sky traversed with lightning
and tempestuous elements, and furious winds evoked by the swirling
dancers. Amid this storm, Nature advances, a wand in her hand,
adorned with her usual attributes, and declaims:

> Enough of troubling the world here
> Furious winds, cease agitating sea and land
> Enough! And now my rule revere.
> Let Zephyr alone in the world command.

The Chorus of Winds answers tempestuously:

> Let us no more torment the world here
> And cease agitating sea and land
> Alas, we must her rule revere
> Let Happy Zephyr alone in the world command.

The Zephyr rises slowly in the air, the fracas gradually evaporates, the
clouds dissipate, and everything becomes harmony and serenity. A
gentle landscape appears, and the Genius of Fire descends in an iri-
descent cloud from the East.

In the theater, too, all seemed calm; an unusual silence reigned on
the parterre and in the loges; the audience appeared stunned by what
they were seeing and hearing; at each couplet they were more troubled, not knowing what attitude to take toward this singular work.

Never had such audacity resonated in this acme of the lyric art. Never had the condemnation of arbitrary power been heard with such violence behind the veil of Asiatic fiction. The King of Ormus kidnaps the wife of his rival and threatens him with death; next to him Count Almaviva, piqued at seeing his valet more happy than he but powerless to prevent his marriage, seemed an amiable libertine. Those who had attended three years earlier the premiere of *The Marriage of Figaro* recognized here the same situation, but in quite another register. In passing from the private sphere to the public scene, from Suzanne's chamber to the Palace of Atar, the story took a deliberately seditious turn. At the same time the tone changed: this was no longer a comedy, nor even a drama, but a story about a people in revolt, with prophetic glimpses heralding a radiant future.

The audience listened to the work in quasi-religious contemplation but manifested nothing when the curtain fell: no whistles, little applause. Rather, they were in a sort of collective stupor, behind which lay a profound malaise. Still, the groundlings loudly demanded the author's appearance, which had never happened at the Opéra. The helpless actors wondered if they should make an announcement and argued about what to do. Then Salieri, who was hanging around backstage, felt himself lifted up and carried onto the stage and delicately placed before the delirious audience. The poet was the one they wanted, but for some reason Beaumarchais refused to show himself. Was it anger? Disappointment? If so, he was quickly reassured, for the three following performances attracted as many spectators as the first, although always with the same reaction of bewilderment and perplexity. There was nothing hostile about this reception; rather, it had a kind of fearful adherence and deep sympathy that they did not dare proclaim.

Upon his return to Vienna, *caro* Salieri, terribly frustrated by his host's demands, showed the original *Tarare* poem to Lorenzo Da Ponte—unbeknownst to Beaumarchais. The composer wanted him to extract a real opera libretto that would please lovers of bel canto, for which he could let himself go and compose music that he loved. Da Ponte stripped the poem of its political and philosophical hodgepodge, transformed the hero into a romantic lover, softened the criticisms of throne and altar, and introduced characters from commedia dell'arte—in short, he transformed it into a tragicomic drama in the grand tradition. Salieri, liberated from constraint, reverted to the Italian style that delighted the Viennese court and flattered the singers' vocal abilities; he privileged arias over recitatives, inserted a few bravura passages, replaced the ballet with a harlequinade trio, and resolutely broke with the spirit of Gluck that Beaumarchais had imposed. Thus revised, not to say deformed, *Tarare* was renamed *Assur, King of Ormus. Assur* was presented to the Viennese court on January 8, 1788, only seven months after *Tarare*, on the occasion of the marriage of Archduke Franz to Elisabeth de Württemberg, in the presence of the emperor.

Tarare is worth less for its own qualities than for its crystallization of a moment in history. Despite its mediocrity, Beaumarchais's opera raised the problems of French society at the end of the eighteenth century: about political freedom, about social inequality, about absolute power and the means to escape it. "The dignity of man is the moral point that I wanted to treat, the subject I gave myself," announced the author, associating his work with Enlightenment philosophy. "The spirit of the nation seems to be in a fortunate crisis. Everyone feels a lively insight that things could be better. People worry, agitate, invent, reform . . . I see in every class a desire to be worth something, to be proud of itself, to spread its ideas, its knowledge, its pleasures, which can only work to the general advantage." It is this crisis of society that *Tarare* tried to express, this general movement toward more happiness and more equity. The plot, with its exoticism and fantasy, denounces the wrongs of the French monarchy by transposing them to the Persian Gulf. And it was endlessly malleable: a revival in 1790 involved rewrites advocating divorce, the marriage of priests, and the freeing of slaves. After the Terror (with the author absent in Hamburg) it became even more radical, and further revivals under Napoleon and during the Restoration adapted both verse and plot to the exigencies of their own times. There was not much left of the original impulse:

> Whoever you may be, King, Brahma, Soldier,
> O Man! Your greatness of this earth
> Does not belong to your estate
> But depends on your character.

Twenty-Four

THE FOLLY AT THE FOOT
OF THE VOLCANO

Tired of seeing our identical houses and our gardens without poetry, I built a house everyone cites.

—Beaumarchais

Beaumarchais's victory over Bergasse did not resemble his victory over Goëzman fifteen years earlier. Its outcome was not a triumphal cry of joy but immense dejection. The Kornman trial had brought him as much unpopularity and even enmity as his first court cases had brought him sympathy. In these two years of struggle the violent sarcasm and insults flowing from the pen of his adversary left him stunned, knocked out; it was a victorious but battered athlete who left the ring. At fifty-seven Pierre-Augustin appeared to be a robust man in full possession of his physical and intellectual means. Despite a slight deafness that worsened over time, his demeanor was that of a wealthy banker showing off his luxury. He was now primarily preoccupied by the construction of his new dwelling in the Faubourg Saint-Antoine and was in no mood to tussle with a runt of a lawyer who was nipping at his soft spots; meanwhile Bergasse made his own reputation by dragging down the veteran. He writes in the third person:

> He was heard to say he was tired of business, that it was time to rest, that he was seriously thinking of retiring to the Boulevard to live in oblivion and completely in philosophy, that he was longing

to have the new house finished, which he called with sweet reverie *The Good Man's Tomb*, in order to give himself up to the company of his spouse, *whom alone he loved*, twenty-some friends to keep him entertained, and a few innocent occupations that might charm his last days.

In prevailing against Bergasse and Kornman, Beaumarchais suffered a serious personal defeat, while Bergasse emerged triumphant from a trial he had lost. As often happens, the judiciary and the political arenas had delivered contradictory verdicts. But for the first time the author of *The Marriage of Figaro* found himself on the wrong side, that of arbitrary power, denounced by his hero five years earlier on the stage of the Théâtre Français.

But Beaumarchais no longer cared about the right side and the wrong side. Basically he had only ever marched in one direction, his own; he had decided to follow it to the end, come what might. A man who ordinarily was so sensitive to the mood of the times, so prompt to grasp what was going on, so able to turn it in his favor— how could he not have felt a bad wind rising? Did his growing deafness make him impervious to rumor? Kornman, Bergasse, and their clan were putting up placards denouncing him as a monopolist of wheat; the working-class people of the faubourg and Les Halles saw him as a tight-fisted employer; and the crowd began to growl when he passed. But he proceeded nonetheless to build a palace of a thousand and one nights in the middle of the Faubourg Saint-Antoine, right across from the Bastille, in the rowdiest part of the capital. Always well informed, he had learned that the king was planning to demolish the Bastille and create in its place a grand square along the lines of the Place Louis XV (today the Place de la Concorde). Consequently, property in the whole neighborhood would rise in value, as he understood.

In June 1787 he acquired, on the adjudication of the City of Paris and for the sum of 204,000 livres, a vast plot situated at the corner of the boulevard Saint-Antoine (future boulevard Beaumarchais, between numbers 2 and 20) and the current boulevard Richard-Lenoir. This parcel was the site of the ramparts of the precinct of Charles V, called the Grand Bastion, and formed a rectangle of about a hectare in area, slightly narrower at the north than the south. Built on a terrain slightly raised from the boulevards, it offered about the same aspect as the terrace of the Tuileries along the quai to the Place de la Concorde. Across from it rose the eight towers of the Bastille, high, massive, and somber, plunging their enormous feet into pools of muddy water: it was a mournful vestige of a bygone age and Pierre-Augustin dreamed of erecting opposite it the most modern and luxurious residence in the capital. His creation of stone and flowers, his audacious utopia, would thumb its nose at the decrepit walls of the fortress, as the affirmation of a new era defying the old. In addition to his own home, shops and rental apartments would be created along the wall of the precinct, below the terrace.

To realize this grandiose project, he thought of hiring Victor Louis, the architect of the Bordeaux theater, a man with daring concepts with whom he had once thought of throwing a bridge across the Seine in one single arch, so as to facilitate navigation even during high tides and ice. He had proposed to finance the bridge himself, if he could impose a toll; once amortized, it would become the property of the city. But political events decided otherwise—he had to reduce his ambition to the construction of his own home and to change architects. He called upon Paul-Guillaume Lemoyne, called Lemoyne the Younger or the Roman, to design the building, and he gave the garden contract to the landscape architect François-Joseph Bélanger, who ten years earlier had created the Saint James Folly. But the real master, commissioner, and conceiver of the whole project would be Beaumarchais himself, who desired to leave to posterity a living testimony of the art of living in the eighteenth century.

Lemoyne's estimate of 300,000 livres increased in line with the requirements of his client, finally reaching (upon delivery) the exorbitant sum of 1,600,300 livres! Work began at the end of 1787 or the start of 1788, and proceeded at a sustained pace, seven days a week, including Sundays. Even before the masons and gardeners were finished, crowds of the curious pressed against the barriers to try to glimpse something of the palace that the master had erected to his own glory.

In the spring of 1789 an inaugural festival was given under the presidency of the Duc d'Orléans. An orchestra formed of the best

Opéra artists played works by Rameau, Gluck, and Beaumarchais himself. Soon his house would become a sort of national monument that Parisians of all classes, as well as provincials passing through the capital, would feel a duty to visit. Tickets of entrance would soon be necessary to regulate the flow. Beaumarchais distributed them to all those who asked, sometimes writing a word in his hand for notable visitors. To the Duc d'Orléans, who wanted to admire his gardens, he wrote: "Hurry, Milord, for my garden has almost been ravaged ten times, and I do not know what remains." Shortly after their reconciliation, Mirabeau accepted refreshment in the Temple of Bacchus, in the company of Sieyès, the author of *What Is the Third Estate?*, and some other deputies. Women, impatient to see the marvels, were welcomed by the yaps of a charming small dog, wearing a fancy collar on which was written, "My name is Follette and Beaumarchais owns me. We live on the boulevard." The most modest female visitor received the same consideration as the finest lady.

To re-create what this residence looked like in the time of its splendor, today we have only the architect's plans, rare sketches, even rarer descriptions, and a posthumous inventory. Razed in 1822 to make way for the Canal Saint-Martin, the grounds had long been abandoned; only the portal and the corner pavilion at the end of the garden remained, which were in turn demolished in 1826. It takes a lot of imagination to try to reconstruct it nowadays.

Let us try, though. The boulevard where the house was situated is still called Saint-Antoine. At the height of the rue du Pas-de-la-Mule the precinct wall formed a cut-off corner. Raising our eyes to the terrace, we perceive on the left a round pavilion, covered with a dome, itself surmounted by a small globe of the earth, on which we read the inscription "Orbi," traversed with a great golden plumped pen in the guise of a weather vane. On the pediment are the words "To Voltaire" and above, this verse from his *Henriade*: "He lifts the blindfold of error from nations." In the center of the corner angle, our carriage crosses under the arch ornamented with two bas-reliefs (attributed to Jean Goujon) of the Seine and Marne rivers, which were recovered from the demolition of the Porte Saint-Antoine and restored at great expense. We pass under a vault that leads us to the garden, and we take an alley to the right to the middle of the domain. This opens on a vast peristyle colonnade, at the center of which, on a rock covered with climbing plants, arises a fine copy of *The Fighting Gladiator* (probably an allusion to the owner's motto, "My life is a combat"), which formerly ornamented the gardens of the Soubise. In the axis of this courtyard, the facade of the house forms a hemicycle of Palladian inspiration, which has nothing in common with the aristocratic and bourgeois residences that could then be seen in Paris. The central idea of the house is the interpenetration of the building and the garden, the ensemble forming a sort of continuum where stone and nature intermingle. "It is a country house that resembles no other, built with Dutch simplicity and Athenian purity," as Beaumarchais described his costly "folly."

On the ground level, the dining room is decorated with a frieze of griffons modeled on that of the Roman Temple of Antonius and Faustino. In front of the casement rises a great goblet in Etruscan form, from which a stream of water pours. On each side two cantilevered staircases follow the wall circularly, coming together at the balcony level. A lantern suspended from the ceiling illuminates this room, whose mantelpiece facing the casement reflects the view of the garden and boulevard.

On the first floor, we traverse a rotunda decorated with six mahogany doors enlivened with mirrors and decorated with cameo friezes, between which are hung eight paintings of bucolic sites and ruins painted by Hubert Robert; the chimneypiece in Carrara marble is supported by caryatids imported from Italy. A cupola thirty feet high projects light onto the parquet flooring, a mosaic of precious wood. This high level of workmanship and pleasure is shared by the other rooms. On one side is the billiard salon, with galleries to allow guests to admire the master's virtuosity, and on the other side is the writer's great office, overlooking the garden and boulevard, staggeringly furnished with pieces unique in eighteenth-century French cabinetmaking, the richest in Europe. The monumental cylindrical secretary was made in 1779 by Jean-Henri Riesener, the maker of Louis XV's famous desk (which can still be admired at Versailles) and who became the Crown's furniture maker. According to some, this desk was given to Beaumarchais by his friends, but it would have taken many very rich ones, for it cost 85,000 livres, one of the highest prices ever paid for a piece of furniture! Conceived and built in imitation of Louis's, it copied its richness and ostentation to the point of parody or provocation: the heavy caryatids in gilded bronze are turned into four sirens possibly evoking the exploits of the *Amphytritus*, supporting the desktop and the rolltop of oak with marquetry of mahogany, boxwood, tulip tree, and ebony.

Indeed, it is the marquetry, executed with rare virtuosity, that attracts most attention; covering almost every surface, the inlay figures include bouquets of flowers, still lifes, and landscapes with ruins inspired by Giovanni Pannini's engravings; at the center of the rolltop lies an oval mosaic, surrounded with leaves in arabesques representing an allegorical scene of Optics, after a Lajour engraving, while on the back another scene by the same artist brings together the main attributes of Astronomy. On the main writing surface, at each side of the desk forming a pulpit, panels of sycamore are encrusted with trompe l'oeil recalling the owner's actions on behalf of America: on the left side, upon crushed leaves, one reads in manuscript letters the title of the 1779 pamphlet "*Observations on the Justifying Memorandum from the Court of London* by Pierre Augustin Caron de Beaumarchais, ship-owner and French citizen, Dedicated to the Nation." The signature is half hidden by a playing card imitating to perfection a jack of hearts. On the right side, upon other leaves, rests a goose quill, where one reads: "*Considerations on the Independence of America.*" A monument raised to glorify the hero of said independence, Beaumarchais's famous desk is today part of the collections of Baron James de Rothschild in Waddesdon Manor near London.

Adjoining the salon, the library is composed of six columned armoires garnished with Bohemian glass doors, with the simple and pure lines favored by Louis XVI style, but whose contents might disappoint many. Beaumarchais apparently was not a bibliophile: the library contains no rare editions, no precious manuscripts, no magnificent bindings.

For the rest, the "Beaumarchais folly" has three stories and two hundred windows; its furniture was made by the greatest cabinet-makers of the day, notably Jacob, the most innovative, whose chairs and tables announce the Empire style. Pierre-Augustin, always on the frontier of progress, installed commodes "in English style" and a hot-air heating system.

Opposite the building, on the other side of the court, an elegant gate gives access to the "Anglo-Chinese" garden. On the same level as the first floor, two assymetrical acres—traversed by a carriageway and, below, by an ice tunnel opening on the rue du Pas-de-la-Mule—appear larger than they really are. They are covered with lawns, massive trees, rare species, flowerbeds, fountains, and especially a waterfall feeding a pool for gondolas, traversed by a Chinese bridge with its obligatory bell flowers. Since the ridiculous often arises from an excessive quest, fish imported from China were combined with frogs taken from the Auteuil marsh, whose croaking mingled with the chirping of Parisian sparrows attracted by the grain, completing the bucolic illusion. At turns in the path, we discover an abandoned Indian cottage, a rockery and grotto, and faux ruins. In all English gardens, on all fashionable promenades, knowledgeable architects flattered the rustic tastes of city dwellers with cottages, ruins, and empty tombs. On the eve of perishing, the ancien régime erected in its hereditary parks these symbols of crumbling, abolition, and death. Nature was no longer creation but annihilation; it represented not the origin but rather the end of a world, the effacement of a civilization. Beaumarchais's garden matched history; it installed absences, becoming a kingdom of memory and nostalgia, a repertoire of qualms. Soon patriotic citizens would come to drink, dance, and make love in these false cottages, in the shadow of false cloisters falsely ruined, among these false mausoleums, for they were nature lovers and disciples of Jean-Jacques Rousseau; they had similarly sensitive hearts and minds full of philosophy.

In the middle of the garden rose a temple to Bacchus decorated with a small Grecian colonnade. Its mysterious entrance concealed a gastronomic lair; and on the pediment was the following inscription in cod Latin:

> Erexi templum a Bacchus
> Amicisque gourmandibus
> [I erected a temple to Bacchus
> and my gourmet friends.]

High at the back, a white marble statue represents a weeping woman leaning against a tree trunk: on its marble plinth is a terra cotta figure representing love and a couplet expressing paternal affection:

You who sows trouble in more than one family,
I ask you, Love, to make my daughter happy.

In the silence of the copses are steles and miniature temples that salute the memory of those departed, like Pâris-Duverney. Such is the retreat, half city/half country, *rus in urbe*, where Beaumarchais hoped to spend his old age in peace, apart from the world and amid his loved ones. In addition to his wife and daughter Eugénie, now twelve, there would be the inseparable Gudin de La Brenellerie, who had just lost his mother, and his favorite sister Julie, who lived in an apartment on the second floor overlooking the courtyard. (There she would die on May 9, 1798, almost exactly one year before her dear "Pierrot.")

Although his new house was ready to welcome him in the spring of 1789, Beaumarchais thought it prudent to delay his move and to remain awhile at rue Vieille-du-Temple. The troubles then agitating the Bastille sector were giving him cold sweats. He began to wonder if he had not committed a folly in building his solitary retreat at the entrance to this frightful neighborhood, like a palace at the foot of Vesuvius—and then having it visited like a museum exhibiting its treasures for all to see!

The Faubourg Saint-Antoine was one of the most dynamic centers of production of the capital and therefore concentrated the strongest working-class population. Each day the rural unemployed flooded into the city in search of work. The furniture industry alone employed hundreds of artisans: woodworkers, sculptors, turners, cabinetmakers, bronze workers, upholsterers, stud makers. But many other trades gave this famous neighborhood its particular appearance: carriage assembly, Venetian glass polishing, ceramics, hat making, coppersmithing, and so on.

During the riots of spring 1789, Beaumarchais expected the worst. "Since the people's effervescence began, my person and my possessions have run the greatest dangers," he recounted. "I was loudly designated as the third victim when they pillaged the houses of [my neighbors] Henriot and Réveillon." He was warned that a porter who had been fired from his establishment, and moreover had been a false witness in the Kornman trial, was threatening to set fire to his hôtel; he alerted the authorities, who did nothing. Realizing that he could count on no one but himself to guard his property, he mounted a watch at night, paced the neighboring streets, observed and scrutinized the quartier for the slightest suspicious clue. He reported the least sign of threat to the police chief, begging him to strengthen the security cordon around his residence.

Beaumarchais was at first glad when the Estates-General were convened: "Do not alarm those minds that only the hope of a great amelioration can sustain in the astonishing quarry which is opening before us." But due to his current unpopularity, he kept himself at a distance from events. Even as the Third Estate reproached him for his wealth and his relations at court, he tried to gain its favor. It was as a simple bourgeois, a "French citizen," that he sat in the first assembly of the district of Blancs-Manteaux on April 21. Some people were surprised, remarking that he ought to be voting with the nobility, to which he haughtily replied: "I have never taken letters of *vétérance* [to make his title hereditary], even after twenty years, because I recognize only a man's dignity. I well knew that by not presenting these letters, I would lose the privileges of nobility and that I would become part of the bourgeoisie. This is my place." The majority of votes were in his favor, and he would soon even be the assembly's president.

Worried that his membership in the local provisional council was not sufficient to win him the sympathy of workers and the unemployed, he spent 12,000 livres for the poor of the parish of Sainte-Marguerite, founded charitable institutions, offered his services to maintain the peace, disseminated humanitarian aid, and made demagogic statements—in vain, for the people still considered him sold to the aristocracy. He supported Gudin's candidacy for the Estates General met in May 1789. In good faith he thought that this was the route to the regeneration of France; he expected the forthcoming Constitution to limit the sovereign's power and abolish the abuses of power that he had never stopped denouncing. But at the first excesses, he took a tough line against the depredations by the screaming populace and the uselessly spilled blood: "And the brigands who burn châteaux call that freedom!"

Many people were surprised that Beaumarchais was not "head of any faction, orator of any club, demagogue of any gathering." He was reproached for not winning a mandate as deputy, for holding himself apart from the political scene, for having the false air of a deserter or even a counterrevolutionary, which ill matched the Figaro that was still fresh in common memory. How could one reconcile the bravery of yesterday's statements with today's caution? Could one recognize the dashing challenger of the established order in the arrogant and overconfident parvenu who had become deaf (literally and figuratively) to popular demands, and who raised his voice only to preach calm and moderation?

All those who blame Beaumarchais for his halfheartedness should be reminded that if he was ahead of his time in denouncing arbitrary power, he never brandished the standard of revolt; he never attacked the monarchy and the nobility as such, only the despotic drift of the former and the exorbitant privileges of the latter. "I am a dramatic author by amusement, but it is very seriously that I am the friend of order and good rules," he had written in 1781 to the Comédiens-Français. Can one imagine Figaro setting fire to the Almaviva château? No, he would have saved it from vandals with his loquacity and cleverness. His mockery and jokes denounced only abuses, never institutions themselves. He was asking for freedom and equality of opportunity—and now they were proclaimed. More a reformer than an agitator, Beaumarchais thought that "to criticize or indict some laws is not to overthrow all laws." He defied partisan passions and the appeals to violence that Marat and Desmoulins habitually issued; he declared himself independent of all parties, hostile to all factions, distrusting everything rather than becoming its dupe or victim. Recent events had scarcely changed him; he remained what he always was: a solitary militant, jealous of his free speech, knowing the cost of liberty and ready to defend it.

If he had lived in his new house, Beaumarchais would have been able to witness from his windows the taking of the Bastille. But on July 14 he was working in his offices at the rue Vieille-du-Temple with the commissioners of the Blancs-Manteaux district, over which he presided at the time, to prepare the collection of the poll tax, to guarantee order in the neighborhood, and to preserve from lynching the unarmed soldiers who were trying to protect themselves from the mob. Suddenly the door flew open and an agitated face appeared: "Monsieur de Beaumarchais, two thousand men are in your garden and they are going to pillage everything." The commissioners jumped up, but Beaumarchais got them to sit back down with a sentence worthy of Corneille: "Messieurs, we can do nothing about something that does harm to me alone; so let us concern ourselves with the public good!" After a flattering murmur, he suspended the meeting, rushed to the Bastille, checked the damage, and found eighty men to guard his palace while the populace occupied the fortress and massacred its soldiers. He saved the life of one of them and gave him refuge for the night. He learned of the awful death of Flesselles, provost of merchandise, and the prison governor, the Marquis de Launay; both were decapitated by the mob and their heads carried on pikes from the Hôtel de Ville to the Palais-Royal.

One of the rooms of the Bastille contained, in carefully arranged boxes, all the archives of the fortress since 1659, when it had become this precious depository. The documents concerned not only prisoners who had been confined there, but those of several other places of detention, as well as innumerable police files: inquiry reports, surveillances, seizures, search warrants, civil records, flagrante delictos, and so on. All Parisian crime and debauchery were gathered here, catalogued and filed away. When rioters erupted into these offices on July 14 in blind fury, they emptied many boxes, dispersed their contents, tore up hundreds of papers, threw files out the windows, burned some records, and tossed others into septic mud. The next day the "visitors" were much more peaceful; they were collectors looking for curious or rare documents. For two days, the collectors gleaned at ease. What they saved remains for historians an inexhaustible source of information on the underside of the ancien régime—some documents still show signs of the pillaging.

On the evening of July 14, driven by patriotic zeal, Beaumarchais had rushed to the aid of this precious depository, still threatened by indelicate visitors. At the head of his force of eighty armed men, he went into the Bastille, descended into the tunnels where the archives lay, and spent several hours choosing bundles of records that interested him. What was he looking for in those basements? He had no lucrative goal; he did not need the few louis that peddling these papers would bring. Did he have a collecting mania? Our man was neither a bibliophile nor a dealer in old papers. Was he hoping to find the real reason for his internment in Saint-Lazare? That is more plausible. Was he seeking compromising evidence against one of his adversaries? We can never know—but he was caught by the new governor in the process of marauding national files, which were confiscated.

On the morning of July 16 the assembly of electors made the decision to demolish the Bastille. Not losing a moment, Beaumarchais asked Jean-Sylvain Bailly, who had just been elected mayor of Paris, for the mission of supervising the demolition work, so that it would not obstruct the major drain alongside it or cause damage to neighboring houses. A few days later the electors of his new district of Saint-Marguerite named him a member of the municipal body, now called the Répresentation de la Commune. He accepted the office without batting en eyelid. Why? Did he want to disprove the reputation for cowardice he had acquired by his apparent indifference to the Revolution? His friend Gudin warned him that this move would cause him trouble; he should have listened.

A new tide of rumors would drag him to the nadir of popular contempt. To the thousand worn-out insults were added particularly serious accusations in these times of food shortages and riots. He was blamed for piling up enormous quantities of wheat in his cellar, for depriving the people and reducing them to famine, for feeding the black market and pushing up prices. At the time grain was scarce and expensive; bakeries were raided and bakers hung. Apart from foodstuffs, he was accused of stockpiling weapons, notably twelve thousand rifles that he had promised to the provisioner Flesselles, who had been murdered on July 14. The revolutionaries requisitioned the contents of his home, but instead of the expected "weapons, grain and flour," they found only thousands of paperback copies of his Voltaire edition! Official warrants of his innocence were tacked to his doors, but they were torn down in the night and replaced with new denunciations.

It was also claimed that Beaumarchais had links with the "principal agents of despotism," that his basements communicated with those of the Bastille, that he had used them to introduce enemy sol-

diers, and that he deserved death for treason. As a result Beaumarchais found himself suspended from the Commune Assembly. In
response he sent his colleagues a verbosely self-justificatory petition,
perfectly constructed and carefully argued (despite a few digressions),
in which he reviewed his career. With a personality dominated by
egotism and personal ambition, a member of the narrow circle of
high finance, enjoying a fortune that isolated him even more from his
peers, Beaumarchais had not observed the world changing around
him; with a singular blindness he failed to note the profound muta-
tions in people's minds and still lived according to the old system,
whose manners, language, and habits of mind he retained. Moreover,
he had been too involved with the ancien régime to be able to contribute anything in the new one. The transnational events of 1789
did not win his adherence, and he remained fundamentally a man of
the ancien régime; but he had to act. He had things to be pardoned
for: his wealth, his talents, his celebrity, his real or presumed influence in business, his "folly." Few victims were better positioned for
punishment by popular revenge. Once the fate of others alerted him
to the dangers he was running, he aimed to regain by every possible
means the favor of public opinion.

He gave 12,000 livres to the Blancs-Manteaux district and the
same sum to the poor of Sainte-Marguerite, especially women and
children, "so as to excite by this fine example more public philan-
thropy." During the first eighteen months of the Revolution, according to Gudin, he spent more than 100,000 francs on charitable work.
This generosity was not devoid of political intent: he was trying to
win respect from his most fervent opponents. He declared to Pierre
Manuel, the chief prosecutor of the Commune of Paris: "*Patrie* without property is a phrase so empty of meaning that those who most
feign to believe in it do not slacken their efforts to become property-
owning patriots, at your expense and mine. *Inde* anger, *inde* quarrels,
inde tolerated pillaging, *inde* all those writings claiming equality on
behalf of those who have nothing and against all people who possess
things."

After a man dies, the inventory of his possessions and his records
often reveals his life's secrets. That of Beaumarchais tells us that to
comfort penniless families, artists, people of letters, and even people

of quality, he had advanced more than 900,000 livres, knowing that he would never be paid back. Several writers borrowed large sums that they never reimbursed. These good deeds extended to former adversaries: he came to the aid of Mme. Goëzman when she was stripped of her fortune and in need. Generous by nature as much as by calculation, he long gave aid of all kinds, buying beds for hospices, offering each year a dowry of 12,000 livres for the marriage of a young man of Faubourg St. Antoine. During the first Festival of the Federation, on July 14, 1790, he lodged eight hundred delegates from the provinces and refused payment. In short, he did not skimp on providing evidence of his fraternalism.

But neither his patriotic largesse nor his humanitarian proclamations could shelter him from the suspicions that were the basis of national justice. Revolutionaries insulted him as a class enemy, assailing him with almost four hundred letters every day. Some were pitiful, some arrogant; some scolded him that his philanthropical offerings were only intended to make up for his past and constituted only a tiny fraction of his former spoils; others issued threats if he did not accede to their requests. He tried to answer everyone with civility:

> The crowd of petitioners who address to me is such that I would need ten secretaries to respond to them, for a dry word is far from sufficing for misery; people need consolation, details, and especially help. Not being able to fill this painful duty for all who are writing to me, I groan and I stop, and the whole result is that I have only two kinds of commerce with the world: strangers who ask things of me and unjust men who insult me, rascals who threaten me without even having seen me. Are you satisfied, Monsieur, by having made me waste my time to tell you useless things, me who has so many useful things to do? Monsieur, if you have the sweet compassion for me that you ask of me for yourself, you will stop insulting someone who has done you no harm and has done no wrong to anyone, other than not being able to oblige everyone at the same time.

Beaumarchais saw that France was going through a transitional period: old laws were disappearing, while new ones had not yet been born. It was a sort of parenthesis in history, when the most barbarous impulses were unleashed. If his petition trumpeted his fidelity to the old power, he was perhaps betting on a quick reestablishment of monarchical authority and playing the card of counterrevolution. If so, that bet was not well placed.

Twenty-Five

"BURIAL OF FIGARO"

As one grows older, the soul becomes sadder, the turn of mind grows darker. There is nothing I can do: I no longer laugh when a malicious person or a rascal insults me for my works. I cannot help it. —Beaumarchais, *"A Word on* A Mother's Guilt*"*

In Revolutionary France politics was everywhere: in the street, the salons, the cafés, the promenades. In the fine arts the political epidemic reigned over all genres, with poetry, novels, comedy, tragedy, opera, all imitating the painter David. What literary taste remained was confined to the literature of sensibility, both emphatic and pitying. That horrified Beaumarchais, but what especially angered him was the dramatic art's inability to disengage itself from current events. As bravos now greeted even the smallest historical fact and patriotic statement, the theater became a kind of tribunal; small incidents in assemblies, clubs, and public places furnished the plot lines for both dramas and comedies. Writers confined themselves to inventing moving characters and placing them in pathetic situations. A simple delivery man offers his savings to those in prison, a tenant farmer returns to his master the goods he has bought at a pittance, a young businessman tears his fiancée from the horrors of the cloister—such plots caused torrents of tears and won their authors effortless fame and fortune. During the Revolutionary years, political pressure constantly prescribed and encouraged so-called "patriotic theater," inflating the flow of officially sanctioned mediocrities.

"The Revolution taking place here has a considerable influence on literature," Beaumarchais wrote to a Russian prince in charge of the theaters there.

> Free peoples, on the whole, lose in elegance what they acquire in forcefulness, and our theater feels the new spirit in France. Our minds are concerned with such great matters and with becoming Republicans; we can no longer incline to the literary graces of the ancien régime; but it must be admitted that, to make our tree grow straight, we have forced it to bend in the opposite direction. Harsh words in the mouths of our actors make the Muses flee; strongholds replace palaces, with an orchestra of cannons; streets take the place of alleys, and you hear "liberty" shouted where you once heard sighs. "Live free or die" instead of "I adore you." These are our games and amusements. Agreeable *Athens* has taken on some of the character of fierce *Sparta*. But since agreeability is our natural element, the return of peace will see us regain our character, and although allied with a more virile tone, our gaiety will once again have the upper hand.

But while dramatic literature was awaiting those happy days, it was deprived of independence and forced to suit the times, condemned to sterility. Competition and the abolition of privileges produced a deceptive freedom that could generate only militant works (almost unreadable today) by conformist authors. Such is the fate of any form of entertainment when it is subjugated to ideological commitment.

On November 4, 1789, the Comédie-Française premiered André Chénier's *Charles IX*. The young poet's play dealt with the French civil wars of religion, and its climax had the king admitting:

> I have betrayed the country, its honor and laws
> May heaven strike me as an example to kings!

The Revolutionary-studded audience went wild. The frenetic ovations marked the play as a landmark in the history of the French theater. Four days later Beaumarchais, both jealous and disapproving of the politicization of French drama, went to see a performance. Afterward he shared the fears that the play inspired in him with the theater company:

> In this time of unbridled license, when people have much less need of being excited than of being contained, these barbaric excesses, whichever side they are heard from, seem to me danger-ous to present to people and are liable to justify their own excesses. The more success *Charles IX* has, the stronger my observation will be, for the play will have been seen by people of all kinds. And then, my friends, what a time—when the king and his family come to reside in Paris—to allude to the plots that might have led them there! What a time to ascribe to the clergy, in the person of a cardinal, a crime that he has not committed (that of blessing the knives of the assassins of Protestants). What a time, I say, when despoiled of all its goods, the clergy becomes prey to public malevolence, since it saves the state by offering its riches! If the plans of muddled people at court had been success-ful, if the clergy had won the great trial of its property, I could conceive why such a work could have been permitted; but in the actual state of things, I admit that I cannot conceive why. I do not intend to blame the author: his work was written, and he must have wanted to see it played. His motives were no doubt pure, but shouldn't the administration be careful in choosing if such a spectacle should be accepted or else postponed?
>
> As for you, Mesdames and Messieurs, if you do not want peo-ple to say that you care only for box office receipts, if you prefer people to think you are citizens as much as actors, if you want your productions to increase without offending anybody, without wounding any rank or order, then meditate on the advice that my friendship offers you, and consider all its aspects. The play of *Charles IX* hurt me inconsolably, it will alienate wise and moder-ate men, Messieurs, and ardent spirits do not need such models! Only eight days ago an innocent baker was hung, decapitated, and dragged through the streets, and it can happen again. What entertainment is there in a theater showing us Coligny [the sixteenth-century Protestant leader] being massacred, decapi-tated, dragged by the order of the court?

> We need to be consoled by portraits of our ancestors' virtues
> more than to be frightened by images of our vices and crimes.

As odious as he found the evocation of the violent wars of religion, Beaumarchais remembered his own Protestant origins and kept in his heart the bitter memory of his father forced to convert in order to practice his vocation as watchmaker. At several points in the course of his career, Beaumarchais had pleaded for equal rights for Protestants. In 1787 the king had granted them civil status: they could finally vote and so were eligible for the Estates General, to which some fifteen of them were elected deputies. In December 1790, despite fierce opposition from the Catholic Church and demonstrations that spilled blood in southwestern France, the Constituent Assembly restored to Protestants all their goods that had been confiscated after the revocation of the Edict of Nantes in 1685, which had put an end to decades of religious toleration. Beaumarchais wrote to the deputy whose speech won the day: "Whatever personal harm the Revolution might do me, I will bless it for the great good it has just done . . . For fifteen years, I have been constantly at work, pleading with our ministers to alleviate the fate of the unfortunate Protestants. Blessed be forever the government that has brought the exiles back into the ranks of French citizens!"

After the panic and popular unrest that marked the autumn of 1789, civil peace was restored. "Affairs in France have taken the best possible turn," Beaumarchais rejoiced,

> and even more than was hoped for, because the new division of the kingdom into eighty-three departments, overturning the old order, is taking place in tranquility. It is almost finished without any dissent, with a rationality, a devotion, and an agreement that are almost universal and will destroy forever the possibility of overturning the new Constitution of this fine kingdom. But what puts the seal on the joy of good patriots is the memorable initiative from the King of the French, Louis XVI, in coming himself to the National Assembly on the fourth of this month, and giving a fine speech [swearing allegiance to constitutional freedom] that I attach, and which inspired universal enthusiasm for him . . . Our France is saved.

A few months later, the deputies, in accordance with *The Declaration of the Rights of Man*, suppressed hereditary nobility. Beaumarchais reacted with amusement, writing to Marie-Thérèse at a spa: "What is going to become of us? We are losing all our honors, reduced to family names, without coats of arms or livery! Heavens! . . . On Sunday I no longer possessed what the name *Beaumarchais* had had, but the decree bears on *noms de terre* [land] but not on *noms de guerre* [war], and it is under the latter that I have always defeated my cowardly enemies!" And so he kept on signing himself "Caron de Beaumarchais," sometimes adding "philosopher-cultivator," in the taste of the day.

With France evidently out of danger, barbarism defeated, spirits pacified, and gaiety rediscovered, Beaumarchais thought normalcy would return, and he intended to profit from this bright interval to return to his favorite occupation. On August 3, 1790, he attended a revival of *Tarare*, followed by *The Crowning of Tarare*, which was supposed to update his opera to the taste of the day. Around the same time he got back to work on *The New Tartuffe, or A Mother's Guilt*, which he had abandoned four years previously. In early 1785, in the preface to *The Marriage of Figaro*, he had announced a third Figaro play: "I keep a crowd of ideas that press upon me, and one of the most moral subjects of the theater today is on my work desk: *A Mother's Guilt*." That January a well-informed gazetteer had let his readers hope for a forthcoming performance: "M. de Beaumarchais will give us after Easter his new play that no longer bears the title *A Mother's Guilt* but rather *A Woman Like So Many*." Of this first draft, no trace remains; the conserved manuscripts correspond to the second period of writing, 1789–90.

If Beaumarchais wanted to create a virtuous successor to his previous brilliant and gay plays, he failed. Too many years had passed since the vivacious follies of *Barber*. The resourceful Rosine, lively and mischievous, would now be a "very unhappy woman of angelic piety"; Suzanne, the charming *soubrette* who had gently played with danger, "is beyond the illusions of youth." Figaro, who once filled the air with teasing sallies, is now no more than a shadow of himself; he laboriously contrives to undo the ruses of his adversary, an Irish hypocrite named Bégearss—and does not always succeed. The lightning flashes he once shot now give way to a dim and trembling lantern. Aging, he lets himself be caught in the trap of morality; and when the count finally offers him money in recognition of his services, he drapes himself in new-found dignity.

Pierre-Augustin thought this final play of the trilogy was "one of the strongest conceptions that could emerge from his head." According to the preface to *The New Tartuffe, or A Mother's Guilt*, its novelty consists of "founding a comedy of intrigue upon the pathos of drama," as indicated in the double title, which alludes both to Molière and to melodrama. But fine sentiments drip from every scene to the point of nausea. All the ingredients of the treacliest melodrama conceivable are present. *Prepare your handkerchiefs*, the author seems to say in his preface: "Come and judge *A Mother's Guilt* with the same generous spirit in which it was composed for you." Here was something to disappoint most admirers of Beaumarchais, for what they had loved about *The Barber of Seville* was its freedom, gaiety, and insouciance (although some judged the author overly casual or tainted with cynicism). But *A Mother's Guilt* is nothing more than a bad play built on a bad plot, featuring mushiness, compassionate sentimentality, mellifluous sensibility, and a lachrymosity that produces laughter instead of tears. In short, it openly stalked emotions instead of touching hearts. It contains many topical allusions: the action takes place in Paris at the end of 1790; the Count is now called "Monsieur" Almaviva and is given a bust of Washington; the villain Bégearss (anagram of Bergasse), in his attempted blackmail, invokes the new law on divorce; and Léon, the illegitimate son of Rosine and Chérubin, speaks against the abuse of monastic vows and supports the right to revolt. In the last scene Figaro exclaims: "What a happy revolution! One day has changed our lives! No one to exploit us! No shameless hypocrite! Everybody's done their duty; don't let's complain if there have been times of trouble. There's gratitude enough in any family when you get rid of a troublemaker." Could this play succeed?

In the spring of 1790 after three years of construction, his magnificent residence on the Boulevard Saint-Antoine was finally finished and ready to welcome him. Persuaded that the risk of civil war was over, he moved in with his family. On May 1 his daughter Eugénie, now fourteen, left her convent to come live with her parents. Pierre-

Augustin composed for the occasion an "Old Gallic and Civic Rondo," one of the most exquisite of his final products, proving that he felt more at ease with popular song than with great dramatic tableaux. Published by its author in fifty copies, the rondo captivated Paris and drew a flock of aspirants for Eugénie's hand, including penniless captains and papa's boys without inheritance.

Faithful to his actors and also eager to stress the historical continuity of his trilogy, it was to the Comédie-Française (now called the Theater of the Nation) where *The Barber of Seville* and *The Marriage of Figaro* had played, that Beaumarchais offered *A Mother's Guilt*. But in January 1791 the National Assembly issued a decree that liberalized the theater and protected authors (for which he had long campaigned); the first article abolished the monopoly privileges of the Comédiens-Français. Now anyone could set up a theater, and many new ones sprang up to satisfy the avid public demand for spectacle. As usual, he launched into a campaign of promotional readings; although these one-man shows could not guarantee success, at least they sparked the public's curiosity. This time the readings took place at his palatial home, where the guests admired the decor before applauding the drama. The premiere took place on June 26, 1792, before a large audience at the new Théâtre du Marais, which he had financed, right by his house. The spectators included Mlle. Contat, the actress who had once played Suzanne and now wanted to see what had happened to "her" after twenty years of marriage.

The play's failure was immediate and resounding. The audience had no appetite for an outdated family tragedy. The French now burned for noble causes: the war against Austria preoccupied them much more than the "interior pains" of the poor Countess. (Mlle. Contat jotted some derisively pungent couplets, using lines from the play, and regaled her guests with them; Beaumarchais was surely one of the first to laugh at this burlesque.) But nothing could save Beaumarchais's last dramatic work from shipwreck; *A Mother's Guilt* was one of the most crushing failures of his career. As the curtain slowly fell amid catcalls from the parterre, the old critic Michel-Jean Sedaine leaned over to Gudin and lamented, "My friend, we have just witnessed the burial of Figaro."

On March 2, 1792, while the play had been in rehearsal, some

Belgian dealers wrote to Beaumarchais, saying they wished to propose an important deal. Scorched by his recent misadventures and disinclined to launch into a new business venture, nevertheless he agreed to hear them out. The next day a certain Delahaye appeared, a bookseller, who offered him not books but munitions. Around the end of 1790, the Austrians defeated insurgents in the Low Countries and seized the rebels' weapons. They sold the weapons to the Dutch merchant Osy of Rotterdam, who sent them to Zeeland and then resold them to a Brussels company, which in turn resold them to Delahaye. The Zeeland admiralty authorized their removal against a deposit equal to triple their value, on condition that they were used only in the colonies.

Our bookseller therefore had 60,000 rifles on hand and promised to supply a second lot of 140,000 later on. He was proposing that Beaumarchais serve as intermediary to sell them to the French government, which had great need of them. The Legislative Assembly was about to declare war on Austria; the French army was insufficiently equipped; the matter was urgent. Nobody seemed better to lead this operation than the financier of international fame, the expert on clandestine armaments, the former director of Roderigue Hortalez. Ten years before Beaumarchais had delivered munitions to the young American Republic; today he was to equip the French armies. How could he possibly pass up a good business deal that would also help his country in a time of danger? Moreover, if he refused he might appear a traitor, for Delahaye had warned him that if the weapons did not go to the army, they would go to the émigrés, those who had left France to fight against the Revolution, who would pay more for them.

Nonetheless, Beaumarchais initially refused Delahaye's proposal, sticking to his decision never again to engage in business. Gudin had warned him against the dangers of commerce in this troubled period, and his other friends advised extreme prudence. But Delahaye was persistent. The émigrés were competitors to be feared, he said, and the munitions should equip not them but the nation's soldiers. Beaumarchais asked himself, "If this major cargo of weapons due to my refusal slips away to the country's enemies, and people come to find out about it, I will be made to seem a very bad citizen." He reflected, weighed the pros and cons, and finally chose "the peril of being useful to his country," to use Gudin's expression. Thus in the spring of 1792, aged over sixty, Beaumarchais launched into one of the most perilous enterprises of his long career. This "Dutch Rifle Affair" almost cost him his life, made him lose a major portion of his wealth, and sacrificed the small amount of rest he could still enjoy. But it also enabled the writer to produce *Compte rendu des neuf mois les plus pénibles de ma vie* (An Account of the Nine Most Painful Months of My Life) divided into "six epochs." It was his last work and one of the most successful; to it we owe our knowledge of his life during the Revolution.

Before he went any farther, Beaumarchais needed more information about Delahaye. He got it, and it seemed excellent. They reached an agreement, and the deposit was made. Beaumarchais submitted the proposal to the Marquis de Grave, who had just replaced the Comte de Narbonne as minister of war. After some discussions the count asked Beaumarchais to negotiate with his vendor. To conclude the deal, the government would loan him 500,000 francs in assignats, the banknotes used during the French Revolution, which were in fact worth only 300,000; for his part, Beaumarchais put up as security his life annuities against a loan guaranteed by the City of Paris for a value of 745,000 francs, which largely exceeded the amount required, and on which he continued to receive interest, estimated at 72,000 francs. The government authorized him to withdraw money on his own account up to 445,000 francs and guaranteed him its diplomatic support in dealings with Holland in case the latter held the weapons back out of fear of Austria.

The agreement was signed on April 3. Three days later the Marquis de Grave sent Beaumarchais, as agreed, the 500,000 assignats. The next day Beaumarchais's clerk and trusted associate, Jacques Gilbert de La Hogue, former director of the Kehl printing works, set out for Holland, bearing 700,000 to 800,000 francs in letters of exchange. When he arrived in Brussels, La Hogue learned that emissaries from the competition had beat him there. The alert had been given; he was expected. While visiting a friend of Beaumarchais, La Hogue met "a man of quality of the enemy party" who asked him if "a certain M. de La Hogue who came from Paris had arrived yet."

The stranger added in a threatening tone, "This is a man who is suspect to us, and he will have a hard time here." Barely had the man turned away than La Hogue leaped into a carriage and flew to Rotterdam. Too late! The Dutch government was already aware of the agreement signed a week earlier in Minister de Grave's office; there had been leaks, and the news had spread like a powder train, which retrospectively vindicated Beaumarchais, who had insisted that the operation be kept secret. But worse was to come.

Less than three weeks later, on April 20, Louis XVI and the Legislative Assembly declared war on Austria. In fact, Louis and the Assembly had contrary ambitions: the former hoped that the Austrian armies would put an end to the Revolution and assist him in reestablishing the old order, whereas the latter hoped that France would have a rapid victory, obliging the sovereign to submit.

For Beaumarchais, the news fell like a bludgeon. Under pressure from Vienna and Brussels, Holland had increased the obstacles to prevent the weapons from leaving; now with the declaration of war, the impasse was total. The weapons were embargoed. Pierre-Augustin addressed memo after memo to the offices of war and the navy and went twice a day to the minister of foreign affairs, loudly demanding a lifting of the embargo. He got no response. When the Marquis de Grave was replaced by Joseph Servan, Beaumarchais alerted him to this affair: "The urgency of a decision from you on retaining the sixty thousand rifles that belong to you in Zeeland and which the Dutch are preventing leaving the port, where two vessels have been waiting for three months, forces me to ask you for the honor and favor of a ten-minute audience: it will take no longer." No response. On May 30, at the end of his patience, he sent Servan a threatening letter that sounded like a civics lesson, with a copy to the minister of foreign affairs.

If only he had listened to Gudin and his other friends! After three days, the minister told him that the affair was now in the hands of the King's Council. What did that mean? Was the king himself opposed to France's intervention to expedite the sending of the rifles? What could have been easier than to require this service of Holland, which remained a friendly power? He wrote to La Hogue that "malevolence was at its height," that France had for some time been witnessing a continual waltz of ministers, and that he no longer knew where to turn. What did the ambassador think? Should he conclude a fictive sale with the Dutch dealers? Send the cargo to Santo Domingo and wait for better days? While he wavered, a rumor ran through the streets that Caron de Beaumarchais had brought from Brabant 50,000 rifles that were now stocked in his cellar, and that he had already sold them to the enemy at an enormous profit.

On June 4 François Chabot, a defrocked Capucin, a deputy of the Legislative Assembly, a notorious sans-culotte, and a specialist in denunciations, calumnies, and debauchery (in short, a miserable man in all respects), mounted the tribune to denounce Beaumarchais as a hoarder of weapons. We remember that in 1789 the "philosopher-cultivator" had been accused of stockpiling reserves of wheat, flour, and weapons; even after a search of his home revealed no such reserves, many remained skeptical about his innocence. Visitors to his English garden had prattled about an "ice tunnel" dug beneath his property. Where could it have led—to the Bastille? Elsewhere? The craziest rumors were circulating; Beaumarchais had proved his innocence in vain, for doubts persisted. In a long preamble Chabot stigmatized all traitors to the country, "in coalition with the rebels from across the Rhine, and thereby with the House of Austria." Then he came to Beaumarchais: "The commissioner of the Louvre section denounces Sire de Beaumarchais for acquiring 70,000 rifles from the Low Countries; and we have had the announcement in the Committee of Surveillance that these rifles were deposited in a very suspect place in Paris. The municipality has knowledge of one of these depots."

Outcries were heard in the chamber: some called for vengeance, while others protested in favor of the accused. Suddenly amid the brouhaha Representative Lacroix stood up, with a giant's stature and a stentorian voice. "The 70,000 rifles that M. Beaumarchais bought," he claimed, "were for the Department of War. About two months ago they were delivered somewhere." Beaumarchais was stunned; he could not believe his ears. The public applauded wildly: a small consolation, for Chabot was setting him up for a lynching. "Hell is now unleashed against these miserable rifles!" he anguished. "Was there ever such stupidity or treachery? And I could be massacred over it!" Pierre-Augustin had wanted to avoid publicity about this arms deal, but once the secret was out, he could not keep quiet. He needed an immediate official denial, for threats to his property and his person were increasing. That very evening he wrote to Servan de Gerbey, the minister of war, asking for a meeting:

> I have the honor of warning you that I have just been *denounced today to the National Assembly* as having sent from Brabant to Paris 50,000 rifles that I keep hidden, they say, in a very suspect place. You might well think that this accusation, *which makes me a member of the Austrian committee, would very much interest the king, who is suspected of being the leader, and that it would be no more suitable for him than for me to let suspicions of this kind ferment.* After all the approaches I have made, *to you as well as other ministers,* to procure these arms for my country, after the uselessness and (I add) the pain, *after the inconceivable indifference with which such patriotic efforts have been repulsed by the current ministry, I would owe it to the king and myself to justify myself loudly* if my patriotism did not still prevent me by the certainty I have that the moment I explain myself publicly, *the door of France will be closed to these arms.* This sole consideration still prevails over *that of my threatened security and the movements that have been noticed around my house.* But *this state of affairs cannot last 24 hours; and it is from you,* as minister, that I am waiting for *the response that I should make to this inculpation* [by Chabot]. I ask you again for a meeting during the day with M. Dumouriez, if he is still [foreign affairs] minister. You are too well informed not to feel the consequences of a delay. My servant has the order to wait for a written reply you will give him for me. There is some virtue, Monsieur, in my conduct, *despite the fright of my entire family,* but the public good above all!

Servan replied that he and Dumouriez would hear his correspondent and set the interview for June 8 at nine in the evening. "Four lost days," sighed Beaumarchais. As the matter was urgent, he decided to respond to Chabot before consulting the ministers.

On the evening of June 8 he presented himself at the Ministry of

War, where Servan and Dumouriez were waiting for him. He recounted the affair and persuaded the ministers to act with the Dutch authorities to finally lift the embargo. Dumouriez promised that a pair of Amsterdam bankers would guarantee him against the competition for the exact value of the cargo (and not three times as much, as Holland had until then demanded). This surely was unjustified but necessary if a deal was wanted. For his part, Servan promised to give him 150,000 of the 750,000 livres deposited as collateral. Beaumarchais would use these funds to conciliate influential people. Upon reaching this agreement, the three men separated, "very content with each other." Four days later no money had come, so Beaumarchais sent a pressing appeal to the minister of war, concluding: "I beg you, do not leave me, when you have my funds, to make immense sacrifices to procure them elsewhere; but whatever your decision in this respect, I ask you not to make me wait."

The same day Servan sent him a note asking him to make contact with Pache, first secretary of war, who would settle the matter. Beaumarchais told himself, "Finally, thank heaven, I am at the end of my troubles! M. Dumouriez has written to [the Dutch bankers] and I will get 50,000 écus, of which I will send 100,000 francs to La Hogue to remove all obstacles; and the rifles will arrive and M. Chabot will see them, and the people will bless me, after having insulted me!" The next morning, "happy as a child," he went to the War Ministry and asked to speak to Pache. He was led to an office, where a man listened to him coldly and replied, "I am not M. Pache, but am occupying his place in the interim. Your affair cannot be concluded. M. Servan left the ministry this morning, and I do not know where your papers are." Beaumarchais, beside himself, went to the artillery offices, where he learned that Servan had taken all his papers with him. As Dumouriez was replacing him as war minister, he ran to him, could not find him, and left a note. The next day, the fourteenth, Dumouriez replied though his aide de camp that the 50,000 écus would be sent the day after next. On the sixteenth, Beaumarchais arrived at the Ministry of War at midday, when Dumouriez gave his audiences. Finding that he had just gone out, Beaumarchais waited in the grand salon. Suddenly the door opened. A bailiff appeared and announced in a loud voice, "M. Dumouriez has just left War, and we do not know who will replace him." Beaumarchais bounded up to the next floor for more information but met not a living soul. The corridors were deserted, and the offices were empty.

The coup de grâce was soon in coming. On June 23 he got a letter from La Hogue: the Amsterdam bankers refused to cooperate, on the pretext that they had not received the order from Dumouriez directly and that the latter had been content with informing the ambassador in The Hague, which smelled of bad faith. In fact, these bankers, having earned so much money serving France, now found it more interesting to serve Holland and Austria. But in fact Dumouriez had not forgotten him: in quitting War, he had informed his successor of the unfortunate arms dealer's contretemps. The new minister heard the long account of the whole affair, "with supporting documents on the table," with a benevolent ear.

Three months had passed since the declaration of war on Austria, and the situation on the ground was very worrisome. As the Duke of Brunswick's Prussian troops advanced, followed by the army of the émigrés, they found little resistance. On July 11 the Legislative Assembly proclaimed the country in danger. All Paris rang with calls to arms and martial songs. Vulcan set up his furnaces on the Invalides Esplanade. No fewer than 258 forges were working full time, each delivering four cannons per day. On boats moored in the river opposite the Tuileries, eighty workshops were engaged in making rifles for the Revolution. It was an emergency: for the past two years, the distribution of weapons to the National Guard had much reduced the supply to the armies. But even a takeover by military authority of rifle manufacturing would not allow each combatant to be armed. All emergency measures were encouraged: a campaign was launched to recover saltpeter from walls, and people spoke of melting down church bells. At the same time 60,000 rifles were rusting somewhere in a port in Holland. Nobody knew the war would last twenty-three years, with brief interruptions.

Twenty-Six

"THE NINE MOST PAINFUL MONTHS OF MY LIFE"

A wise man in a time of revolution does not deal either in weapons or in wheat.　　　　　*— Gudin de la Brenellerie*

On July 26, 1792, the Duke of Brunswick, general of the coalition armies arrayed against Revolutionary France, issued a manifesto to the French that provoked both stupor and anger. He summoned the population to submit to its sovereign. "If the Château des Tuileries is invaded or damaged," he declared, "if the least violence is done there, the least outrage to Their Majesties the King, Queen and the Royal Family, and if I am not immediately assured of their safety, their well-being, and their freedom," then the allies would take "exemplary vengeance that will be forever remembered, by delivering the city of Paris to military execution and total subversion, and putting those rebels guilty of murder to the suffering they will have merited." The arrogance of the ultimatum was equaled only by its clumsiness and its absurdity. Clearly Louis XVI had indeed maintained relations with the enemy. Parisians, far from letting themselves be intimidated, were livid, while the frightened court organized its defense and awaited the worst. The agitation was so widespread that Beaumarchais judged it prudent to send his wife, daughter, and sister away; they took refuge in Le Havre so that if the situation worsened, they could sail for America. He remained behind with his friend Gudin in the vast residence on the boulevard Saint-Antoine. On

July 30 he watched from his window as five hundred federated soldiers from the Commune of Marseilles passed by, singing at the top
of their lungs warlike stanzas exalting "sacred love of country." Bare-
foot, lacking uniforms and rifles, armed only with their faith and a
few pikes, they would carry onto the field of battle this burning
hymn, whose words and music would serve as their talisman—"La
Marseillaise."

Amid the general exasperation, the Affair of the Dutch Rifles
burst out again. Beaumarchais was once more on the stand, accused
of preventing patriots from taking possession of the weapons, of
instigating the obstacles that had kept them in Holland. Once more
he sent La Hogue back to try to negotiate with the Dutch authorities; but nothing seemed to pacify the public opinion that was rising
against him. Those most aroused accused him of "a lack of civic
spirit" and of "treason." Targeted by the populace's wrath, he knew
his life was in danger and called for aid from Claude Bigot de Sainte-
Croix, newly named to foreign affairs. The minister did not respond,
but would not have helped anyway, for events were rushing forward
and the trap closing around him.

On August 8 he learned that a band of six criminals disguised as
national or federated guards was getting ready to enter his home with
thirty accomplices. They claimed to be sent by the municipality to
search for hidden weapons. In reality, they wanted to extort from
him "with bayonet in the kidney, knife at the throat," the 800,000
francs he was supposed to have received from the Treasury. The next
day he demanded "safeguard" from the mayor of Paris.

But the mayor had far too many other fish to fry. On August 4 the
Faubourg Saint-Antoine *section* had set a deadline of five days for
the Legislative Assembly to decree the overthrow of the king. If the
deputies did not force Louis XVI to abdicate by August 9, the people
of Paris would rise up.

On the ninth, the Assembly broke up without daring even to
debate the matter, burying its head in the sand. Parisians wanted to
kill the king as a traitor to the country and take their revenge on the
moderate Assembly. The ultimatum fixed by the local *sections* expired
that very night at twelve. Orders of insurrection circulated to all *sections*; to the sound of the drums, rifles were loaded, sabers sharpened,

and cannons hitched. Arms were gathered everywhere. The committee of federated soldiers intended to play a leading role; the next day these soldiers from the provinces would give a national dimension to the capital's revolt. The ones from Marseilles gathered at the Club des Cordeliers, where Danton harangued them. In the Faubourg Saint-Antoine, Santerre of the National Guard assembled battalions of militants. Paris held its breath.

Suddenly at midnight the tocsin sounded its lugubrious moan from the Saint-Antoine and Cordeliers church towers—this was the signal. On both banks of the Seine a shouting crowd spread onto the streets: federated soldiers, sans-culottes, militants from the *sections*, and workers were all heading toward the Tuileries. Passing along the boulevard Saint-Antoine, agitators booed "that infamous Beaumarchais, that enemy of the country who keeps sixty thousand rifles in Holland, and does not want to bring them here." In sight of his house, the troops formed. Assured that he had hidden in his cellars a whole arsenal to exterminate the people, women screamed, "We have to set his place on fire!" But the mob reached the Carrousel without firing.

By the early morning the Tuileries was in a state of siege. Fifteen hundred soldiers, including nine hundred Swiss guards of proven fidelity, desperately defended the palace, but the king had already left, finding refuge with his family at the National Assembly. A hellish butchery began. On this day, August 10, a monarchy eight centuries old collapsed; a new body, the Commune, set itself up in the Hôtel de Ville. With power issuing directly from "the people," the Commune claimed to exercise sovereign authority over Paris and immediately substituted itself for the municipality.

The next day, Saturday, August 11, the municipality had seals put on the Château des Tuileries. The Assembly voted to convene a National Convention (named in imitation of the United States) elected by universal suffrage and charged with giving France a new constitution. It declared Louis XVI "provisionally suspended from his duties, until the National Convention has pronounced the measures it believes it must adopt to guarantee the sovereignty of the people." That very evening, Parisians gathered at intersections to read, by the gleam of torches, the decree announcing the deposing of the king. Three days later the royal family was conducted to the Temple prison.

Beaumarchais had spent August 10 gripped by desperate worry. In the evening he saw the soldiers coming back; the *bonnets rouges* discharged their rifles and threw firecrackers. He went to bed, but the next morning a stranger awakened him, warning that the women of Saint-Paul would shortly arrive with the crowd to search his house, especially underground, where he was suspected of hiding weapons. This would be the fifth time his house was searched; nothing was ever found. But Beaumarchais could do nothing to prevent it; calumny was heedless. To reduce breakage to a minimum, he decided to open all the furniture—bedrooms, cabinets, desks, chests of drawers, armoires—so that no lock would be forced. Shortly afterward the "murmuring hoi polloi" pressed against the garden fence, threatening to tear it down if the gate wasn't instantly opened. Beaumarchais had nothing to hide and tried once more to prove it. "Come on in!" he cried, intending to confront the furious horde. At this moment Gudin and two other friends begged him to flee; finally convinced by their reasons, he left the garden via the subterranean passage that led to the rue du Pas-de-la-Mule. Bad luck: a sentinel there cried out, "There he is, running away!" Pursued by the crowd, Beaumarchais managed to outrun them and take refuge in the rue des Trois-Pavillons (today rue Elzévir) at the home of his friend Gomel, who had escaped to the countryside.

Later he would write down the story in a letter to his daughter Eugénie, safe in Le Havre with her mother. The tale "might be useful for the history of the Revolution," he said. The horde had forced his door, hurling death threats at him. "I knew it to be hot-tempered, sheep-like to the point of criminality," and yet capable of "a natural justice that pierces through the disorder," he wrote with admirable impartiality. He harbored no grudge toward these undesirable visitors and even rendered homage to their honesty. Let him recount this "mad day" to his dear Eugénie:

> While I was shut up in an impenetrable asylum, thirty thousand souls were in my house. From attics down to caves, locksmiths opened all the armoires, and masons rummaged underground,

probed everywhere, lifting stones even over the septic tanks and making holes in the walls, while others dug in the garden deep enough to find virgin soil. All of them passed twenty times through the apartments but some said, to the great regret of the brigands (there by the hundreds): "If we don't find anything here that relates to our search, the first who steals the least bit of furniture or a buckle will be hanged and then we'll cut him in pieces." Ah, when I was told that, I regretted not having stayed, in silence, to contemplate this crowd in the clutch of fury, to study its mixture of aberrations and a natural justice that pierces through the disorder! You remember those two lines I put in the mouth of Tarare that were so applauded:

> When good people are grumbling away
> It's always someone leading them astray.

They really applied in this case: cowardly wickedness had misled the people about me. While ministers and committees were praising the selflessness and civic virtue of your father on the affair of the rifles from Holland, of which they had proof in hand, someone sent the people to his house, as if to an enemy traitor who hides many weapons, hoping to pillage them! . . . Finally, after seven hours of severe searching, the crowd melted away, on the orders of I know not which leader. My people swept up an inch and a half of dust, but not a chandelier was lost. The children stole the green fruits: I would have liked them to be riper, but at their age there is no wickedness. A woman in the garden picked a gillyflower; she paid for it with twenty slaps in the face; they wanted to dunk her in the fountain.

I went home. They had been careful to the point of drawing up a document, garlanded with a hundred signatures, that attested that they had found nothing suspect in my possession. And I had it printed with all my thanks for leaving my house intact; and I published it, my child, first because praise encourages the good, and also because it is a thing worthy of attention by good minds, this mixture in the people of blindness and justice, of total oblivion and pride; for if, while given to disorder,

they can be humiliated if they are thought to be capable of steal-
ing, there is something in them. If I live a while longer, I want to
reflect on that. My child, I dined at home as if nothing had happened. My people, who all behaved marvelously and as devoted
servants, told me all their details. One said: "Monsieur, they were
thirty times in the caves and not a single wineglass was swiped."
Another: "They emptied the kitchen fountain, and I rinsed goblets for them." She: "They rifled through all the linen cupboards
and not a towel was missing." He: "One of them came to tell me
your watch was by your bed; here it is! Your glasses, your pencils
were on the writing table and nothing was taken."

No doubt Beaumarchais owed this favorable treatment to the esteem
in which residents of the area generally held him. They had not forgotten his generous gifts to the poorest among them. "If he had not
been loved," noted Gudin, "if he had not been dear to his servants,
all his goods would have been dissipated by pillaging."

On the evening of this trying day, Beaumarchais took the air in his
garden, meditating on the disaster he had narrowly escaped. His
entourage vainly repeated that he ran no danger in sleeping at home;
shuddering, he thought of the threats he had received. Had he not
been warned that an association of miscreants was getting ready to
raid his house? Perhaps it had slipped into the crowd just now? And
who knew if the marauders were not still hidden in the copses? No, it
was better tonight to sleep at his neighbor's, without a light, after
making sure that he was not followed. Once there he sent back his
valet, telling him to close the street door securely, while he barri-
caded himself in, accompanied only by a servant of his friend. Then
he got undressed and went to bed.

At midnight the terror-stricken servant entered his room. "Get
up, Monsieur. People have come looking for you; they are beating at
the door. Someone at your house betrayed you; the house is going to
be looted." Beaumarchais leaped up: "Is there a way one might get
out of here?" "No, sir. But hurry; they are going to break the door
down! What will my master say?" "He will say nothing, my friend,
for I am taking my person away so they will respect his house. Go
open, and I will go down with you." More dead than alive, he went

down to the kitchen that gave onto the courtyard; through a window he saw hundreds of maniacs surging through the carriage entrance, slovenly men and women, sans-culottes armed with pikes, hairy and sweaty, oaths in their mouths, their fists raised. The servant came back to him and gasped, "It's you they want!" "Well, they will find me here."

Believing his last hour had come, Beaumarchais thought of his family, especially of Eugénie. Standing behind an armoire, leaning on his cane, he saw

> tallow candles go by, go up, go down, enter apartments. People were walking in rooms over my head. The courtyard was guarded, and the street door open. Me, on tiptoe, holding my breath, I occupied myself with obtaining perfect resignation and recovered my sang-froid. I had two pistols in my pocket: I debated whether I ought or not to use them. My conclusion was that if I used them, I would be hacked up on the spot and would hasten my death by an hour, removing the last chance of crying for help and perhaps obtaining it on the way to the Hôtel de Ville. Determined to suffer everything, unable to divine from whence came this excess of horror after the visit to my house, I was calculating the possibilities when, as the light made the tour down below, I heard someone open my door. I judged that it was the good servant who, perhaps in passing, had imagined he had got rid of the danger that threatened me. The greatest silence reigned.
>
> I saw through the windows of the first floor that all the armoires had been opened. I thought I had found the meaning of all these enigmas: the brigands, I told myself, had gone to my house; they had forced my people, on pain of having their throats cut, to tell them where I was. Terror had made them speak: they had come here, and finding the house as good to pillage as my own, they had kept me for last, sure that I could not escape.
>
> Then my painful thoughts turned to your mother and you, and to my poor sisters. I told myself: My child is safe, my age is advanced, my life is a small thing, and this only accelerates a natural death by a few years; but my daughter, her mother, they

are safe! Tears fell from my eyes. Consoled by this reflection, I concerned myself with the end of my life, thinking it was upon me. Then, feeling my head emptied by so much contention of mind, I tried to deaden it and not think of anything. I looked mechanically at the lights coming and going; I said: *The moment is coming*; but I was an exhausted man whose ideas start to ramble, for it was four hours that I had been standing in this violent, deathlike state. Then, feeling my weakness, I sat down on a bench and there awaited my death, without being otherwise frightened.

Drawn from his reverie by footsteps behind the door, he bounded up, as if moved by a spring, and held his breath, an icy sweat on his forehead. Suddenly the door opened; by the light of the candle, he saw a white form coming toward him and recognized Gomel's servant in a nightshirt, candelabra in hand. "Come, sir, they are asking for you," he said in a firm tone. "What, you are going to hand me over? I will go without you. Who is asking for me?" "Monsieur Gudin, your clerk." "What, my clerk?" "He is there with these gentlemen." Beaumarchais thought he was dreaming: his clerk here, at this hour? The servant insisted: "Come up, it is not you they are looking for. Monsieur Gudin will explain everything."

He followed the servant to the first floor. There—oh surprise—he met his clerk, Gudin de La Ferlière, the younger brother of his dear alter ego, who had been working for him for more than ten years. Gudin had left home at eleven o'clock, wearing his uniform as a National Guard, with saber and rifle, to make sure everything was back in order and to watch over Beaumarchais's house. As he was walking on a neighboring street, along came a patrol led by a brave café owner Gibé, also in uniform, who recognized him and accosted him gaily. "Eh, Monsieur Gudin, do you want to come with us?" he said. "You will be better off than all alone." Gudin joined them, but seeing them double their pace, he cried out: "You are going too fast! This is not how to patrol!" "We are not patrolling; we are going to search a house in which we hear there are weapons." And of course this house was none other than that of Gomel, where Gudin knew Beaumarchais was spending the night. Feeling betrayed, convinced that this troop had been ordered to kidnap or massacre him, he shuddered to find himself part of the expedition but was determined to brave everything to save his employer or else perish with him.

At the head of the troop, the commissioner read his mission's orders, which consisted of searching the house and seizing any weapons that might be found. Gudin was sure that there weren't any, but what would become of Beaumarchais if he was discovered in this suspect site? He took Gomel's servant aside and whispered, "Is your master's friend in this house?" "Yes." "Where is he hiding?" "I don't know." "But we have to find him and warn him of the peril. If not . . ." While the apartments were lit and visited, Gudin noiselessly separated from his comrades, remained in the dark holding his breath, and then tiptoed into the bedroom. He looked everywhere for Beaumarchais and called out to him softly, but the latter had already hidden down in the kitchen. More and more worried, Gudin rejoined the commissioner and visitors, who went up floor by floor to the attic.

Finally the National Guards completed their inspection of the premises to their satisfaction, finding no weapons, they left. Outside they gave an account of their mission to the massed crowd, who dispersed in silence, probably disappointed at going back empty-handed; only the women refused to leave. "Enraged that nothing was found, [they] claimed the search had been sloppy, and that in eight minutes they would go in and find the hiding place." As they tried to enter by force, the commissioner abruptly closed the door.

Broken by fatigue and nerves, Beaumarchais tried to get back to the sleep so brutally interrupted. As the sun was throwing its first light, he turned over in his mind the events of that night. "I will write it down, twenty people will verify it, but nobody will believe me, and everybody would be right," he told himself. "All the major traits of my life have a singular quality, but this beats them all. The horrible truth seems only an improbable dream: if anything gives it credence, it is the impossibility of believing that someone could imagine anything so improbable."

But he was not yet at the end of his woes! Ever since his family had departed for Le Havre, Beaumarchais had been living alone with Gudin in the immense residence, which these days appeared quite empty. Entrenched in the library, they philosophized on the misery of the times, on the trials they had just traversed, and those that probably awaited them.

On August 23 at five in the morning, Gudin de La Brenellerie was awakened by the noise of voices and running footsteps. He perceived armed sentinels guarding all the exits from the house. He rushed into his friend's bedroom and found him surrounded by men of severe aspect, who were putting seals on his affairs and confiscating his papers. Amid his inquisitors, Pierre-Augustin appeared implacable, seeming to direct operations. When they were finished, they pushed him out the door. The miserable Gudin remained alone in the vast hôtel, now watched over by the servants, "whose looks made one wonder whether they were there to save the effects or else give the signal for looting."

Taken to the town hall, the accused was put into a barely lit passage and left there for a solid nine hours without a chair to sit on, without seeing anyone. Finally, at about four in the afternoon, he was led to the office "of surveillance," presided over by a man named Panis, who began the interrogation. Surprised that his statements were not written down, he was told: "This is only a summary procedure. It will be more formal when we have lifted your seals." But he was notified that he had been arrested for refusing to import into France 60,000 rifles for which he had been paid in advance. That night he slept in the Abbaye prison.

Constructed in 1635 by the abbots of Saint-Germain-des-Prés, long a military prison, under the Revolution the Abbaye became the site of detention for all suspects of the crime of damaging the nation: Royalist conspirators, refractory priests, the relatives of émigrés, and king's guards, but also simple workers who had held jobs in aristocratic households. The next day thirty-two Swiss and twenty-six king's guards who had escaped the Tuileries carnage were imprisoned there, ten to each cramped cell, one of which was the place where Beaumarchais had spent his first night as a prisoner.

On the afternoon of August 24 two municipal officers came to find him to take him back to his home, where they lifted the seals and made an inventory of his papers. It took all night. Then he was led back to the town hall and put in the corridor he had previously occupied. Again he was left to rot for several hours, then was taken once more to the surveillance office for a tribunal presided over by Citizen Panis.

> Monsieur, we have been given a summary of the examination of your papers. On this subject, only praise is to be given. But you spoke of a portfolio on the business of the rifles that you are accused of holding in Holland. This portfolio has been twice inspected by these two gentlemen [indicating the two officers who had escorted the detainee to the Abbaye] and they have affirmed that we will be quite astonished. You are pure.

Beaumarchais started to read a document, but the tribunal interrupted him. Panis said in a firm tone: "Sir, that is enough. There has been some horror here. M. de Beaumarchais should be given an honorable attestation of his innocence and civic spirit, and an apology for the trouble caused, for which the national emergency is to blame."

A secretary, after benevolently gazing at the accused, took up a pen to write the attestation. Then a small man with a hooked nose in black entered the room and murmured a few words in the president's ear. Who was it? "Shall I tell you, my readers?" Beaumarchais would recount. "It was the great, the just, the merciful MARAT!" When he left, Panis rubbed his head, seemingly embarrassed, and resumed speaking: "I am very sorry, Monsieur, but I cannot free you. There is a new denunciation." "Tell me what it is and I will clarify things instantly." "I cannot. It would only take a word or a single gesture from you to some of your friends waiting outside to destroy the effect of the search that is going to be made." "Monsieur, may my friends be sent away; I will be a prisoner in your office until the search is over. Perhaps I can shorten it for you if you tell me what it is about." "You sent five trunks of suspect papers to a woman at 15, rue Saint-Louis in the Marais. Order has been given to fetch them."

> Beaumarchais replied: Gentlemen, I give to the poor with pleasure all that is found in the five trunks indicated and will answer for anything that is suspect in them. Or rather, accept my declaration that there is no trunk of mine in the house you mention.

> Only one bundle exists in the house of one of my friends, with
> titles to the property I safeguarded after the warning about loot-
> ing that might take place at my house on the night of the ninth
> to tenth and about which I informed M. Pétion in writing. While
> these five trunks are being searched, also search my bundle; here
> is the signed order to my friend's servant to give it to you; you
> will also examine that. Another trunk of papers and old records
> was stolen from me the same day this bundle left my house; have
> that found, and I cannot do any more.

All that was executed on the spot, and the attestation signed by all
the municipal officials was given to Beaumarchais. While waiting for
the trunks to arrive, they went out for lunch, while the prisoner
remained in the surveillance office, under a single guard. As they
were going out, an individual wrapped in a tricolor scarf came in,
pointed to Beaumarchais, and screamed, "I possess irrefutable proof
of his treason. He did want to deliver to the enemy the arms that he
was paid for!"

Turning toward his judges, Beaumarchais replied with sang-froid:
"You see, Messieurs, that this gentleman does not know what he is
talking about." The maniac swore: "You neck will answer for it!"
"Fine, as long as you are not my judge."

When the tribunal went to lunch, Beaumarchais remained alone
with his Cerberus, meditating yet again on his bizarre destiny. The
bundle arrived, but no news of the five trunks. Time passed, night
fell, and no one came back. The office boy said he was going to bed
but could not leave him alone in that room. So he shut Beaumarchais
up in a closet with a mattress on the floor. After thirty-two hours the
municipal officers, recognizing the "purity" of this detainee, came to
tell him: "In the trunks were found old rags from nuns that the lady
had sheltered. We know you are innocent of all the accusations.
While waiting for the office to open, we are sending you home.
Tomorrow we will inspect your bundle and you will have a certificate
in due form." After signing a promise to present himself to the Committee of Surveillance any time he was required, Beaumarchais finally
went home, after five sleepless nights, escorted by two gendarmes to
keep watch over him.

The next morning he was brought back to the Abbaye under guard and expressly forbidden to speak to anyone outside "without a written order from the municipality." He again met those who had been his companions in misfortune: D'Affry, a "venerable old man"; Thierry de Ville d'Avray, former chamber valet to Louis XVI; Montmorin father and son; Sombreuil, former governor of the Invalides, "and his virtuous daughter," who was imprisoned with her father; the Abbé de Boisgelin, Lally-Tollendal; Lenoir the alms treasurer, aged eighty-two; Gibé, a notary—a total of 192 people "stuffed into 18 tiny rooms." They talked about events or philosophized about their sorry fate. For several days bad news had abounded: the Austro-Prussians were marching across France, Longwy had surrendered, and Verdun was seriously threatened. Everyone was persuaded that France had been betrayed. The angry populace muttered against priests and aristocrats. The Commune's Committee of Surveillance stirred up hatred, while Revolutionary journalists like Marat, Fréron, and Gorsas pushed people to vengeance. "Terror is on the march," observed a prisoner, "and they will take advantage of it to have our throats slit here." Replied Beaumarchais, "It doesn't seem like it."

Like his fellow detainees, he expected to meet his death and was persuaded that any enterprise to avoid it was futile; What good would it do to appeal to an authority from which he expected nothing? And so Beaumarchais took up his pen to rebel against injustice, to censure calumny, and to denounce this new form of arbitrary power, just as he had once denounced the privileges of the old order, and with the same audacity. Imprisoned, harried, and persecuted, he dared to speak out; when the most elementary prudence might have obliged him to keep quiet, he raised his voice against the venality of ministers and wrote a memorandum on the corruption of leaders. Of course, the tone was not the same as when he had been fighting against the Maupeou parlement; the years had tempered his fieriness, blunted his verve; nor did the moment lend itself to witticisms. But he remained the champion of the rights of man that he had always been, and he continued, against all odds, to believe in the triumph of justice.

Thanks to the active complicity of his unfortunate companions, he managed to write a petition addressed to the Committee of Surveillance. Thierry lent him paper, and d'Affry his portfolio to serve as a writing desk, while the young Montmorin, seated on the ground, served as lectern. It took insane courage to launch such a challenge to the Dantons, Marats, and Robespierres on the eve of the September Massacres:

> For five days, I have been stuck alternatively between a *dark corridor of the town hall and the filthy prison of l'Abbaye*, without being seriously questioned about the facts of such importance, although I have not stopped asking for it, although I have brought and *left in your office the portfolio* that contains my entire justification and glorifies me as a citizen. Yet my house and my papers have been strictly searched—and have furnished your commissioners only honorable testaments about me! *My seals have been lifted*; I alone am under the seal of a prison that is uncomfortable and unhealthy due to the excessive number of prisoners being sent here. Forced to account rigorously *to the nation* for my conduct in this affair, which became distressing only *through the faults of others*, I have the honor of warning you that if you refuse me the justice of hearing my defense and my means of acting, *I will see myself forced, to my great regret, to address a public memorandum to the National Assembly, in which, having detailed the facts, supported by unimpeachable pieces of evidence, I can only be more than exonerated. But even publicizing my defense will be the death knell for the success of this immense affair.* And to imprison me in secret will not preserve anybody from my pressing demands, since my memorandum will already be in the hands of some.
>
> Messieurs, how we lack weapons! Sixty thousand rifles would have long since been in France, *if each person had done his duty.* I alone did so and in vain; and *you are not hastening to know who the guilty ones are!* I have repeated *that I offered my head as hostage for the care I took, the sacrifices I have made, to bring this great assistance*; I told you that *I despise this malevolence*; and because I asked for the name of my vile informers and for the pleasure of confounding them, instead of continuing my barely begun interrogation, you have made me remain *thirty-two hours without those who were supposed to interrogate me coming back to*

the office! And without the sweet compassion that should have taken care of me, I have spent two days and a night *without knowing where to lay my head*! And the affair of the rifles is without any clarification—and the only man who could enlighten you, *you have sent him into the secrecy of a prison when the enemy is at your doors*! What more could our implacable enemies do to hurt us, *a Prussian or Austrian committee*? Pardon the just pain of a man who attributes this wrong more to great difficulties than to ill will. But *since nothing is done without an order*, for these five unhappy days *I have been frightened by the disorder that reigns in the administration of this city.*

On August 29, 1792, the sixth day of his detention, around five o'clock in the evening, as he and Thierry were reminiscing about the old days, a clerk opened the door: "Someone is asking for Monsieur Beaumarchais. A Monsieur Manuel with some municipals." When the clerk left, Thierry worried: "Was he not among your enemies?" "No, alas, we have never seen each other. It is said to begin thus: a bad omen! Has my time come?" In the lobby he found out who Manuel was (a state prosecutor), and said to him: "Monsieur, without knowing each other, we have had a public mix-up about my tax contributions. Not only have I paid them exactly, but I have paid those of others who did not have the means. My affair must have become quite grave if the state prosecutor of the Commune of Paris, leaving his public duties, comes here to bother with me!"

"Monsieur, far from leaving my duties," said Manuel, "it is to concern myself with them that I have come to this place; and is not the first duty of a public officer to come tear from prison an innocent who is being persecuted? Your informer Colmar is unmasked; his *section* has taken away the tricolor of which he is unworthy. He is chased out of the Commune and I think is even in prison. You have the right to sue him. It is to make you forget our public debate that I have asked the Commune to absent myself for an hour to get you out of here. Leave at once!"

At these words the prisoner fell into his arms, tears in his eyes. "I will never forget this man, nor this moment," he later wrote. Nor was he likely to forget him, for Manuel was none other than the lover of his mistress, Amélie Houret. Thus it was to her and his rival that he owed his liberation. If he had been detained another six hours, he would have been lost: the town hall was closed down, the doors were barred, and the September massacres began on the following Sunday.

We can best appreciate Beaumarchais's luck, his "fine escape," if we know what happened then, a few days after his release. The day before, while the enemy continued its advance and the Prussians laid siege to Verdun, Danton had demanded incursions into homes "to find the thirty thousand traitors and eighty thousand rifles that are hidden." The next day there was a curfew at six; the maddest rumors ran through the working-class districts; people spoke of a conspiracy by aristocrats and priests that Marat had been denouncing for months in *L'Ami du Peuple*. Fear degenerated into murderous madness. The Commune's Surveillance Committee was enjoined to judge all detainees without distinction, arrests were increased, and men armed with pikes and rifles ran to the prisons. About three thousand persons were condemned due to their birth, their fortune, their faith, or their opinions. Prisoners were crowded into all the places of detention in the capital: in the Chatelet, the Conciergerie, the Carmes, and the Abbaye. There a "Revolutionary tribunal" was improvised, presided over by a certain Maillard, a bailiff nicknamed "chief executioner." Secret prisoners, cut off from the outside world, lived in anguish. One by one, as the name of each was called, they filed like cattle to the abattoir. People were strangled, or had their heads cut off; they were raped, tortured, dismembered.

Let us find out who Beaumarchais's savior was.

Twenty-Seven

THE LAST MISTRESS

*Having passed the age of pleasing, I must flee the misery of
loving.*   *—Beaumarchais to Amélie Houret*

When everything was in upheaval around him, when his fame
declined to near oblivion and success turned its back, Beaumarchais
clung desperately to what procured at least the illusion of happiness:
his fine house, his family, and a few faithful friends. But what was
all that worth, without the pleasures of the senses? Even amid all-
consuming activity, he had found in libertinage one of the principal
mainstays of existence; now the silence of the flesh bore a foretaste of
death. Nothing was more alien to him than meditating on his final
end. On the contrary, animated by a furious impulse to live, he
continually cultivated desire as the most precious benefit a person
possesses to exorcise the poison of anguish. A world without desire
would resemble an extinguished world, bereft of society and movement. To desire was to exist. Pleasure was the motive for thought,
the end point of action.

We know about Beaumarchais's amorous adventures in the ten
last years of his life only very imperfectly, because his descendants
took care to destroy all the evidence. In 1787, in the middle of the
Kornman affair, Pierre-Augustin had met Amélie Houret de La Marinaie, whose lover he soon became. We know from his correspondence with her (or at least what remains of it) that he officially kept

her and for a while formed a second household with her under his roof.

The first public mention of this liaison with Amélie Houret appears in the *Courrier des Spectacles* on 16 Prairial of the Year VII (June 4, 1799, or only eighteen days after Pierre-Augustin's death): "A very lovely woman has letters burning with love from Beaumarchais; she was well worthy of inspiring them. But as he was over fifty years old when he wrote them, there is reason to believe that they are less the work of his heart than of his mind. Apparently, they will appear in print someday." This announcement was intended to attract the family's attention and fully succeeded. Five months later, when Amélie died in turn, the owner of these letters (probably the author of the announcement) offered to sell them to Mme. de Beaumarchais; she asked advice from Gudin, who dissuaded her from doing so. However, she did acquire her husband's letters and destroyed them all. Or so she thought—as often happens in such cases, the seller had kept some back, which passed from hand to hand until they ended up in the collections of the British Library in London, where they are still kept today.

Who was this mysterious Amélie Houret, Comtesse de La Marinaie, born Duranty? We know only that she was married against her will to Comte Houret de La Marinaie, that this marriage was not happy and ended in a divorce in January 1796. She had previously embarked on amorous adventures: chronically in debt, she used her charms to obtain financial help from her lovers. Apart from Beaumarchais, whose liaison with her was intermittent and stormy, she was the mistress of Pierre Manuel, former bookseller who in 1791 was named the chief prosecutor of the Commune. Much later she would fall madly in love with a man ten years younger than she, known only by his initials H.C., whom some people believe was Hector Chaussier, author of many vaudevilles. This was an unhappy passion, for the young man finally admitted to his mistress that "love chained him to the feet of another." His moral sketch of her:

> Amélie should please any sensitive and enlightened man; she is prodigiously witty, but also full of sentiment. I cannot conceive how such naturalness and vivacity, strength and judgment, can be

allied. Her mind, light or deep according to circumstance, naïvely brilliant and just, leaves nothing to be desired to the delicate observer who knows how to feel it; but few men are capable of hearing it and admiring it . . . This woman suffered great miseries; she bore them with remarkable courage and paints them with a painful and poignant energy that tears the soul! She recounts her life to whomever wants to hear it; she speaks truth to everybody, finds it simple to say to a man "I despise" you when he appears contemptible to her . . . She has applied her pride to disdaining all that women seek out of vanity. There is in her soul a continual and constant disdain for what men commonly esteem: disdain for riches, honors, luxury, prejudices.

Although she cultivated the arts and letters, Amélie Houret de La Marinaie never published any work during her lifetime.

Her correspondence with Pierre-Augustin (of which only fragments remain) gives no details about the circumstances of their meeting but allows us to suppose that it was she who took the initiative. Tormented by a husband with whom cohabitation was becoming impossible, she came to ask advice of Beaumarchais, who was then in the midst of the Kornman trial and a recognized champion of the cause of women. No doubt her constant need for money inclined her to choose as defender a man capable of giving her, in lieu of a legal solution, at least significant compensation. Sure of her charms, in the prime of her youth, she used consummate art to seduce the gray-bearded millionaire. No dupe, he resisted (or pretended to), less out of concern for his tranquillity as he claimed, than to have time to dream about this fresh prey who was offering herself to him. Eroticism is never without the imaginary, nor the imaginary without discourse. The eighteenth century did not know how to make love without talking about it; it talked beforehand to raise the level of desire, during lovemaking to enhance it, and afterward to relive it in thought. "You only know how to make love on a bed," we recall that Beaumarchais had once written to Mme. de Godeville. "It is sometimes charming on a sheet of paper." Deferring the satisfaction of the senses is part of the art of enjoyment. To awaken in writing the voluptuous image of the temptress, to postpone the pleasure with the *idea* of pleasure, was the refinement of libertinage. For Beaumarchais, who would soon reach the age of sixty, it was also a way of warming a somewhat vacillating ardor. He wrote to her:

> Now, imperious lovely, what do you want to do with me? First, I no longer want to see you; you are a firebrand, and whether you yourself burn or not, you set fires everywhere. Yesterday, leaving you, it seemed there were embers on me. My poor lips, ah ye gods, just for having pressed them to yours, were as ardent as if they had been devoured in the fire of fever. No, no, I do not want to see you any more, I don't want your breath to put fire in my breast . . . I am happy, cold, tranquil. What would you offer me? Pleasure? I don't want any more of that kind. I have given up your sex; there will be no more for me . . . No more kissing sessions; I will become mad . . . I, suspended like a fly in the webs of Arachne, would let myself be sucked dry, let my reason wander, lift my almost extinguished senses; and that miniature woman with her colossal ideas would make a puppet of my heart. No, no, let's stop, there is still time; send me what you think, feel, want, require of me; I am your advisor, your respectful admirer, not yet your friend. God preserve me from your charms!

Encouraged by this first success, the clever woman pushed her advantage, painting her situation in the blackest colors: married to a rich man who deprived her of everything, she lived in a state of extreme precariousness and could not even provide for her mother. Moved by her tale of misery (and also no doubt by her pretty features), Beaumarchais rushed to rescue her.

Their turbulent liaison would last almost until Pierre-Augustin's death in 1799. As we have seen, in 1792 she rescued him from prison by appealing to her other lover, the Commune's chief prosecutor, Manuel. The two lovers at first established a relationship of torrid eroticism, whose excesses Beaumarchais expressed in unfettered language. Nowhere else in his writing, not even in his letters to Mme. de Godeville, does he so shamelessly evoke desire, nor manifest such disdain for convention. Never had he pushed verbal license so far.

Such passages allow us to see a Pierre-Augustin both sincerely infatu-
ated and trying to seduce. After about ten years the passionate declarations would end, but in the meantime the lovers would overturn
the last barriers of decency and reduce respect for each other to
naught. A pure language of sex came to prevail between the two
lovers, an idiom of connivance, direct and brutal, as is used between
partners in debauchery when nothing is forbidden and the violence
of the words serve only to regenerate bodies that have become blasé.

Beaumarchais knew that he had only limited time left to love.
Now it was his turn to play the role of Bartholo, caught in the nets of
this adventuress thirty years younger than he, summoned to deploy a
sexual valor equal to the one he obligingly described on paper. Did
these excesses hasten his death, as was rumored at the time? Certainly
they had the effect of darkening his last years, for while he took some
pleasure from them, he also suffered cruel torments. Jealousy became
the assiduous companion of his days and especially his nights.

Here are portions of two letters previously published only in
hard-to-find scholarly journals. The first bears no date, but the context tells us it was written the day before the second one, which is
from 11 Vendémiaire of the Year VII (October 2, 1798). Beaumarchais plays the jealous and obscene old man with touching natu-
ralness:

> To punish me for having treated you casually, you played the
> strumpet, or rather you let yourself be treated like a whore by
> someone you did not love [Manuel]! Do you understand me
> now? It was about your cowardly prostitution that I was rightly
> complaining! It is a crime to have fucked another while your
> lover, by divine drunkenness, was sucking your cunt and your ass,
> as a devout person takes the Eucharist. The crazy things I did to
> you you have now doubly covered with indelible dishonor: first
> by letting them be done to you by another, then by divulging
> disdainfully that I rendered you that charming homage that you
> call *tiberiads* [sodomy], solely in order to present yourself as a
> devoted victim of the tyrannical subjection into which my mon-
> key put you! *Heaven! My monkey made you the divinity of my wor-*
> *ship!* You don't love me any longer, I sense, despite everything

you write. I am not complaining; I am too old and unfortunate
to be lovable . . . What pleased me on your part was the exclusive
happiness with which my tongue supplemented the weakness of
my penis! When I thought I had made you taste the pleasure that
fucking is for me, I accepted it from you with the simplicity of a
giving back that you seemed to grant out of love for the one who
idolized you. This time is passed, Amélie, and the unreasoned
charm of the reciprocity of the religious worship by which two
lovers try to prove to each other that everything about the other
is dear, is finished for us two. You will not have the advantage
over me of a sacrifice that you want to flaunt. I have sucked your
rosy mouth. I have devoured the tips of your tits. I have put with
delight both my fingers and my tongue into your cunt imbibed
with spunk. I have licked your asshole with the same divine pleasure that my tongue has sought yours. When, pardoning my
weakness, you have spilled the spunk of loving by moving your
sweet cunt over my mouth altered by this divine come, I have let
you do to me what pleased you. This time of delirium is passed.
Even if I had an extreme need for animated consolation, I will
not go to your place tomorrow to discuss the differences in our
ways of loving each other. Yours is rendered austere and prudish
only for the insipid pleasure of wanting to prove to me that your
love is the more delicate! Your sad superiority saddens me and
destroys my naïve happiness . . . But can't you write back before
midnight?

The second letter was written by Beaumarchais between the lines of
her reply:

This love I have proved to you, you have dragged through the
mud; you have called *tiberiads* the crazy worship I have rendered
to you alone! And more libertine than I am, if that is what libertinage is, you have dishonored our games and our love by the
publicity you have given them . . . To what virtue, what wisdom
have you returned, if you say you have no other lover, since
you constantly receive that nothing man, that naked man
[Manuel], between your arms and your thighs? . . . You put vice

into the pleasure of delivering yourself and virtue into the same act without pleasure! Either you are raving or lying or dissimulating . . . Were you as beautiful as Venus, you would have been pardoned here if one did not believe that you have made me your dupe! You no longer have with me that ecstasy that excuses love and its pleasures. What will you do with me in your bed, in your arms? You have dissected our love and what remains is only a skeleton that has lost its life and beauty . . . Remember, poor dear, that it is unworthy of us that you provoke my weaknesses by your carnal embraces, by those lascivious liberties that ecstasy alone warrants, and that you would fail in what you owe to us two if you forgot yourself to the point of showing me everything that I do you the justice of believing that you will not show to anybody anymore. Imagine what I must think of you if you compromised the majesty of our sentiment by letting me kiss your buttocks, by opening me up with your dainty fingers as you have a hundred times when you were not yet reformed; or at least, if you show all, don't say "do nothing" or indecently call up the vestiges of the virility that your friend is ashamed to feel when your hand goes under his belt. Yesterday morning, while talking to me of something else, did you not unbutton that which a well-born mistress does not unbutton without carnal intention? What do you want from me if you no longer feel anything?

Amélie's portion of the letter concludes with a request for four orchestra seats for the theater ("and please slip six livres in adroitly"). These two letters are unambiguous: it is indeed a rupture between the two lovers. How could they reconcile Amélie's aspiration to chastity with Pierre-Augustin's insatiable carnal appetite? Moreover, how could they reconcile that appetite with the impotence he freely admits to his mistress, since he noted its preliminary signs twenty years previously with Marie-Madeleine de Godeville? The only explanation (in my opinion, one that some of this correspondence confirms) does no honor to our hero or to his muse. Beaumarchais's letters testify in effect not to active eroticism but to certain practices (petting, fellatio, cunnilingus, masturbation) that often accompany men's declining sexual activity and for which his mistress perhaps felt a legitimate repulsion. Her sentiments for him may not have changed; no doubt with time, her gratitude toward her benefactor gave way to the tenderest affection. Proof of this is that exactly two months before Beaumarchais's death, when their separation was already confirmed, Amélie did something extraordinary to get her old lover back: she went so far as to beg Mme. de Beaumarchais to effect this rapprochement! This was a mad effort, to which Marie-Thérèse replied in a tone of offended dignity:

> I do not hide, Madame, that I am very astonished that you address me in order to reach Monsieur de Beaumarchais. You well know that we each have very separate apartments, and that we each have the freedom to receive the people we like, and nothing is less in my character than to go to inspect my husband's place and make indiscreet demands or fault his conduct for whatever reason. This confidence, this respect that is due him, is my way of proving my attachment. Each person has his own . . . Allow me to tell you, Madame, that this *fear of displeasing me* seems unfounded, and I have difficulty believing that you really thought of that for an instant . . . I do not know on what you base the idea that you are *odious* to me. That is an evil word! Let us reduce it to what is meant: there are incompatible social unions, and ours, Madame, would be of this kind, in the strictest meaning of the term.
>
> I cannot believe, despite the four lines that you sent me, that the happiness of the man I love and honor (to whom *I have proved it in a solid manner*) depends on re-attachment to a liaison that has become more absurd and more impossible than ever— and surely I am not alone in this opinion, if one had to collect opinions.
>
> You have a form of attachment so beyond my scope that I can only be astonished and remain silent. But, Madame, there is one thing I truly understand: which is that if reason became your guide, you would be the first (out of the attachment for this same friend) to feel how inconvenient it would be for him to have a rapprochement that would bring neither of you any felicity what-

ever, and would produce the most awful effect on the minds of a multitude of people with whom you shared your conquest. As for all the letters that you have received, publicity is not a banal safeguard, Madame.

W. M. Beaumarchais

Twenty-Eight

WANDERINGS

*O my weeping country! O wretched Frenchmen! What good will
it have done you to demolish Bastilles if brigands come to dance
on the ruins and massacre us on their debris?*
        —*Beaumarchais,* **Nine Most Painful Months**

While Paris was engaged in massacre, Beaumarchais took refuge near
Versailles. Still, he bombarded the minister of war with letters for an
audience so as to obtain permission to fetch the famous rifles from
Holland. He finally received a summons to appear before the Council of Ministers on September 12, 1792.

Introduced into the council hall, he was invited to sit at the end
of the table, like an accused man before his judges: Danton (minister
of justice), Roland (minister of the interior), Servan (minister of
war), Lebrun, and Clavière (whom we have already met). Beaumarchais presented himself as a victor convinced of his rights and sure of
obtaining justification. But they treated him casually, with condescension, even rudeness. Everyone appeared convinced that he was
deliberately not supplying the armies in order to make a substantial
profit. Was it not thanks to speculation that he possessed his immense
fortune? Clavière poured out his rancor. But Lebrun did not want to
compromise himself openly; Servan did not say a word; and Roland
appeared worried and in a hurry to return to his affairs. As for Danton, he led the discussion with authority but more or less ignored the
real issue.

The meeting ended with profound disagreement between the two parties and on a gaffe by Roland that almost cost the life of the "soldier-citizen." Leaving the council, whose meetings in principle were supposed to remain secret, he declared publicly that they had debated a question "that will never finish before the end of the war, that of the rifles of M. Beaumarchais." In a few seconds the statement spread around the city, igniting a powder keg. A violent popular demonstration was improvised against the enemy of the country, and it was a miracle that he managed to escape being lynched. Setting aside counsels of prudence from his friends and listening only to his indomitable will to win, Beaumarchais appealed directly to the National Assembly and asked to be heard by the weapons commission. He was told the same day that he would be heard "with pleasure" on September 15 at eight in the evening. Beaumarchais went to the meeting, his portfolio under his arm, and spoke keenly for three hours, producing supporting evidence.

As soon as he withdrew, these gentlemen began their deliberation. Examining his conduct since the start of the affair, they judged it "irreproachable, in both substance and form," and wrote an attestation that was submitted on the nineteenth. At the same time the military committee and the weapons commission asked Lebrun to prepare everything that Citizen Beaumarchais would need to travel to Holland the next day, specifically passports for him and for M. de La Hogue, an advance of 50,000 German florins, and complementary funds that Lebrun promised to send to the French ambassador in The Hague.

On September 21, the day after the French victory over the Prussian and Austrian armies at Valmy, the day the monarchy was abolished, and the eve of the proclamation of the Republic, Beaumarchais took the small amount of gold he had at home in reserve and deposited with his banker écus that were destined for the national treasury (when he had been paid back) in order to have credit for the same sum in Holland. He took the *poste* to Le Havre with Gudin. Understanding the perils that awaited him, he left behind a "Protest Against the Ministers," which he deposited in one of the secret drawers of his famous rolltop desk, and kept a copy. "In case of misfortune," he asked that it be opened in the presence of commissioners who would inventory his papers. This vitriolic indictment accused the

principal ministers of preventing the rifles from leaving the port of
Veere; he blamed Lebrun especially for never paying him the deposit
required to have the embargo lifted—despite his solemn promises
before the military authorities. He ended with these words:

> I protest with all my power against the treachery of the current
> minister, and I make him responsible to the Nation for all the evil
> that this has brought, and that in this I am only executing what I
> severely warned them I would do in my letter, in the form of a
> memorandum sent to M. Lebrun on August 19 of this year,
> where I told him bluntly "After having explained to you what a
> new minister cannot divine, if the minister goes ahead and
> thwarts these plans, then I am forced to declare, Monsieur, that
> here my responsibility finishes, that I am placing the burden on
> the executive power, which I had the honor of forewarning."

But his mision had not been kept secret.

After a brief stay in Le Havre, taking time to embrace his wife,
daughter, and sister, he embarked for England, hoping for a change of
scene. Disembarking at Portsmouth on the thirtieth, he reached London on October 2 but stayed only twenty-four hours, time enough
to meet his bankers and correspondents, the Le Cointe brothers,
whom he informed of his need for money, since he had been able to
bring only 30,000 francs with him. The bankers gave him credit for
10,000 pounds sterling and told him: "End this as soon as you can;
do not lose a minute!" He also devised with them a plan that would
foil the resistant Dutch authorities: the Le Cointe brothers would
pretend to buy the famous rifles, supposedly destined for the West
Indies, and then would have them transported first to England, then
to a French port.

The agreement concluded, Beaumarchais embarked for Holland;
after a six-day crossing, "the most painful in forty years," he arrived
in The Hague, "sick to death," and went to the French ambassador
Emmanuel de Maulde to give him the orders from Lebrun. "This
order is positive, and I will obey it exactly; but you will find this
country full of obstacles," he warned Beaumarchais. "Has M. Lebrun
sent you the guarantee?" "No, not yet." "The minister told me he

would give you an order to lend me two or three hundred thousand francs if I needed them, from all the funds you have." "I do not have any." "Then while waiting for the guarantee to arrive, I am going to require a notarized affidavit from the Dutch seller that he is making me a legal expropriation and a similar delivery, at Tervere itself. Since I am dealing with cunning people in Paris—"

"You can, if you want, spare yourself all these difficulties," the ambassador interrupted, and told the astonished Beaumarchais that Lebrun had recommended a certain "Constantini," who proposed to buy the entire cargo for 7.8 florins apiece, to be paid in gold on the spot. "This is only a florin less than the government price, which you will earn back by all the trouble you will save yourself. This man appears to have the confidence of the ministers. He obtained from them the exclusive right to supply to the government with everything that can be got out of Holland. And the difficulties that people could give you in France will not affect him, it appears, at least if I may believe his words."

Beaumarchais refused flatly, indignant at such a proposal: "Monsieur, tell M. Constantini that I reject his offer with contempt, as I have rejected others under the knife at the Abbaye, and that he will not have my rifles. For a long time this affair has not been merely commercial for me. Of course my country will have them; but it will have them from me alone, at the first price I sold them for, and not a florin more. No banditry will take place."

"Banditry?" Were they trying to make a profit on these rifles by buying them more cheaply from Beaumarchais in order to resell them dearly to France? And who was hiding behind this "Constantini," which was no doubt an alias—Lebrun? Clavière? Both? Others? Who was this Corsican adventurer who came out of the shadows, without past or future, and who seemed to have entry everywhere, unlimited funds, and powerful enough support to have the embargo lifted? It was a mystery. A certain number of clues, though, threw suspicion on Lebrun, who was perhaps maneuvering to discourage Beaumarchais enough to make him sell his arsenal at a loss to Constantini, a straw man, in order to resell them at a high price to the French government. This would explain the minister's repeated postponements and lack of response.

On October 16 Pierre-Augustin wrote to Lebrun to remind him of his promises. He received no answer. Ten days later he tried again. Still nothing. On November 9 he threatened to go into permanent exile or to spill the beans. The same day Lebrun finally replied: he had just discovered a fact known since the beginning, that the rifles were not new but had been used by a free corps of Dutch patriots at the time of the last attempted revolution, then had been sold to the Belgians, who had used them during their own revolution; finally Dutch merchants had bought them and sold them to Beaumarchais. Lebrun wrote:

> I agree that a guarantee of fifty thousand florins demanded to lift the embargo put on old rifles will disengage you from great embarrassment, that of knowing where to place them. I agree that the treaty passed between you and ex-minister Lajard is very advantageous. But be of good faith, citizen, and agree in turn that we would indeed be dupes to approve of such a treaty and to adhere to it. Our views and our principles did not agree with those of our predecessors. They gave the impression of wanting what they did not want; and we are good patriots and good citizens; sincerely desiring to do good, we fulfill the duties of our office with as much loyalty and probity as honesty.

Lebrun ended with a falsehood that underlay his whole diplomatic correspondence: "For some time, I no longer meddle in the purchase of arms. These mercantile operations scarcely agree with the kind of work and expertise required by my department."

Nevertheless, the Revolutionary armies were going from one military success to another. After they defeated Brunswick's troops at Valmy, they forced the Austrians to evacuate Champagne, Verdun, and Longwy and chased them back across the border. Led by the general Custine, the French troops invaded the Palatinate, the Rhineland, and took Speyer, Worms, Mainz, and Frankfurt. Another general, Montesquiou, entered Savoy, and Anselme took Nice, where tricolor cockades now blossomed. At the beginning of October the Austrians lifted the siege of Lille and retreated to Belgium, which Dumouriez entered on the twenty-seventh with 40,000 men. On

November 6 he soundly defeated the Austrians at the village of Jemmapes. Under these blows, the Imperial powers had to abandon Brussels, Mechelen, Leuven, Liège, Ghent, and Namur. Within a month, the Revolutionary armies had taken almost all of Belgium and were pursuing their advance into Holland. Dumouriez was getting ready to "bring liberty to the Batavians" as he had to the Belgians. He sent two armed launches to Middelburg to ask the Estates of Zeeland for passage across the Scheldt estuary so as to bombard the Château of Antwerp. Middelburg, on the island of Walcheren, was so close to Veere that Beaumarchais thought his rifles were nearly within his grasp. Those rifles, so long and wrongfully held by the Dutch government, were finally going to be liberated by French troops! But that proved to be an illusion.

But at this precise moment, Pierre-Augustin's head was on the block in Paris. On November 28, 1792, Deputy Lecointre presented to the Convention a long report denouncing Beaumarchais as a "member of the clique of conspirators"; he also implicated two former ministers, the Marquis de Grave and Scipion Chambonas. He characterized Beaumarchais as a "man vicious by essence and corrupt by inclination, who has reduced immorality to a principle and villainy to a system." He accused him of having secret correspondence with Louis XVI and of despoiling the nation's wealth. He denounced the dealings over the Dutch rifles as "the fruit of collusion and fraud." So, "given the fraud and the criminal connivance that reigned in both the deal of April 3 and the transaction of late July between Beaumarchais, Lajard and Chambonas, therefore Pierre-Augustin Caron, called Beaumarchais, will be put under arrest."

The Convention voted unanimously in favor of the accusation, guaranteeing the guillotine. On November 30 seals were again put on the house in boulevard Saint-Antoine, and on the warehouses of the Voltaire edition in Strasbourg; Lebrun sent a dispatch to the French ambassador in The Hague for the arrest and extradition of the guilty party. That same day Beaumarchais learned of the accusation from The Hague gazette, which devoted a long article to his "fraudulent deals." Beaumarchais judged it prudent to sneak away in the night. Hearing of his flight, the British ambassador, Lord Auckland, remarked that he was "a victim in his fortunes to the Revolution, to which his talents so much contributed. It is said that his house and papers are seized on some charges. I cannot pity him." Pierre Manuel, his savior from the Abbaye, probably at the urging of Amélie, warned him of the danger he was in and pressed him to go to London as quickly as possible. Decidedly doomed to stormy Channel crossings, Beaumarchais endured a tempest, in the course of which he witnessed the shipwreck of a vessel carrying French émigrés. While meditating once more on his bizarre destiny, he expected after a brief stay in London to return to Paris, "for it was time the National Convention learned about everything."

Arriving in London "by miracle," he hurried to open messages that his friends had dared not send him in The Hague and came across this phrase: "If you are reading this in England, give thanks on your knees, for God has preserved you!" There followed details about the trap that the Ministers Clavière and Lebrun had laid for him after his arrest. The extraordinary courier who was instructed to bring him back to Paris "hands and feet bound" had received another, quite singular command: to make sure the prisoner did not arrive alive. Those in high places feared the self-defense so often threatened by this "strange minister of foreign affairs." He later wrote "What man would have believed this blind rage from ministers? Ah, well—that was their plan. As sent from Paris."

Happy to have escaped both the nation's razor and the mercenary's knife, blessing Heaven to have reached London, the asylum for escapees from all kinds of regimes, Beaumarchais thought of his family, "wandering and desolate," of his wife, child, and sisters. But he was unable to communicate with them without divulging the secret of their presence in Le Havre and thus putting them in danger. So he took the risk of writing to them by means of the press: he inserted an open letter in Le Courrier de l'Europe of December 11, 1792. This was also his last contribution to this paper, for after sixteen years of existence it would cease to appear after December 28. In reality, this "Letter to My Family" aimed not so much to make contact with his kin as to defend himself publicly against the serious accusations of the Convention. He denied, for example, having had recent correspondence with Louis XVI, alluding to letters that dated back to 1775 and concerned the American war. Did he forget that he had continued to write to the king until 1786? But the letters that interested the Convention were not these either, but the ones he supposedly wrote against the Revolution for the Austrian armies, in favor of the émigrés. As there is no better defense than to attack, Beaumarchais denounced those who, disdaining every law, had tried to make him disappear between The Hague and Paris. He named no names, but the supposedly guilty parties could easily recognize themselves if they opened that issue of the gazette.

Accused of collusion with the enemy, Beaumarchais was soon branded with a new mark of infamy, again unjustified. On the pretext that his "Letter to My Family" was dated from London, he was declared to be an émigré, although he was entrusted with a mission by the French government, as his passport proved. This declaration was most serious, for the laws specified very heavy punishment for fugitives: banishment for life from national territory, deprivation of civil rights, and seizure of all goods, which became the property of the state. Such reprisals against Beaumarchais were not long in coming. On the night of December 16, with no prior warning, eight men went to his house, occupied only by his wife, daughter, and sisters, and installed three guards. That day he started writing a "Petition to the National Convention," arguing against the arbitrary power and summarizing all his tribulations since 1789. The declaration was dramatic in its very conciseness, and his indignation was forcefully expressed. But some passages reveal the voice of an irredeemably wounded man:

> For my part, citizens, my tumultuous life has at last become burdensome. As a result of the liberty I acquired by the Revolution, I have a score of times been nearly burned out, hanged high, or shot; I have suffered in the last four years from fourteen accusations, each as absurd as atrocious; I have seen myself dragged off to your prisons twice for summary execution without a trial; I have received in my house a visit by forty thousand men of the sovereign people, though I have committed no other crime than to have a pleasant garden; I have been denounced by you for two separate acts called *treasonable*; all your seals have been placed on my house for the third time this year, without anyone telling me

why; and people were sent to arrest me in Holland and perhaps
to slit my throat en route back to France (while I find myself safe
in London). I now propose, O citizens, to return at once freely
to Paris, either as a prisoner on parole until my case is heard, or
else with the *whole city* or *my house as prison*, if that is more suitable. When this precaution is taken and my life is guaranteed, I
will leave instantly for Paris. I even have some hope of still being
useful to my country.

This was not simply talk: Beaumarchais had every intention of
returning to France and was actively preparing for it. He longed to
see his kin and his home, and especially to plead his cause before the
Convention and rehabilitate himself in public opinion. But that was
another illusion. Times had changed since the Goëzman affair. His
London friends pleaded with him that he would be throwing himself
into the lions' den, that he was running back to the guillotine, but he
listened to nobody. So they resorted to a most unexpected stratagem
to save him: they put him in prison!

The Le Cointe house, Beaumarchais's bankers, had advanced him
10,000 pounds sterling before his trip to Holland. This sum was to
be used as part of the deposit for buying the rifles, but now he found
himself unable to reimburse it. So his banker had him held as an
insolvent debtor in the King's Bench prison—less to secure his person than to force him to remain in England, where he ran no risk. "It
was too much to lose both his money and his friend," Beaumarchais
remarked ironically in a letter to Gudin.

Arrested on December 28, he was transported to the King's
Bench, where he was treated as a distinguished guest. Installed in a
private apartment outside the prison walls, he received much consideration from the penitentiary personnel and had the right to receive
visitors and other detainees who were guilty of indebtedness. Here he
was far from the horrible cells of the Abbaye or, worse, the scaffold
already erected for him.

The English authorities, however, did not appreciate the presence
of Beaumarchais on their soil. They had not forgotten his more-than-
suspect maneuvers twenty years ago, when he had been the secret
agent of the King of France, nor his tussles with the Chevalier d'Éon,

which had supplied the press with scandal, nor his help to the American rebels. What was this arms dealer doing in England? What suspicious operation was he up to now? After his precipitate arrival in London, the British ambassador to The Hague had warned Whitehall, "He will do all possible mischief to us." Some in Prime Minister William Pitt's entourage feared that he would try to spread Revolutionary ideas. But curiously, his arrest had been desired and arranged by his best friends, notably Le Cointe. All these questions Beaumarchais tried to answer in his "Letter to the British," published on December 29, 1792.

Using his forced inactivity for his own benefit, Beaumarchais wrote the "sad story" of his misadventures from March to December 1792, entitling it *An Account of the Nine Most Painful Months of My Life*. Here he refuted point by point the accusations of Lecointre before the National Convention. It was written in six "epochs"; the first was finished in the beginning of January 1793. His banker Paul Le Cointe sent four printed copies to William Pitt, who devoured it as an adventure story and asked for the sequel. Apart from the simple literary pleasure it provided, the prime minister found therein much information that he had sought elsewhere, about the men who were governing France during this troubled period. Danton, Marat, Dumouriez, Lebrun—heretofore he could barely put a face to their names, let alone a character, but now they came to life before his eyes; he discovered the pettiness and baseness of some, the blackness and cupidity of others, and the badly disguised ambition of them all. These muddled, unstable, and agitated functionaries, overcome by events, were trying in vain to perform thankless tasks and all trying to keep their heads on their shoulders. But what pleased Pitt most was the portrait of France given over to anarchy, where the currency was collapsing and an economic debacle loomed.

In fact, France was traversing a particularly critical period. The trial of Louis XVI, starting on December 16, lasted until January 18. That day the deputies of the Convention voted for the king's death. On January 21 at 10:20 a.m. the blade of the guillotine fell on the royal neck; when the news reached Great Britain, it provoked anti-French riots. Pitt used the pretext of the execution of the king to break off diplomatic relations with France and brought Britain into the conflict alongside the Austrians and Prussians. From the French standpoint, the moment could not have been more badly chosen, for French troops, having crossed European borders from the Scheldt to Savoy to "liberate" neighboring peoples, were now suffering major reverses.

The entry of Britain and the Low Countries into the coalition revived interest in Beaumarchais's rifles, ownership of which was now claimed by all parties. Holland possessed a long head start in this race for the weapons, since the cargo was held in its waters, but a British frigate was anchored in the Veere bay to keep watch on the port. While appetites for these arms were sharpening (it was said they would prove more dangerous to the users than to the enemy), in Paris the banker Perregaux was able to raise 10,000 pounds sterling as bail money to free Pierre-Augustin. On February 1, 1793, Beaumarchais left prison "on condition of not leaving the city." By a public contract the bankers purchased the rifles, and by a private and secret contract Beaumarchais reserved the right to buy them back within two months—what is called in legal terms the right of repurchase. "The ten thousand pounds sterling mortgaged on these same arms" constituted the exchange that he would pay back in April. By this astute scheme, he prevented the cargo from being seized, which it would surely have been as long as its fate remained uncertain.

Upon his arrival in Le Havre, Beaumarchais embraced his wife, daughter, and sisters, who had come to welcome him; they found him pale and weak from his ordeals but more determined than ever to win justice. On February 10 he received the information that he had impatiently awaited: "The National Convention decrees that there will be a two-month reprieve in the execution of the decree of accusation against Citizen Caron Beaumarchais, and during this time he will furnish his defense so that the National Convention can pronounce definitively." (The seals on his effects and papers would be lifted on February 14.) Justice Minister Garat gave him the good news and enjoined him to reach Paris as soon as possible. On the twenty-sixth, after five months of absence, he finally set foot in his home, surrounded by those close to him. Since the Parisian population, and especially that of his neighborhood, manifested frank hostility to him, he prepared to publish his *Nine Most Painful Months*, written during his stay in the London prison. Stripped of its digressions, revised, and corrected, the new version (which still ran to 350 pages!) would be published in six thousand copies. Still as practical as ever, he also published in a small format, for people in a hurry, several extracts from the sixth "epoch" that amounted to only thirty-two pages.

Reading this self-justificatory account, one is struck by the firm tone and the audacious statements. Aged over sixty, the gentleman had not lost his vigor—only his gaiety. Although his family and friends recommended that he maintain a prudent silence, he made a brilliant reappearance on the legal scene, persuaded that great publicity for his cause could only animate minds in his favor. The introduction to the first "epoch" not only presented his self-defense but was a judicious critique of the Revolutionary style as marked by hyperbole and swollen by vanity. Danton's words to the Assembly—"Audacity, still more audacity, always audacity!"—best suit Beaumarchais in publishing his *Nine Painful Months* in March 1793. Ten years previously Figaro had audaciously mocked those who "take the trouble to be born and nothing else." At the time, Parisians applauded this line, including those at whom it was aimed. But in 1793, when Beaumarchais refused to submit to bullying by the villains who now governed France, he was alone; even those who might have supported him remained silent out of fear of reprisals. For already the Terror was lurking, escorted everywhere by the hydra called denunciation.

Standing before the Convention, Beaumarchais summoned all of France to be his judges. Was he naïve or presumptuous to do so? More simply, his was the testimony of a man who had always had faith only in the individual and was more interested than his judges in the interests of the citizen. An isolated voice might and should stand up to hatred and corruption, he believed, even at the risk of losing his head, especially when the conscience of a whole people was being insulted. Doubtless he fully measured the risk he was taking. His purpose was not only to claim his own rights but to defend a larger cause that was more noble and everlasting: that of truth. His relatives and friends tried to caution him, for his own and their sakes, in vain. At the beginning of March 1793, when the destiny of France was hanging in the balance and its territory was threatened, when its regime seemed most unstable, Beaumarchais finished his sixth "epoch" with a prophetic hymn calling for peace among all the nations of Europe:

O my weeping country! O wretched Frenchmen! What good will it have done you to demolish Bastilles if brigands come to dance on the ruins and massacre us on the debris? *True friends of liberty*, remember that its first oppressors are license and anarchy. Join my cries of protest and let us demand laws from the deputies who owe them to us, who were elected by us for this purpose! Let us make peace with Europe; was not the finest day of our glory when we declared it to the world? Let us strengthen our domestic government. Let us organize ourselves without disputes and storms, and especially, if possible, without crimes. Your maxims will be established and will spread much better than by war, murder, and devastations, *if people see you happy as a result of them*. Are you happy? Let us be truthful. Is it really by the blood of Frenchmen that our land is watered? Speak up! Is there a single one of you who has had no tears to shed? *Peace, laws, a constitution!* Without these blessings, there is no country, and above all no liberty!

Frenchmen! I am over sixty years old and with some experience of people. In sticking to my hearth, I have proved that I have no more ambition. No man on this continent has contributed more than me to making America free: *judge if I adore the liberty of our France*! I have let the whole world speak, and I will again be silent after these few words. But if you hesitate to take a generous part, I tell you with pain, Frenchmen, that we have only a moment more to exist as free; and then the premier people of the world, in chains, will become the shame and opprobrium of this century, and the terror of other nations!

On April 7 the deadline of the repurchase option, signed with the Le Cointe brothers, expired. Beyond that date the arms would become the property of the bankers. On that day Beaumarchais learned that his file was now in the hands of the finance committee. For many weeks his case, judged so urgent a year ago, had been dragging from office to office. Indifference, negligence, ill will, and meanness all combined to delay the proceedings. By mid-April, not only had no decision been taken, but the seals had still not been lifted. Another month would pass before the February 10 decree was enforced.

On May 7 Beaumarchais was summoned to the Committee of Public Safety, which a month before had replaced the Committee of General Security and sat at the Louvre in the wing called Equality (today Flore). Three days later he appeared officially before his accuser Lecointre, whose list of charges were refuted one after another. The "citizen-soldier" was deemed innocent, and his arms deal was generally approved; better still, he was unanimously instructed to take possession of his goods in the Low Countries. For this purpose he was given the title of commissioner of the Republic on a secret mission and was promised 600,000 Dutch florins in assignats. Coming from a government that the day before had still considered him suspect, this abrupt turnaround proved at least that the *Nine Painful Months* had had an effect.

Beaumarchais declared himself ready to return to Holland, this time on condition that "all protection and safety be agreed over [my] initiative, so that nothing arrest its course. If [I] was forced to travel, [my] goods would be under the safeguard of the Republic employing [me]. And finally, all justice would be rendered to [my] patriotic zeal." But new obstacles arose to oppose his mission. First, how was he to transfer the funds that had just been granted him without wasting any time? He suggested moving quickly so as to not "make the exchange fall" and charged Perregaux with the operation, as the banker most suiting the taste of the Committee of Public Safety, using all the necessary discretion; moreover he was among his friends. Then began a race against the clock, which sorely tested his nerves. The Committee of Public Safety was handling too much at once and could not be concerned with him. As formerly with Lebrun, he was again obliged to sit in antechambers (up to seven hours a day) and to attend meetings that lasted whole nights. He protested and invoked his age, but they mocked him; he was increasingly deaf and needed an ear trumpet. Still, he insisted and tried ten times, twenty times, but nobody wanted to hear him. Realizing that "each day a new obstacle is forged," he told himself that someone was hiding something from him, that so much ill will was perhaps aimed only to discourage him. If so, his enemies did not know him well. Paralyzed by indecision, negligence, delays, prevarications, and incessant interrogations, he begged the committee to put an end to this pointless situation.

At this juncture news arrived from England that the Le Cointe brothers, tired of waiting in vain for the purchase of the arms when the resale was a month overdue, had sold the cargo stored in Veere. Far from feeling desolate, Beaumarchais exulted: "Thanks to the genius of France, this letter [from the Le Cointes] puts the arms back in my hands. With alacrity, zeal, and intelligence, I still hope to manage to prevent them going to others. The sale is made, but not the delivery; and I see with joy that I can prevent it from happening. I am writing to Holland to prevent it. This stick that I am placing in the wheel spokes, and which I alone can disengage, will make my Englishman more accessible to my demands." What was he referring to? This stratagem, "the stick in the spokes" by which he intended to prevent delivery of the rifles, was quite simple: he would break his contract with Le Cointe by offering him "a retraction payment."

During the meeting of May 19, devoted to "this final secret work," Beaumarchais persuaded the Committee of Public Safety to increase the sum of 600,000 florins allocated on the fourteenth for buying back the cargo. The committee decided that "these arms will be bought from Le Cointe, en bloc, as he has acquired them, by ultimatum up to the sum of 800,000 florins of Holland, which will be paid back in kind, in England or Holland as he chooses. Soon the 922 cases and 27 tons will arrive in one of the ports or border towns of the French Republic, following the preferred route." The Committee of Public Safety would hold 800,000 florins at the disposition of Le Cointe; Beaumarchais would be given "all passports considered necessary"; and 104,000 florins would cover the exit guarantee and warehousing costs. "If circumstances require"—in other words, in case of difficulties on the part of the Dutch—delivery of the rifles would be demanded in America in order to satisfy the clause stipulating their departure from Europe. During the session of May 22, however, new quibbling arose between committee members and the very new commissioner of the Republic: they caviled, whittled, and wangled the 800,000 florins down to only 104,000 to be reserved for him—in short, they made his task impossible. At the same time, far from being disarmed, his old enemies laid into him. The Corsican bandit "Constantini" invented the word *figarotisme* to designate "connivances" and "turpitudes," while Lebrun denounced his "intrigues" and "malevolence."

Finally on June 27, the eve of his departure, Beaumarchais commended his family to Barère, the Committee of Public Safety member with whom he got along best. The two men, united by mutual confidence, said good-bye and wished each other good luck—without believing it. At the moment of parting Beaumarchais whispered in his companion's ear, "I am sure that you envy my fate, and that you find me too happy to be able to go." To which Barère replied, "That is true, but I do today what I have been doing every day for a year: I make my courage for the day to come."

Twenty-Nine

THE PRISONER OF ALTONA

Days of crimes and disgrace, that a vestige of fear today makes us call the time of Terror, but that History will call the reign of the execrable ones!
— *Gudin*, **Histoire de Beaumarchais**

Traveling under the identity "Pierre Charron, Lausanne merchant," Beaumarchais left Paris on June 28, 1793, for Basel, where the Committee of Public Safety had promised to send him 700,000 florins via Perrégaux. The funds had predictably not arrived. Beaumarchais wrote a letter to the committee that remained unanswered. Rather than go back to France, where he would exhaust himself in vain efforts, he decided to go directly to England. Shortly after his arrival in London, more bad news hit him: Le Cointe had resold the rifles and would deliver them to the anti-Republican armies in the Vendée via Guernsey. Here he was, caught between a rock and a hard place: on one side, his government was preventing him from buying the rifles back for want of money; on the other, if the rifles passed into enemy hands, the government would take him for a traitor. Then a magnificent idea crossed his mind.

First, Beaumarchais had to become the owner of the arms by buying them back from Le Cointe. With his own money, he paid him 1,000 guineas, plus 32,000 florins, representing the profit he would make on this sale, plus, finally, 10,000 pounds sterling, all of which made him the new owner of the cargo. Now he had definitively deprived the counterrevolutionary army of the rifles they were impatiently awaiting. All that remained was for Beaumarchais to bring the weapons to Le Havre without arousing the British authorities' suspicions. They were ignorant of the repurchase agreement, which had been signed privately. But how could he transport the weapons outside British jurisdiction? Here Figaro showed the full measure of his genius by drawing up a plan.

He would recruit a foreign buyer to ostensibly buy the rifles from Le Cointe. This buyer would then resell them on Beaumarchais's behalf to an American company, in a fictional sale. The ship transporting the cargo from Zeeland to New York would necessarily have to stop in France, where the merchandise would be unloaded. The American company would be called Chevallié and Company, the name of Beaumarchais's agent in New York. Beaumarchais also chose the buyer: a businessman named Schultz in Hamburg, on whom he could count. Schultz would be led to believe it was a simple commercial transaction. To make the operation seem all the more plausible, Le Cointe went to Hamburg in person.

Unfortunately it was easier to trick the Cabinet of St. James than Scotland Yard, which already had some suspicions about the mysterious Pierre Charron. Its finest detectives sniffed around the Le Cointe bank and soon spotted Beaumarchais's allies. Following the portly, deaf sexagenarian with a strong French accent, they came to the residence of Captain Swinton at 5 Sloane Street near Hyde Park, where the neighbors seemed to know him. (He had built a house near there around 1785.) On August 14 he received a ministerial letter—"very polite"—that gave him three days to clear out of Britain, on pain of arrest. On the sixteenth he embarked for Ostend, where he arrived three days later, at the end of his strength. After recovering, he set off for the Low Countries and passed a few hours in Veere, where he surveyed his two ships (which had been "at the dock" for more than a year) but did not linger because the enemy was at his heels. Arriving at Antwerp, he fell gravely ill and took refuge with a surgeon who cared for him—and who, if he pierced the disguise, did not denounce him. Beaumarchais remained there almost three months, suspended between life and death. During his forced retreat, news trickled in from France: the assassination of Marat on July 13, the successive defeats of the Republican armies (they abandoned Mainz to the Prussians and surrendered Valenciennes); the Girondin revolts in Lyons, Bordeaux, and Marseilles against the Convention; popular fury at the lack of foodstuffs in Paris. On September 5 the Reign of Terror began by unleashing a massive "purification": the prisons overflowed with suspects, and the guillotine was working overtime. Marie-Antoinette was condemned on October 14 and mounted the scaffold two days later. With no news of his family and unable to receive any, Beaumarchais lived in anguish. On October 8 he managed to send a note to his wife through Perrégaux.

Barely convalescent, he reached Rotterdam, where he had a meeting with Le Cointe; meanwhile Schultz, the Hamburg buyer, presented a request to the United Provinces to lift the embargo on the arms, and since they were to pass from Veere to New York, he also asked to be exempted from the enormous ensurance deposit, which had risen to three times the purchase price. According to the official list of successive owners, the weapons were passing directly from the bookseller Delahaye to the banker Le Cointe—Beaumarchais was not once mentioned. Everything was going well; it was time to inform Chevallié in New York about the "imbroglio" and to give him the necessary instructions.

The Committee of Public Safety, lacking news of its commissioner, lost patience and called him to account. Beaumarchais sent back a twenty-page report. The Committee of Public Safety acknowledged the report, seemed convinced of the good faith and effectiveness of its agent, and took encouraging measures in his favor. The times were not at all inclined to clemency, however. The Law of Suspects, voted by the Convention on September 17, relied on the widest and vaguest definition; "suspects" included not only political opponents, émigrés and their relatives, but also the wealthy, opportunists, cannon salesmen, suppliers of weapons and provisions—in short, all those whom the Convention wished to be rid of. Was there any citizen more "suspect" than Beaumarchais, who was abroad, probably plotting against the Republic? There were abundant reasons to put him on the list, not only of suspects but also of émigrés; doing so would allow them to seize all his goods and put them up for sale. Nevertheless, at the request of Mme. de Beaumarchais on 25

Frimaire of the Year II (December 15, 1793), the "Committee of Public Safety . . . declares that Citizen Beaumarchais is fulfilling a secret mission and consequently orders that he not be treated as an émigré." Three days later a second order lifted the seals on his property.

Despite this precarious mark of relative goodwill, the expatriate did not dare return home until he had delivered his famous rifles. He lurked around them in Zeeland, tracked by the foreign police, resorting to intrigues, prevarications, and hasty plots. He was a curious and somewhat pathetic figure, this aging Figaro, condemned to live clandestinely and improvise a breathless existence; he never went to sleep without wondering if tomorrow he would be strong enough to continue, and if the day would lead someplace where he could lay his head. These black thoughts sometimes brightened: ripping open a packet from Paris, he devoured a letter from Eugénie written on January 24: "We are living in a very retired way, seeing few people, going out seldom. A more dissipated life would displease me; I do not miss the pleasures—only you. You are always in my thoughts." In Frankfurt, where he arrived incognito, exhausted by his continual wandering, the anguish did not leave him. Bits of frightening rumors arrived from Paris, where the Terror was raging. The prisons were overflowing with "suspects," distrust reigned everywhere, and famine was setting in; churches and aristocratic houses were being looted. What would become of his own sumptuous residence, located amid a populace racked by hunger and misery? Unprotected women were living in this vast home stuffed with wealth; while it was assumed that they had enormous means, in fact they were suffering the common fate. Despite assurances given to Beaumarchais, the authorities did not lend a sou to his family, whose resources were steadily diminishing.

Still in Frankfurt in March 1794, he was even more afraid, despite his reassuring words to Eugénie, for the despoilment appeared imminent. His fears were well founded: a denunciation arrived at the new "Committee of General Security," which transmitted this note to the director of domains: "We are informed, Citizen, that the buildings situated in Paris belonging to the said Beaumarchais appear still at the disposition of relatives or agents. We exhort you not to lose sight of the interests of the Republic entrusted to you; keep us informed of the measures you will take." After verification, the director of domains realized that Citizen Beaumarchais had been crossed off the list of émigrés of the preceding 25 Frimaire, and so it was impossible to affix seals to his goods for the third time. The authorities ruled anew: in contempt of the obvious truth, they declared that the "individual" in question would be treated as an émigré and his property would be confiscated.

Foreseeing a seizure within twenty-four hours, Mme. de Beaumarchais and the Gudin brothers hastily destroyed documents attesting to the ties between the man in exile and the ancien régime. Crazy with fear, cloistered in their huge house, Marie-Thérèse and Eugénie awaited the worst. The Terror had all of Paris trembling, aristocrats and common people, rich and poor, masters and valets, innocent and guilty; the number of guillotined reached the hundreds and soon the thousands. The Revolutionary Tribunal increased the death sentences; its justice was expeditious and without appeal, delivering to the charnel house the enemies of the Revolution and even its recent friends.

On March 20 the agents of the Convention came once more to put seals on Beaumarchais's house. A decree placarded on the walls informed passersby that the house was now "national property." The family were obliged to leave: Marie-Thérèse found lodging in a small apartment at 18, rue du Paradis-Poissonnière but vigorously contested the order from the Committee of General Security, founded on "an error of fact," she argued. Not discouraged, she complained that due to the unjustified sequestration, her husband's affairs had suffered irreparable damage: his furniture was ruined, his storehouse housing the Voltaire edition had been "ruined by water leakage, his fonts and characters were useless, other furniture nonrepaired, the creditors unpaid." The tax agents who confiscated his goods had snatched everything she possessed, even the rental income from the boutiques opening on the boulevard, and she found herself without any means, isolated with her daughter in this modest lodging where she felt no safer than in the boulevard Saint-Antoine. She decided to leave Paris with Eugénie and take refuge in Boissy-Saint-Léger, leaving her house in the care of her sister-in-law Julie and Gudin. As her husband had given her power of attorney to administer his affairs and property, she informed the Convention that she was putting an end to its management, thereby disengaging her responsibility. But she soon had to make other statements of allegiance that were even more painful. Revolutionary laws ordered that the wives of émigrés had to divorce their husbands, on pain of being considered suspect themselves and suffering the same punishment as their husbands. Officially requested on 6 Floréal of the Year II (April 25, 1794), the Beaumarchais divorce was pronounced on the following 28 Thermidor (August 15). It would last only three years, until Pierre-Augustin's return to France and their remarriage.

Far from attenuating the resentment of his judges, Beaumarchais's perfectly valid way of obeying the law without betraying his sentiments only irritated them more. On July 4, 1794, for no given reason, the Committee of Public Safety ordered the arrest of Mme. de Beaumarchais, her daughter, and her sister-in-law Julie: the two commissioners of Boissy were ordered to "put under arrest the woman Beau Marchet [*sic*] and her daughter, and take them to detention in Paris." First transported to Saint-Lazare, the two women were then sent away for lack of space; the same problem arose at Madelonnettes, where they no longer knew where to put the prisoners; a house of arrest in Plessis-Égalité could not receive them either. The prison hotel business had never done so well; Dame Guillotine liberated dozens of places a day, but still it was hard to find lodgings in any Paris prison. The unhappy women were then taken to a British Benedictine convent, where they were finally admitted. The same day five other commissioners received orders to go to Saint-Antoine "to effect the arrest of Marie-Émilie [*sic* for Julie] Caron Beaumarché [*sic*] as suspect and sister of the émigré." Julie would be taken to Plessis-Égalité, while Gudin, miraculously spared, remained the sole and faithful guardian of the premises.

At the former convent Mme. de Beaumarchais and her daughter shared their space with fifty detainees, among them the "widow Lamoignon," the "wife of Rivarol," the "widow Suffren," and especially the "widow Tourzel, aged 44," former governess of the royal children, and her two daughters, Mme. de Charost and her younger sister Pauline de Tourzel, twenty-one, future Comtesse de Béarn, who would devote a whole chapter of her *Memories at Forty* to her stay in the former convent. Pauline's first impression was no doubt similar to what Eugénie de Beaumarchais and her mother felt:

> We were very sad arriving there. During the committal formalities, they made us enter a great hall that in better times had been the Benedictine refectory; we threw ourselves on the chairs without exchanging a single word. A small, old, and very thin man, dressed in a camisole that only went halfway down his body, covered with a nightcap, a broom in hand, was occupied with cleaning the hall. He approached us with an air between mockery and interest and told us: "Mesdames, eight days ago, I was like you, sad and silent. It appears that you are one of us. In eight days, you will be playing your part like me." He took up the broom and continued to sweep.

This singular personage was none other than the Comte de Cassini, son of the famous astronomer César-François Cassini de Thury, who had succeeded his father as director of the Paris Observatory and whose work relating to the division of France into *départements* had not prevented him from being considered suspect.

Mme. de Tourzel and her daughters had been at the English Benedictines' for three months (they had been arrested in April 1794) when Mme. and Mlle. de Beaumarchais arrived there at the beginning of July. Pauline de Tourzel improvised as cook; using some dried vegetables bought outside, and the remains of meat and bread distributed by the guards, she was ingenious at preparing each day "feasts in her fashion."

"In the beginning, we enjoyed the greatest freedom inside the house," remembered the Comtesse de Béarn. "Of course, it was freedom in a prison, but at least we could see and visit each other. Among most of the prisoners there was benevolence, almost a paternal union. Still, out of fear of *sheep* [spies] listening to our words, even our sighs, each was on guard not to express anything but good signs. Moreover, our life was so exposed that nobody could find anything suspect."

Pauline then recounts how the Comte de Cassini, who drew very well, organized on the staircase landing a sort of small academy where he taught art to the ladies. In the garden Mme. Aynar rigged up a swing that became the main entertainment of the young ones. Most likely Eugénie and Pauline, who were about the same age, shared in Cassini's art lessons and in the games in the garden. Continued the Comtesse de Béarn:

> Time passed rather sweetly, but soon the horizon darkened again. Since we had been shut in the prison of the former convent of the English Benedictines, we had seen many people enter; we were now more than three hundred prisoners, and nobody had yet been called before the fatal tribunal. But we began to speak of plots, and the prison regime became more rigorous. Several of us were taken away and led to the scaffold . . . From this moment, everything changed in our way of living. Uncertainty replaced tranquillity; terror entered our hearts. Our fears became more serious when we were warned that my mother's name had been pronounced by one of those mouths out of which came death sentences. We thought our last day had arrived. We prepared ourselves, we encouraged each other, we went so far as to seek information on how the death sentence was carried out. Resigned to our fate, we occupied ourselves by preparing clothing that would make the executioner dispense with laying a hand on us. One day we thought these preparations were going to become useful. The covered cart that took designated victims was at the door of the house; the clerk's voice called us. We were terrified, but happily it was only a matter of transferring all the female prisoners elsewhere, and consequently my mother, my sister and myself were part of the convoy about to leave.

In fact, on 6 Thermidor (July 24, 1794) the female prisoners were transferred to the former monastery of Port-Royal (established in 1625 by the abbess Angélique Arnaud in the Faubourg Saint-Jacques, today the maternity hospital of Port-Royal), which under the Revolution had been given the derisory nickname Port-Libre or "The Mire." The convoy was composed of forty-four women and a child of three. Upon arriving in Port-Libre, they beheld a group of victims being led to the scaffold. On 9 Thermidor (July 27) a new prisoner, whose name alone inspired horror and fright, unexpectedly arrived: they rushed to glimpse Georges Couthon, the theoretician of the Great Terror. Was it possible—Couthon a prisoner? Suddenly they understood that they had nothing more to fear, that the awful nightmare was ending, that their liberation was near. The next day Couthon mounted the fatal cart, accompanied by Robespierre, Saint-Just, and their friends. A new era was opening. Ten days later, on August 8, 1794, Mme. de Beaumarchais and her daughter were released; Julie had to wait a few more months before going home.

Marie-Thérèse's first thought upon leaving Port-Libre was of her husband, still a refugee in Germany. She was able to write to him that everyone was well: "As a mother, I had to use everything to save my dear child from the fate of so many innocent and respectable girls who are today rehabilitated, mourned, and cried over, but which so much sorrow and so many tears and tardy justice will never bring back!" But she barely had time to lament; it was urgent to put a roof over their heads and find money to live on, for their house in Saint-Antoine was still under sequestration, and any income was going into public coffers; even the credit notes in her husband's desk had passed into the hands of treasury agents; the house was threatened with confiscation. Marie-Thérèse wanted authorization to reenter, but Eugénie was too scared to go in and trembled at the idea of living alone with her mother in this immense residence "that has so often exposed us to the rabble's insults," as she wrote to her father. Still, it was urgent that a family member occupy it, both to preserve it from damage and to protect it, as much as possible, against the rapacious tax collectors. Julie would take charge. At sixty years of age, crippled with rheumatism, she came to live with an elderly maid in this deserted palace that was guarded by sergeants of the Republic, whose walls still bore in giant letters: "National Property."

The two sisters-in-law, who had maintained a curious correspondence, tried to survive as best they could in these hard times, when privations affected the whole population. Famished queues formed at the doors of shops. The assignats depreciated after the Terror, but with effort Marie-Thérèse managed to procure a bundle of them that she shared with Julie. Bread had become so scarce that she implored a friend who had moved to the country to find grain or flour in the provinces.

While his family labored under these difficulties and placed all their hopes in his return, Beaumarchais pursued his own sad existence as a proscribed person, moving from Ostend to Basel, from Cleves to Frankfurt, from Nijmegen to Hamburg, with no apparent purpose, always incognito, his money and credit exhausted. Sought by the police everywhere, he was tortured by pain in the bladder and most of all was worried about his family. When he left Frankfurt for Holland on June 4, he wrote to his agent in New York: "I learn that my poor family is wandering and thorn outside my home, or retired somewhere I know not, maybe with friends in the country, without my being able to find out what they are living on, nor how women can bear this ultimate degree of misery, which would overwhelm many a man." Overcome by doubt, he despaired of ever seeing his native land again, of embracing his wife and daughter—or of spending his last days as a free man in a free nation. "If I thought I could help my family by having myself transported, even in a litter, to where they have taken refuge, carrying with me the accumulated proofs of my efforts and my sacrifices, I would not hesitate. But I am told that having been declared an émigré, I will not be heard at all, but would be arrested as soon as I set foot in France, and I would be dead before being able to defend myself. And then they would be certainly lost . . . I have no more contact with the men of my country," he concluded in the depth of his despair. Some days he would be tempted, as the young Chevallié advised, to go to America, "the only country where one can breathe in peace." But fleeing and letting himself be stripped of all his goods, especially his famous cargo, without reacting—would that not be cowardly, or tantamount to admitting guilt?

What man in his situation and at his age would not think himself beaten? But his despairing moments did not last. Soon, despite lassitude and illness, the man of action regained the upper hand. Even when he was at the bottom of the abyss, and everything seemed lost, plans and ideas surged up. A new scheme now entered his head, already solidly constructed, equipped with a strategy, ready to be used. As always, he would make a big splash and take the leading role.

To start with, he must drop the masks! He had to stop living clandestinely and present himself under his real name. Why? Beaumarchais intended to meet the ministers of The Hague to propose—a general peace! This might be his last role, but surely it would also be the most grandiose he had ever conceived in his craziest dreams. At sixty-three, Figaro would become the peacemaker of Europe!

He could not have chosen a better moment for such an initiative, for the soldiers of Year II were going from victory to victory. Beaumarchais was therefore in a strong position; the threat of a French invasion of Dutch territory should be a weighty argument to convince the stadtholder ministers. His plan was simple: he would get the United Provinces to cede the rifles to the French Republic. This done, the Republic would immediately decree the end of hostilities. In other words: *Give us back our weapons, and we will offer peace.* It was a strange concept, in truth, to receive rifles with one hand and hold out an olive branch with the other! Naturally, Beaumarchais could undertake nothing without the approval of the Committee of Public Safety. He communicated his peace plan and begged the committee to support his efforts.

While passing through Basel in July 1794, he learned of the arrest of his family and his own inscription on the list of émigrés. Anguished, he nevertheless headed for the Low Countries to pursue his mediation effort. Arriving in Nijmegen, he learned of Robespierre's fall and execution. His wife, daughter, and sister were saved. Comforted, he continued on to The Hague, where he requested an audience with the Dutch councilor Laurens Pieter Van de Spiegel. The interview took place on the evening of August 20. Beaumarchais spoke at length, describing his conduct during the Revolution and mentioning the different purchases he had made for France in the course of his many trips abroad. Then he passed on to the political changes in France after Robespierre and said he thought the new government would aspire to peace. The current state of French opinion, he averred, was aroused against England, Prussia, and Austria and did not envisage peace with those nations. But Holland could be the ideal terrain for European peace talks. The French, in their current hatred of any monarchical system, would feel less repugnance about dealing with a republic whose form was close to their own. It went without saying that nobody was better placed than he to start the peace process between the nations concerned. The Committee of Public Safety should assume responsibility: if it remained hostile to negotiations with the coalition, it risked keeping France in its state of distress and isolation. In conclusion, he offered "to be imprisoned here in some fortress and to write only what would be approved, to communicate the answers and to conduct this affair in the fashion judged most suitable here."

The Dutch authorities could not believe that Beaumarchais was acting on his own initiative; they were certain that he was an emissary of the French government. In any case, his proposals aroused various reactions. The French armies were then advancing and converging on Maastricht, the key city of Holland, which led the Baron de Bielfeld, secretary to the Prussian ambassador in The Hague, to remark: "In this situation more critical than ever, it would not be astonishing if the government of the Republic of the United Provinces lent an ear to the peace-making proposals with which the famous Beaumarchais, in the village of Voorburg near here, is probably entrusted."

Beaumarchais sent the Committee of Public Safety a report on his conversation with the councilor: "I wrote to Paris everything that I had just said, in the hope that I had conceived it as much for the great good of Europe as for the deliverance of my immense cargo. I received no response, although I since found out, very indirectly, that my conduct was strongly approved." While his approach seemed to be welcomed in France, on the coalition side opinions were mixed: Holland appeared convinced of the possibility of an armistice but wondered about the conditions; Prussia and England speculated that they were being manipulated and should be mistrustful. Ambassador Keller summed up the general opinion in a report to the king of Prussia: "The councilor appears to believe (and this is perhaps an effect of the insinuations of Sire Beaumarchais) that the French government is tired of a ruinous war and desires its end, but Sir Van de Spiegel is persuaded (as I am) that the French, after the major successes they have just had, want nothing of a partial accommodation."

We will never know what happened. During his peace discussions, Beaumarchais found himself once more the object of violent attacks, this time from his longtime enemy Lecointre, the Convention deputy who in 1792 had accused him of complicity with Louis XVI. Having changed camp after Thermidor, Lecointre now denounced Beaumarchais as an agent of Robespierre. Supposedly the former intimate of the Trianon and friend of princes, the émigré had now become a Jacobin, an advocate of the guillotine and terrorism! And yet this is what Beaumarchais read in *Le Moniteur*. Lecointre challenged the members of the Committee of Public Safety who had entrusted Beaumarchais with a mission abroad and confided in him "immense treasure." To the émigrés taking refuge in Holland, the news was a bombshell, and they now treated him as a Jacobin. The ministers of the stadtholder now saw him as an agent of the Terror trying to trick them. And so they withdrew their protection and asked him to leave their country.

Chased out of Holland for the second time, condemned as undesirable in England, considered a traitor in his own country, he found refuge in Germany, or more exactly in Hamburg. This tiny republic at the mouth of the Elbe, a major commercial port and one of the prime financial centers in northern Europe, was crawling with businessmen, double and triple agents, émigrés from everywhere. Lodging in an attic apartment where a glacial wind blew, obliged to live meagerly, Pierre-Augustin confided on paper: "In my poverty, I had become thrifty to the point of extinguishing a match and keeping it to use again. I had not noticed this habit except after reflection: that I had been brought to this by my poverty-stricken situation. This is not worth mentioning—except that I had fallen suddenly from 150,000 livres of income to the state of lacking everything."

Installed in Altona, a charming Danish enclave separated from Hamburg by a long avenue of trees, Beaumarchais led a withdrawn life, especially avoiding the many French émigrés who populated Germany's foremost port. Divided into factions according to their political opinions, everyone agreed to keep him at a distance, treating him as a renegade. He represented to them, if not the bloodiness of the Jacobins, at least the death knell of the ancien régime to which he owed everything, right down to his name. How could he be one of the émigrés? What was he doing here if not spying on them? Wasn't that his former profession? Was he not working undercover for the

Committee of Public Safety as he had worked formerly for the king of France?

This suspicion appeared all the more plausible given that Hamburg had become the center of international espionage. Its neutrality and its geographical situation made it the obligatory transit point for carriers of dispatches and secret agents of all kinds. Since the start of the Revolution the British government had maintained plots and intrigues there, an easy task since France had no diplomatic service present. After the execution of Louis XVI, the Hamburg Senate had refused to grant credentials to the Republic's representative, Le Hoc. Here too foreign corps were recruited for the British army, which sailed regularly from Cuxhaven. On its side, the French government maintained observers in the city or the region, notably in Altona, where the post of vice consul was occupied by the Greek Stamati, who had entered the diplomatic ministry in 1793. Other correspondents included Israel, Hamburg's currency exchanger, and Pierre Fauchet, one of the first to warn the authorities that the Prussians wanted to leave the coalition.

Did Beaumarchais perform secret activities within this spy nest? It was presumed that he did, whispered about, but nothing was known. One thing is almost certain: although his letters often mention his retired life, remote from Hamburg's intense financial activity, he did maintain relations with businessmen and influential bankers. No doubt he made contact with Jacques de Chapeaurouge and the Comte de Ricé, associated with the House of Orléans, and with Pierre Bellamy, a compatriot, half-dealer, half-spy, who would later work for Talleyrand. "The banking networks are critically important at this time," Beaumarchais noted. "It is there that information, both financial and political, circulates the fastest and most reliably." In short, we have every reason to think that even in exile his business demon pushed Beaumarchais to operate in ways that were barely admissible, hence unadmitted, and consequently secret.

At the same time as his exile became prolonged, a single idea distracted him to the point of obsession: to go back to France, find his family, erase his name from the list of émigrés, and take hold of his fortune—or what remained of it. To do so he had to win the confidence of the Committee of Public Safety by any means, even by spying on Royalist conspirators—and especially by repatriating the 60,000 rifles currently held by the British. Some hope remained, for at the end of April 1795 the British government still had not officially confiscated them. On the thirtieth, he sent "all the new and current members of the Committee of Public Safety" his seventh and final "epoch," published two years earlier in response to the denunciations from the same Lecointre. In nineteen numbered paragraphs, he retraced the epic of the rifles from his first negotiations with Lebrun to the recent "scandal" created by Lecointre at the Convention. "It is not a hand that I am holding, but the French Republic," he declared, then denounced the injustice of his proscription. His own government had abandoned him, had put his goods under seal and his family in prison, but he was stubbornly pursuing the struggle. The importance of his mission justified all sacrifices, despite the blunders and the bad faith on the French side, despite the deliberate sabotage and the maneuvers of dishonest ministers. At the end of April 1795 encouraging news arrived from England: the rifles were now the property of the American merchant and hence of "Pierre-Augustin Caron Beaumarchais, commissioned, wandering, persecuted, not an émigré."

Meanwhile Marie-Thérèse was keeping busy. Aided by her daughter and her friends, she made various attempts to obtain the excision of her husband's émigré status. She sent an appeal to the legislation committee, which sent her to the Paris *département*, which was subordinated to the Committees of General Security and Public Safety. Before every set of administrators, ten and twenty times over, she retraced the rifle story, enumerated the sequence of seals, searches, and interrogations, and produced her certificates of civic duty and patriotic zeal from before, during, and after her stay in the Abbaye. Petitions, requests, memoranda, minutes, and attestations rained down on the ministerial offices. Moreover Marie-Thérèse, Eugénie, and Julie presented a petition to demand that Beaumarchais be struck off the list of émigrés. Thereafter events moved quickly; a month later, the deputy from Gard presented to the Convention a report and draft decree: "Caron Beaumarchais will be removed from the list of émigrés, the seals on his furniture and the confiscation of his goods lifted, with the restitution of income." Nothing now opposed the exile's return! Nothing, that is, except the impromptu obstructions that were the French bureaucracy's redoubtable specialty. A few days later the dossier was frozen—nobody knew why—in one of those administrative cogs that seemed the devil's invention. As long as she had been struggling with its monstrous mechanics, Mme. de Beaumarchais thought she had flushed out all the traps.

By a troubling coincidence, on May 19, 1795, during Marie-Thérèse's administrative ventures, the Martin Theater (formerly the Molière) announced the premiere of a one-act verse comedy entitled *Figaro Returns to Paris* written by a certain Hyacinthe Dorvo. The plot was simple: two old bachelors, one a rabid Royalist and the other an impenitent Jacobin, have a niece, an orphan aged sixteen. Each wants to choose for her a husband who conforms to his own politics. Figaro arrives, returning to the capital after the Terror, reconciles the two brothers, and allows the niece to marry her own preferred suitor. In this topical play, with its winking title, the author exploits a situation that was the subject of many dinner table debates. The audience would not fail to react to the explicit allusions to *The Barber of Seville.*

While in Hamburg Beaumarchais saw as few people as possible but at least chose his society well. Among his familiars was Abbé Louis, the future minister of finance (under the name of Baron Louis), for whom Beaumarchais secured a job in a Hamburg commercial house; the man would always be grateful. During his forced leisure, Beaumarchais wrote about all sorts of subjects, but the situation in Europe especially preoccupied him. He had always loved politics "madly" and he had dreamed of a career as a statesman. Even lacking power, he had elaborated strategies in relation to the current power struggles among governments. He continued to advocate his grand plan for the "general peace" and thought—with good reason—that recent events would make it topical once more.

In April a separate peace put an end to the war between Prussia and France. This treaty signed by both parties stipulated an immediate end to hostilities: France would occupy Prussian possessions on the west bank of the Rhine "until the general pacification" of the Germanic empire. In return, she "would welcome the good offices" of the King of Prussia in relation to the German princes who desired to negotiate. This peace did not damage either signatory. In with-drawing from the coalition, Prussia left Austria with the whole onus of the war on the Rhine, which could only help Paris. On May 16 France imposed peace on the Netherlands, which she recognized as the Batavian Republic, a free and independent power. The Batavians ceded to France Dutch Flanders, Maastricht, and Venlo and pro-posed to pay 100 million florins "as indemnity and compensation for war costs." Secret articles also stipulated that the cost of maintaining the French army of occupation would be incumbent on The Hague. Such were the conditions imposed on the Batavian patriots who had been hoping to deal as equals with the Committee of Public Safety.

Never had the international context seemed more favorable to the Pax Europaea so promoted by Beaumarchais. Accepting the basic outlines of the current conjuncture, he even conceived of an entente cordiale with England. This grandiose project was totally unrealistic, at least for the time being. But Beaumarchais, overflowing with enthusiasm, always ahead of his times, characteristically erected improbable utopias that would become tomorrow's realities. Forbid-den from parts of Europe, a refugee living under an alias, suspected by everybody, his goods confiscated, his family in desperate straits, lacking mandate and support and means, he asked for an interview with William Pitt, prime minister of Great Britain. Certainly his ini-tiative had a hidden agenda (he always knew how to make the nation's interest coincide with his own), and he hoped to tear his cargo of rifles from the claws of the British lion. This was dangerous speculation, as the banker Perrégaux (flabbergasted by the man's audacity) remarked, for demanding his weapons would amount to claiming that he was their owner, when in principle they belonged to an American merchant. In any case, the meeting never took place, since Pitt replied to Beaumarchais that his presence in England was considered undesirable.

In June 1795 the British government proceeded to estimate the value of the rifles. As could be expected, the estimated figure was about half their real value. Beaumarchais's man in the United States was obliged to accept this bargain and to sign the transaction. Now the cargo became the property of Great Britain—a bitter epilogue to a cruel affair that the "soldier-citizen" had carried around like a boulder, at the cost of a thousand torments and enormous financial losses, forcing him into an exile that had also saved his life.

On June 27 a British flotilla of fifty sails bearing a contingent of 4,000 émigrés wearing British uniforms appeared in the Bay of Quiberon in Brittany. Commanded by Comte Louis Charles d'Hervilly and Joseph de Puisaye, they entrenched themselves in the Quiberon fort and occupied Carnac and Auray. Soon they were joined by bands of Breton peasant Royalists called *chouans* under the leadership of François de Charette, a counterrevolutionary commander. A month later Republican troops commanded by General Lazare Hoche pushed the Royalists back to the peninsula; only a few émigrés (including Puisaye) managed to reach the English fleet. The chouans and émigrés would be tried in Auray by a military commission; the former were acquitted, but 748 émigrés were condemned to death and shot in conformity with the law and on the formal order of the commissioner Jean-Lambert Tallien. Charette managed to escape.

Not surprisingly, Beaumarchais intervened in this affair, advising clemency toward the defeated, even as he risked appearing as one of their sympathizers. To take their part, just when he was struggling to obtain his removal from the list of émigrés, seemed either a miscalculation (at best) or double-dealing (at worst), but it was quite simply a matter of conscience. At the time he wrote his appeal, he was ignorant of the bloody repression ordered by Tallien, but he could foresee a frightful slaughter; he pleaded in favor of these émigrés only out of human sentiments, because the civil war appalled him and because one always draws more advantages from a generous pardon than from vengeance. However, the Committee of Public Safety never received his plea, dated August 5, because Mme. de Beaumarchais, to whom he had sent it, judged it prudent to do nothing.

Every day Pierre-Augustin expected to hear that his name had been crossed off the list. A first announcement on August 14 proved incorrect. Marie-Thérèse knocked on every door, used her contacts, harassed all the heads of offices, waited in antechambers—all in vain. She was at this time seriously worried about the health of her daughter. At the start of August Eugénie contracted a mysterious illness that kept her in bed for ten days hovering between life and death.

Nothing was said to her father until she was well; cared for at great expense by a renowned doctor, she would be completely cured. But the old exile, finding the time passed slowly, assailed his Parisian correspondents with questions and was angry to learn that his appeal for clemency for the Quiberon émigrés had not been communicated. Perrégaux tried to explain that it was unwise to give lessons in magnanimity to the Committee of Public Safety when his own repatriation depended on its goodwill.

Around the end of the year hope was reborn. Beaumarchais expected to be home before Eugénie's nineteenth birthday on January 5. But the proceedings had been interrupted due to the troubles agitating the country since autumn. The Vendée revolt regained strength, thanks to Charette. On October 5 in Paris the Royalists attempted a coup d'état against the Assembly, and the army had to intervene: General Bonaparte had strafed the insurgents on the steps of the Saint-Roch church, which still bears the traces. The last days of October saw the Convention (which had been ruling since September 1792) disappear, giving way to the Directory. With this new power, the horizon seemed clearer and optimism returned. Pierre-Augustin consented to the engagement of Eugénie to Andre Toussaint Delarue, former aide-de-camp to Lafayette in the National Guard, and the groom pleased him. "This fine young man," he later confided, wanted the young girl even "when it was thought she no longer possessed anything."

In January 1796 civil peace seemed reestablished in France, and Marie-Thérèse took further steps to obtain the decree that would allow Beaumarchais to come back. She addressed a petition to Merlin de Douai, the new chief of police. She obtained a surcease on the sale of the confiscated furniture, and she got Robert Lindet to compose an elegy to the exile that not long ago would have got him guillotined. He pleaded anew for Beaumarchais in April 1796 to the head of police, Cochon de Lapparent, who had just replaced Merlin. Finally on June 1 the Directory approved the removal of Beaumarchais from the list of émigrés, putting an end to three years of exile. The last obstacle to his return to France was gone. Marie-Thérèse transmitted the good news to her husband and, in the throes of joy, wrote a note to her friend Perrégaux:

My good friend,

I do not know if I am the first to impart the happy news, but at least I can confirm it: the final striking-off the list was signed day before yesterday, and I got it yesterday at three. I have just sent it to Pierre, and I hope that he will set off without losing any time, assuming he has provisions. All this is done with good grace; and we owe much of it and eternal gratitude to my son-in-law's brother-in-law.

The lifting of the seals and confiscations is ordered, but I cannot deliver myself yet to complete celebration; I still have to work to put an end to this long and disastrous adventure, and sweep the paths so that one sees only roses and lilies-of-the-valley, whereas we have drunk absinthe in long draughts.

Thirty

"TANDEM QUIESCO"
(I REST AT LAST)

A man descends as he rose, dawdling where he ran . . . then disgust and illness . . . an old and feeble doll . . . a cold mummy, a skeleton . . . vile dust, and then—nothing! Brr! In what abyss of reverie have I fallen, as if into a bottomless well? I am cold.
—*Speech cut from* **The Marriage of Figaro**

Ten days later Beaumarchais received the official papers announcing his removal from the fatal list. He felt he was losing the "faculty of turning phrases" but quickly informed his New York correspondents: "After four years of suffering and three years of an exile and a banishment followed by incalculable losses, I have just received, my dear friends, my diploma of reentry as honorable as can be . . . I am leaving for Paris in three days, as foreign to everything that has happened in the last three years as the unhappy La Perouse [a captain who disappeared in 1788] if fate should bring him back." And he concluded with a sibylline sentence that would assume its full meaning a little later: "Count on new and very energetic courage on my part; I have an idea that you will see me with you, in a form that will suit everybody very well."

On June 18, 1796, he obtained his passport for France and started off for Paris via Holland. Arriving in Antwerp, he asked Perrégaux to keep his return a secret: "Another note to add to yesterday's from Rotterdam to Thérèse, mother of Eugénie. But don't make her wait, for you would be delaying the meeting between her, my daughter, and myself on the route where I will wait for them. Keep my arrival to yourself, my friend. Until I show myself in public, I will see in my little corner only my intimate family."

When the very stout Beaumarchais arrived in Paris on July 5, 1796, his kin gave him an emotional welcome. Then he visited his house in Saint-Antoine, which had been uninhabited for more than two years. He found both the building and the garden in a deplorable state and could not live there, for the confiscation had not yet been lifted; he would instead live in the modest apartment rented by his wife.

The financial situation he found on his return was as desolate as his garden. His formerly immense fortune had been ravaged not only by the general crisis but by the confiscation of his revenues. Masses of papers and archives had disappeared, stolen by successive occupants of the house. His letters of credit had been seized. He had to get to work without delay to reconstitute his patrimony, or at least part of it. The state owed him enormous amounts, starting with the 745,000 francs in life annuities that he had deposited as a guarantee at the start of the Dutch Rifle Affair and that he had never touched, for a total of 300,000 francs. On the other hand, the half-million assignats that he had received from the government had rapidly devalued and were not sufficient to cover his expenses: the surety bond to the Dutch, payment for the weapons, the repurchase from Le Cointe, the fictional transactions, the bribes distributed here and there, the salaries of agents, his daily and traveling expenses, and so on. His last years would be consumed with vain attempts to recuperate these funds.

These worries did not sap his joy, however, when he led his daughter to the altar only five days after his return. On July 10 Eugénie married Toussaint Delarue, the "fine young man" whose constancy and disinterestedness Beaumarchais had appreciated. "She, her mother, and I thought we ought to recompense this generous attachment," he wrote, and so "five days after my arrival, I made him this fine present." (A year later he remarried Marie-Thérèse de Willermaulaz, a simple formality after their forced divorce in 1794.) Another great happiness of these first days was to finally embrace his old and faithful friend Gudin de La Brenellerie, who came on purpose from his hermitage in Burgundy. Gudin wrote, "To see each other again after so many years, after so many awful events, was not like being torn from the dangers of a shipwreck and finding yourselves on the rocks; rather it was like escaping the grave and embracing after an unhoped-for resurrection."

Like all the émigrés who had returned to France, Beaumarchais barely recognized the country he had left. Everything had changed so much! Like so many others who had been shaped under the ancien régime, he felt that nostalgia for "the sweetness of life" that Talleyrand described. That the French Republic did not win his wholehearted approval goes without saying. Still, it was mainly the institutions that irritated him and made him skeptical; the men now in power actually appeared very superior to those of the defunct monarchy. A letter to the son of his American correspondent in April 1797 expresses this view:

> Dear Charles, Yesterday I had a dinner that will long remain in my memory for the choice of guests that our friend General Dumas had gathered at his brother's. Once upon a time when I dined with great men of state, I was always shocked by the pack of people whose birth alone made them socially acceptable: idiots of nobility, imbeciles in office, men vain about their wealth, impudent youths, flirtatious women, etc. If it was not Noah's ark, it was at least the court of King Pétaud [where every beggar wants to command]. But yesterday, out of twenty-four people at the table, there was not one whose personal merit had not put him in the place he occupied. It was—if I may say so—an excellent cross-section of the French Republic. And I silently regarded them, recognizing in each the great merit that distinguished them all.

Must we attribute to his deafness, almost total now, the merit he saw in all these guests? In any case, the names he cites suggest that he was indeed in good company: General Jean Moreau, François-Antoine Boissy d'Anglas, Joseph Jérôme Siméon (the great jurist), Charles Cochon de Lapparent (the police chief, "one of the powerful men who knows best how to turn to the nation's advantage a difficult ministry"), Vincent Vaublane (of the Council of Five Hundred), the young François-Étienne Kellermann ("who, wounded, brought us twenty-five flags from Bonaparte"), Jean-Étienne-Marie Portalis (of the upper chamber), and more.

While reviewing the men whom he regarded as the nation's elite, Beaumarchais could not have suspected that four months later, on 18 Fructidor (September 4), a coup d'état would banish almost half of them. Of course this coup cooled much of his Republican sympathy. Gudin notes that henceforth "he recognized neither men nor affairs any longer; nor did he understand anything about the forms or means used in these times stripped of rules and principles, when the just appeared absurd, when the most inimical appeared the most able. He uselessly invoked the Reason that had enabled him to triumph so many times, but Reason was now foreign. One might daresay Reason was a kind of émigré whose name made suspect anyone who invoked it."

Three weeks later the Parisian public saluted the return of the former enfant terrible of the French scene—four months late! But what did that matter—the homage was all the warmer. On May 5 a theater performed *A Mother's Guilt* with the actors of the old Comédie-Française in the main roles; Beaumarchais came up on stage and savored this ovation as a balm for his wounds. For a long time he had felt no joy comparable to these intense minutes; this audience seemed to reach out to him, to exclaim its admiration and gratitude, paying him back a hundredfold for his long years of exile; he remembered that evening for the rest of his life.

But the euphoria of meeting his audience again dissipated, and Pierre-Augustin had to confront torments on all sides. Even reestablished in his fine residence, he felt only bitterness and sadness. He had built it to prepare for a gentle old age, sheltered from need, amid family and friends—but instead he saw only reasons to despair; each day brought new troubles, as if bad luck were chasing him.

More and more often he thought of America, that distant republic whose baptismal font he had once helped carry and that today owed him several million livres; his effort to recoup the funds consumed his last years. He addressed volumes of letters to U.S. officials, and even to the American people as a whole, informing them about the ingratitude and injustice of which he had been victim. In fact, he was fighting not for himself but for his only daughter Eugénie, to whom he willed this American debt as his sole legacy. It was in her name that in 1795 he had written from Hamburg a memo to Congress to remind it once more of the breadth of his sacrifice and of the unjust contempt with which he had been recompensed. The style may lean toward the pathetic, but no American citizen could read it today without a pang in his heart. America no longer resembled that young Republic of twenty years before that had been fighting for its independence: it was not yet a world power, of course, but it was already a prosperous nation, in full economic expansion, promised a great future, and entirely able to honor the debts it owed its unhappy creditor, who, broken by age and illness, deprived of any resources, made his last stand for the recognition of his rights.

> Americans! I served you with indefatigable zeal, and in my lifetime I have received only bitterness in return, and I am dying as your creditor. Suffer that in dying, I bequeath to my daughter as dowry what you owe me. After me, due to other injustices against which I could not defend myself, perhaps there will remain nothing in the world for her; and perhaps Providence wants her to have a resource after my death, thanks to your delayed settlement. Adopt her as a worthy child of the State! Her unhappy mother and my widow will take her to you. May she be regarded among you as the daughter of a citizen! But if after these final efforts, if after all that has just been said, against any possible appearance, I can still fear that you reject my demand, if I can fear that you refuse arbitrators to me and my heirs, desperate and ruined as much by Europe as by you, and your country being the only one where I might without shame reach out my hand to the inhabitants, what would remain for me to do but to beg heaven to give me a moment of health to allow me to travel to America? Arriving among you, mind and body enfeebled, unable to sustain my rights, would I then, proof in my hand, have myself carried on a wooden stool to the entry to your national assemblies and, holding out the cap of liberty that no

man more than me has contributed to proffering you, would I
cry out to you: "Americans, give alms to your friend, whose accumulated services have had only this recompense: *Date oblum
Belisario!*"

Pierre Augustin Caron de Beaumarchais

From Hamburg, April 10, 1795

Several times in the last years he thought of taking his family to
America; not only would he be received as a liberator, but once he
was on the spot he would be able to obtain at least part of the funds
owed him, which would allow him to spend the remainder of his days
in honest comfort. What had been a vague temptation whose realization he postponed, after his return to France appeared to be an imperious necessity, his only means of escaping poverty (whose specter
loomed on the horizon) and living in a land of freedom. Obviously
the ideal would be to have the French government send him there
on an official mission—why not as ambassador? Did he not have all
the qualifications for this eminent post? Not only had he finally
learned English, he was a pioneer in French intervention alongside
the insurgents; he had kept faithful correspondents across the
Atlantic, had many American friends, and enjoyed undeniable prestige in the eyes of the founding fathers of the United States. Perhaps,
too, the Americans would decide to reimburse the ambassador of the
French Republic for the debts they had contracted from the agent of
Louis XVI . . .

The moment appeared propitious to solicit this post because
Franco-American relations had never been so strained, and he considered himself the only mediator capable of restoring peace. For one
thing, France was contesting the commercial and friendship treaty
America had made with England in 1794, which it considered to violate agreements signed with France in 1778. For another, the two
countries were embroiled in a maritime struggle: it has been estimated that French corsairs inspected more than eight hundred American vessels between 1797 and 1800. The situation did not change
when Charles de Talleyrand-Périgord was named minister of foreign
relations in July 1797. This former émigré, who had been newly
crossed off the famous list, had often crossed paths with Beaumar-

chais. In Hamburg, where Talleyrand had disembarked after his return from America, the two men had shared connections in financial milieux. On their return to France they saw each other and even knit a friendship (if anyone could really call himself a friend of Talleyrand). Three months after his installation in the aristocratic Hôtel de Galliffet, Talleyrand received the official letter proposing the candidacy of Beaumarchais for the post of French ambassador to the United States. Disingenuously titled "Demand for a Passport in Whatever Form," this extraordinary letter has not been published since 1885:

> Citizen Minister,
>
> Your stay in America has put you in a position to know the interests that have long summoned me to that continent, if the still more powerful interests of my unhappy family in France had not fixed all my attention on my return to my country. But the very honorable justice that the Directorate has rendered in restoring my status of citizen has returned to me only an eighth of my fortune, dilapidated during four years of proscription. I can no longer delay so necessary a voyage; the fate of my family depends on it.
>
> This great country owes me part of its liberty. I know, as do you, that I would be welcomed there with honor and consideration. I would indeed like to turn to France's advantage the memory that this people keep of the great service I rendered them when it shook off the oppression of the very unjust England.
>
> I add, Citizen Minister, that perhaps nobody else except you would have the means to bring these two great republics closer, when some want to disunite them and when their joint interest is to arrest the insolent and intolerable usurpations by the English that threaten the entire world!
>
> A profound knowledge of the interest of the three nations, a firm head, a conciliatory spirit, joined with my long experience in human events, give me the presumption to believe that I might honorably fulfill to the Continental Congress this mission, if you and our five directors judge me worthy of this important trust. My very weakened hearing would not even be an obstacle; the

delegate of a powerful republic has no need to be spoken to in whispers when dealing with its interests. The mystery commonly practiced by royal negotiators is beneath his high diplomacy.

This is certainly not a post of honor that I want to take away from anyone more able than I. It is certainly not preferential treatment or pecuniary interest that I am striving to win; it is simply an offer that I make, with no personal interest, of every-thing of which I am capable; and I would not be hurt by any refusal, provided that this offer is regarded as proof of my patri-otism and *that one deigns to put me into action*!

I attach to this letter a copy of my courageous response to the manifesto of the King of England in 1779. I had printed it in favor of the Americans whom I served in all manners, hoping that their liberty would one day flow back to France. Offer it to the executive Directory and they will recognize in it the free and republican spirit that has animated me since those days, the truths that I spoke to our incapable ministers when everything in France was on its knees to them. This answer cost me disgrace at our court. I was derisively called *French Citizen*; but it also brought me from England, from the opposition, a host of letters labeled with this known, honorable, but dangerous address: "*To the only free man in a country of slaves: M. Beaumarchais.*" And I received such letters.

In support of this, I pray Citizen Reubell [one of the five original directors] to recall the great memorandum that I sent him from my attic in Holstein in 1795 on our *badly made peace with Spain* and on the secret intents of the English in opening a passage to the Pacific Ocean by the *Lake of Nicaragua*. I offered easy means of turning this information to France's advantage and making her in a few years the prime maritime nation of the world. Today this superb plan could find its application; it serves to prove that the exile who sent it was an excellent citizen. I offered it then and I offer it again. Nobody can judge it better than Citizen *Talleyrand*.

Moreover, if it is thought that at sixty-six years of age, I pre-sume too much about my strength, then I abandon my claim and confine myself to asking you for a simple passport *as merchant and as republican.* I will be no less a good Frenchman in Philadelphia during the six months I will spend there; and I will serve my country without a mission as if I had been presented with the most magnificent diploma.

> With respectful attachment,
> Caron Beaumarchais
> 16 vendémiaire, Year VI [October 7, 1797]

In the margin is written in Talleyrand's hand: "This passport cannot be granted."

Eight months later, undiscouraged, Beaumarchais reiterated his demand to the finance minister Ramel:

I am perhaps the only Frenchman who under two regimes has never asked anything of anybody, and yet among my great achievements I include with pride having *contributed more than any European to make America free*; to rescue her from her British oppressors: Today they are doing their utmost to make her our enemy. My affairs call me there and I may be able to foil their intrigue, for if there I cannot be paid, at least I have some honor. If Reubell, who has always treated me honorably, listened to me for only a quarter hour on this subject he would desire to restore me to a situation where I may serve my country. I offer this and I can do so without it costing anything and without wanting either a position or recompense.

These repeated attempts were not presumptuous, for they seemed to be responding to the wishes of the Americans themselves. The latter sent special envoys to Paris, charged with negotiating between the Directory and President John Adams. They had in fact requested Beaumarchais's arbitration, which seemed a good augury for his candidacy for the rank of ambassador. But Talleyrand considered his old friend inclined to be everyone's dupe.

In January 1798 a commission named by the Directory to examine Beaumarchais's accounts found that the state owed him 997,875 francs, including the sum deposited as a security at the start. The amount was much less than he was demanding but sufficient to deal with his most pressing debts and to pay property tax on his two hundred windows. But to imagine that Beaumarchais would be content with that would be to misjudge him. Very discontentedly, in fact, he denounced the compromise and demanded that other inspectors review his case. This was a bad idea; the second commission appointed by the Directory proved tougher than the first. The commission examined his accounts one by one with implacable rigor; once a month throughout 1798 he debated these auditors point by point, subject for hours to a torrent of questions, objections, and contradictions. He contested, argued, refuted, and pleaded with a stubbornness that won admiration but did not convince the commissioners, who refused, among other things, to take into account the arbitrary confiscation of his goods when he had been mistakenly put on the list of émigrés.

The result of this counterexpertise was a turnabout: not only was Beaumarchais no longer considered a creditor of the state, he was now its debtor! The treasury that three months earlier had owed him almost a million now claimed that he had to pay 500,000 francs to obtain the restoration of his titles to income. Harassed by the bailiffs, not knowing where to turn, he went to Finance Minister Ramel:

> For six years I have been suffering, and for two, since returning to Paris, I have been asking for justice as a grace. I swear that my situation is becoming intolerable. I would have solved the whole world's problems with all I have written on this detestable matter, which wears out my reason and ruins my old age. To have oppositions slapped on me when I am a patient creditor! Still languishing, still waiting, without ever receiving anything! Rushing around and knocking on doors and never getting anywhere is the torment endured by a slave or a subject of the ancien régime, and not the way a French citizen should live. Let me put a pallet in the attic of your mansion, and you will be told every day: *he is still here.* You will then realize that a desolate man, uprooted for six years and ruined, may be excused for wanting someone to deign to bother with him.

Ramel was not deaf to this appeal; he gave the order to suspend the pursuit of Beaumarchais and to reexamine his accounts. But meanwhile the author of *The Marriage of Figaro*, at the end of his resources, had to make the most painful sacrifice possible: he would sell his house in Faubourg Saint-Antoine. He thought he found the perfect buyer in the person of General Bonaparte. The young conqueror of Italy was said to have harvested the trophies not merely of glory but also of fortune.

Beaumarchais followed fervently the exploits of the twenty-eight-year-old general, already extremely famous. When Mathieu Dumas, Beaumarchais's son-in-law's brother-in law, introduced him to General Desaix, he seized the occasion to convey to Bonaparte a formal sales proposal, in which he vaunted the advantages and charms of his house:

> Paris, 25 Ventôse Year 6 [March 16, 1798]
>
> To General Bonaparte:
> Citizen General
>
> A country house in the middle of Paris that resembles no other, built with Dutch simplicity and Athenian purity, is offered to you by its owner. If anything could console him for the pain of selling it, after having built it in happier times, it would be that the place might suit the man, as amazing as he is modest, to whom he is pleased to offer it. Do not say *no*, General, before having seen it carefully. Perhaps it would seem worthy of sustaining the loftiness of your conceptions in its cheerful solitude . . . Whether you accept it or not, permit an old man who is not accused of loosely offering words of esteem, to obtain from you permission to assure you of his esteem and the respect that a man of your age inspires in a man of his. In finishing my letter, General, I am tormented with an idea; a fear of having failed the frankness in my nature if I did not tell you my whole secret. I am trying to excite your curiosity to satisfy my own. The fame of your actions has reached me only through a haze and I am unable to attach to the *Buonaparte* whom I have seen the many high deeds, without which they remain to me only historical facts! Whether or not you ought to acquire my country here, at least come see my garden, so that I might tell myself when you are in England: he was there, I had him here, he sat in this chair, he appeared to know me thanks to the interest I took in his glory.

In the final analysis, I feel that I like my own pleasure more than yours: this is why I insist on begging you to come let yourself be tempted by my house at the boulevard and gate of Antoine.

Fifteen days later Beaumarchais got a four-line response, without a word about the house. He recognized the legendary laconic style of Napoleon:

> Paris, 11 Germinal Year VI
>
> General Desaix has given me, Citizen, your kind letter of 25 Ventôse. I thank you for it. I will seize with pleasure any circumstances that present themselves to make the acquaintance of the author of *A Mother's Guilt*. I salute you,
>
> Bonaparte

Did this mean that for Napoleon, Beaumarchais was above all the author of the third play in the Figaro trilogy? This seems unlikely, since he had never seen it on the stage and had never had it performed privately. No doubt the future emperor wanted to prove his amiability by recalling to the author the recent triumph of his play. (As for *The Marriage of Figaro*, after reading it again in 1816, Napoleon summarized the comedy as "a topical play to debase the nobles by amusing them.")*

In the spring of 1798, still persecuted by an administration that was ever more exacting and fussy, Pierre-Augustin suffered a cruel loss. On May 9 his sister Julie died at the age of sixty-three in her apartment in her brother's home. What can we say of the role she played in his career? Three years younger than he, pretty and prickly, she had just as much of the "Caron spirit" as he: a mixture of gaiety, insouciance, malice, vivacity, and effrontery. Like him, she distrusted grand sentiments; she wrote hasty letters full of freshness and fantasy and possessed the stuff of a real writer. She had sacrificed everything for this brother whom she admired above anyone else.

Despite his successive failures, Beaumarchais's situation had no-

---

*In 1809, when the Empire wanted to tear the house down to extend the boulevard, Eugénie presented at a party a petition to Napoleon for just compensation; they were offering one-third of what Beaumarchais had paid for it.

ticeably improved since his return to France, thanks to his persever-
ance, the good management of his interests, and his genius for business. He did not boast of the improvements (his correspondence
stresses the heavy losses), knowing that it was never advisable to display one's ease when one was the creditor of the state. His fortune
was considerably reduced, but he still had almost a million in capital
and 20,000 francs in income.

Whatever the trials he had undergone in recent years, Beaumarchais never let himself be alienated by them. Neither the Terror, nor
banishment, nor the loss of his goods had made a dent in his untiring
curiosity about the people and happenings of his century. Always
devoted to the public good, he showered the Directory with his
advice, as he had formerly done to Louis XVI and to the Convention.
Reubell consulted him on the treaty with Spain, and Baudin des
Ardennes, member of the upper chamber, submitted proposals for a
tax on salt and for press freedom. Together they exchanged views on
the Constitution, and Beaumarchais did not forgo severe criticism of
government policy: "For a long time, I have been shivering at the
shocking waste of public money! No minister says, *Let us control ourselves and economize and put our finances in order*; all of them cry,
Money, money! The Directory does not know which one to listen to."
Not content with dispensing commentaries, proposals, and reservations, he contributed incognito to speeches and organized political
dinners at his home, thus playing again in later life the role of covert
adviser at which he had once excelled.

This is how Beaumarchais appears toward the end of his life:
"happy inside," as he declared, as prompt to become inflamed for a
noble cause or to dash off party verses as he had been in his youth.
The man of science and progress had lost nothing of his craving for
discoveries of all kinds. On the contrary, in the final years of his life
he proved most curious about advances in science and technology.
Still on the frontier of progress, he was as interested in the *aéram-
bules* of the aeronaut Baron Scott as he had once been in the balloons
of the Montgolfier brothers, and he warmly endorsed their inventor
to Neufchâteau, minister of the interior. Persuaded that aerial navigation was the transportation of the future, he deplored the failed
experiments of aeronauts, the Robert brothers, and the young Jean-
François Pilâtre de Rozier, attributing their failures to the form of

their engines: "Balloons! Always balloons! Can one steer spherical bodies?" Scott then developed a project for an aircraft in the form of a fish; Beaumarchais encouraged his work. Then, remembering his own troubles over the watch escapement mechanism, he had Scott's work published, "to assure him at least the honor of his fine invention, by publicizing the date that he made it." After the Revolution Scott wrote a second, longer pamphlet, supplementing it with his most recent research, which Beaumarchais sent to Neufchâteau along with an enthusiastic recommendation.

Another grand project close to his heart was Ferdinand de Lesseps's plan for a Panama canal. In 1796, while still in exile in Hamburg, he had written an important memo for Director Reubell in which he proposed joining the Atlantic and Pacific oceans by the construction of a waterway through Nicaragua. The text is unfortunately lost, but Gudin de La Brenellerie supplies a rather precise summary. Beaumarchais warned the Directory that Pitt was preparing "in a circumspect way" to invade the province of Nicaragua in the isthmus north of Panama.

> This fine province encloses a lake of eighty leagues around that spills most of its waters into the Saint-Jean River in the Gulf of Mexico and less into the Pacific Ocean. Only modest work would be sufficient to make these rivers navigable by vessels and to form an easy communication via this lake between the Atlantic Ocean and the Southern Sea. Ships would cross in a few months the space that separates Europe from China and the East Indies. The nation that is the mistress of this lake and the canals that joined the two seas would be infallibly the mistress of world commerce.

Beaumarchais thought Pitt had designed to make Britain into this mistress. He warned the Directory that Pitt was fortifying with secret garrisons the outposts that the British occupied among the Mosquitos [*sic*], the "savages" who wandered or lived on the northern bank of this lake and the Saint-Jean River.

Never a domestic man, Beaumarchais loved surrounding himself with luxury and wealth and detested anything that smacked of selfish and solitary quietude. He concerned himself with everything, intervened in everything. There was no lack of causes, good and less good, and his passion for action knew no bounds. When he learned that the remains of the great Maréchal Turenne, seized in the vandalism of the Terror, were exposed in the Jardin des Plantes among animal bones, he grabbed pen and paper, and five months later the seventeenth-century hero received a worthy tomb. French plenipotentiaries had been savagely massacred in Radstadt? He sent an urgent letter to Director Jean-Baptiste Treilhard: they must cause a "mass uprising"! And neither the theater nor literature was absent from his thoughts. One day he pleaded on behalf of authors against actors; the next day he made himself the advocate of Mme. Vestris, once a famous tragic actress, now abandoned by fortune and success.

On May 17, 1799, Beaumarchais spent the evening at home, surrounded by his family and a few friends. Gudin noted that "never had his mind been more free and more brilliant." He had played his usual game of cards with the bookseller Bossange, and as it went on longer than usual, his old valet came in to tell him it was late and time to go to sleep. The next morning, when the faithful servant entered his bedroom, he found his master inanimate in bed, on his right side, victim of a heart attack.*

Beaumarchais left this life at sixty-seven years and four months, not only "without wanting to," as Figaro would say, but even "without knowing it." "He had often told me that he wanted to end this way," Gudin recounted. "It was the most desirable and happy death for the person concerned, but the most frightening for a family. It would be impossible for me to describe the surprise, fright, and pain of his family, the sorrow they felt, and what I feel at the loss of such a friend."

When he had his house built, Beaumarchais had inscribed on the threshold "Tomb of the Gentleman," and along one of the darkest paths of his garden, near the little Temple of Bacchus, he had chosen for his resting place a shady copse called "the Green Room." Here he was buried in the presence of his relatives and close friends. Jean-

---

*Gudin's devotion continued beyond the grave; he published seven volumes of his friend's papers in 1809 and died thirteen years after him, in 1812.

François Collin d'Harleville read the adieu that Gudin had composed but that emotion prevented him from pronouncing. In an undated document, Beaumarchais summarized his own life:

> What was I then? I was nothing but myself, and myself I have remained, free in the midst of fetters, calm in the greatest of dangers, making headway against all storms, directing speculations with one hand and war with the other; as lazy as an association, and always working; the object of a thousand calumnies, but happy in my home, having never belonged to any coterie, either literary, or political, or mystical, having never paid court to any one, and yet repulsed by all.

But no posthumous homage could compare with the one—so just, measured, and true—that his widow made a few days after his death:

> Our loss is irreparable. The companion of twenty-five years of my life has died and left me only useless regrets, a horrible solitude, and memories that nothing will erase . . . He would graciously pardon and willingly forget the insults and bad turns. He was a good father, a zealous and useful friend, a born defender of all those absent ones whom people attacked in front of him. Superior to the small jealousies so common among people of letters, he advised them, encouraged them, and served them with his purse and his advice. In the eyes of philosophy, his end should be regarded as a favor; he is taken away from this laborious life, or rather it has been taken away from him without debate, with none of the heartbreak of the awful separation from those who were dear to him. He left life without being aware, as he entered it.

On his tomb, he had these simple words engraved:

TANDEM QUIESCO [I REST AT LAST]

BEAUMARCHAIS AND AMERICA

There is an age coming when noble minds will forgive one another the sins and weaknesses they were guilty of in the past! We'll see a gentle love take the place of the stormy passions that once divided them.　　　　　**—Count, A Mother's Guilt**

When Beaumarchais died on the night of May 17–18, 1799, he had still not received satisfaction for his financial claims against the United States. During the thirty-six years that followed his death, from 1799 to 1835, all successive governments in France and all the ambassadors of these governments would support in vain the claims of the heirs of Beaumarchais against the United States. Various ministers would intervene in their favor without success. On 28 Germinal of the Year XI (April 18, 1803), Talleyrand, then at foreign affairs, wrote the French ambassador in Washington:

> I invite you, citizen minister, to support with your influence the claims of the Beaumarchais family, to demonstrate the loyalty and national honor that it invokes. A French citizen who risked for the service of Americans his whole fortune, and whose zeal and activity were so essentially useful to them during the war that won them their freedom and their rank among nations, might no doubt claim some favor. At least he should be listened to when he demands only good faith and justice.

Thirteen years later, in response to insistent and repeated requests from Eugénie de Beaumarchais, the U.S. government had Albert Gallatin, treasury secretary, ask the Duc de Richelieu, foreign affairs minister, if the French government would consent to formally declare that the million deposited on June 10, 1776, in the hands of Beaumarchais "had nothing in common with the supplies made by the said Beaumarchais to the United States." The Duc de Richelieu wrote a declaration attesting that the French government had been absent from any commercial transactions by Beaumarchais with the United States. This was the official version; as we know, this sum had indeed been used to acquire weapons and military equipment for the insurgents. But still Beaumarchais was responsible for it to his country alone. Nothing authorized the United States to ask him to account for it, let alone to deduct this million from its debt. At least it was hoped that the U.S. would believe in Richelieu's attestation, if only as a diplomatic gesture. But they did nothing of the sort.

In 1822 Eugénie de Beaumarchais, his sole heir, submitted a new plea to Congress, imploring that body for justice. "After having examined the mentioned documents," she said,

> you will wonder no doubt why I have been asking for justice so many years without being heard. Will you still refuse me? Is it to recompense Beaumarchais for his devotion to your cause that his daughter must be deprived of his fortune, and end her life in a vain and cruel hope, like her father, whose existence was shortened by torment and pain? Until his last breath, he begged you to rule on his claim. He said to you: "My conduct toward you was devoted and disinterested; my correspondence, my commercial contracts testify to this; they are in your hands, they have been minutely examined; examine them again." The proofs that these frequent examinations have established are authenticated by irrefutable testimony, including (I find with pride) from some of your compatriots: their veracity cannot be put in doubt. Decide with equity and impartiality! Or at least, name special commissioners to settle this difference and put an end to this unequal struggle; I will accept them with confi-

dence as my judges. But I beg you for a rapid decision to be taken.

In 1824 Eugénie de Beaumarchais crossed the Atlantic with one of her sons to solicit Congress in Washington. But an inflexible majority rejected the claim. Only in 1835 did the heirs receive the happy news that the United States had finally settled their ancestor's account. But instead of the 2,280,000 livres stipulated in Alexander Hamilton's report of 1793, only 800,000 livres were to be paid, or a little less than a third—and without any penalty for late payment (almost a half-century!) and not immediately. Should the heirs take it or not? They accepted the transaction but understandably neglected to express their gratitude.

Beaumarchais loved the United States unhappily. If he had thought at first that helping the American insurgents would win him big profits, his intelligence was too keen for him to believe that for long. Very soon he understood that he was working to found a new nation in a new world, for the triumph of the Enlightenment and the glory of the King of France. Was that not a sufficient source of pride? He put into this adventure a disinterestedness and a generosity that were not recompensed at their just price—far from it! But what did that matter, since he achieved there the finest political victory of which he could ever dream. He knew nothing of the new world; he never set foot there (not being a good enough sailor), and his deal with Arthur Lee was only a vast misunderstanding, but he served nations. His enthusiastic and unreflective action, naïve and puerile in certain respects, seemed typical of the American fashions that were causing a furor everywhere: in women's hairstyles as in wallpaper, novels, and opera ballets. A powerful current was pushing France toward America and America toward France, without any real reciprocal knowledge, two nations so different from each other, converging in the faith of imaginations. Beaumarchais had engaged in something that arose from aesthetics and fashion, something frivolous, a showy grandeur, a comic heroism. A hatred of England and the thirst for vengeance were certainly present, but went hand in hand (to the point of dominating his consciousness) with the feeling of serving humanity in the conquest of a new era of justice and liberty. Despite his troubles and disappointments, he always kept at the bottom of his heart that idealistic and utopian image of the American people, himself following the advice that he had given Théveneau de Francy: "Do as I do: despise petty considerations, petty measures, and petty feelings. I have associated you with a magnificent cause."

Bibliography
Évelyne Lever's Acknowledgments
Index

BIBLIOGRAPHY

I. MANUSCRIPT SOURCES

Institut de France
Archives de l'Académie des Sciences

Archives Nationales
Série O^1 (Maison du roi): 843–47: Comédie-Française, 1668–1790 3065 B: Performance of *Mariage de Figaro* à Gennevilliers (October 6, 1783).

Série X^{2B}: 1338: Minutes of the Parlement criminel: Beaumarchais and others, 1770–1774 (1 carton). Affaire Goëzman: interrogations, confrontations, letters, notebook of Goëzman's porter.

Série Y Châtelet de Paris: 10941–42: Summary of minutes made and received by Pierre Thiérion, commissioner at the Châtelet (1755–62). 11089: Office of Berton and predecessors, Levié, Formel. 11334: Office of Pierre Chénon. 12436: Office of Dorival and predecessors.

Série Z^{1Q}: 1 à 98: Bailiwick and royal captaincy of Varenne du Louvre.

Série AF II: 214–19 (1793–95): Committee of Public Safety: War.

Série BB^{30}: 175–78: Beaumarchais trial.

F^7: 5617, pièce 9: Passport of Beaumarchais. 4633, item 311: Décree of the National Convention. 4591: Committee of Public Safety.

Série H^1: 1468: Beaumarchais's deposition.

Bibliothèque Nationale de France
F.fr. 6680–87: "Mes Loisirs ou Journal d'événements tels qu'ils parviennent à ma connaissance" by the Parisian bookseller S.-P. Hardy (1754–89).

F.fr. 13734: Régnaud, "Histoire des événements arrivés en France depuis le mois de septembre 1770, concernant les parlements et les changements dans l'administration de la justice et dans les lois du royaume."

N.a.fr. 4388–89: Journal of the Marquis d'Albertas.

Fonds Joly de Fleury: 2082

Archives des Affaires Étrangères
Political Correspondence: Spain, v. 540, 541, 580.
Political Correspondence: England, v. 502, 503, 504, 511, 515, 516, 517, 522, 528, 531.
Political Correspondence: Holland, v. 584.

Bibliothèque Historique de la Ville de Paris
Ms. 1312–21: "Registre de la Correspondance littéraire et typographique sur la nouvelle édition des *Œuvres complètes* de M. de Voltaire, commencé le 10 juin 1779."
Ms. 12304: "Théâtre".

Bibliothèque de la Comédie-Française
Archives Beaumarchais.

Bibliothèque Municipale de Tonnerre
Family papers and correspondence.
Cote R: Negotiations between Chevalier d'Éon and Beaumarchais. *Campagnes du Sr Caron de Beaumarchais* (R. 22)

Library of Congress (Washington)
Thomas Jefferson Papers.
George Washington Papers.

The Pierpont Morgan Library (New York)
Ma-Heineman Ms. 247: *Beaumarchais letters to Mme de Godeville* (1777–79).

II. PUBLISHED SOURCES
Affiches, Annonces et Avis divers, ou Journal Général de France.
Antoine, Michel, and Didier Ozanam. *Secret Correspondence from the Comte de Broglie to Louis XV.* 2 vols. Paris, 1956–61.
Bachaumont, Louis Petit de. *Mémoires secrets pour servir à l'histoire de la République des Lettres en France, depuis 1762 jusqu'à nos jours ou Journal d'un observateur.* 36 vols. London, 1777–87.
Bergasse, Nicolas. *Mémoire sur une question d'adultère, de séduction et de diffamation, pour le sieur Kornman, contre la dame Kornman, son épouse, le sieur Daudet de Jossan, le sieur Pierre-Augustin Caron de Beaumarchais, et M. Lenoir, conseiller d'État et ancien lieutenant-général de police.* S. 1., 1787.
———. *Observations du sieur Bergasse sur l'écrit du sieur de Beaumarchais ayant pour titre* Court Mémoire en attendant l'autre, *dans la cause du sieur Kornman.* S. 1., August 1788.
———. *Mémoire du sieur Bergasse dans la cause du sieur Kornman, contre le sieur de Beaumarchais et le prince de Nassau.* S. 1., 1788.
Campan, Mme. *Mémoires de Madame Campan, première femme de chambre de Marie-Antoinette.* Paris: Mercure de France, 1988.
Clairambault-Maurepas. *Chansonnier historique du XVIIIe siècle.* Edited by E. Raunié. 10 vols. Paris: Quantin, 1879–84.

Collé, Charles. *Journal et mémoires sur les hommes de lettres, les ouvrages dramatiques, et les événements les plus mémorables du règne de Louis XV (1748–1772).* Edited by Honoré Bonhomme. 3 vols. Paris: Firmin Didot, 1868.

Courrier de l'Europe, gazette anglo-française. 32 vols. London [and Boulogne-sur-Mer], 1776–92.

Diderot, Denis. *Correspondance.* Edited by Georges Roth and Jean Varloot. 16 vols. Paris: Ed. de Minuit, 1955, 1970.

———. *Oeuvres complètes.* Edited by Roger Lewinter. 15 vols. Paris: Club Français du Livre, 1969–73.

Du Deffand, Marquise. *Lettres à Horace Walpole 1766–1780.* Edited by Mrs. Paget Toynbee. 3 vols. London: Methuen, 1912.

Grimm, Diderot, Raynal, Meister, etc. *Correspondance littéraire, philosophique et critique.* Edited by M. Tourneux. 16 vols. Paris, 1877–82.

Gudin de La Brenellerie, Paul-Philippe. *Histoire de Beaumarchais.* Memoirs based on the original manuscripts by Maurice Tourneux. Paris: Plon, 1888.

———. *Aux mânes de Louis XV et des grands hommes qui ont vécu sous son règne, ou Essai sur les progrès des arts et de l'esprit humain, sous le règne de Louis XV.* Aux Deux-Ponts, à l'Imprimerie ducale, 1776.

Gustave III, King of Sweden. *Gustave III par ses Lettres.* Edited by Gunnar von Proschwitz. Stockholm, Norstedts/Paris: Jean Touzot, 1986.

Hardman, John, and Munro Price, eds. *Louis XVI and the comte de Vergennes: Correspondance, 1774–1787.* Oxford: Voltaire Foundation, 1998.

Hardy, Siméon-Prosper. *Mes loisirs, ou Journal d'événements tels qu'ils parviennent à ma connaissance.* Text dated 1774. Critical edition by Christophe Bosquillon. Edited by Daniel Roche. 2 vols. DEA d'Histoire, Université Paris I, 1993–94 (typed text).

———. *Mes Loisirs. Journal d'événements tels qu'ils parviennent à ma connaissance (1764–1789).* Vol. 1, *1764–1773.* Edited by Maurice Tourneux and Maurice Vitrac. Paris: Alphonse Picard and Son, 1912.

Histoire de L'Académie des sciences. Paris: de l'imprimerie royale, 1754.

Houret de la Marinaie, Amélie. *Quelques traits d'une grande passion, ou Lettres originales de feue Amélie Ho[uret], comtesse de La M[arinaie], écrites pendant le cours des années 3, 4 et 5 de la République française.* Paris: Desenne et Pigoreau, Year X, 1802.

Impartial (L'), October 14, 1834.

Inventaire après décès de Beaumarchais, (L'). Edited by Donald C. Spinelli. Paris: Honoré Champion, 1997.

Journal de L'Institut Historique. vol. 1, pp. 73–158, 212.

Journals of the Continental Congress (1774–1789). Washington: Library of Congress, 1904–37.

La Fortelle, M. de, (pseud. of Chevalier d'Éon). *La vie militaire, politique et privée de Demoiselle Charles-Geneviève-Louise-Auguste-Andrée-Thimotheé Éon ou d'Éon de Beaumont . . .* Paris: Lambert, Onfroi, Valade, Esprit & "chez l'auteur," 1779.

———. *Lettre d'un habitant de la lune, ou Mémoire en forme de lettre pour feu Caron de Beaumarchais, ancien horloger, musicien, orateur, fournisseur de fusils, pour ses péchés auteur dramatique, et pour sa félicité, aujourd'hui demi-dieu, demeurant ci-devant boulevard Saint-Antoine, actuellement habitant de la*

Lune, contre M. Mary Lafont, membre de la troisième classe de l'Institut historique. Cause pendant devant le public. Paris, Delaunay, 1834.

Lettre de M. Morande, auteur et rédacteur du Courrier de l'Europe, à M. de Beaumarchais. London, July 6, 1787.

Lévis, Duc de. Souvenirs-Portraits, from Lettres intimes de Monsieur, comte de Provence, au duc de Lévis. Edited by Jacques Dupâquier. Paris: Mercure de France, "Le temps retrouvé" series, 1993.

Loménie, Louis de. Beaumarchais and His Times: Sketches of French Society in the Eighteenth Century from Unpublished Documents. Translated by Henry C. Edwards. New York: Harper, 1857.

Louis XV. Correspondance secrète inédite de Louis XV sur la politique étrangère avec le comte de Broglie, Tercier, etc. Edited by E. Boutaric. 2 vols. Paris: Plon, 1866.

Louis XVI. Correspondance secrète inédite sur Louis XVI, Marie-Antoinette, la cour et la ville, de 1777 à 1792, publiée d'après les manuscrits de la bibliothèque impériale de Saint-Pétersbourg. Edited by M. de Lescure. 2 vols. Paris: Plon, 1866.

Manuel, Pierre. La Bastille dévoilée. 3 vols. Paris, 1789.

———. La police de Paris dévoilée. 2 vols. Paris: Garnery/Strasbourg, Treuttel/ London, de Boffe, Year II (1795).

Marie-Thérèse. Correspondance secrète entre Marie-Thérèse et le comte de Mercy-Argenteau, avec les lettres de Marie-Thérèse et de Marie-Antoinette. Edited by M. le Chevalier Alfred d'Arneth and M. A. Geoffroy. 3 vols. Paris: Firmin-Didot, 1874.

Marmontel, Jean-François. Correspondance. Edited by John Renwick. 2 vols. 1974.

Mercier, Louis-Sébastien. Tableau de Paris. Edited by Jean-Claude Bonnet. 2 vols. Paris: Mercure de France, 1994.

———. Le Nouveau Paris. Edited by Jean-Claude Bonnet. Paris: Mercure de France, 1994.

Mercure de France, September 1753.

Métra Louis-François. Correspondance secrète, politique et littéraire. 18 vols. London: John Adamson, 1787–90.

Mirabeau, Honoré Gabriel Riqueti, Comte de. Réponse du Cte de Mirabeau à l'écrivain des administrateurs de la Compagnie des Eaux de Paris. Brussels, 1785.

———. Sur les actions de la Compagnie des Eaux de Paris. London, 1785.

Morande, Charles Théveneau de. Le gazetier cuirassé, ou anecdotes scandaleuses de la cour de France. A cent lieues de la Bastille [London], 1771.

Oberkirch, Baronne d'. Mémoires. Edited by Suzanne Burkard. Paris: Mercure de France, "Le temps retrouvé," 1970.

Pidansat de Mairobert. L'Espion anglais ou Correspondance secrète entre Milord All'-Eye et Milord All'Ear. Rev. ed. 10 vols. London: Adamson, 1784–85.

Pièces relatives aux démêlés entre Mademoiselle d'Éon de Beaumont, chevalier de l'ordre royal et militaire de St. Louis & ministre plénipotentiaire de France, &c., &c., &c. Paris, 1778.

U.S. government. Annals of Congress (1789–1824).

———. Bills and Resolutions of the House of Representatives and the Senate (1823–73).

———. *Register of Debates (1824–37)*. 14 vols. Washington: Gales and Seaton.
———. *Report of the Committee of Claims, to whom was referred, on the twenty-fourth December last, the petition of Amélie Eugénie de Beaumarchais, heir and representative of Caron de Beaumarchais, deceased*. City of Washington: A. & G. Way, Printers, 1806.
Voltaire, François-Marie Arouet, dit. *Correspondance*. Edited by Théodore Besterman. 13 vols. Paris: Gallimard, Bibliothèque de la Pléiade.

III. BIBLIOGRAPHIC REFERENCES
Brenner, Clarence D. *A Bibliographical List of Plays in the French Language, 1700–1789*. Berkeley: University of California Press, 1947.
Cordier, Henri. *Bibliographie des œuvres de Beaumarchais*. Paris: Quantin, 1884. Slatkine reprints 1967.
Cioranescu, Alexandre. *Bibliographie de la littérature française du dix-huitième siècle*. 3 vols. Paris: Éditions du CNRS, 1969.
Morton, Brian N., and Donald C. Spinelli. *Beaumarchais: A Bibliography*. Ann Arbor: University of Michigan Press, 1988.

IV. WORKS BY BEAUMARCHAIS
Œuvres complètes. Edited by Gudin de La Brenellerie. 7 vols. Paris: Léopold Collin, 1809.
Œuvres complètes. 6 vols. Paris: Furne, 1826.
Œuvres complètes. Edited by Saint-Marc Girardin. Paris: Firmin-Didot, 1845.
Œuvres complètes. Edited by Édouard Fournier. Paris: Laplace, Sanchez et Cie, 1876.
Œuvres. Edited by P. Larthomas and Jacqueline Larthomas. Paris: Gallimard, "Bibliothèque de la Pléiade," 1988.
Notes et réflexions. Introduction by Gérard Bauër. Paris: Hachette, 1961.
Parades. Edited by Larthomas. Paris: SEDES, 1977.
Le Tartare à la légion. Edited by Marc Cheynet de Beaupré. Le Castor-astral, 1998.
Théâtre. Edited by Jean-Pierre de Beaumarchais. Paris: Le Livre de poche/Classiques Garnier, coll. "Classiques modernes," 1999.
Théâtre complet: Réimpression des éditions princeps avec les variantes des manuscrits originaux publiées pour la première fois par G. d'Heylli et F. de Marescot. 4 vols. Paris: Académie des Bibliophiles, 1869–71.

V. CORRESPONDENCE OF BEAUMARCHAIS
"Correspondance de Beaumarchais avec la Comédie-Française." *Revue rétrospective*, 2nd. ser, vol. 7 (1836), pp. 433–67.
Farges, Louis. "Beaumarchais et la Révolution. Lettres et documents inédits." *La Nouvelle Revue*, no. 37 (1885), pp. 548–71.
"Lettres de vieillesse." Edited by Louis Thomas. *Revue de Belgique* vol. 44 (1905–06), pp. 301–16, and vol. 46, pp. 51–54.
"Deux lettres de Beaumarchais. Lettres de l'exil." Edited by Louis Thomas. *Mercure de France*, July 16, 1907, pp. 278–89.

Marsan, Jules. *Beaumarchais et les affaires d'Amérique. Lettres inédites.* Paris: Ed. Champion, 1919.

Lettres de jeunesse (1745–1775). Edited by Louis Thomas. Paris: E. de Boccard, 1923.

Lettres inédites de Beaumarchais, de Mme de Beaumarchais et de leur fille Eugénie. Edited by Gilbert Chinard. Paris: A. Margraff / Baltimore, MD: Johns Hopkins, 1929.

"Une lettre de Beaumarchais et de sa femme (1798)." Edited by Marie-Jeanne Durry. *Le Divan.* Paris: 1937, pp. 135–42.

Correspondance. Edited by Brian N. Morton. 4 vols. Paris: Nizet, 1969–78.

Quinn, Renée. "Beaumarchais et Amélie Houret: Une Correspondance inédite." *Dix-Huitième Siècle*, no. 7 (1975), pp. 35–47.

For the Good of Mankind: Pierre-Augustin Caron de Beaumarchais, Political Correspondence relative to the American Revolution. Edited and translated by Antoinette Shewmake. University Press of America, 1987.

Lettres galantes à Madame de Godeville. Edited by Maurice Lever. Paris: Fayard, 2004.

VI. PRINCIPAL BOOKS AND ARTICLES CONSULTED

Aldridge, Alfred Owen. *Franklin and his French Contemporaries.* New York: New York University Press, 1957.

Analyses & Réflexions sur . . . Beaumarchais, Le Mariage de Figaro. Paris: Ellipse Edition Marketing, 1985.

Arnault, Antoine Vincent. *Souvenirs d'un sexagénaire.* 4 vols. Paris: Dufey, 1833.

Arneth, Alfred Ritter von. *Beaumarchais und Sonnenfels.* Vienna: Wilhelm Braumüller, 1868.

Arnould, E. J. *La Genèse du "Barbier de Séville."* Dublin: Dublin University Press and Paris, Minard, 1965.

Azeau, Henri. *Complot pour l'Amérique, 1775–1778: le rêve americain de Beaumarchais.* Paris: R. Laffont, 1990.

Baetens, Jan, ed. *Le combat du droit d'auteur.* Paris: Les Impressions Nouvelles, 2001.

Bailly, Auguste. *Beaumarchais.* Paris: Fayard, 1945.

Beaumarchais. Exposition at the Bibliothèque Nationale. Catalog by Annie Angremy. Paris, 1966.

Bauer, Gérard. *Beaumarchais: Notes et réflexions.* Paris: Hachette, 1961.

Bayet, Jean. *La Société des auteurs et compositeurs dramatiques.* Paris: Arthur Rousseau, 1908.

Beaumarchais, Jean-Pierre de. "Un inédit de Beaumarchais, *Le Sacristain.*" *Revue d'Histoire Littéraire de la France*, no. 74 (1974), pp. 976–99.

——. *Beaumarchais, le voltigeur des Lumières.* Paris; Gallimard, "Découvertes," 1996.

——. "À l'approche du bicentenaire: Beaumarchais, voltigeur des Lumières." *Revue des sciences morales et politiques* (1999), pp. 1–16.

Benoit, Marcelle, ed. *Dictionnaire de la musique en France aux XVIIe et XVIIIe siècles.* Paris: Fayard, 1992.

Berthe, Abbé Léon-Noël. "Deux amis à la cour de Versailles: une correspondance inédite de Beaumarchais et Dubois de Fosseux." *Dix-huitième siècle*, no. 6 (1974), pp. 288–97.

Bettelheim, Dr. Anton. *Beaumarchais: Eine biographie*. Frankfurt: Rütter et Loening, 1886.

Boncompain, Jacques. *Auteurs et comédiens au XVIIIe siècle*. Paris: Librairie Académique Perrin, 1976.

Bonnassies, Jules. *Les Auteurs dramatiques et la Comédie-Française à Paris, aux XVIIe et XVIIIe siècles*. Paris: Léon Willem-Paul Daffis, 1874.

Bonneville de Marsangy, Louis. *Madame de Beaumarchais d'après sa correspondance inédite*. Paris: Calmann Lévy, 1890.

Borgal, Clément. *Beaumarchais*. Paris: Éditions universitaires "Classiques du XXe siècle," 1972.

Boussel, Patrice. *Beaumarchais, le parisien universel*. Paris: Berger-Levrault, "Illustres inconnus," 1983.

Broglie, Duc de. *Le Secret du roi. Correspondance secrète de Louis XV avec ses agents diplomatiques, 1752–1774*. 2 vols. Paris: Calmann Lévy, 1878.

Brown, Gregory S., and Donald C. Spinelli. "The Société des Auteurs Dramatiques, Beaumarchais, and the 'Mémoire sur la Préface de *Nadir*.'" *Romances Notes*, vol. 37, no. 3 (Spring 1997), pp. 239–49.

Castries, Duc de. *Beaumarchais*. 1972; reprint Paris, Tallandier, 1985.

Cousin d'Avallon. *Vie privée, politique et littéraire de Beaumarchais, suivie d'anecdotes, bons mots, réparties, satires, épigrammes et autres pièces propres à faire connaître le caractère et l'esprit de cet homme célèbre et singulier*. Paris: Michel, Year X (1802).

Cox, Cynthia. *The Real Figaro. The Extraordinary Career of Caron de Beaumarchais*. New York: Coward McCann, 1963.

Dalsème, René. *La vie de Beaumarchais*. Paris: Gallimard, "Vies des hommes illustres," 1928.

Darnton, Robert. *La Fin des Lumières. Le mesmérisme et la Révolution*. Paris: Librairie Académique Perrin, 1984.

Descotes, Maurice. *Les grands rôles du théâtre de Beaumarchais*. Paris: Presses Universitaires de France, 1974.

Didier, Beatrice. *Beaumarchais ou la passion du drame*. Paris: PUF, 1994.

Doniol, Henri. *Histoire de la participation de la France à l'établissement des États-Unis d'Amérique*. 6 vols. Paris, 1886–99.

Donvez, J. *La Politique de Beaumarchais*. Paris, 1981.

———. "La Reconnaissance des États-Unis par l'Espagne." *Revue historique* (October–December 1957), pp. 279–83.

Durand, John. *New Materials for the History of the American Revolution*. New York: Henry Holt, 1889.

Estrée, Paul d'. "Le nègre de Beaumarchais (1766)." *Nouvelle Revue Rétrospective*, vol. 10 (September 1896), pp. 182–90.

———. "Un locataire masqué de l'hôtel de Hollande, Roderigue Hortalez et Cie (1776–1788)," *La Cité* (July–October 1920), pp. 81–92.

Europe. Revue Littéraire Mensuelle. April 1973 (issue devoted to Beaumarchais).

Fay, Bernard. *Beaumarchais ou les Fredaines de Figaro*. Paris: Librairie Académique Perrin, 1971.

————. *L'ésprit révolutionnaire en France et aux États-Unis, à la fin du XVIIIème siècle*. Paris: Champion, 1925.

Feuchtwanger, Lion. *Beaumarchais, Benjamin Franklin et la naissance des États-Unis*. Translated by Sabatier. Geneva: Slatkine and Paris: Champion, 1977.

Fredet, Jacques. "Maison Caron de Beaumarchais, boulevard et porte Saint-Antoine, bâtie par Lemoyne le jeune." *Paris, formes urbaines et architectures*, Les Cahiers de l'Ipraus, no. 1 (1998), pp. 67–97.

Free, Lloyd R. "Image de l'Amérique chez Caron de Beaumarchais." In *L'Amérique des Lumières. Partie littéraire du colloque du bicentenaire de l'indépendance américaine (1776–1976)*. Paris-Geneva: Librairie Droz, 1977.

Frischauer, Paul. *Beaumarchais: Der Abenteurer im Jahrhundert der Frauen*. Zürich: Bibliothek Zeitgenössischer Werke Verlag, 1935.

Funck-Brentano, Frantz. "Documents sur Beaumarchais." *Nouvelle Revue Rétrospective*, vol. 10 (September 1896), pp. 160–82.

Gaiffe, Félix. *Le Mariage de Figaro*. Paris: SFELT, Éditions Edgar Malfère, 1942.

Gaillardet, Frédéric. *Mémoires du chevalier d'Éon*. 2 vols. 2nd ed. Paris: Grasset, 1935.

Gallet, Michel. *Demeures parisiennes à l'époque de Louis XVI*. Paris: Le Temps, 1964.

Gatty, Janette C. *Beaumarchais sous la Révolution. L'affaire des fusils de Hollande d'après des documents inédits*. Leiden: E. J. Brill, 1976.

Geoffroy, A. "Beaumarchais en Allemagne." *Revue critique d'histoire et de littérature* (July 2, 1870), pp. 13–16.

Giudici, E. *Beaumarchais nel suo e nel nostro tempo: Le Barbier de Séville*. Rome, 1964.

Grendel, Frédéric. *Beaumarchais ou la calomnie*. Paris: Flammarion, 1973.

Guichard, Léon. "Beaumarchais et Mozart. Note sur la première représentation à Paris des *Noces de Figaro*." *Revue d'Histoire littéraire de la France*, no. 3 (July–September 1955), pp. 341–43.

Hallays, André. *Beaumarchais*. Paris: Hachette, "Les Grands Écrivains Français," 1897.

Howarth, William D. *Beaumarchais and the Theater*. New York: Routledge, 1995.

Huot, Paul. *Beaumarchais en Allemagne. Révélations tirées des Archives d'Autriche*. Paris: Librairie internationale, 1869.

Joubin, A. "Le Mariage rompu ou Le naufrage de Figaro, d'après des lettres inédites de Beaumarchais." *Revue des deux mondes* (August 1, 1937), pp. 538–61.

Kates, Gary. *Monsieur d'Éon Is a Woman: A Tale of Political Intrigue and Sexual Masquerade*. New York: Basic Books, 1995.

Kinosian, Craig Kasper. *Beaumarchais, Mozart and Figaro*. Unpublished Ph.D. diss., University of California, Los Angeles, 1988.

Kite, Elisabeth S. *Beaumarchais and the War of American Independence*. 2 vols. Boston: Gorham Press, 1918.

Lafon, Mary and Jean-Bernard Lafon. *Cinquante ans de vie littéraire*. Paris: Calmann Lévy, 1882.

Lafon, Roger. *Beaumarchais, le brillant armateur*. Paris: Société d'éditions géographiques, maritimes et coloniales, 1928.

————. "Les années d'activité maritime de Beaumarchais." *Mercure de France* 204 (May 15, 1928), pp. 75–93.

Larthomas, Pierre. *Beaumarchais: Parades.* Paris: SEDES, 1977.

———. "Les Manuscrits des oeuvres dramatiques de Beaumarchais." In Béatrice Didier et Jacques Neefs, eds., *Sade, Rétif, Beaumarchais, Laclos. La Fin de l'Ancien Régime.* Paris: Presses Universitaires de Vincennes, 1991.

Latzarus, Louis. *Beaumarchais.* Paris: Plon, "Le roman des grandes existences," 1930.

Lemaître, Georges. *Beaumarchais Who Wrote "The Barber of Seville" and "The Marriage of Figaro," and Helped Finance the American Revolution.* New York: Alfred A. Knopf, 1949.

Lebois, André. "Beaumarchais et les insurgents d'Amérique." *De l'Armorique à l'Amérique de l'Indépendance. Deuxième partie du colloque du bicentenaire « Indépendance Américaine ». Annales de Bretagne et des pays de l'Ouest,* vol. 84, no. 2 (1977), pp. 173–82.

Lever, Maurice. *Théâtre et Lumières. Les spectacles de Paris au XVIIIe siècle.* Paris: Fayard, 2001.

Lintilhac, Eugène. *Beaumarchais et ses oeuvres. Précis de sa vie et histoire de son esprit, d'après des documents inédits.* 1887; reprint Geneva: Slatkine, 1970.

Loménie, Louis de. *Beaumarchais et son temps. Études sur la société en France au XVIIIe siècle, d'après des documents inedits.* 2 vols. 1880; reprint Geneva: Slatkine, 1970.

Manceron, Anne et Claude. *Beaumarchais, Figaro vivant.* Paris: Dargaud, 1968.

Maréschal de Bièvre, Comte. "Les tribulations de M. de Beaumarchais, exploitant forestier." *Revue des Études Historiques* (July–September 1933), pp. 379–402.

Morton, Brian N. "Beaumarchais et le prospectus de l'édition de Kehl." *Studies on Voltaire and the Eighteenth Century,* vol. 81 (1971), pp. 133–47.

Paer, A. *Centenaire du « Mariage de Figaro » de Caron de Beaumarchais.* Brussels, 1884.

Perkins, James Beck. *France in the American Revolution.* Boston and New York: Houghton Mifflin, 1911.

Perrault, Gilles. *Le secret du roi.* 3 vols. Paris: Fayard, 1992–96.

Petitfrere, Claude. *Le Scandale du « Mariage de Figaro », prélude à la Révolution française.* Brussels: Éditions Complexe, 1989.

Pinon, Pierre. "La Maison de Beaumarchais." In *Les Canaux de Paris.* Paris: Délégation à l'Action Artistique de la Ville de Paris, 1994.

Pinsseau, Pierre. *L'étrange destinée du chevalier d'Éon (1728–1810).* Paris: Raymond Clavreuil, 1945.

Pollitzer, Marcel. *Beaumarchais, le père de Figaro.* Paris: La Colombe, 1957.

Pomeau, René. *Beaumarchais, l'homme et l'oeuvre.* Paris: Hatier-Boivin, "Connaissance des Lettres," 1956.

———. *Beaumarchais ou la Bizarre destinée.* Paris: Presses Universitaires de France, 1987.

———. "Le manuscrit du *Sacristain.*" In Béatrice Didier and Jacques Neefs, eds., *Sade, Rétif, Beaumarchais, Laclos. La Fin de l'Ancien Régime.* Paris: Presses Universitaires de Vincennes, 1991.

———. *Voltaire en son temps.* 2 vols. Paris: Fayard/Voltaire Foundation, 1995.

Proschwitz, Gunnar et Mavis von. *Beaumarchais et le « Courrier de l'Europe ». Documents inédits ou peu connus.* 2 vols. Oxford: Voltaire Foundation/Taylor Institution, 1990.

———. « Le *Courrier de l'Europe* et la guerre d'Indépendance." *Annales de Bretagne*, vol. 84, no. 11 (1977), pp. 235–45.

———. « La Révolution et la littérature: une lettre inédite de Beaumarchais." In *Mélanges de langue et de littérature française offerts à Pierre Larthomas*. Paris: Collection de l'École Normale Supérieure de jeunes filles, 1985.

———. « Le Comte de Vergennes, Beaumarchais et le *Courrier de l'Europe.*" *Revue d'histoire diplomatique* (1988), pp. 351–70.

———. « Du Nouveau sur Beaumarchais éditeur de Voltaire." In *Le Siècle de Voltaire: Hommage à René Pomeau*. Oxford, 1987, 2:735–46.

———. "Gustave III, Beaumarchais et *Le Mariage de Figaro*." In *Influences: Relations culturelles entre la France et la Suède*. Göteborg/Paris, 1988.

———. "Une Affaire politico-commerçante." In Béatrice Didier and Jacques Neefs, eds., *Sade, Rétif, Beaumarchais, Laclos. La fin de l'Ancien Régime*. Paris: Presses Universitaires de Vincennes, 1991.

Proust, Jacques. « Beaumarchais et Mozart: une mise au point." *Studi francesi* (1972), pp. 34–45.

Revolution des auteurs, La, 1777–1793. Exhibition at the Théâtre National de l'Odéon, catalog. Paris: Société des Auteurs et Compositeurs Dramatiques (SACD), 1984.

Revue d'histoire littéraire de la France. No. 4 (July–August 2000), no. 5 (September–October 1984), and no. 6 (November–December 1974).

Ricard, Antoine. *Une Victime de Beaumarchais*. Paris: Plon, 1885.

Richard, Pierre. *La Vie privée de Beaumarchais*. Paris: Hachette, "Les Vies Privées," 1951.

Robinson, Philip, ed. *Beaumarchais: homme de lettres, homme de société*. Oxford, Bern, Berlin, Brussels, Frankfurt, New York, and Vienna: Peter Lang, "French Studies of the Eighteenth and Nineteenth Centuries," 2000.

Robiquet, Paul. *Théveneau de Morande. Étude sur le XVIIIe siècle*. Paris: Quantin, 1882.

Rouff, Marcel. "Un opéra politique de Beaumarchais," *La Révolution Française*, t. 59 (July–December 1910), pp. 212–29, 333–58.

Roulleaux-Dugage, Georges. "Beaumarchais musicien." *Revue hebdomadaire*, 11 March 1911, pp. 235–66.

Ruault, Nicolas. *Gazette d'un parisien sous la Révolution. Lettres à son frère 1783–1796*. Edited by Anne Vassal and Christiane Rimbaud. Paris: Librairie Académique Perrin, 1976.

Seebacher, Jacques. "Autour de Figaro: Beaumarchais, la famille de Choiseul et le financier Clavière." *Revue d'histoire littéraire de la France*, no. 62 (1962), pp. 198–228.

Sgard, Jean. *Dictionnaire des Journalistes (1600–1789)*. Grenoble, 1976.

Shérer, Jacques. *La Dramaturgie de Beaumarchais*. Paris: Nizet, 1964.

Shewmake, Antoinette. *For the Good of Mankind: Pierre-Augustin Caron de Beaumarchais, Political Correspondence Relative to the American Revolution*. Edited and translated by Antoinette Shewmake. New York: University Press of America, 1987.

Spinelli, Donald. *L'Inventaire après décès de Beaumarchais*. Edited by Donald C. Spinelli. Paris: Honoré Champion, 1997.

Stillé, Charles J. *Beaumarchais and the Lost Million: A Chapter of the Secret History of the American Revolution.* Philadelphia, 1886.

Sungolowsky, Joseph. *Beaumarchais.* New York: Twayne, 1974.

Thomas, Louis. *Curiosités sur Beaumarchais.* Paris, 1944.

Thomasset, René. *Beaumarchais écrivain et aventurier.* Paris: Nathan, 1966.

Valles, Ch. de. *Beaumarchais magistrat.* Paris, 1927.

Van Tieghem, Philippe. *Beaumarchais par lui-même.* Paris: Seuil, "Écrivains de toujours," 1960.

Vercruysse, Jérôme. "L'Imprimerie de la Société littéraire et typographique de Kehl en 1782," *Lias,* no. 13 (1986), pp. 165–233.

Vier, Jacques. *Le mariage de Figaro, miroir d'un siècle, portrait d'un homme. Le mouvement dramatique et l'esprit.* Paris: Minard, "Archives des lettres modernes," 1957, 1961.

Vizitelly, Ernest Alfred. *The True Story of the Chevalier d'Éon, his experiences and his metamorphoses in France, Russia, Germany and England, told with the aid of state and secret papers.* London: Tylston and Edward and A. P. Marsden, 1895.

Watts, G. B. "Catherine II, Charles-Joseph Panckoucke, and the Kehl edition of Voltaire's *Oeuvres.*" *Modern Language Quarterly* (1957), pp. 59–62.

———. "Panckoucke, Beaumarchais and Voltaire's First Complete Edition." *Tennessee Studies in Literature* (1959), pp. 91–97.

ÉVELYNE LEVER'S
ACKNOWLEDGMENTS

Before closing the French manuscript that I have reread, I must give heartfelt thanks in the name of Maurice Lever, my husband who died on January 28, 2006, to all those who helped and sustained me so that this book might appear. My affectionate gratitude goes first to Claude Durand and Denis Maraval, our old friends and editors at Fayard who allowed Maurice to write a biography of twelve hundred pages in three volumes! May François Samuelson, who defended this project with all the intelligence and authority that we expect of him, find here the expression of our deep friendship. It was he who formerly enabled the Sade biography (translated by Arthur Goldhammer) to be published by John Glusman at Farrar, Straus and Giroux. Alas, a Beaumarchais of twelve hundred pages could not see the light of day in the United States—although this devil of a man was the most American of Frenchmen. Thus it was necessary to reduce this book to the some four hundred pages that are offered here. John Glusman was an editor both warm and attentive, and Susan Emanuel a magnificent translator. I must thank all those who permitted the final realization of the work, in particular Nathalie Reignier. They may be assured of my sincere gratitude.

INDEX